Refreshing the Singapore System

Recalibrating Socio-Economic Policy for the 21st Century

Refreshing the Singapore System

Recalibrating Socio-Economic Policy for the 21st Century

W. L. Terence Ho

World Scientific

NEW JERSEY • LONDON • SINGAPORE • BEIJING • SHANGHAI • HONG KONG • TAIPEI • CHENNAI • TOKYO

Published by

World Scientific Publishing Co. Pte. Ltd.

5 Toh Tuck Link, Singapore 596224

USA office: 27 Warren Street, Suite 401-402, Hackensack, NJ 07601

UK office: 57 Shelton Street, Covent Garden, London WC2H 9HE

Library of Congress Cataloging-in-Publication Data
Names: Ho, W. L. Terence, author.
Title: Refreshing the Singapore system : recalibrating socio-economic
policy for the 21st century / W. L. Terence Ho.
Description: Hackensack : World Scientific, [2021] |
Includes bibliographical references and index.
Identifiers: LCCN 2021015321 | ISBN 9789811236532 (hardcover) |
ISBN 9789811236549 (ebook) | ISBN 9789811236556 (ebook other)
Subjects: LCSH: Economic development--Singapore--History--21st century. |
Social planning--Singapore--History--21st century. | Singapore--Economic policy. |
Singapore--Economic conditions. | Singapore--Social policy.
Classification: LCC HC445.8 .H599 2021 | DDC 330.95957--dc23
LC record available at https://lccn.loc.gov/2021015321

British Library Cataloguing-in-Publication Data
A catalogue record for this book is available from the British Library.

For any available supplementary material, please visit
https://www.worldscientific.com/worldscibooks/10.1142/12265#t=suppl

Desk Editor: Lai Ann

Typeset by Stallion Press
Email: enquiries@stallionpress.com

"Terence Ho unites technical expertise, historical depth, and personal experience to answer two urgent questions for policymakers in Singapore and around the world: What is the secret recipe that has fostered five decades of miraculous growth in Singapore, accompanied by rising shared prosperity? And how must that recipe be updated — or revamped — to meet the challenges of today and the decades ahead? You won't find a better guide to these questions than Ho's authoritative book."

David Autor
Ford Professor of Economics, Massachusetts Institute of Technology

"This book traces the evolution of Singapore's socioeconomic policies over the past two decades, as it confronted — and continues to confront — the twin challenges of slowing economic growth and rising societal inequality. Ho offers a comprehensive account of the full range of Singapore's policy responses, drawing on his firsthand experiences in the government sector. This essential reference comes at a particularly timely juncture for taking stock, with Singapore at a political and economic crossroads as it navigates the post-Covid world."

Davin Chor
Associate Professor and Globalization Chair, Tuck School of Business, Dartmouth College

"How does Singapore manage its social welfare system? *Refreshing the Singapore System* is now the go-to book on this important topic."

Tyler Cowen
Holbert L. Harris Professor of Economics, George Mason University
Co-host of the *Marginal Revolution* economics blog

"In an increasingly polarised age, political polemic is often assumed to be synonymous with public policy. What is forgotten is that public policy is a sifting of what is politically and technically possible from the ideal. Terence's arguments for a recalibration of Singapore's socio-economic policy will neither satisfy those who want to adopt a Scandinavian model nor those who want less 'government distortion'. However, for those who are willing to grapple with the practical dilemmas of governing in a real political entity, they will draw insights from Terence's measured arguments."

Goh Mui Pong
Head, Monetary Authority of Singapore Academy

"*Refreshing the Singapore System* is an important contribution to understanding the policy ecosystem in Singapore and how different policy domains interact and interrelate. The book is extensively researched, well-organised and cogently articulated. The policy complexities and conundrums are clearly communicated and aided by visual models which make comprehension of even the most complicated interplays intuitive. Mr Ho has done the policy community in Singapore a significant service through his contribution of this book which deserves to be read by and will benefit both the specialist and the layperson."

Devadas Krishnadas
Chief Executive Officer, Future-Moves Group

"*Refreshing the Singapore System* is an excellent primer for more informed discourse on Singapore's unique social policy in chat rooms, living rooms and boardrooms islandwide."

Augustin Lee
Chief Executive Officer, Singapore Central Provident Fund Board

"*Refreshing the Singapore System* is an excellent first-hand account and a great primer on the thought processes behind Singapore's well-honed economic and social policies. Terence's book brings to us the unique view of the seasoned policy planner. More importantly, his time in the Service also traces the pressures faced by modern Singapore — an evolving social compact, faster population ageing, a greater need for human capital optimisation amidst a more volatile global financial system, and an unprecedented pandemic."

Leong Wai Ho
Managing Director (Research), Modular Asset Management

"During his two decades in Singapore's civil service, Terence Ho was involved in, or had a ringside seat to, many of the more contested public policies. After the pandemic, many of these would have to be rethought as the social contract is debated and renegotiated. A prerequisite of such rethinking is a deep understanding of how Singapore's key socioeconomic policies have evolved in the last two decades. *Refreshing the Singapore System* is a highly readable, sympathetic and coherent account of these policies, their underlying philosophy, and how they've been enhanced in recent years."

Donald Low
Senior Lecturer and Professor of Practice in Public Policy,
Hong Kong University of Science and Technology

"This book is informative, fair and, above all, clear. It is written in a style which not only makes it easy to read but a pleasure to read. There is much substance here. I have no hesitation in recommending this book to any reader, whether a student, businessperson or voter. All can gain a better understanding of Singapore, the socio-economic policies it has followed as well as the challenges and choices Singapore and its citizens are addressing and will have to continue to address."

Victor Mills
Chief Executive, Singapore International Chamber of Commerce

"A fascinating, thorough and thoughtful examination of public policies in Singapore, a country widely recognised for its economic achievements which has also been pioneering important new approaches to social welfare and labour markets. The book carefully examines the data on issues such as poverty, inequality, social mobility and the evolution of a distinctive Singapore model that doesn't fit neatly into categories designed for the Western world, and is particularly interesting on the sophisticated methods developed to align economic and social policies in a fast-changing environment."

Sir Geoff Mulgan
Professor of Collective Intelligence,
Public Policy and Social Innovation, University College London
Former Chief Executive of Nesta,
the UK's innovation agency for social good

"I found Terence Ho's book an honest and balanced treatment of the policy challenges and options in Singapore. It offers a comprehensive and clear coverage of existing policies. It also presents — in a matter of fact manner — a spectrum of alternative recommendations, smattered with personal views from Ho's leadership rounds in several ministries. I will be using this book as a key resource for my teaching and research."

Irene Y. H. Ng
Associate Professor and Director of the Social Service Research Centre,
National University of Singapore

"*Refreshing the Singapore System* presents a ringside view of the many important changes to Singapore's socio-economic policies over the past two decades. Given his involvement in many of these policies, Terence Ho is able to present a highly informative narrative of these changes, carefully documenting the important features, explaining well the rationale for each one, comparing the results with relevant empirical work where available and formulating integrative frameworks to link the different pieces. Policy discussions in Singapore can often be lively, and the book now affords every participant the opportunity to discern the recent Singapore approach across the entire web of key policies. For a small country, this mosaic is both complex and highly deliberative. Terence's work will be a valuable contribution to the needed public discourse on how the system should continue to evolve given the dynamic changes in Singapore society and the environment the country will face."

Peter Ong
Chairman, Enterprise Singapore
Former Head of the Singapore Civil Service and Permanent Secretary
(Transport, Trade and Industry, and Finance)

"For those interested in innovative policy regarding skills development, Singapore has long been seen as an important example. In his book *Refreshing the Singapore System*, Terence Ho provides a very useful insider's perspective on the components of Singapore's human capital policies and how they are evolving in the face of new labor market challenges."

Paul Osterman
NTU Professor of Human Resources and Management,
MIT Sloan School of Management

"*Refreshing the Singapore System* presents excellent discussions about the implications and trade-offs of the various policy options over the years, and with specific focus on the policy response to the COVID-19 crisis, as well as the challenges confronting this small nation going forward. It is a must-read for anyone who is keen to gain insights into the intricacy of Singapore's economic and social policies."

Irvin Seah
Senior Economist and Head of Strategic Projects, DBS Bank

"The author has skillfully supported his easily understood socio-economic model of Singapore with quantitative evidence. It is a very good addition to the body of writing on the Singapore economy. Anyone interested in public policies that have shaped the Singapore economy into its present form should read this book."

Mun-Heng Toh
Honorary Fellow, National University of Singapore Business School

"Terence Ho's book is a useful reference of Singapore's social and economic policies in recent years. It records and analyses exhaustively specific actions taken by the government on both sides of the national balance sheet — enhancing assets and ensuring their fair distribution. Both sides are related of course. Without a fair distribution, which means taxes and transfers, there will be no satisfactory social compact which conduces effort and steady productivity growth. Only then can the asset side show steady improvement. The market is never completely self-regulating.

Without good governance, the market undermines itself through accumulation of monopoly power and income inequality. There is perhaps no government in the world which addresses as thoroughly the factors affecting both sides of the national balance sheet as the Singapore Government. If there is a fundamental criticism of the government, it must be that it fine-tunes too much. Ho's book examines in detail the nuts and bolts, including the emergency measures taken in response to the COVID-19 pandemic."

George Yeo
Senior Advisor, Kuok Group
Former Minister for Information and the Arts, Health, Trade and Industry, and Foreign Affairs in the Singapore Cabinet

For Pippa and Ben

Acknowledgements

This book owes much to the advice and input of Senior Minister Tharman Shanmugaratnam, who played a pivotal role in shaping many of the social policy innovations described herein.

Many others have been similarly generous with their time and expertise. I would like to thank, in particular, Prof. Paul Cheung, Dr Goh Mui Pong, Asst. Prof. Koh Choon Hwee, Mr Devadas Krishnadas, Dr Kuan Ming Leong, Prof. Donald Low, Mr Irvin Seah, Mr Tan Kok Kong and Mr Tee Koon Hui for their detailed feedback and contributions to the book. Mr Ang Boon Heng, Mr Jeremy W. Z. Lim and Mr Sky Chua provided valuable assistance on data-related issues, for which I am grateful.

I also wish to acknowledge the input of Mr Terence Chan, Mr Chin Yi Zhuan, Ms Chong Soo Fern, Mr Musa Fazal, Ms Kirsten Ho, Ms Kong Kum Peck, Mr Kwa Chin Lum, Mr Augustin Lee, Mr Matthew M. H. Lee, Ms Lee Yan Ye, Mr Peter Lim, Ms Sinni Lim, Mr Lim Tze Jiat, Assoc. Prof. Irene Y. H. Ng, Prof. M. Ramesh, Mr Sim Feng-Ji, Mr Tan Juanhe, Mr Tan Pei-En, Prof. Tan Thiam Soon, Ms Tong Mun Ling, Ms Xie Jiayin and Dr Yip Chun Seng.

Finally, my appreciation goes to my editor at World Scientific, Ms Lai Ann, for her patience and dedication in seeing this book through to publication.

The opinions expressed in the book are my own and do not represent the views of the Singapore government, or the views of any of the above-mentioned persons. Any errors in the book are mine alone.

Contents

List of Abbreviations

A*STAR	Agency for Science, Technology and Research
AI	Artificial intelligence
ALP	Applied Learning Programme
ASEAN	Association of Southeast Asian Nations
ASPIRE	Applied Studies in Polytechnic and ITE Review
BEST	Basic Education for Skills Training
BTO	Build-To-Order
CAYE	Contribute-As-You-Earn
CDC	Community Development Council
CECA	Comprehensive Economic Cooperation Agreement
CET	Continuing education and training
CFE	Committee on the Future Economy
CHAS	Community Health Assist Scheme
CIP	Co-Investment Programme
COVID-19	Coronavirus disease 2019
CPF LIFE	CPF Lifelong Income for the Elderly
CPF	Central Provident Fund
CPFIS	CPF Investment Scheme
CPI	Consumer Price Index
DPAP	Development Projects Advisory Panel
DRC	Dependency Ratio Ceiling
DSA	Direct School Admission
EDB	Economic Development Board
EDBI	EDB Investments

EITC	Earned Income Tax Credit
ELP	Earn and Learn Programme
EP	Employment Pass
ERC	Economic Review Committee
ESC	Economic Strategies Committee
ESG	Environmental, social and corporate governance
FCF	Fair Consideration Framework
FDI	Foreign direct investment
FDW	Foreign domestic worker
FTA	Free trade agreement
FTSE	Financial Times Stock Exchange
FY	Financial year
GDP	Gross domestic product
GLC	Government-linked company
GNP	Gross national product
GP	General practitioner
GST	Goods and Services Tax
GSTV	GST Voucher
HDB	Housing and Development Board
HHI	Herfindahl-Hirschman Index
ICT	Information and communications technology
IHL	Institute of higher learning
ILTC	Intermediate and long-term care
IMF	International Monetary Fund
ITE	Institute of Technical Education
ITM	Industry Transformation Map
JGI	Jobs Growth Incentive
JSS	Jobs Support Scheme
KiFAS	Kindergarten Fee Assistance Scheme
LLE	Large local enterprise
LQS	Local Qualifying Salary
LRIS	Lifetime Retirement Investment Scheme
LTVP+	Long-term visit pass plus
MA	MediSave Account
MAS	Monetary Authority of Singapore
MBF	Market-Based Skills Recognition Framework
MCO	Movement Control Order

MICE	Meetings, incentives, conventions and exhibitions
MNC	Multinational corporation
MOE	Ministry of Education
MOF	Ministry of Finance
MOH	Ministry of Health
MOM	Ministry of Manpower
MOST	Modular Skills Training
MP	Member of Parliament
MSF	Ministry of Social and Family Development
MTI	Ministry of Trade and Industry
MWR	Money's worth ratio
NIE	National Institute of Education
NIEC	National Institute of Early Childhood Development
NII	Net Investment Income
NIR	Net Investment Returns
NIRC	Net Investment Returns Contribution
NPCEC	National Productivity and Continuing Education Council
NTU	Nanyang Technological University
NTUC	National Trades Union Congress
NTUC's e2i	NTUC's Employment and Employability Institute
NUS	National University of Singapore
NWC	National Wages Council
OA	Ordinary Account
OECD	Organisation for Economic Co-operation and Development
PAP	People's Action Party
PCP	Professional Conversion Programme
PEA	Payout eligibility age
PET	Pre-employment training
PGP	Pioneer Generation Package
PIAAC	Programme for the International Assessment of Adult Competencies
PIC	Productivity and Innovation Credit
PISA	Programme for International Student Assessment
PMET	Professionals, managers, executives and technicians
PPP	Public-private partnerships Purchasing power parity

PR	Permanent resident
PSLE	Primary School Leaving Examination
PWM	Progressive Wage Model
R&D	Research and development
RA	Retirement Account
RRA	Retirement and Re-employment Act
S&CC	Service and conservancy charges
S&P 500	Standard and Poor's 500
SA	Special Account
SARS	Severe Acute Respiratory Syndrome
SCC	Student Care Centre
SDF	Skills Development Fund
SEC	Special Employment Credit
SEP	Self-employed person
SERS	Selective En Bloc Redevelopment Scheme
SES	Socio-economic status
SGD	Singapore dollar
SIRS	Self-Employed Person Income Relief Scheme
SIT	Singapore Institute of Technology
SMA	Singapore Medical Association
SME	Small and medium-sized enterprise
SMU	Singapore Management University
SSA	Social service agency
SSG	SkillsFuture Singapore
SSO	Social Service Office
SUSS	Singapore University of Social Sciences
SUTD	Singapore University of Technology and Design
TAFEP	Tripartite Alliance for Fair and Progressive Employment Practices
TFP	Total factor productivity
TLC	Temasek-linked company
UBI	Universal basic income
UI	Unemployment insurance
UK	United Kingdom of Great Britain and Northern Ireland
UNDP	United Nations Development Programme

UNESCO	United Nations Educational, Scientific and Cultural Organization
UPLIFT	Uplifting Pupils in Life and Inspiring Families Taskforce
UPSR	Ujian Pencapaian Sekolah Rendah (primary school achievement test)
US	United States of America
USD	United States dollar
USSFTA	United States-Singapore Free Trade Agreement
VA	Value added
VAT	Value-added tax
VERS	Voluntary Early Redevelopment Scheme
VWO	Voluntary welfare organisation
WCS	Wage Credit Scheme
WIS	Workfare Income Supplement
WISE	Work Improvement through Secondary Education
WSG	Workforce Singapore
WSQ	Workforce Skills Qualifications
WSS	Workfare Skills Support

Introduction and Overview

Singapore's rapid ascent from Third World to First since becoming an independent nation in 1965 has won it international acclaim as an economic miracle. A relatively poor country at independence, Singapore has catapulted to ninth in the world in 2019 in terms of per capita nominal gross domestic product (GDP) (in US dollars), and second in the world in purchasing power parity terms, according to World Bank data.[1] The Swiss-based Institute for Management Development, in its influential *World Competitiveness Yearbook*, ranked Singapore the world's most competitive economy in 2019 and 2020.[2]

Impressive achievements in social development have accompanied the city-state's economic success. Singapore was ranked first among 174 economies in the World Bank's 2020 Human Capital Index,[3] and 11th among 189 economies in the Human Development Index published by the United Nations Development Programme (UNDP) in 2020.[4] Life expectancy at birth was 83.6 years in Singapore, fourth highest among those ranked by the UNDP. In 2019, home ownership among resident households was 90.4%, and the literacy rate 97.5%.[5] In the Organisation for Economic Co-operation and Development (OECD) Programme for International Student Assessment (PISA) test in 2018, Singapore 15-year-olds came in second in reading, mathematics, and science, finishing only behind their peers from China.[6]

These were achieved with relatively low levels of public spending — total government expenditure in 2019 (excluding special transfers[7] and spending from government endowment and trust funds) stood at 15.4% of GDP, with expenditure on social development less than half of the total, at 7.3% of GDP, despite having risen significantly in the previous five years.[8] This compares with the OECD average public social expenditure of about 20% of GDP in 2019.[9]

Low tax rates, flexible labour markets, emphasis on individual self-reliance, along with state subsidies for public housing and education, have underpinned Singapore's development trajectory and continue to be foundations for Singapore's socio-economic system. Unlike most advanced market economies, Singapore does not have a statutory minimum wage or unemployment insurance. Aside from exceptional support provided during the COVID-19 pandemic, only those with minimal income or family support are eligible for state unemployment benefits.

This raises the question — is Singapore's socio-economic system, so successful during the years of rapid economic expansion, sustainable in the future as income growth slows, the population ages, and social divisions emerge? Can Singapore's policy approach show the way for other countries, developed or developing, or will it buckle under the pressures of rising social demands?

Singaporean academics and commentators have weighed in. Economist Linda Lim (2014) argued that development challenges in the 21st century had cast doubt on the sustainability of Singapore's policies.[10] In a collection of essays, Donald Low and Sudhir Vadaketh (2014) challenged the Singapore Consensus, arguing that fundamental changes to Singapore's system of governance are needed.[11] Sociologist Teo You Yenn (2017) gave voice to the nation's conscience in her bestselling book *This Is What Inequality Looks Like*, in which she made the case for a reframing of Singapore's approach towards poverty and inequality.[12]

In fact, Singapore's socio-economic system has evolved significantly in the past two decades. The stresses and strains from a maturing economy and ageing society, along with technological change and global economic competition, have necessitated a significant overhaul of social security. Policy innovation has been spurred by the challenges of sustaining income growth and social mobility, ensuring income security, and addressing inequality.

Over the past 19 years, as I served in various capacities in the Singapore Public Service, two questions have preoccupied me. First, how can Singapore continue to make a good living in a globalised, hypercompetitive world? And second, how can the fruits of economic progress be distributed in a way that is equitable and inclusive, without undermining the ethic of hard work and self-reliance that underpins the Singapore System, if at all possible?

In my first job as an economist in the Ministry of Trade and Industry, I monitored macroeconomic trends and specific economic sectors. Subsequently, at the Ministry of Education, I was involved in university and technical education policy reviews. This gave me occasion to reflect on the fundamental role of the education system in building up human capital, shaping the distribution of skills and incomes across the population, and enabling social mobility.

As General Manager of the South East Community Development Council from 2007 to 2009, I was at the frontline delivering social and employment assistance to South East District residents during the Global Financial Crisis. My colleagues and I regularly met with the then-Ministry of Community Development, Youth and Sport (now Ministry of Social and Family Development) to receive guidance and provide feedback on social assistance policies.

At the Ministry of Finance (MOF) from 2010 to 2013, I was the director in charge of public sector performance and organisation, and also for a time Second Director of Fiscal Policy. From 2013 to 2016, I oversaw economic strategy and resourcing for economic programmes across the public sector. The common theme in my work was optimising fiscal and manpower resources for public outcomes.

My focus switched to labour market issues when I joined the Ministry of Manpower (MOM) in 2016. Here, I was responsible for manpower planning and policy, spanning foreign workforce policy, local employment facilitation, and labour market research. As the labour market links economic and education policy with socio-economic outcomes through jobs and incomes, my stint at MOM brought together various strands of my public sector experience, crystallising my thoughts on the two questions that had occupied my mind since joining the Public Service.

The answers to these questions, I came to realise, were to be found in Singapore's socio-economic system, the set of intertwined policies and institutions that collectively determine the path of economic development and distribution.

During my six and a half years with MOF in the 2010s, I had a ringside seat to the annual Budget deliberations that sought to address both economic and social challenges. During this period, many programmes and policy innovations were initiated to shore up the socio-economic system in order to sustain fairness and inclusivity.

Some of these initiatives were manifestly impactful; others appeared incremental in nature. Cumulatively, they have brought Singapore a long way since the early 2000s. From a system with limited redistribution or risk pooling, apart from significant state subsidies for housing and education, Singapore now has a more comprehensive social security system, albeit without certain staple features of other systems, notably unemployment insurance and a minimum wage.

A reframing of my original questions is in order: is the refurbished Singapore System now fit for purpose? What further changes, if any, are needed to sustain Singapore's social compact in the future?

This book seeks to address these by alternately looking back, looking around, and looking ahead.

Singapore serves as a useful reference point in comparative models of welfare capitalism. In Singapore's socio-economic system, human capital formation and personal effort (individual responsibility or self-reliance) take centre stage. Job and social protections play a supporting role, but one that is expanding. **Looking back** at the changes to the Singapore System over the past 15–20 years reveals the shifts in policy thinking that have accompanied structural changes to Singapore's society and economy. This book aims to unpack the driving forces and socio-economic trends that have motivated the introduction of new policies and programmes, with the government trying, amid these changes, to hold fast to the core tenet of individual responsibility.

Looking around shows how Singapore strives to achieve social outcomes both in ways that are similar to, and others that are strikingly different from, the approaches taken by other advanced capitalist economies. While countries have different contexts and characteristics, they face many similar challenges, being subject to common global trends and driving forces. Policies adopted by countries ahead of Singapore in demographic and social transition may pave the way for Singapore. Conversely, policy innovations developed in Singapore could be adapted to address challenges elsewhere. Certain features of other models can be grafted onto a country's socio-economic system at minimal cost, while others can only be adopted by jettisoning existing elements and accepting new risks and trade-offs.

Looking ahead points to how the Singapore System may evolve in the years ahead. The challenges of job disruption, income volatility, inequality, and social mobility will only intensify, even as Singapore seeks to rebound from the depredations of COVID-19. Heightened political contestation, amplified by social media, is also reshaping the social compact between the government and citizens. These internal dynamics will undoubtedly exert a growing influence on social policy. At the same time, with fewer low-hanging fruits to pluck, policy choices will entail greater risks and sharper trade-offs, with far-reaching ramifications for Singapore's economy and society. The political leadership will need to carefully consider when it is necessary to abandon long-cherished policies and mental models, and conversely when to double down on the well-tried strategies that have brought Singapore success thus far.

Book Overview

Singapore's socio-economic system can be understood as a suite of interlocking policies and institutions founded on a set of core principles or values. These principles include:

- Self-reliance or individual responsibility towards self, family, and community, also described as "Reward for Work, and Work for Reward"
- Living within one's means, both at the household and national level, where fiscal prudence and conservatism guide budget planning
- Maintaining an open, competitive economy for Singapore and its citizens to earn a good living, and to provide the state with the resources for public spending and investment
- Subjecting enterprises and public services to market discipline

— Social investment, particularly in education and skills, for a competitive workforce and self-reliant citizenry

Singapore is often seen as pushing the concept of self-reliance to extremes. In fact, Lee Kuan Yew, the city-state's first Prime Minister, expressed the need for a balance between the *yang* of economic competition among individuals, and the *yin* of collectivism, or social support.[13] The People's Action Party (PAP), which has been in continuous power since Singapore became self-governing[14] in 1959, pursued a social democratic agenda from the outset. It eschewed liberalism in favour of a communitarian ideology, even while tapping on market mechanisms for financial discipline.[15] The continuity of the PAP's rule has meant no sudden disjoint or reversal in policy direction, but rather an evolution in approach as impelled by changing economic and social circumstances.

The notion that an individual should provide for himself and his family as a matter of personal responsibility, rather than rely on the state, remains at the heart of Singapore's socio-economic system. Community and state lend support, not to replace individual effort, but to augment it while reinforcing self-responsibility. Self-reliance, though a moniker adopted by the government, is perhaps not the best description of the Singapore way. This is in consideration of the significant and growing resources committed by the state towards social investment and social support, as well as the part played by the community. ***Personal effort with collective support***, in my view, is a more accurate description of Singapore's approach.

The ethos of self-help is enshrined in the Central Provident Fund (CPF), a system of mandatory savings that forms the bedrock of social security in Singapore. Through their CPF savings, citizens and permanent residents provide for their own housing, healthcare, and retirement needs, supplemented by significant government subsidies that are tiered according to household means. To encourage work and enterprise, taxes are kept low and fiscal redistribution limited. The unemployed are required to tap on personal savings, along with family and community help, before turning to the state for financial support as a last recourse.

The success of Singapore's export-led industrialisation, founded on political and macroeconomic stability, a skilled and disciplined workforce, as well as excellent infrastructure and connectivity, has propelled economic growth, raising incomes and living standards for most Singaporeans. However, affluence has brought about greater income dispersion and rising living costs. At the same time, structural forces including global competition, technological change, and an ageing population, are reshaping Singapore's social contract and socio-economic system.

In response to these challenges, the government has acknowledged the need for greater public support to augment personal effort. Structural transfers (including the Workfare Income Supplement, Silver Support, and the Goods and Services Tax Voucher, which will be described in subsequent chapters) have been introduced and enhanced, while social insurance (CPF LIFE, MediShield Life, and CareShield Life) has taken on a critical role in healthcare and retirement provision, alongside mandatory savings. Other changes, major and minor, have been set in motion across Singapore's socio-economic policy domains, leveraging collective help to complement individual effort.

In designing these changes, the government has hewn to its core principle of upholding individual responsibility and personal effort. For instance, Workfare rewards work; social insurance premiums are often paid for by one's own CPF savings. In lieu of a statutory minimum wage, the government is expanding the implementation of sector-specific "progressive wages" which are tied to productivity and skills upgrading, and hence more in keeping with the spirit of "Work for Reward". Upstream intervention continues to be prioritised — public investment in education and skills has been enhanced, brought forward to early childhood, and extended through life. Tax incentives encourage community giving, while welfare benefits remain residual rather than universal.

All in all, the strengthening of social support over the past two decades has been significant. Assistance is provided in a way that is consistent with the government's socio-economic principles, but the principles themselves are being interpreted more broadly to accommodate new forms of social support.

Notwithstanding, the demographic and structural challenges facing Singapore are immense, and will test the limits of the Singapore System in the years to come. Mindsets and policies must therefore adapt — to embrace an older workforce with fewer local-born citizens, reduce reliance on foreign workers, and support inclusive growth.

This requires employers to invest in developing the local workforce and provide opportunities for reskilling and training on the job, while reducing overall manpower reliance through productivity improvement. Locals must be willing to take up redesigned jobs traditionally viewed as blue-collar work. Policies need to be continually reviewed and refreshed, taking a systems perspective that integrates upstream (e.g. social investment, cost management) and downstream policy levers (e.g. redistribution). Collective support must be calibrated to provide sufficient assurance to citizens, to prevent socio-economic fissures from fracturing societal trust amid rising costs and widening inequality. This will make possible inclusive and sustainable economic growth, with the ultimate aim of bettering citizens' lives and enabling self-actualisation.

Organisation of the Book

Before examining the Singapore System in detail, it is useful to first consider the aims of socio-economic development, against which the performance and adequacy of the Singapore System can be assessed. While this book is primarily about Singapore, it is also an exploration of how public policy can contribute to human welfare or well-being in the broadest sense.

The aims of development are taken up in Chapter 1, which sets up a framework to understand and compare socio-economic systems, and what they must deliver in terms of socio-economic outcomes that underpin citizen well-being.

Chapter 2 takes stock of how Singapore has progressed in terms of key socio-economic indicators over the decades, and where it is today. This sets the stage for an overview of the Singapore System in Chapter 3, which also outlines the socio-economic forces impelling change, and the main policy responses, in broad strokes, since 2001.

Chapters 4–6 examine key downstream elements of the Singapore System — namely, fiscal redistribution (Chapter 4), social security (Chapter 5), and social assistance (Chapter 6), detailing how policies in each of these areas have evolved in response to emerging trends and challenges, particularly since the turn of the century. Where pertinent, research is cited and references made to international practices, inviting the reader to reflect on the policy choices that Singapore and other countries are facing.

Chapters 7–9 address major upstream drivers of socio-economic outcomes: education (Chapter 7), manpower (Chapter 8), and economic policy (Chapter 9). Again, the approach is to look back at how these have evolved, look around at systems elsewhere, and look ahead to emerging gaps and opportunities.

Chapter 10 discusses the financing of public policies and programmes to achieve socio-economic outcomes. Finally, Chapter 11 surveys the impact and implications of COVID-19 on the Singapore System, while reflecting on recent political developments in Singapore and how these may affect policymaking. I conclude by looking at how the Singapore System may adapt and shape Singapore society in the years ahead.

This book does not analyse socio-economic outcomes by gender or race, nor does it cover policies relating to disability or workplace injury, which are also part of the social safety net. Community relations, social capital, and societal fault-lines that go beyond socio-economic issues are also outside the book's scope. For reasons of space, focus, and the author's areas of expertise, these would be better treated elsewhere.

As the Singapore Story unfolds, the Singapore System will continue to evolve. I hope, through this book, to bring the reader up to date on Singapore's socio-economic development and policy innovations in the first two decades of the 21st century, and to situate Singapore's experience in the wider international discourse on public policy.

Endnotes

1. Among sovereign states only. Based on World Bank, "GDP Per Capita (Current US$)" and "GDP Per Capita, PPP (Current International $)", World Development Indicators, last updated 19 March 2021, https://data.worldbank.org/indicator/NY.GDP.PCAP.CD; https://data.worldbank.org/indicator/NY.GDP.PCAP.PP.CD.
2. IMD International (Institute), *The World Competitiveness Yearbook 2020* (Lausanne: IMD International, 2020).
3. World Bank, *The Human Capital Index 2020 Update: Human Capital in the Time of COVID-19* (Washington DC: World Bank, 2020).

4. United Nations Development Programme (UNDP), *Human Development Report 2020: The Next Frontier — Human Development and the Anthropocene* (New York: UNDP, 2020).
5. Source: Singapore Department of Statistics.
6. Organisation for Economic Co-operation and Development (OECD), *PISA 2018 Results (Volume I): What Students Know and Can Do* (Paris: OECD Publishing, 2019).
7. Special transfers refer to one-off transfers (as opposed to structural transfers) to households and businesses for various purposes, such as to share budget surpluses or offset business costs.
8. Ministry of Finance (MOF), *Analysis of Revenue and Expenditure: Financial Year 2020* (Singapore: MOF, 2020).
9. OECD Social Expenditure Database, accessed 2 May 2021, https://www.oecd.org/social/expenditure.htm.
10. Linda Y. C. Lim, "Singapore's Success: After the Miracle," in Robert Looney, ed., *Handbook of Emerging. Economies* (London: Routledge, 2014), 203–226.
11. Donald Low and Sudhir Thomas Vadaketh, eds., *Hard Choices: Challenging the Singapore Consensus* (Singapore: NUS Press, 2014).
12. Teo You Yenn, *This Is What Inequality Looks Like* (Singapore: Ethos Books, 2017).
13. Lee Kuan Yew, *From Third World to First: The Singapore Story: 1965–2000* (Singapore: Times Editions, Singapore Press Holdings, 2000).
14. Internal self-government preceded merger with Malaysia from 1963 to 1965, and Singapore's independence in 1965.
15. Chua Beng Huat, *Liberalism Disavowed: Communitarianism and State Capitalism in Singapore* (Singapore: NUS Press, 2017).

Chapter 1

Socio-Economic Policy

The ultimate purpose of economic development is to better people's lives — not just in the material sense, but all the way up Maslow's hierarchy of needs, from the base of physiological needs to the summit of self-actualisation.[1]

Economic and human development, in fact, go hand in hand. Human development may be defined as "the process of enlarging people's choices".[2] In his book *Development as Freedom*, Indian economist and philosopher Amartya Sen (1999) makes the case that economic development is in essence an increase in freedom, with freedom being both the objective of development as well as its means.[3] Throughout history, it is typically in cities and states with both security and ample resources that intellectual pursuits and the arts have flourished.

Addressing poverty is therefore foundational. Across the world, charitable initiatives and social enterprises play a role in addressing the specific needs of the underprivileged or vulnerable. However, sustained, large-scale poverty alleviation requires economic development. China is a case in point. According to the World Bank, over 800 million people have been lifted out of extreme poverty since the initiation of Chinese economic reforms in 1978;[4] China's poverty rate fell from 66% in 1990 to 0.5% in 2016, as measured by the percentage of people living on the equivalent of US$1.90 or less per day in 2011 in purchasing power parity terms.[5]

In Ghana, strong economic growth over the past three decades helped the country to achieve the first Millennium Development Goal of reducing the poverty rate by more than half, from 47.9% in 1991 to 12.7% in 2016.[6] Similar development elsewhere is narrowing global inequality.

Albeit on a smaller scale, Singapore's rapid industrial development in the 1960s through to the 2000s has uplifted its citizens from a relatively low income base, and in so doing greatly expanded opportunities for employment and education, along with intellectual, sporting, and artistic pursuits.

Many Singaporeans in my parents' generation would grasp at any chance to earn a decent salary, never mind the conditions of the job or whether they enjoyed the work. Like others in my generation, growing up in the 1980s, we were told to study hard and pursue a career in professions such as medicine, law, and engineering (usually in that order of priority) so as to earn a good living. A number of my peers dutifully took up law at university and, only later in life, returned to their passion for writing or baking, whether as a hobby or full-time. Today, many more, though importantly not all, Singaporeans have the opportunity to follow their passion, to pursue self-actualisation in the choice of their career or vocation.

Compared with the past, many more (though not all) young Singaporeans have the opportunity to study or work abroad, or to travel to far-flung places across the globe. Many enjoy sports and adventure activities that were unthinkable for most Singaporeans a generation ago, with some denizens of this tropical island state even having aspirations to compete in the Winter Olympics!

Singapore's founding Prime Minister Lee Kuan Yew famously said in 1969 that poetry was "a luxury we cannot afford".[7] Today, some may argue that Singapore's literary scene has not yet attained maturity, but there is no doubt that Singapore Literature has taken root, with poetry, books, and plays enjoyed in Singapore and finding their way to overseas audiences via anthologies, tours, and festivals.

The long and short is that economic development matters, not just to material well-being, but also to the opportunities, expression, and self-actualisation of citizens.

The Socio-Economic System

Economic development is about both growth and distribution. The interplay of social and economic policy and institutions (the socio-economic system) sets the conditions for economic growth and also influences how

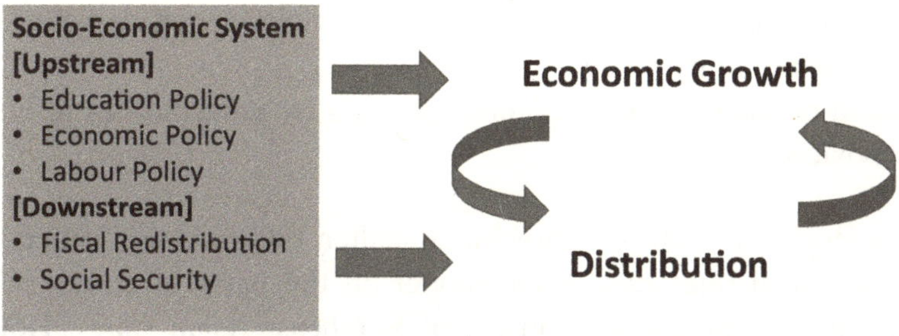

Figure 1.1 Socio-Economic Policies Affecting Economic Growth and Distribution

income and wealth are distributed across households and individuals through market opportunities and post-market transfers. Economic growth affects how resources are distributed through labour and asset markets, while distribution affects growth through channels such as investment, consumption, and access to education (Figure 1.1).

The characteristics of a country's socio-economic system may be a function of history, culture, politics, and society. The state almost always plays a central role through laws, policies, and institutions, regardless of the extent to which it is directly involved in the provision or delivery of social support. Other important actors that may shape social and economic development include companies, non-governmental organisations such as charities and social enterprises, as well as religious organisations, community groups, and families.

In capitalist economies with social welfare aims, the socio-economic system is often referred to as a social welfare regime. These are in turn categorised in the academic literature into various "welfare state models" or "models of welfare capitalism".

The East Asian Model of Welfare Capitalism

In his seminal work, *The Three Worlds of Welfare Capitalism*,[8] Danish sociologist Gøsta Esping-Andersen (1990) classified contemporary Western welfare states into three types:

— Liberal regimes, emphasising market solutions to social problems and limited, means-tested assistance

— Conservative regimes, centred on community-based assistance and traditional family values
— Social democratic regimes, characterised by universalism in welfare provision

Ian Holliday (2000),[9] Christian Aspalter (2006),[10] and others have argued for a distinct East Asian model on the basis of commonalities among East Asian states, inclusive of Southeast Asian states. Holliday (2000) characterised mature East Asian economies including Singapore as "productivist" welfare regimes, where social policy, primarily in the form of human capital investment, supports economic objectives, in contrast to other welfare regimes where the focus is on social protection and redistribution. This approach often characterises welfare as supporting the industrialisation objectives of the developmental state.[11]

The East Asian model has been described as having features of the liberal model such as limited coverage of welfare entitlements, as well as features of the conservative model such as a significant role for family and community support, reinforcing existing social structure.[12] Kwong-leung Tang (2000) identified common characteristics of East Asian regimes including low government spending, flexible labour markets, and the targeting of social security at politically important groups.[13] The state's regulatory role is typically also cited in the literature.

Beyond economic development strategy, some posit that the commonalities in East Asian models are due to cultural factors such as Confucianism;[14] others point to institutional legacies from colonial heritage, as well as conservative-leaning authoritarian governments. At the same time, Holliday (2000), Ian Gough (2001),[15] and others have attempted to map out intraregional variations within the broad East Asian typology and chart out different paths each state has taken.

Attempts to compare and classify welfare regimes have often considered the following dimensions:

— Institutionalisation of social rights (e.g. whether or not there is a commonly acknowledged right to certain forms of social support as a citizen)
— Policy instruments or content of welfare programmes

— Share of welfare provision borne by the state and other actors
— Redistributive outcomes

Much attention is also given to the state's motivation. For instance, Aspalter (2001) adopts an actor-based perspective, pointing to greater political or democratic contestation, as well as pressure from social movements, as motivating the evolution of East Asian welfare regimes.[16]

While political considerations shape the underlying logic and evolution of welfare systems, this book focuses on unpacking the aims of socio-economic policy to analyse how various policy instruments in a given system work together to further these fundamental aims. After all, these aims have to be pursued by all but the most tyrannical governments, whether motivated by electoral performance in a functioning democracy or by the desire for political legitimacy in an authoritarian regime. There is a brief discussion on recent political developments in Chapter 11, but the reader who is interested in understanding politics, ideology, and governance in Singapore is encouraged to delve into the literature that explores these issues and their interplay in greater depth.[17]

Aims and Outcomes of the Socio-Economic System

A pithy articulation of the objective of socio-economic policy is the pursuit of inclusive growth, which the OECD defines as "economic growth that is distributed fairly across society and creates opportunities for all".[18]

Notwithstanding, it is useful to unpack the aims of the socio-economic system from the fundamental starting point of human well-being. This forms the bedrock of the social contract or social compact, which is the implicit agreement among members of a society to cooperate for mutual protection and benefits. The willingness of people to support a particular form of government, or set of policies, depends inter alia on:

(a) Tangible benefits in the form of security and economic gain
(b) The perceived fairness of the system in terms of opportunities, as well as what each citizen or group of citizens contributes and receives in return
(c) A sense of belonging, through shared national identity, ethnicity, culture, history, as well as social inclusion

These fundamentals can be distilled into the following objectives which a country's socio-economic system must help to deliver:

- Financial security
- Prosperity, or improvement in living standards
- Perceived fairness in opportunities and outcomes
- Social inclusion across class or socio-economic status

Each is vital to the social compact, and hence to social cohesion and a well-functioning society.

These are in turn supported by the following socio-economic outcomes, or indicators of well-being[19]:

1. **Income security** (inclusive of employment, income adequacy/stability, and retirement adequacy) and **affordability** (particularly of necessities such as food, housing, and healthcare) provide citizens with financial security.
2. **Real income growth** contributes to rising living standards or prosperity.
3. **Social mobility** (or economic mobility), the ability of those from less well-off backgrounds to climb the income ladder, reflects fair opportunities in a dynamic society.
4. **Income/wealth distribution** (or **inequality**) may affect perceived fairness of outcomes and social inclusion.

These outcomes are interlinked. For instance, income growth may determine income security for vulnerable groups. How a country achieves income growth shapes income distribution, which could in turn affect social mobility. Likewise, social mobility could influence income distribution as well as economic vitality, and hence income growth. These relationships are depicted in Figure 1.2.

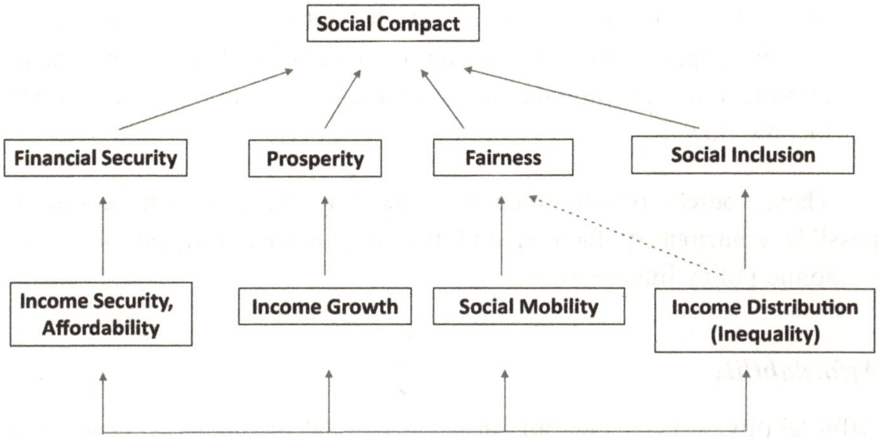

Figure 1.2 Socio-Economic Outcomes Underpinning the Social Compact

Income Security

Income security may come under threat from:

— Unemployment, particularly structural unemployment (caused by job-skills mismatch) and long-term unemployment, which can result in erosion of skills and human capital and consequently a decline in employability. Retrenchment is just one possible cause of unemployment, but is typically disruptive to a worker's finances given its sudden and involuntary nature, and it may be difficult for the worker to re-enter employment quickly at a similar wage level.

— Income volatility, associated with economic cycles or contingent work arrangements such as freelance or gig work. An uneven income stream can make loan servicing difficult, and hamper financial and retirement planning, especially for those with less financial buffer.

— Low, stagnant wages, which can result in the working poor being unable to make ends meet or to save enough for retirement.

— Insufficient retirement income, which could be due to low wages, gaps in employment, high consumption, debt, inadequate investment returns, or having capital tied up in illiquid assets that do not generate income flow.

These sources of economic precarity may themselves have several possible contributory factors, and typically attract a range of socio-economic policy interventions.

Affordability

Affordability is a key outcome in itself. Even if incomes rise faster than the price level for lower-income households in general, particular households and individuals may struggle to cope with the rising prices of certain essential goods and services (e.g. food, healthcare) if these essentials form an outsized share of their expenditure. Affordability may also be a concern for retiree households without income from employment.

Real Income Growth

Growth in real income, or income after adjusting for inflation, is generally a good indicator of rising purchasing power and economic well-being. However, it has several limitations. It does not account for non-market activity such as caregiving by family members, which adds value but does not show up in income statistics. Measures of aggregate income do not factor in the distribution of income, while individual and household incomes do not take into account the availability of public goods and amenities that are not priced, such as nature and clean air, or conversely, disamenities such as pollution, crowds, and queues.

To derive real income, nominal income must be deflated by a price index such as the Consumer Price Index (CPI), which is the price of a representative basket of goods. As consumption patterns change, the basket of goods that underpins CPI changes. CPI tracks changes in the aggregate price level, weighted by the items in the most recently defined expenditure basket. It does not track changes in living cost arising from changes to the composition of the basket itself. Hence, as consumption norms change, CPI growth may understate the experienced rise in living costs. Consequently, it is possible for people to feel poorer even as their real incomes grow.

Social Mobility

Social mobility may refer to a number of different concepts. Intragenerational mobility refers to the ability of an individual to move between socio-economic classes within his own lifetime, while intergenerational mobility refers to the ability to move between classes from one generation to the next.

Within intergenerational income mobility, a further distinction may be drawn between:

- Absolute intergenerational mobility, which is the ability of children to earn higher incomes than their parents, and
- Relative intergenerational mobility, which is their ability to move into a higher income percentile within their cohort as compared with their parents.

Absolute mobility is important for a sense of societal progress, while relative mobility (the typical focus in discussions on social mobility) is necessary for a sense of fairness.

While income inequality has been on the rise in many advanced economies since the 1980s, at least there is evidence that relative intergenerational mobility in countries such as the United States (US) and United Kingdom (UK) has been stable. Raj Chetty et al. (2014) found evidence that relative income mobility in the US had not changed significantly over time across birth cohorts from 1971 to 1986.[20]

On the other hand, absolute income mobility in the US has declined sharply — about 90% of those born in the early 1940s had higher real incomes than their parents, compared with just over 50% of those born in the early 1980s (Chetty et al., 2016).[21] Erzsébet Bukodi and John Goldthorpe (2018) found no overall decline in social mobility in the UK since the 1950s, although a person born to parents in managerial or professional positions remained 20 times as likely to find a similar job in adulthood than a person born to working-class parents.[22]

For those inclined to view the glass as half-empty, it is disappointing that relative income mobility in these countries does not appear to have improved despite efforts to widen educational opportunities for those from lower-income households. Furthermore, Miles Corak (2013) suggested that rising income inequality in the US is likely to lower intergenerational income mobility going forward, with the wealthy better able to transmit economic advantage to their children.[23]

Distribution of Incomes and Wealth (Inequality)

Although the income gap between rich and poor countries has narrowed in recent decades, inequality within countries has been on the rise. Between the mid-1980s and late 2000s, the Gini coefficient, a standard measure of income inequality, rose in 17 out of 22 OECD countries for which long-term data is available.[24] The 2008–2009 Global Financial Crisis shone the spotlight on Wall Street excesses, eliciting critiques of the system of market capitalism in which the crisis played out. The Occupy Wall Street protest against inequality sprung up in New York in 2011 and inspired copycat movements elsewhere.

The focus on inequality in developed economies has continued unabated into the 2010s and 2020s. French economist Thomas Piketty's *Capital in the Twenty-First Century*,[25] a book which traces historical trends in wealth and income inequality in Europe and the US, and promulgates a highly redistributive public policy agenda, shot to the top of the *New York Times* bestseller list in 2014. The book's thesis — that a return on private capital exceeding economic growth over the long term could lead to an upward spiral in wealth concentration — fuelled intense debate in academic circles and the popular press.[26] Piketty himself was dubbed a "rock star" economist, his celebrity status within the international elite reflecting the global zeitgeist.

Certainly, inequality may impinge on our sense of fairness. However, inequality and economic unfairness are not identical; Christina Starmans,

Mark Sheskin, and Paul Bloom (2017) cited evidence that people are more concerned with the latter than the former.[27] Hence, it is important to distinguish between inequality of outcomes and inequality of opportunities.

Inequality of outcomes across individuals in a society may have various causes, which can be placed on a scale from most objectionable to least:

1. Economic exploitation, discrimination, differential bargaining power
2. Differences in educational or employment opportunities
3. Differences in endowment or inheritance of wealth and other resources
4. Differences in endowment of innate ability or skills
5. Luck or chance through life
6. Differences in effort, application, or risk-taking

Of the above, #1 and #2 are clearly inimical to fairness and ought to be addressed. Some would argue for taxes and transfers to offset #3 and #4 (the lottery of birth) as well as #5 (the lottery of life).[28] Most would accept unequal outcomes stemming primarily from #6, particularly if differential rewards spur effort, enterprise, and innovation.[29] Interestingly, there is some evidence that one's own life experience may influence beliefs regarding the causes of inequality, and hence one's support for redistribution. A University of Michigan survey of US citizens conducted in 2017 found that those in the wealthiest 5% who had climbed the economic ladder were least supportive of wealth redistribution, whereas those in the top 5% who were born into wealth had attitudes towards inequality and redistribution similar to those of the general population.[30]

High inequality may stoke feelings of resentment and undermine societal trust,[31] especially if the less well-off think that the system is stacked against them. Hence the nature and causes of inequality matter — whether wealth arises primarily from inheritance, or is gained through work or enterprise, and how legitimate each of these routes to riches is perceived to be.

Beyond fairness, it is also worth considering how inequality is related to the other socio-economic dimensions of interest, viz. financial security, living standards, fair opportunities, and sense of belonging.

While it would be unconscionable to have abject poverty coexist alongside an excess of wealth in any society (whatever the cause), an unequal distribution of income or wealth does not always imply a lack of financial security or inadequate living standards among those at the lower-end of the income distribution.

If we are principally concerned with financial security and living standards, is this then a problem of indigence rather than inequality? Clearly the two concepts are linked, but a distinction can be drawn between absolute poverty and inequality. American philosopher Harry Frankfurt (2015), for example, argued that we are morally obligated to eliminate poverty, but not necessarily to reduce inequality.[32]

Measures of income inequality do not factor in the consumption of public goods and amenities which the state may make available at free or nominal cost, or informal transfers made between members of a family, clan, or community, which are especially common in developing countries.

What really matters, in fact, is distribution of utility, not distribution of incomes or even equality of consumption. Beyond a point, there is diminishing marginal utility from spending. A $10,000 luxury watch is unlikely to bring its owner a thousand times more utility than a reliable $10 watch; the greater disparity is between someone who has a watch and someone who does not, rather than between two people with watches of different quality. The general standard of living depends on affordable food and consumer products, and not on whether the wealthy are splurging on fine dining or luxury goods. This argument, while downplaying the significance of income inequality, may in fact support the case for higher taxes on the wealthy since there is diminishing marginal utility from wealth and consumption.

Some maintain that inequality must remain front and centre of the socio-economic agenda, and not just for reasons of fairness or concerns about indigence.

One set of concerns is whether inequality has an impact on economic growth and outcomes for society as a whole.

A 2014 OECD report highlighted that income inequality could have a negative impact on medium-term growth, a key reason being that the poorer members of society are less likely to invest in education.[33] Epidemiologists Richard Wilkinson and Kate Pickett (2009), in an influential book entitled *The Spirit Level: Why More Equal Societies Almost Always Do Better*,[34] argued that inequality has pernicious effects on societies. They claimed that in 11 social and health dimensions (such as physical health, drug abuse, education, and imprisonment), outcomes were significantly worse in countries with greater inequality, whether rich or poor, although there was subsequent debate over the robustness and replicability of their findings.[35]

Inequality may also undermine democracy if the rich are able to exert outsized political influence through political donations, for instance. While a concern in some countries, this is less likely in Singapore where there are caps on election spending by political parties; as it turned out, all political parties in the 2020 general election spent considerably less than their entitlement of $4 per voter.

Importantly, inequality may erode social mobility if the better-off can translate their wealth into permanent advantage for their descendants. Alan Krueger (2015) found a strong correlation between income inequality and intergenerational income elasticity (the degree to which one's parents' income predicts one's own income) across countries, a relationship which he dubbed the "Great Gatsby Curve".[36]

Inequality may, in fact, affect the lived experience of the individuals with lower income through higher costs and social exclusion. Their consumption basket and ability to participate in society may be affected by their position in the income ladder, and more so as the ladder extends, with rungs further apart.

With the gentrification of older residential precincts in Singapore, such as Tiong Bahru, traditional coffeeshops and provision stores have given way to hipster cafes selling more expensive food and desserts. These cafes can afford to pay higher rents because there is sufficient demand from middle-class Singaporeans for their fare. Through the mechanism of land and rents, the average prices of food and goods are raised in line with what the majority of Singaporeans can afford and are prepared to spend on. This increases prices for lower-income earners and reduces their choices.

A no less significant impact on the lower-income arises from social exclusion. For instance, a child with financial constraints may have to forgo the opportunity to join her friends for a meal at a restaurant after a class or school activity. Hence, inequality may directly affect one's sense of social belonging. This is the reason many developed countries are concerned with relative poverty, and not just absolute levels of poverty.

Should reducing the inequality of economic outcomes be a policy objective, then? Clearly, excessive inequality could undermine the social compact through various channels, but it is less clear what level of inequality is acceptable, or that less inequality is always better in the way that less poverty or higher living standards always is.

There may be a case to focus public policy on outcomes that are affected by inequality viz. affordability and living standards for those at the middle to lower end of the income distribution, access to education and economic opportunities as drivers of social mobility, and social inclusion, which contributes to social cohesion. Notwithstanding, it remains useful to track inequality and understand what is driving it, given the many potential links between inequality and socio-economic outcomes that matter.

Mapping Interlinkages in the Socio-Economic System

Of the five socio-economic outcomes/indicators that underpin the social compact viz. real income growth; income security (employment, income stability/adequacy, and retirement adequacy); affordability or cost of living; inequality; and social mobility, at least three — income growth, income security, and affordability — can be represented in a flowchart that shows how various policy levers may affect these outcomes (Figure 1.3).

This **Socio-Economic Flowchart**, as I call it, can be used to elucidate how various parts of a socio-economic system affect employment, incomes, savings, and consumption. The flowchart shows that there are many ways for the government to influence outcomes — upstream via

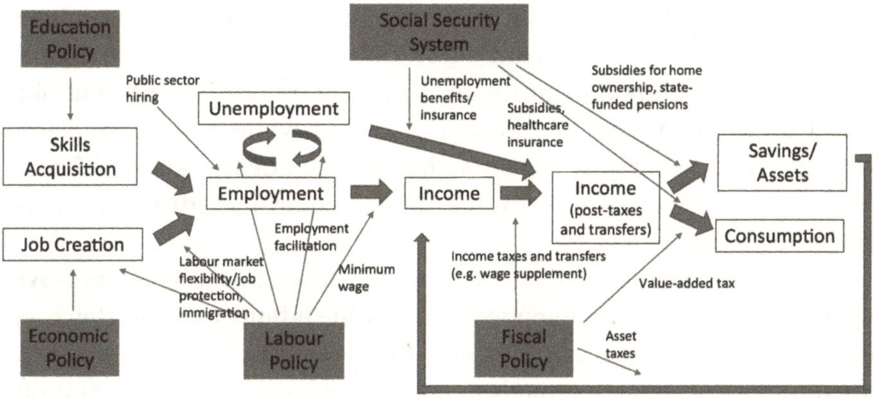

Figure 1.3 Socio-Economic Flowchart

interventions in the education system and job market, downstream via taxes and transfers, subsidised provision of public services, social insurance/risk pooling, or any combination of levers. Although not depicted in the flowchart above, monetary policy is also important for price stability, which affects consumption, savings, and investment.

A useful distinction may be drawn between curative and preventive social policies.[37] Curative policies refer to social transfers and other interventions to shore up incomes and mitigate inequality so as to insulate citizens from the market. This is linked to the concept of "decommodification", which captures "the degree to which welfare states weaken the cash nexus by granting entitlements independent of market participation" (Esping-Andersen, 1999).[38] In contrast, preventive and productivist policies focus on helping people adapt to a competitive labour market through asset-building strategies, particularly investment in human capital, as the cornerstone of the social investment state (Sherraden, 2003; Morel et al., 2012).[39]

The Socio-Economic Flowchart will be used in subsequent chapters to analyse changes to the Singapore System, as well as specific issues such as how to boost the wages of low-income workers.

A socio-economic system typically has an internal logic whereby various interlocking policies and institutions work together to support the economy and provide for citizens' needs.

For instance, in the Danish "flexicurity" system, a **competitive, open, market economy** is supported by a flexible labour market. The relative lack of job protection is compensated by a **comprehensive and generous social security system** that protects incomes while helping displaced workers return to employment through **active labour market policies**. To finance universal social security, the system requires a **redistributive fiscal system** with high taxes.

Singapore shares similarities in terms of a having a **competitive, open, market economy** supported by a **flexible labour market**. However, it relies on full employment to provide social security, with state-provided **unemployment benefits modest** and restricted to the less well-off. Instead, there is strong **emphasis on retraining and employment facilitation** to get workers quickly back into employment. Relatively **limited redistribution** allows for low taxes.

It is often useful to identify the underlying philosophy or guiding principle underpinning a system. This could be, for instance, self-reliance in the case of Singapore, or social rights based on citizenship in the case of the Nordic social democracies. In Chapter 3, I suggest that the Singapore System may be best characterised as personal effort with collective support, with the emphasis on individual responsibility sustained even as state assistance has been significantly enhanced.

This chapter has introduced five socio-economic indicators — income growth, income security, affordability, inequality, and social mobility — as the foundations of the social compact, and described how various policy levers may work together within a socio-economic system to deliver these outcomes. This sets the stage for a deeper exploration of how the Singapore System works, and how it must continue to evolve in order to sustain these outcomes.

Endnotes

1. Abraham Maslow, "A Theory of Human Motivation," *Psychological Review* 50(4) (1943): 370–396.
2. Paul Streeten in United Nations Development Programme (UNDP), *Human Development Report 1999* (New York: Oxford University Press, 1999), 16.

3. Amartya Sen, *Development as Freedom* (New York: Alfred Knopf, 1999).
4. "The World Bank in China: Overview," World Bank, accessed 1 May 2021, https://www.worldbank.org/en/country/china/overview.
5. Tan Weiping, "China's Approach to Reduce Poverty: Taking Targeted Measures to Lift People out of Poverty," presentation at Addis Ababa, 18 April 2018; World Bank, "Poverty Ratio Headcount at $1.90 a Day (2011 PPP)," World Development Indicators, last updated 19 March 2021, https://data.worldbank.org/indicator/SI.POV.DDAY?locations=CN.
6. World Bank, "Poverty Ratio Headcount at $1.90 a Day (2011 PPP)," last updated 19 March 2021, https://data.worldbank.org/indicator/SI.POV.DDAY?locations=GH.
7. Cited in Peter Hyland, "Singapore: Poet, Critic, Audience," *World Literature Written in English* 23(1) (1984).
8. Gøsta Esping-Andersen, *The Three Worlds of Welfare Capitalism* (Princeton: Princeton University Press, 1990).
9. Ian Holliday, "Productivist Welfare Capitalism: Social Policy in East Asia," *Political Studies* 48(4) (2000): 706–723.
10. Christian Aspalter, "The East Asian Welfare Model," *International Journal of Social Welfare* 15 (2006): 290–301.
11. The developmental state refers to the model of state-directed economic planning and development, characteristic of Japan and East Asian economies. See Chalmers Johnson, *MITI and the Japanese Miracle: The Growth of Industrial Policy, 1925–1975* (Stanford: Stanford University Press, 1982).
12. Yih-Jiunn Lee and Yeun-Wen Ku, "East Asian Welfare Regimes: Testing the Hypothesis of the Developmental Welfare State," *Social Policy & Administration* 41(2) (2007): 197–212.
13. Kwong-leung Tang, *Social Welfare Development in East Asia* (London: Palgrave, 2000).
14. Catherine Jones, "Hong Kong, Singapore, South Korea, and Taiwan: Oikonomic Welfare States," *Government and Opposition* 25(3) (1990): 446–462.
15. Ian Gough, *Welfare Regimes in East Asia and Europe*, paper delivered at the Annual World Bank Conference on Development Economics Europe 2000 (Paris, 27 June 2000).
16. Christian Aspalter, *Conservative Welfare State Systems in East Asia* (Westport: Praeger, 2001).
17. See, for instance, Kenneth Paul Tan, "The Ideology of Pragmatism: Neo-liberal Globalisation and Political Authoritarianism in Singapore," *Journal of Contemporary Asia* 42(1) (2012): 67–92; Chua Beng Huat, *Liberalism*

Disavowed: Communitarianism and State Capitalism in Singapore (Singapore: NUS Press, 2017).

18. "Inclusive Growth," Organisation for Economic Co-operation and Development (OECD), accessed 1 May 2021, http://www.oecd.org/inclusive-growth/.
19. For a wider set of indicators on inclusive growth and well-being, see OECD, *Opportunities for All: A Framework for Policy Action on Inclusive Growth* (Paris: OECD Publishing, 2018); OECD, *How's Life? 2020: Measuring Well-Being* (Paris: OECD Publishing, 2020).
20. Raj Chetty, Nathaniel Hendren, Patrick Kline, Emmanuel Saez, and Nicholas Turner, "Is the United States Still a Land of Opportunity? Recent Trends in Intergenerational Mobility," *American Economic Review* 104(5) (2014): 141–147.
21. Raj Chetty, David Grusky, Maximilian Hell, Nathaniel Hendren, Robert Manduca, and Jimmy Narang, "The Fading American Dream: Trends in Absolute Income Mobility Since 1940," *Science* 356(6336) (2017): 398–406.
22. Erzsébet Bukodi and John H. Goldthorpe, *Social Mobility and Education in Britain* (Cambridge: Cambridge University Press, 2018).
23. Miles Corak, "Income Inequality, Equality of Opportunity, and Intergenerational Mobility," *Journal of Economic Perspectives* 27(3) (2013): 79–102.
24. OECD, *Divided We Stand: Why Inequality Keeps Rising* (Paris: OECD Publishing, 2011).
25. Thomas Piketty, *Capital in the 21st Century* (Cambridge: Harvard University Press, 2014).
26. For a contrary view, see N. Gregory Mankiw, "Yes, r>g. So What?" *American Economic Review: Papers and Proceedings* 105(5) (2015): 43–47.
27. Christina Starmans, Mark Sheskin, and Paul Bloom, "Why People Prefer Unequal Societies," *Nature Human Behaviour* 1(4) (2017): 1–7.
28. On the role of chance in conferring outsized rewards in the winner-takes-all economy, a useful reflection is Facebook co-founder Chris Hughes's book, *Fair Shot: Rethinking Inequality and How We Earn* (New York: St. Martin's Press, 2018).
29. The Gallup World Poll includes a question on people's satisfaction with opportunities to get ahead by working hard.
30. Alain Cohn, Lasse J. Jessen, Marko Klasnja, and Paul Smeets, "Why Do the Rich Oppose Redistribution? An Experiment with America's Top 5%" (28 May 2019), http://dx.doi.org/10.2139/ssrn.3395213.

31. According to the 2020 Edelman Trust Barometer (published by public relations and marketing consultancy firm Edelman), high income inequality is associated with lower trust in government, with the impact of inequality on trust exceeding that of economic growth.
32. Harry G. Frankfurt, *On Inequality* (Princeton: Princeton University Press, 2015).
33. OECD, "Focus on Inequality and Growth," December 2014, https://www.oecd.org/social/Focus-Inequality-and-Growth-2014.pdf. Based on Federico Cingano, "Trends in Income Inequality and Its Impact on Economic Growth," OECD Social, Employment and Migration Working Paper No. 163, 2014, http://dx.doi.org/10.1787/5jxrjncwxv6j-en. A 2015 International Monetary Fund study also found that increasing the income share of the poor and the middle class actually increases growth while a rising income share of the top 20% results in lower growth (Era Dabla-Norris, Kalpana Kochhar, Nujin Suphaphiphat, Frantisek Ricka, and Evridiki Tsounta, "Causes and Consequences of Income Inequality: A Global Perspective," IMF Staff Discussion Notes, 15 June 2015).
34. Richard G. Wilkinson and Kate Pickett, *The Spirit Level: Why More Equal Societies Almost Always Do Better* (London: Allen Lane, 2009).
35. See, for instance, Christopher Snowdon, *The Spirit Level Delusion: Fact Checking the Left's New Theory of Everything* (London: Democracy Institute/Little Dice, 2010).
36. Alan Krueger, "The Great Utility of the Great Gatsby Curve," *Brookings Social Mobility Memos*, 2015.
37. Julian Le Grand, "Treating Poverty," *Guardian*, 21 September 1999.
38. Gøsta Esping-Andersen, *Social Foundations of Postindustrial Economies* (New York: Oxford University Press, 1999), 43.
39. Michael Sherraden, "From the Social Welfare State to the Social Investment State," *Shelterforce: Journal of Affordable Housing and Community Building* (March/April 2003); Nathalie Morel, Palier Bruno, and Joakim Palme, eds., *Towards a Social Investment Welfare State? Ideas, Policies and Challenges* (Bristol: Policy Press, 2012).

Chapter 2

Singapore's Socio-Economic Trends and Performance

To understand the Singapore System, context is crucial. The socio-economic indicators identified in Chapter 1 provide the canvas against which we can trace the evolution of Singapore's policies. This chapter surveys the key trends in income, unemployment, inequality, and social mobility in Singapore, focusing on the period up to 2019, in view of the significant economic dislocation in 2020 arising from the COVID-19 pandemic. 2020 data is discussed separately in Chapter 11, together with the implications of COVID-19 for Singapore's future.

Singapore has recently joined the ranks of wealthy nations, but international comparisons of GDP per capita overstate Singapore's relative standard of living.

Export-led industrialisation and sustained economic growth propelled Singapore's per capita GDP from $1,581 (US$517) in 1965 to $88,991 (US$65,233) in 2019 (Figure 2.1).[1]

Adjusted for inflation, this was a 5.1% per annum real increase from $5,790 to $83,330 (in chained 2015 SGD), or from US$4,088 to US$59,073 (in constant 2010 USD).[2]

Singapore's significantly exceeded those of Mexico and South Africa, two economies that had similar per capita GDP in 1965, and also bettered those of leading industrialised economies such as the US, UK, and Japan (Figure 2.2).

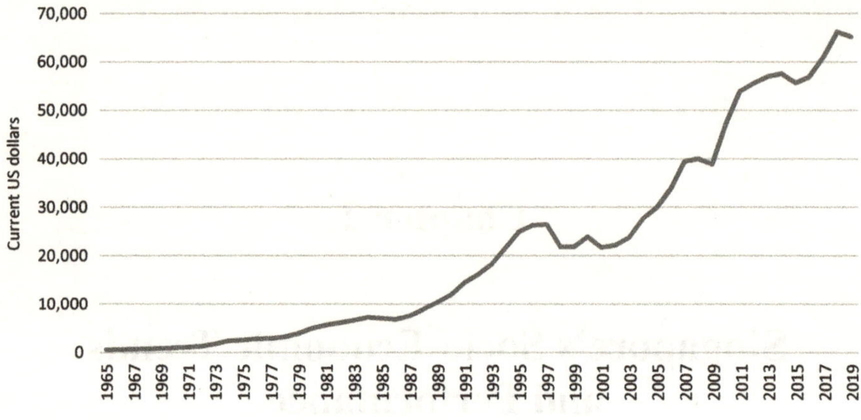

Figure 2.1 Singapore's GDP per Capita

Source: World Bank, World Development Indicators, last updated 19 March 2021.

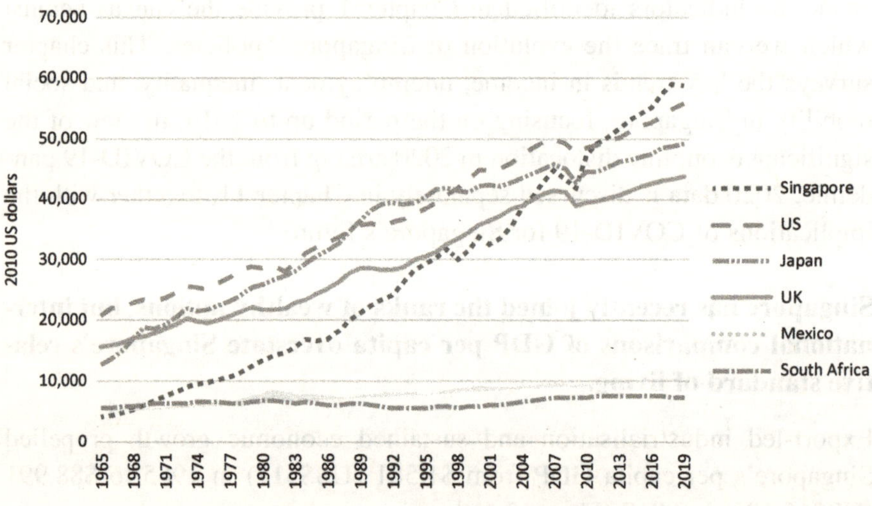

Figure 2.2 Real GDP per Capita

Source: World Bank, World Development Indicators, last updated 19 March 2021.

Singapore has one of the world's highest per capita GDP in nominal or purchasing power parity (PPP) terms (Table 2.1), a commonly used metric to compare economic well-being across countries. However, much of its GDP comprises corporate profits, given that many multinational

Table 2.1 Countries with Among the Highest GDP per Capita (2019)

Economy	**GDP per Capita (Current USD)**	**Economy**	**GDP per Capita (PPP) (Current International $)**
Luxembourg	114,705	Luxembourg	121,293
Switzerland	81,994	**Singapore**	**101,376**
Ireland	78,661	Qatar	96,491
Norway	75,420	Ireland	88,241
Iceland	66,945	Switzerland	70,989
United States	65,281	United Arab Emirates	69,901
Singapore	**65,233**	Norway	66,832
Qatar	64,782	United States	65,281

Source: World Bank, World Development Indicators, last updated 19 March 2021.

corporations have global or regional headquarters in Singapore. As a result, Singapore's wage share of GDP, at around 40% in 2019, is lower than those of many advanced economies.[3]

Income data provides a better indication of how well-off Singaporeans are. In wage terms, Singapore is up among the leading advanced economies, especially in recent years, but not at the stratospheric levels suggested by comparisons of per capita GDP.

In fact, Singapore incomes are in and around those of advanced economies. In 2019, Singapore's median gross monthly income from work of full-time employed residents[4] (including employer Central Provident Fund (CPF) contributions) was $4,563, or about $55,000 a year. This was higher than Hong Kong's median income, and comparable to the UK's, but somewhat lower than incomes in the US and Finland before taxes (Table 2.2). Adjusting for PPP, however, would place Singapore ahead of these economies.

Incomes in Singapore have grown considerably since 1965. The median worker's pay in 2015 was about 6.5 times that in 1965, after adjusting for inflation; the real wage of workers at the 20th percentile was over five times that of lower-income workers in 1965.[5]

While growth in employment income dipped in the first half of the 2000s as the global electronics slowdown and Severe Acute Respiratory

Table 2.2 Median Income of Full-Time Employed in Selected Economies (2019)

Economy	**Median Income Among Full-Time Employed (SGD)**
United States	5,421
Finland	4,794
Sweden	4,572
United Kingdom	4,418
Singapore (residents)	**4,000** **(4,563 including employer CPF)**
Japan	3,358
Hong Kong	3,308
South Korea	2,739

Note: Data for Sweden, Japan, and South Korea pertain to all workers (full-time and part-time). Median income for full-time workers would be higher.

Source: Comprehensive Labour Force Survey, Manpower Research and Statistics Department, Ministry of Manpower (MOM) (Singapore); national statistical agencies (other economies).

Syndrome (SARS) exerted a toll on Singapore's economy, income growth rebounded strongly in the second half of the decade and continued into the 2010s, where it has been broadly sustained across different income strata (Figure 2.3). Between 2001 and 2019, real median income from work of full-time employed residents grew by a cumulative 44%, compared with 12% in the US and 8% in the UK.[6]

In 2019, an international comparison of median wealth per adult (in USD) by Credit Suisse in its annual *Global Wealth Databook* found Singapore just behind France and the UK but ahead of Spain and Italy.[7]

In tandem with income growth, living standards have risen significantly.

Singaporeans have seen marked improvements in measures of human development (Table 2.3) and material living standards. In the years following Singapore's independence, many moved from zinc-roofed houses

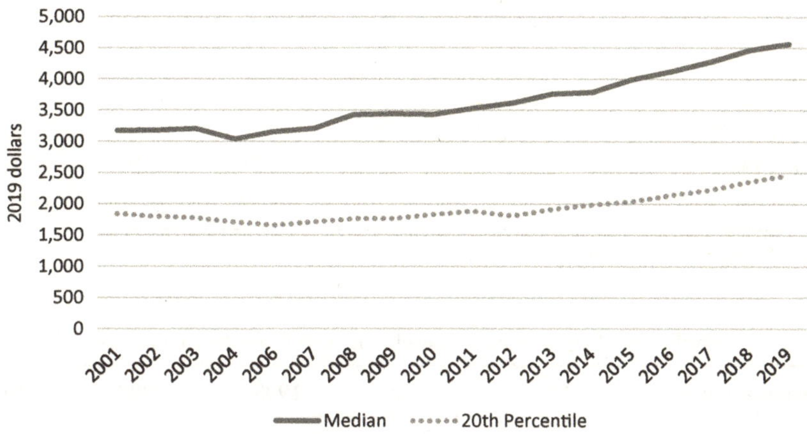

Figure 2.3 Real Gross Monthly Income from Work of Full-Time Employed Residents

Note: Data includes employer CPF contributions. Data for 2005 not available.
Source: Manpower Research and Statistics Department, MOM.

without proper sanitation to modern apartments. Television sets and washing machines became staple items in households (Table 2.4), and many more families could afford private cars, overseas holidays, and domestic help.

The labour market has been mostly tight over the years, with unemployment remaining low as labour force participation increased.

The overall unemployment rate declined steadily from around 9% in 1965 to below 3% in the early 1980s.[8] While unemployment spiked in 1985–1987 during Singapore's first post-independence recession, the unemployment rate remained below 3% from 1989 to 1997.

The annual average resident unemployment rate[9] was elevated between 1998 and 2005, reflecting the impact of the Asian Financial Crisis, post-dot-com slowdown, and SARS. Between 2006 and 2019, it remained below 4%, except for 2009 (Figure 2.4). Even during the Global Financial Crisis, wage support for employers in the form of the Jobs Credit Scheme limited the magnitude and duration of the spike in unemployment.

Table 2.3 Life Expectancy, Literacy, and Years of Schooling

	1965	1985	2005	2020
Life expectancy at birth (residents) (years)	64.5	73.9	80.1	83.9
Literacy rate (15 years and over)	60.2%	85.7%	94.1%	97.1%
Mean years of schooling	—	5.7	9.3	11.3

Source: Singapore Department of Statistics.

Table 2.4 Percentage of Households with Consumer Durables

Consumer Good	1978	1988	1998	2008	2018
Washing machine	15	73.5	90.6	94.7	96.1
Air-conditioner	7.8	19.4	58.3	74.7	79.7
Car	23.8	29.8	35.9	38.3	35.3
Personal computer	NA	11.2	47.9	77	81.4
Mobile phone	NA	NA	51	94.5	98
Television	86.9	97.9	98.5	99.5	97

Source: Household Expenditure Survey, Singapore Department of Statistics.

Singapore's unemployment rate has been lower than those of most advanced economies over many years, up to 2019 (Table 2.5).

Singapore's long-term unemployment rate, defined as unemployment of 25 weeks (approximately six months) or longer, has also been relatively low. While it climbed after the Asian Financial Crisis of 1997–1998 and remained elevated in the first half of the 2000s, it declined to 0.6%–0.8% between 2010 and 2019 (Figure 2.5).

The labour force participation rate has steadily increased over the years as more females and older workers joined the workforce, plateauing at about 68% since 2015 (Figure 2.6). However, male labour force participation has fallen slightly between 2001 and 2019. The number and incidence of discouraged workers (i.e. those no longer looking for work as they think they will not succeed in their search) have been fairly stable in the decade up to 2019 (Figure 2.7).

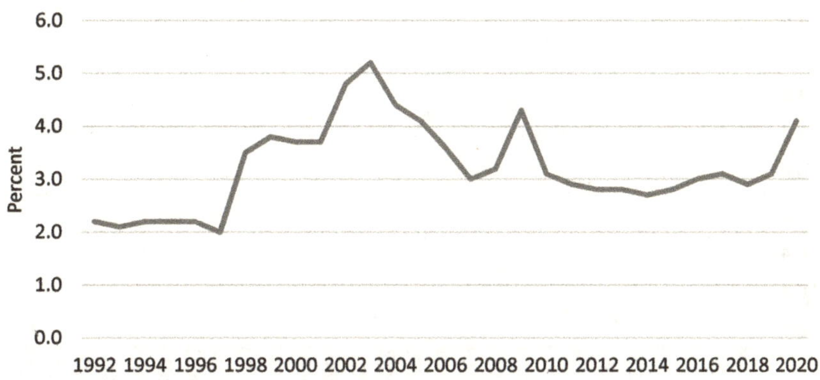

Figure 2.4 Annual Average Resident Unemployment Rate

Source: Labour Force Survey, Manpower Research and Statistics Department, MOM.

Table 2.5 Unemployment Rates in Selected Economies (2019)

Economy	Unemployment Rate (%)	Economy	Unemployment Rate (%)
Japan	2.4	Denmark	5.0
Singapore	**3.1**	Australia	5.2
Germany	3.1	Canada	5.7
United States	3.7	Finland	6.7
South Korea	3.8	Sweden	6.8
United Kingdom	3.7	France	8.4
Switzerland	4.4	Spain	14.1

Source: World Bank, World Development Indicators, last updated 19 March 2021.

Singapore's success in uplifting a broad swath of its populace in a generation has widened income dispersion.

In the 1950s, Singapore was already a cosmopolitan city with a small elite of Western-educated professionals, successful traders, and businessmen. However, the bulk of the population was poor by international standards. In 1955, a decade before Singapore's independence, the modal wage of male workers in regular employment was \$100–\$120 per month.[10] Nearly

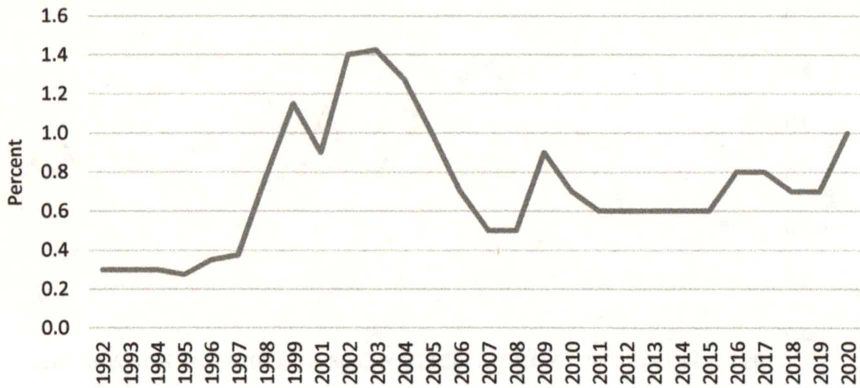

Figure 2.5 Annual Average Resident Long-Term Unemployment Rate

Note: Data not available for year 2000.

Source: Labour Force Survey, Manpower Research and Statistics Department, MOM.

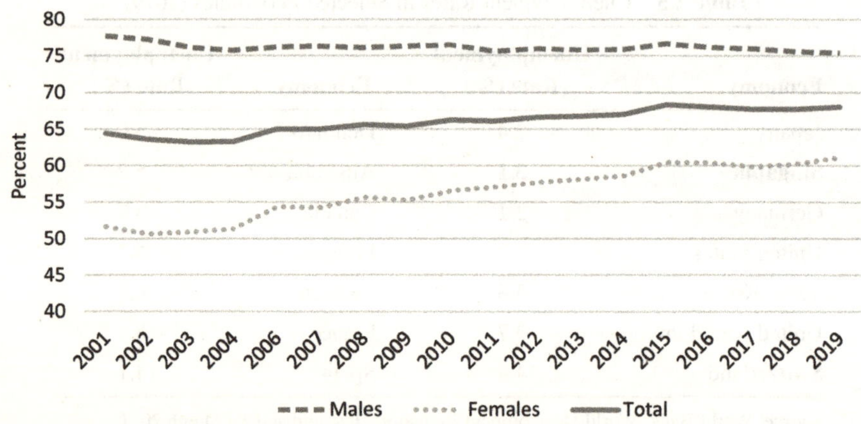

Figure 2.6 Resident Labour Force Participation Rate

Note: Data not available for year 2005.

Source: Comprehensive Labour Force Survey, Manpower Research and Statistics Department, MOM.

a fifth of households, accounting for about a quarter of residents, earned below the state-defined minimum income standard in the early 1950s.

Through the 1970s, 1980s, and 1990s, GDP soared and incomes rose broadly, the proverbial tide lifting all boats. Employment growth between 1983 and 1996 was heavily skewed towards high-paying occupations.[11]

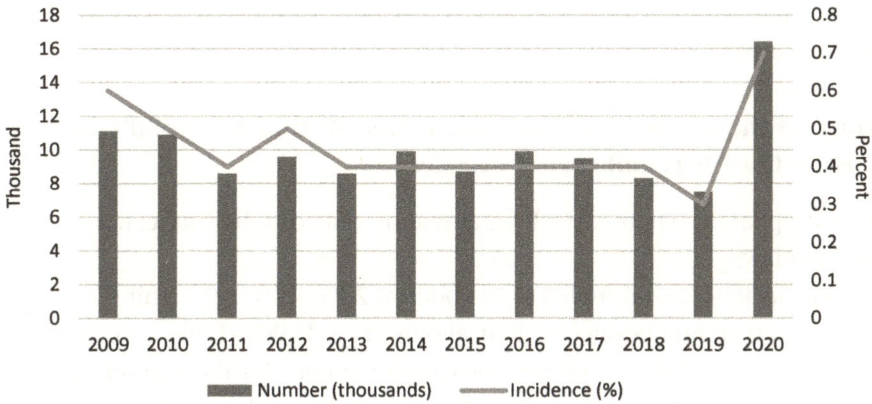

Figure 2.7 Residents Discouraged from Seeking Work

Note: Incidence of discouraged workers refers to discouraged workers as a percentage of the labour force, inclusive of discouraged workers. The spike in 2020 was due to the COVID-19 pandemic.
Source: Comprehensive Labour Force Survey, Manpower Research and Statistics Department, MOM.

Managerial and professional jobs accounted for three-quarters of employment growth during this period, while growth in production and related jobs was negligible. This reflected the increasing educational and skills profile of the workforce. Given the rapid rise in incomes and living standards, it was easy for Singaporeans to rally around the singular focus on economic growth.

Today, the context is somewhat different. With economic growth since 2011 slower than in previous decades, wage growth is also set to slow, bringing issues of distribution to the fore in public discourse.

While the rising tide may have lifted all boats in the years of rapid economic expansion, it lifted some much more than others. The expansion in job opportunities rewarded those possessing educational qualifications and skills with outsized income gains. Private residential property prices skyrocketed, growing by about 16 times between 1975 and 2011, compared with growth of about 10 times in nominal GDP per capita in this period.[12] Consequently, land and property owners saw their wealth expand even more quickly.

Singapore's extraordinary success at lifting its people into the middle and upper middle classes has widened the income and wealth distribution from a narrow elite sitting atop a broad base to more widely dispersed income strata.

Many of the less well-off today are better off than the middle-income class in the 1990s and earlier decades.

This is apparent whether we look at real income or other indicators of living standards.

For instance, households in the bottom 20%–40% are earning more in real terms than middle-income households in the 1990s (Table 2.6). Average monthly household income per household member for the second quintile in 2018 ($1,715) was higher in real terms than the average of the third (middle) quintile in 1998 ($940, or about $1,273 in 2018 dollars), and average of the fourth quintile in 1993 ($929, or about $1,361 in 2018 dollars).[13]

A person in the bottom 20% today is likely to have better-quality consumer durables, more food choices, and greater opportunities to travel abroad than a person in the middle-income group in the 1990s and earlier decades. For instance, 61% of households in the bottom quintile in 2018 had air-conditioning, compared with 56% of the middle quintile in 1998.

The proportion of resident households (excluding retiree households) earning below $1,000 in nominal work income rose to 4.8% in 2003, before gradually declining to 2.0% in 2019 (Figure 2.8). Those in the next income tier of $1,000–$1,999 fell from over 12% in 2000 to just under 6% in 2019. At the other end of the income spectrum, however, the proportion of households earning $20,000 or more surged from 2.5% in 2000 to 15.6% in 2019.

With the vast majority better off relative to previous generations and to other countries, it may be tempting to dismiss the issue of inequality as irrelevant. However, as discussed in Chapter 1, inequality may have pernicious effects on growth, social mobility, and social cohesion, unless the effects of inequality can be adequately addressed.

Hardship does in fact exist in Singapore, even if not to the extent experienced in poorer countries. Teo You Yenn (2017) struck a chord with many readers with her description of the daily challenges that lower-income Singaporeans face, ranging from lack of privacy in crowded, cramped homes to limited control over their time.[14] With this in mind, it is worth taking a closer look at recent trends in inequality in Singapore.

Table 2.6 Average Monthly Household Income from All Sources per Household Member

	1st Quintile	2nd Quintile	3rd Quintile	4th Quintile	5th Quintile
1993	$240	$422	$620	**$929**	$2,071
1998	$304	$608	**$940**	$1,424	$3,215
2003	$281	$635	$1,004	$1,572	$3,790
2008	$419	$1,019	$1,659	$2,608	$6,557
2013	$577	$1,387	$2,208	$3,471	$8,837
2018	$715	**$1,715**	$2,741	$4,291	$10,238

Note: Income data includes permanent transfers such as Workfare Income Supplement.
Source: Household Expenditure Survey, Singapore Department of Statistics.

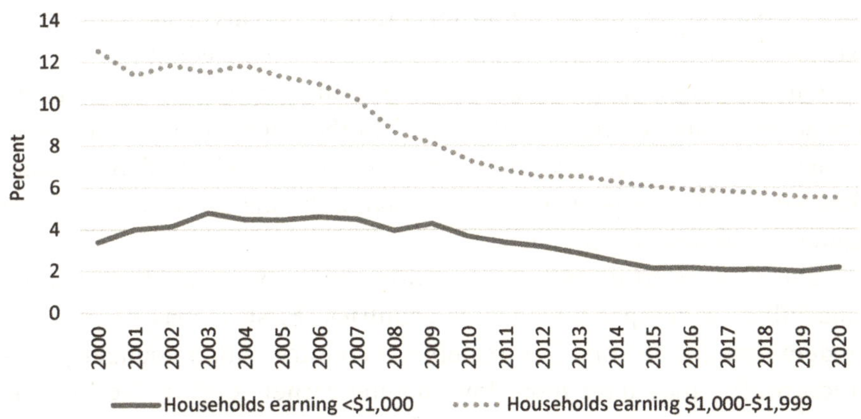

Figure 2.8 Proportion of Lower-Income Households (Excluding Retiree Households)
Note: Based on monthly household income from work, including employer CPF contributions.
Source: Manpower Research and Statistics Department, MOM.

Among resident households in Singapore, there has been a declining trend in income inequality over the past decade.

Measure 1: Gini Coefficient of Household Income per Household Member

The Gini coefficient is a standard measure of inequality, ranging from 0 (where income is equally distributed among all households or persons)

to 1 (where all income accrues to only one household or person). Singapore's household income Gini coefficient declined in the 1980s from around 0.44 in 1980 to around 0.41 in 1990.[15] It then rose through the 1990s and early 2000s to a high of 0.482 in 2007, thereafter stabilising and then gradually declining to 0.452 in 2019, the lowest since 2001 (Figure 2.9). Factoring in government taxes and transfers, which have grown over the years, brings down the Gini to 0.398 in 2019.

Adopting the OECD's method to adjust for different household sizes (square root scale instead of per household member),[16] Singapore's Gini coefficient was 0.411 in 2019 before accounting for taxes and transfers, and 0.352 after.

While Singapore's pre-tax-and-transfer Gini coefficient is lower than those of most OECD countries, the Gini coefficient is higher than most after accounting for taxes and transfers (Table 2.7). This is due to the more extensive redistribution through higher taxes in OECD countries.[17]

One may argue that as a city, it would be more appropriate to compare Singapore's Gini coefficient with those of other global cities, which tend to have higher inequality than the countries to which they belong. However, Singapore is also a nation, making the impact of inequality on national cohesion also pertinent.

The Gini coefficient has limitations as a measure of inequality, especially for comparisons across countries. First, it may be affected by demographic factors. For example, a country with a younger population profile may have more low-income earners even if the lifetime expected income of the young workforce is high. A more accurate picture of inequality should take into consideration the dispersion of expected lifetime wealth and not just current income. Notwithstanding, the median ages of most of the countries in Table 2.7 are fairly close to that of Singapore, apart from Germany and Japan where the population is older, and the US and Australia which have a younger profile.

Second, unlike measures of relative poverty (such as the proportion of population living with less than half the median income), the Gini coefficient may be skewed by very high-income earners. A broad rise in lower-income earners' wages is unlikely to reduce Singapore's Gini by much unless incomes at the upper end fall.

While Singapore publishes the income Gini coefficient adjusted for taxes and transfers, this does not capture implicit government subsidies

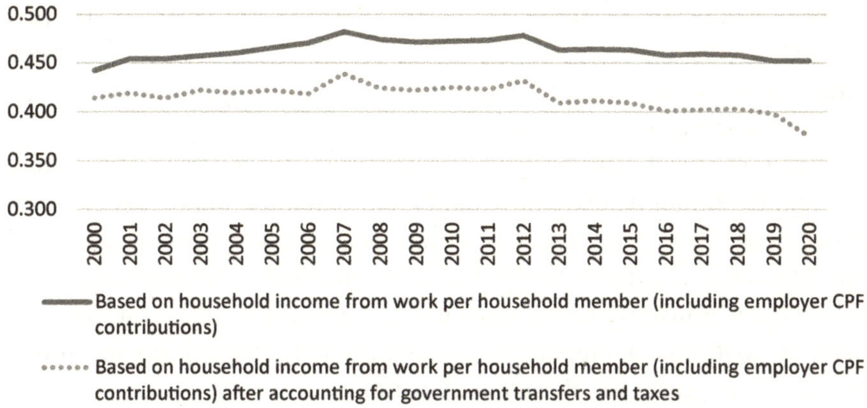

Figure 2.9 Singapore's Household Income Gini Coefficient

Source: Singapore Department of Statistics

Table 2.7 Pre- and Post-Taxes-and-Transfers (TT) Income Gini Coefficient (OECD Measure) for Selected Economies

Country	Pre-TT	Post-TT	Difference	Year
Switzerland	0.386	0.299	0.087	2017
South Korea	0.402	0.345	0.057	2018
Singapore	**0.411**	**0.352**	**0.059**	**2019**
Canada	0.427	0.303	0.124	2018
Sweden	0.428	0.275	0.153	2018
Norway	0.429	0.262	0.167	2018
Denmark	0.446	0.264	0.182	2017
Australia	0.454	0.325	0.129	2018
Germany	0.500	0.289	0.211	2017
Japan	0.504	0.339	0.165	2015
US	0.505	0.39	0.115	2017
Finland	0.509	0.269	0.240	2018
UK	0.513	0.366	0.147	2018
France	0.529	0.301	0.228	2018

Note: Singapore's Gini coefficient is based on household income from work (including employer CPF) among resident employed households, whereas those of OECD economies are based on income from all sources (including non-work income from investments and property, which tends to be more unequally distributed than income from work), among all resident households.

Source: Singapore Department of Statistics; OECD database, retrieved 8 April 2021 (other countries).

for public housing or the extra interest paid by the state on the first $60,000 of CPF balances, which are forms of progressive redistribution. Variations in social institutions and modes of social transfer make cross-country comparisons of the magnitude of social transfers difficult.

The Gini coefficient after taxes and transfers also does not capture transfers from family, clan, or community, which are important in socio-economic systems that emphasise family or community provision of welfare. The tax and transfer wedge (i.e. the reduction in the Gini as a result of taxes and transfers) understates the government's role, as it does not factor in government support for community help through tax incentives and matching grants for charitable donations.

Measure 2: Ratios of Top or Median Incomes to Bottom Incomes

Inequality may also be tracked by looking at income ratios, such as the ratio of the 90th to 10th percentile household incomes (P90:P10 income ratio, Figure 2.10) or the ratio of 50th to 20th percentile individual incomes (P50:P20 income ratio, Figure 2.11).

The P90:P10 household income ratio shows a sharp rise in inequality between 2000 to 2008, before a gradual decline up to 2015, followed by a slight pick-up. The P50:P20 income from work ratio indicates a rise in inequality up to 2008, and a gradual decline from 2015 to 2019.

Despite slight variations in the trend across the Gini coefficient and income ratio measures, they all point to a rapid rise in inequality up to 2008, followed by a levelling-off or decline with some fluctuations from year to year. This break in trend owes in part to efforts to raise income at the lower end. However, in absolute dollar terms, the gap between the top and bottom incomes continues to grow.

While real wage growth at the 20th percentile exceeded median wage growth between 2014 and 2019, lower-income households also saw their expenditure grow faster than the median.

In the five years between 2014 and 2019, P20 incomes of Singapore residents and citizens grew, in real terms, faster than the median (Table 2.8).

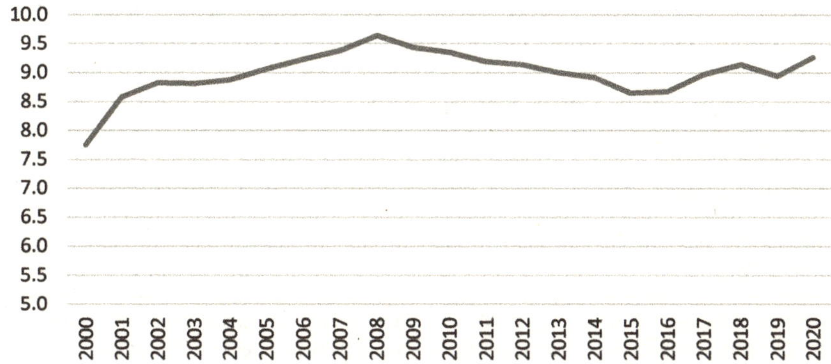

Figure 2.10 Ratio of Monthly Household Income from Work per Household Member (Including Employer CPF Contributions) at the 90th Percentile to 10th Percentile Among Resident Employed Households

Source: Singapore Department of Statistics.

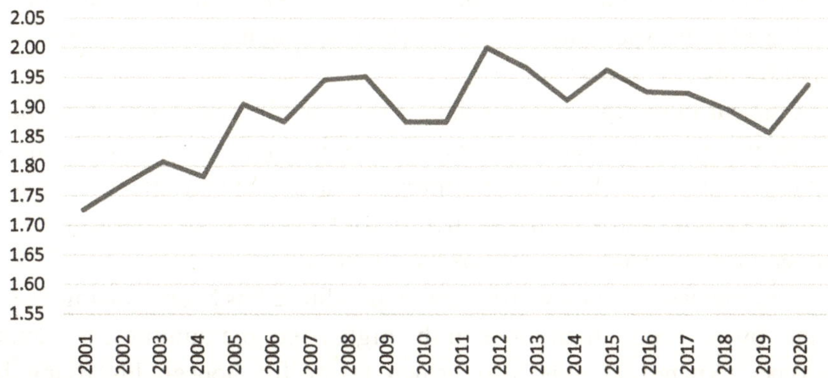

Figure 2.11 Ratio of 50th to 20th Percentile Gross Monthly Income from Work of Full-Time Employed Residents

Source: Singapore Department of Statistics.

Notwithstanding positive real income growth at the 20th percentile, many lower-income Singaporeans may not feel better off. The P20 comprises different individuals and households over time. It does not track a particular citizen or household longitudinally. Some may have risen up the income deciles while others may have fallen. A longitudinal data study

Table 2.8 Annualised Change in Real Gross Monthly Income from Work (Including Employer CPF) of Full-Time Employed Residents and Citizens

	June 2009–June 2014	June 2014–June 2019
P20 (Residents)	2.3%	4.4%
P50 (Residents)	1.9%	3.8%
P20 (Citizens)	1.6%	4.6%
P50 (Citizens)	2.1%	3.9%

Source: "Singapore Citizens in the Labour Force," MOM occasional paper (23 January 2020), with data updated by Manpower Research and Statistics Department, MOM.

using administrative data would be necessary to have this picture. Another group who may not feel better off are retirees, who do not gain from rising employment income.

It is also important to consider expenditure. For this, we can look at the Household Expenditure Survey, which is conducted once every five years (Tables 2.9, 2.10).

A caveat in interpreting this data is that not all households in the bottom income quintile may in fact be poor. Some may be households in or near retirement, with little or no employment income but possessing significant accumulated wealth — such households may be able to rely on their savings to spend in excess of their incomes.

Nonetheless, it is noteworthy that expenditure has been growing faster for the lower-income than those in the higher-income quintiles. By housing type, expenditure has also grown faster for households living in Housing and Development Board (HDB) flats compared with those living in private properties. This could reflect changes in their consumption basket. For instance, private tuition and enrichment programmes for children are viewed by many families today as essential rather than discretionary complements to school-based learning. Bubble tea has become an everyday indulgence, mobile phone plans that come with handset upgrades once in two years are the norm, and overseas travel, even if to nearby destinations, is commonplace. The resetting of social norms as general affluence increases could have a significant impact on the finances of lower-income households.

Table 2.9 Average Annual Change in Average Monthly Household Income and Expenditure from All Sources Between 2012/13 and 2017/18

Percentile	Nominal Income Growth	Expenditure Growth
1st–20th	2.8%	3.0%
21st–40th	2.7%	1.2%
41st–60th	3.0%	0.4%
61st–80th	1.6%	0.8%
81st–100th	2.9%	0.0%

Source: Household Expenditure Survey, Singapore Department of Statistics.

Table 2.10 Average Annual Change in Average Monthly Household Income and Expenditure per Household Member from All Sources Between 2012/13 and 2017/18

Percentile	Nominal Income Growth	Expenditure Growth
1st–20th	4.4%	4.4%
21st–40th	4.3%	2.9%
41st–60th	4.4%	2.2%
61st–80th	4.3%	2.1%
81st–100th	3.0%	1.7%

Source: Household Expenditure Survey, Singapore Department of Statistics.

Real income growth does not account for lifestyle inflation arising from a changing consumption basket as social norms evolve; hence, people may feel cash-strapped even if their real incomes grow.

Consumption norms have changed tremendously in a generation. Growing up in an upper-middle-class family, my indulgences as a youth were a plate of noodles at the school canteen and a drink from the vending machine. Today, students often congregate in casual restaurants and hipster cafes. I had my first trip outside Southeast Asia at the venerable age of 13; my daughter visited Australia, South Korea, and Taiwan before turning four. Like many other parents, I send my pre-schoolers to various learning and enrichment programmes which I did not have the opportunity to experience as a child in the early 1980s.

As spending norms and societal expectations change, inflation as measured by CPI may understate the experienced rise in living costs, as highlighted in Chapter 1. Wage growth for lower-income households may thus be quickly eaten up by rising expenditure.

Income from work may be diverging from wealth, but this is difficult to ascertain.

Any empirical study that aims to explain individual income from work or relate it to other variables or outcomes must take into consideration that an individual's wage may no longer be a good proxy for how well-off he or she is. First, the spouse of a high-income earner may choose to stay out of the workforce or take on a job for personal fulfilment rather than remuneration. This makes household income per household member a more pertinent indicator.

Second, income from work and wealth are diverging as more households accumulate and pass on wealth, often in the form of property, and generate investment income from their assets.[18] Data from the Household Expenditure Survey conducted once every five years shows that income from non-work sources is rising. The share of non-work income out of household income for the 5th (richest) quintile increased from 4.1% in 2007/08 to 10.3% in 2017/18, while that for the 4th quintile increased from 4.1% to 7.3% over the same period. However, data on the distribution of household wealth is not available.

In Singapore, the stock of wealth has grown significantly over time, fuelled by both the rise in income and considerable property price appreciation. A landed property in a good location that cost a mere $100,000 in the 1970s could be worth several million dollars today, the appreciation in its value far outstripping general inflation. This has greatly enhanced the capacity of the well-off to pass on wealth to their children.

However, in the absence of capital gains taxes and related filing requirements, household wealth can only be proxied by other indicators such as housing type. Consequently, it is difficult to measure or monitor wealth inequality in Singapore.

To understand inequality, we have to look beyond incomes to the distribution of wealth.

In most countries, whether advanced or developing, wealth tends to be more unequally distributed than income.[19] A study of 28 OECD economies found that wealth concentration was twice the level of income concentration, with the wealthiest 10% of households holding on average 52% of total household wealth, and the least wealthy 60% of households holding just over 12%.[20]

The OECD study found that up to a quarter of households had negative net worth i.e. their liabilities exceeded the value of their assets. This is, however, unlikely to be the case in Singapore where the bulk of the populations owns HDB flats whose value has appreciated over time, holding stable in recent years. Moreover, there are strict loan-to-value caps in place for property loans so that households are not saddled with excessive debt.

Notwithstanding, at the upper end of the wealth spectrum, many of Singapore's wealthy have multiple private properties and considerable equity holdings. Anecdotally, it would seem that the scions of wealthy families can live off investment income quite comfortably, regardless of their own income from employment.

With society stratifying, there are concerns that various advantages in addition to wealth are passed on, such as a good education and professional connections that can be a significant advantage in the job market. This could further constrain social mobility, which is a cornerstone of the social compact.

Social mobility is vital for the legitimacy of Singapore's meritocracy narrative.

In a fair and dynamic society, anyone should be able to move up the income and wealth ladder regardless of one's family background or starting position. Intergenerational social mobility is particularly vital for the legitimacy of the Singapore's brand of meritocracy and the national narrative that anyone can succeed by dint of hard work. One of the four abiding principles of governance spelled out by Prime Minister Lee Hsien Loong in 2004 is "Reward for Work, and Work for Reward".[21] There is a concomitant commitment on the part of the government to ensure opportunities for all citizens.

Singapore's relative social mobility remains high compared with other advanced countries.

A 2015 study by the Ministry of Finance (MOF) compared the incomes of fathers and their eldest sons (at average ages 48 and 30, respectively), with the sons drawn from cohorts born between 1978 and 1982.[22] Unsurprisingly, given the general growth in incomes, absolute mobility was strong. The real median income of the sons at age 30 exceeded that of their fathers at age 48 by about 35%, with 61% of sons earning more than their fathers.

Singapore also fared well in relative mobility compared with the US and several other advanced economies. 14% of children born to the lowest income quintile of parents reached the top quintile of their own cohorts, higher than in the US, UK, Denmark, and Canada (Table 2.11).

Table 2.12 shows that 14.3% of children born to parents in the bottom 20% of incomes reached the top (5th) quintile upon growing up. In a completely mobile society, one would expect children from the lowest income quintile families to have an equal chance (20%) of landing in any of the five income quintiles at working age. Notwithstanding, Singapore exhibits a higher degree of intergenerational mobility than the US, where only 7.5% of children born in the lowest income quintile families reached the top quintile.

MOF also assessed if mobility had changed over time by comparing the correlation between the income ranks of children and their fathers for two different cohort groups. The income correlation coefficient was 0.21 for the 1969–1973 cohorts, and 0.22 for the 1978–1982 cohorts, suggesting little change in mobility between these two cohort groups over a period of nearly a decade. As the MOF paper highlighted, this could reflect the continued expansion of education and job opportunities into the 1980s and 1990s, which sustained income mobility for the 1978–1982 cohorts. However, it is possible that income mobility may overstate wealth mobility.

Table 2.11 Percentage of Children Who Reached the Top 20% of Income Among Children Born to Parents in the Bottom 20% of Incomes

Singapore	14.3
Canada	13.5
Denmark	11.7
United Kingdom	9.0
United States	7.5

Source: "Income Growth, Inequality and Mobility Trends in Singapore," MOF occasional paper (August 2015).[23]

Table 2.12 Percentage of Children Who Reached Each Income Quintile Among Children Born to Parents in the Bottom 20% of Incomes

	Child's Quintile				
	1st	**2nd**	**3rd**	**4th**	**5th**
United States	33.7	28.0	18.4	12.3	7.5
Singapore	24.0	22.0	20.9	18.8	14.3

Source: "Income Growth, Inequality and Mobility Trends in Singapore," MOF occasional paper (August 2015).

While social mobility in Singapore has remained relatively high up to this point, it is expected to be more challenging to sustain.

To borrow Senior Minister Tharman Shanmugaratnam's metaphor, the income "escalator" is slowing as the Singapore economy matures and growth slows. With a wider dispersion of income and wealth, there is a greater likelihood of social stratification where it is harder for citizens to escape the gravitational pull of their own income and wealth strata.

Among the forces that could hamper social mobility is assortative marriage, where the wealthier and better educated tend to marry one another, passing on to the next generation wealth, resources, a good education, as well as social and professional networks that could give them a leg-up in their careers.

The heavy investment of the more well-off in their children's education, including preschool education, is an important factor that we will circle back to in Chapter 7 on education policy. At the other end of the income spectrum, the less well-off may have fewer resources, time, or (for some) inclination to invest in their children's education. How the state can come in to offset this disadvantage will also be discussed in Chapter 7.

Summarising Outcomes

In recent years, Singapore has managed to:

- Sustain real income growth despite being at the income levels of advanced economies;
- Keep unemployment and structural unemployment low prior to the COVID-19 pandemic;
- Stem the rise in income inequality, although inequality post-taxes and transfers remains high compared with other countries, and there is little data to monitor trends in wealth distribution; and
- Maintain relatively high intergenerational income mobility powered by the expansion of educational opportunities in the past.

However, it is expected that these outcomes will be increasingly difficult to sustain. In particular, it will take tremendous effort to hold back the tide of rising inequality amid intense global economic competition, and to keep social mobility going against the currents of inherited advantage.

Endnotes

1. Unless otherwise stated, all dollar figures in this book refer to Singapore dollars. The average exchange rate in 2019 was 1 US dollar to 1.36 Singapore dollars.
2. Sources: Singapore Department of Statistics; World Bank, World Development Indicators.
3. Sources: Singapore Department of Statistics; Organisation for Economic Co-operation and Development (OECD), *OECD Compendium of Productivity Indicators 2019* (Paris: OECD Publishing, 2019), 100.

4. While most income and manpower-related data released by the Ministry of Manpower (MOM) are for Singapore residents (citizens and permanent residents), the trends for Singapore citizens mirror those for Singapore residents closely as citizens have consistently formed about 85% of the resident population. For data on labour market outcomes for Singapore citizens, see MOM, "Singapore Citizens in the Labour Force" (occasional paper, 23 January 2020), https://stats.mom.gov.sg/iMAS_PdfLibrary/mrsd-Singapore-Citizens-in-the-Labour-Force.pdf.
5. Tharman Shanmugaratnam, Budget Statement, 2015. Wages of lower-income workers in 1965 are proxied by employees of rubber slipper factories, who earned $87 a month ($340 in 2015 dollars) according to the *Ministry of Labour Annual Report 1965*.
6. US data is based on median earnings in 2019 dollars of full-time employed workers (employees and self-employed) (Table P-43, Current Population Survey, Annual Social and Economic Supplements, US Census Bureau). UK data is based on median weekly earnings at 2019 prices of full-time employees (Annual Survey of Hours and Earnings, UK Office for National Statistics, https://www.ons.gov.uk/employmentandlabourmarket/peopleinwork/earningsandworkinghours/bulletins/annualsurveyofhoursandearnings/2019#measuring-this-data).
7. Credit Suisse Research Institute, *Global Wealth Databook 2019* (Credit Suisse, October 2019), 117.
8. Sources: Singapore Department of Statistics, Ministry of Manpower.
9. It is more pertinent to look at the resident unemployment rate rather than the overall unemployment rate, given that foreign workers comprise about a third of the Singapore workforce, and the vast majority are required to leave Singapore if they are without employment. Resident unemployment rate is only available from 1992 onwards.
10. Sydney Caine, *Report of the Committee on Minimum Standards of Livelihood* (Singapore: Government Printing Office, 1957), 13–26.
11. Monetary Authority of Singapore (MAS), "Quality of Employment Growth in Singapore 1983–96," MAS occasional paper 2, 1997, https://www.mas.gov.sg/~/media/MAS/Monetary%20Policy%20and%20Economics/Education%20and%20Research/Research/Economic%20Staff%20Papers/1997/MASOP002_ed.pdf.
12. Sources: Urban Redevelopment Authority, Singapore Department of Statistics.
13. For older data, see Singapore Department of Statistics (DOS), *Trends in Household Income and Expenditure, 1993–2003* (Singapore: DOS, September 2005).

14. Teo You Yenn, *This Is What Inequality Looks Like* (Singapore: Ethos Books, 2017).
15. Ministry of Finance (MOF), "Income Growth, Inequality and Mobility Trends in Singapore," MOF occasional paper, August 2015.
16. The OECD's square root scale implies more resource sharing as household size increases. Adopting the square root scale reduces the Gini coefficient by more for countries with larger household sizes, such as Singapore.
17. Ibid.
18. Such trends have been observed in other mature economies. For instance, the United Kingdom Institute of Fiscal Studies estimated that inheritances would increase lifetime incomes by an average of 14% for those born in the 1980s, compared with just 8% for those born in the 1960s. Those born in the 1980s to parents in the top fifth of the wealth distribution would enjoy a 29% boost to lifetime income from inheritance, compared with 5% for those born to parents in the bottom fifth. See Pascale Bourquin, Robert Joyce, and David Sturrock, "Inheritances and Inequality over the Life Cycle: What Will They Mean for Younger Generations?" *IFS Report* R188 (London: The Institute for Fiscal Studies, April 2021).
19. World Economic Forum (WEF), *The Inclusive Development Index 2018* (WEF, 2018), 4.
20. Carlotta Balestra and Richard Tonkin, "Inequalities in Household Wealth Across OECD Economies: Evidence from the OECD Wealth Distribution Database," OECD Statistics Working Paper No. 2018/1, 2018.
21. Lee Hsien Loong, speech at the opening of the Commonwealth Association of Public Administration and Management Biennial Conference, 24 October 2004, https://www.nas.gov.sg/archivesonline/data/pdfdoc/2004102401.htm.
22. MOF, "Income Growth, Inequality and Mobility Trends in Singapore."
23. Data for US from Raj Chetty, Nathaniel Hendren, Patrick Kline, and Emmanuel Saez, "Where is the Land of Opportunity? The Geography of Intergenerational Mobility in the United States," *Quarterly Journal of Economics* 129(4) (2014). Data for UK from Jo Blanden and Stephen Machin, "Up and Down the Generational Income Ladder in Britain: Past Changes and Future Prospects," *National Institute Economic Review* 205(1) (2008): 101–116. Data for Denmark from Simon Halphen Boserup, Wojciech Kopczuk, and Claus Thustrup Kreiner, "Stability and Persistence of Intergenerational Wealth Formation: Evidence from Danish Wealth Records of Three Generations" working paper, 2014. Data for Canada from Miles Raymond Corak and Andrew Heisz, "The Intergenerational Earnings and Income Mobility of Canadian Men: Evidence from Longitudinal Income Tax Data," *Journal of Human Resources* 34(3) (1999): 504–533.

Chapter 3

Singapore's Socio-Economic System — Distinctive Features and Adaptation to Emerging Challenges

Former Prime Minister Lee Kuan Yew expressed in his memoirs that Singapore's approach towards redistribution was guided by the "need for balance between individual competition and group solidarity". He wrote, "If winner takes all, competition will be keen, but group solidarity weak… with rewards evenly distributed, the greater the group solidarity, but the weaker the total performance because of reduced competition."[1] In this paradigm, a trade-off between economic growth and equity is inescapable.

Wary of the fiscal strain imposed by welfare spending in the West, Lee's government sought to uphold self-reliance and reinforce the Confucian value of taking responsibility for one's family, both as a means of sustaining economic dynamism through hard work as well as to keep state finances on an even keel.

This has remained the organising principle of Singapore's socio-economic system — one that is centred on individual effort and self-sufficiency through income from work, accompanied by strict fiscal rectitude. The pursuit of economic growth has primacy as it is seen as the means of achieving all other objectives — creating jobs, raising incomes, improving living standards, providing financial security, and giving the state the resources for public spending and redistribution.

In the 2005 Budget speech, Prime Minister Lee Hsien Loong summarised Singapore's approach:

> *Our social compact is rather different. It is based on personal responsibility, with the family and community playing key roles in supporting people through difficulties. The state will provide a safety net, but it should be a last resort, not a first resort, and should focus on the minority who need help the most. We thus avoid state welfare, which will erode our incentive to achieve and sap our will to strive. Our social compact enables us to keep taxes low, and lets people keep the fruit of their labour and businesses the rewards of their enterprise. And when we do well and have budget surpluses, we can distribute some of them back to Singaporeans.*[2]

The Singapore System has some similarities to other East Asian and Southeast Asian models of welfare capitalism, as highlighted by Christian Aspalter (2006),[3] as well as M. Ramesh and Mukul G. Asher (2000). Ramesh and Asher observed that while Southeast Asian economies had relatively weak commitments to social insurance, such as pensions or unemployment insurance, they had put in early and relatively large investment in basic healthcare and particularly education.[4]

Notwithstanding, Singapore has taken self-reliance further and for longer than other Southeast Asian economies. Ramesh (2004) noted, "Singapore is a special case in the region because of its tenacity in resisting the expansion of state provision of income protection, and because of the extent to which it has gone to encourage and/or compel individuals to meet contingencies on their own."[5] American political scientist Ron Haskins (2011) described Singapore as a "crucible of individual responsibility" that has created "one of the best educated, most disciplined, and most self-reliant populations in the world".[6]

The Singapore Approach: Personal Effort with Collective Support

Singapore's socio-economic system is geared towards financial self-sufficiency or "self-reliance", in line with the principle of "Reward for

Work, and Work for Reward". The key features of the Singapore System may be summarised as follows:

1. **Growth-oriented economic and labour policy** to create good job opportunities
2. Heavy **investment in education and skills** to help citizens take up the jobs created
3. Strong **support for reskilling and job matching**, along with **employment incentives** for unemployed or at-risk workers
4. **Minimal unemployment benefits** to encourage a quick return to work
5. **Low taxes** to encourage work and enterprise
6. **Limited universal subsidies**, so as not to encourage dependency on the government, except for education and public housing
7. **Targeted help for the needy**, in keeping with fiscal prudence
8. Reliance on **mandatory savings** for the key needs of housing, healthcare, and retirement, supplemented by limited risk pooling (social insurance)
9. Encouragement of **family and community support**, through tax incentives and subventions

These features are captured in the Socio-Economic Flowchart, with preferred pathways denoted by dark solid arrows (Figure 3.1).

Over the years, Singapore's political leaders have renewed the warning against adopting Western-style welfare spending, seeing this as a sure path to fiscal perdition.[7] Also at risk is the culture of personal responsibility, which welfare entitlements are viewed as undermining.

Prime Minister Lee Hsien Loong observed that in other developed countries, "welfare has drained fiscal resources and, more damagingly, eroded the work ethic and encouraged an entitlement mentality."[8] In an interview at the St. Gallen Symposium in 2015, then-Deputy Prime Minister (DPM) Tharman Shanmugaratnam said of the Singapore way, "it's about keeping alive a culture where I feel proud that I own my home and I earn my own success through my job. I feel proud that I'm raising my family. Keeping that culture going is what keeps a society vibrant."[9]

The Singapore government's preferred dictum is that "economic growth is the best social welfare programme,"[10] or its variant, "a job is the best welfare" and full employment "the best protection for our people".[11]

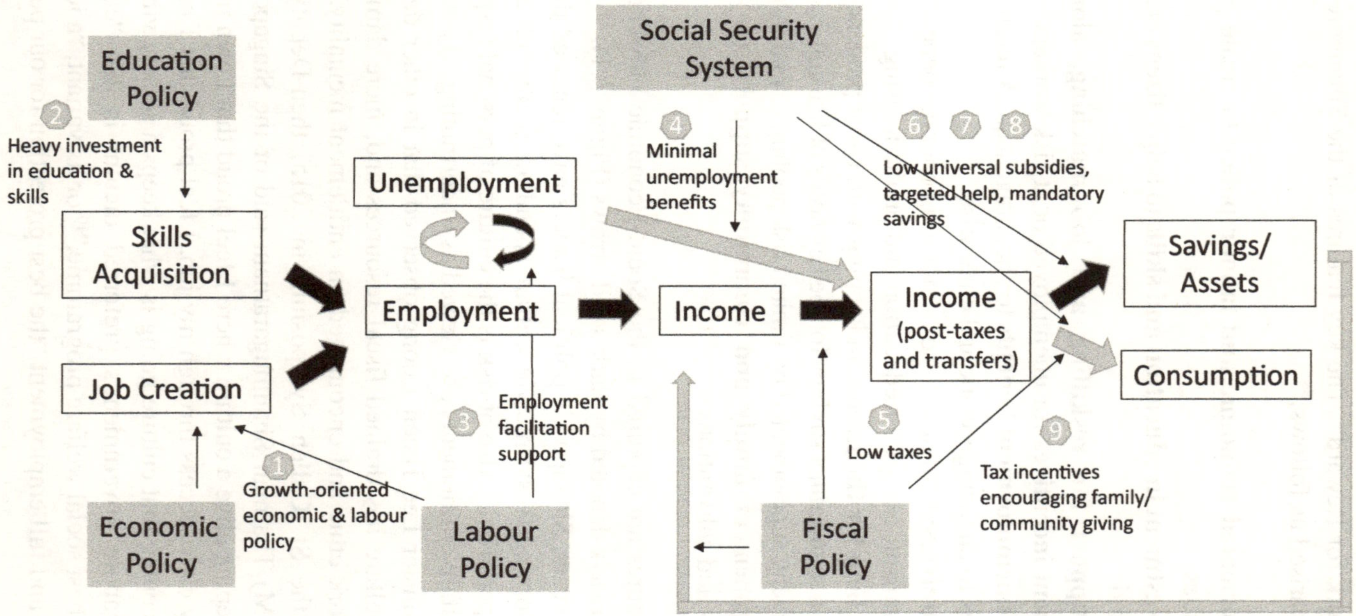

Figure 3.1 Singapore's Socio-Economic Flowchart

This belief finds expression in two ways. First, in the emphasis on job creation as the cornerstone of Singapore's development strategy and industrial policy, and indeed, socio-economic policy. Second, in public policies that have traditionally promoted individual self-reliance over government welfare provision or social risk pooling.

Accordingly, the government has tended to avoid social provision or subsidies on a universal or population-wide basis, with two notable exceptions — public housing and education.

Education and housing are viewed as social investments rather than expenditure, given that housing is an asset that can appreciate in value, while education raises the human capital of individuals and the nation. In the early years after Singapore's independence, the government provided highly subsidised public housing and loans to promote home ownership, so as to give citizens a tangible stake in the country and its future. Recognising the importance of education to economic growth and jobs, the government made high-quality and affordable public education available to all.

While subsidised basic education features prominently in most countries, particularly in East Asia, housing is not a typical welfare programme in Western models, nor is state involvement in housing provision a feature common to most East Asian economies.[12]

In other areas such as public healthcare and transport, the government also provides significant capital grants and operational subsidies to corporatised service providers, but support to end users tends to be means-tested, with a greater focus on cost recovery and fiscal sustainability. A key principle in the provision of subsidised services is co-payment in order to avoid overconsumption.

Singapore can thus be considered a "social investment state" focused on building up citizens' human capital and housing assets, enabling them to compete in the labour market, rather than insulating them from market forces, as would be the case in Western social welfare states.[13]

While at one level Singapore's emphasis on lean government and market discipline has commonalities with free market libertarianism, the state in fact plays a central role in directing and regulating economic and social development. This is consistent with what Senior Minister Tharman has called an "activist" approach to policymaking where the government need not be large but must be focused on areas requiring intervention, such as the provision of public goods.[14] There is no assumption that markets or society, left entirely to themselves, will deliver optimal outcomes; at the same time, government efforts are aimed at supporting rather than suppressing the initiative of market participants and community stakeholders. In his 2015 interview at the St. Gallen Symposium, then-DPM Tharman described Singapore's approach as "achieving a paradox of active government support for personal responsibility, rather than active government support to take over personal responsibility or community responsibility".[15] Asked whether he believed in the concept of a social safety net, he spoke instead of a "trampoline" helping those suffering setbacks to bounce back up.

In brief, the Singapore System is characterised by active state intervention that supports and reinforces, rather than replaces, individual and community responsibility. Self-reliance is a useful label but does not adequately capture the role of the government in topping up the incomes and savings of citizens, investing in education, or offsetting the cost of housing and healthcare. **Personal effort with collective support** is my preferred appellation for Singapore's approach. Over time, state assistance has been stepped up and has taken new forms, but the emphasis on self-help has remained a constant.

In the early 2000s, Singapore's social security system comprised three officially recognised pillars:

a) Home ownership through subsidised public housing
b) Central Provident Fund (CPF), a compulsory savings programme that provides for housing, healthcare, and retirement needs
c) Healthcare assurance in the form of government subsidies for medical treatment, a savings plan (MediSave), basic insurance (MediShield), and state assistance for the most needy (MediFund), collectively known as the "S+3M" framework

In keeping with the principle of individual responsibility, CPF is based on fully funded individual savings accounts, in contrast to unfunded or pay-as-you-go pension systems financed by tax collections. Likewise, individuals are expected to pay for medical expenses with their own savings in their MediSave accounts (introduced in 1984), although this was complemented in 1990 by a basic low-cost insurance plan called

MediShield, with an endowment fund called MediFund set up in 1993 to provide a safety net for those unable to afford even subsidised treatment.

Singapore has traditionally eschewed direct unemployment benefits and limited social assistance to a small base of the most needy families, consistent with its emphasis on self-reliance. The mainstay of public welfare has been the Public Assistance Scheme, a safety net of last resort for the elderly poor and disabled who are without family support.

While Community Care (ComCare) was introduced in 2005 to provide short- to medium-term assistance for needy families during periods of job or income loss, it remains fairly restricted in coverage, and is not considered part of the mainstream social security system.

In contrast to a number of advanced economies where pensions, public healthcare, and unemployment benefits constitute the bulk of social security spending, the emphasis on public housing and individual savings (Figure 3.2) in the Singapore System reflects an asset-based, social investment approach. A stylised comparison of the Singapore System with other socio-economic models is given in Table 3.1.

As described in Chapter 2, Singapore's socio-economic system has worked well for the vast majority of Singaporeans over the decades. Incomes rose rapidly along with life expectancy and literacy, while unemployment remained consistently low. These outcomes buttressed the social compact, enabling the logic of self-reliance, and provided the state with the political mandate and resources to pursue an economic growth agenda.

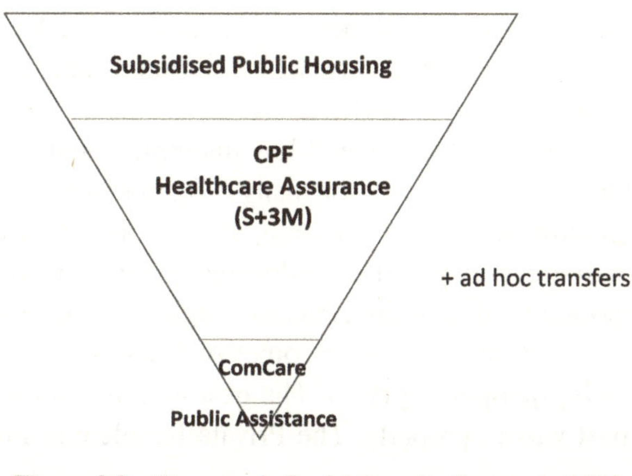

Figure 3.2 Singapore's Social Security System in 2006

Table 3.1 Stylised Comparison with Other Socio-Economic Models

	Labour Policy	**Social Security**	**Fiscal Policy**
Continental Europe Corporatist e.g. Germany, France	High job protection, rigid labour market	High income protection: occupational social security. Corporatist social service provision.	High taxes, redistribution across life cycle
Nordic Social Democratic/ Flexicurity e.g. Denmark, Norway	Low job protection, flexible labour market	High income protection: universal social insurance. Public social service provision. Active employment facilitation support.	High taxes, redistribution
Anglo-Saxon Liberal e.g. United States, United Kingdom, Canada	Low job protection, flexible labour market	Moderate income protection: targeted social assistance, private savings, and insurance.	Moderate taxes, redistribution
Singapore (Personal Effort with Collective Support)	Low job protection, flexible labour market	Low income protection: modest and targeted social assistance, mandatory savings. Active employment facilitation support.	Low taxes, redistribution

It is worth noting that political and social stability, low corruption, and high trust[16] in government agencies and institutions, have contributed significantly to strong economic and social outcomes over the years. These features of the Singapore System did not come about by chance, but were shaped by a suite of policies aimed at fostering social harmony, clean government, and strong institutions, which although not covered in this book, are well-documented elsewhere.[17]

In addition to rising incomes and low unemployment, two other features underpinned social security for many Singaporeans.

First, **large families**. It was not uncommon in the past for families to have seven or more children. Less educated parents, in their old age, would be supported by their more educated, higher-earning children without having to depend on their own incomes or savings.

Second, **rising property prices**. The best investment one could have made in the past was in property. The Private Residential Property Price

Index grew at a compound annual rate of 7.7% from 1975 to 2013, before dipping and then climbing back to an all-time high in 2020 (Figure 3.3). The Housing and Development Board (HDB) Resale Price Index grew even faster at a compound annual rate of 8.1% between 1990 and 2013, although it declined by a cumulative 10% in the subsequent seven years (Figure 3.4). Many Singaporeans continue to invest the bulk of their wealth and CPF savings in property.

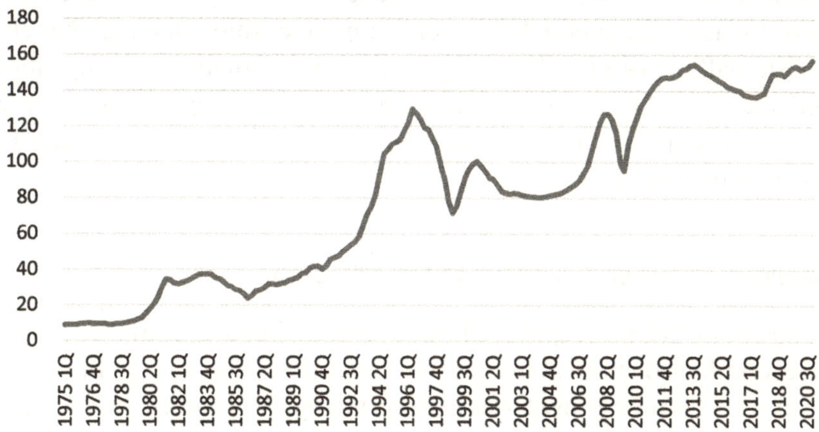

Figure 3.3 Private Residential Property Price Index

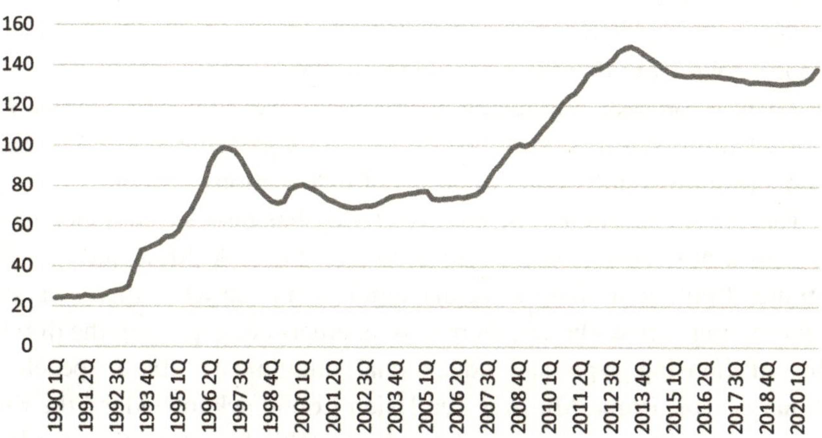

Figure 3.4 HDB Resale Price Index

Emerging Challenges

Entering the 21st century, emerging challenges have necessitated a refreshing of Singapore's socio-economic system, but without a fundamental departure from the core tenet of personal effort with collective support.

These challenges include a maturing economy; rising inequality and social stratification arising from Singapore's economic progress; changing demographics, with the ageing population and shrinking family size making healthcare and retirement adequacy key concerns; and the rising cost of living as Singapore has become a more cosmopolitan, global city.

Externally, the global driving forces of international competition, economic volatility, and technological advances have changed how Singaporeans make a living, the income shocks they are subject to, and the protection they require.

Maturing Economy and Social Stratification

Singapore's GDP per capita and incomes continued to grow strongly in the second half of the 2000s and into the 2010s (Figure 2.3, Table 2.6). However, economic growth has slowed since 2016 and is set to remain weak given the global economic fallout from COVID-19, as well as the maturing of Singapore's economy. Notably, the state-commissioned Committee on the Future Economy,[18] which released its report in 2017, envisaged average GDP growth of 2%–3% per year over the following decade, down from the 3%–5% annual GDP growth target articulated in the 2010 Economic Strategies Committee and the 2003 Economic Review Committee reports. When the pie is not growing as quickly, public attention invariably shifts to issues of distribution.

The greater dispersion of incomes today has also led to concerns of growing stratification along socio-economic lines. A 2017 study by the Institute of Policy Studies on social capital found that while there was still social mixing across classes, there was an emerging gap along the dimensions of housing type and educational attainment.[19] In a speech in February 2018, Prime Minister Lee Hsien Loong acknowledged the risk, observing that "any society which has been stable for a long time tends to stratify."[20] These concerns were echoed by other Members of Parliament (MPs) in the 2018 debate on the President's Address.

The more highly educated and affluent are more likely to marry one another than across socio-economic strata. According to studies, assortative mating (also known as homogamy) accounted for about a third of the increase in inequality in the United States between 1967 and 2007 and about 11% of increased inequality in OECD countries between the early 1980s and early 2000s.[21] In Singapore, the proportion of young married couples whose educational qualifications match (at a fairly granular level) rose from 42% in 2000 to 52% in 2010 and 56% in 2020, with around 80% of young married university graduates having a graduate spouse.[22] The affluent are able to pass on wealth and advantages to children through investment in education as well as access to personal and professional networks, giving their children an advantage in school and in their careers. In particular, wealth passed on in the form of property and assets grows with successive generations, which may lead to entrenched inequality.

Sustaining social mobility will become more difficult, requiring the state to put greater investment into education and creating opportunities for all in order to level the playing field.

Ageing Society

Singapore's citizen population aged 65 and above is expected to increase from about 590,000 in 2020 to over 900,000 by 2030, making Singapore one of the world's fastest ageing nations.[23] The proportion of citizens aged 65 and above rose from 10.1% in 2010 to 16.8% in 2020 (Figure 3.5), and is projected to be about one in four by 2030.[24] According to the United Nations, the share of Singapore's population aged 65 and above is expected to increase by 20.9 percentage points between 2019 and 2050, the largest projected gain by any country besides South Korea,[25] while the median age will rise to 52.8 years.[26]

Fertility rates have been below replacement level since 1977. The decline has been marked of late, reaching 1.14 in 2018 and 2019, and an all-time low of 1.1 in 2020, despite substantial financial incentives and subsidies given to encourage parenthood.[27] This reflects changing societal norms and attitudes regarding marriage and parenthood, improving educational attainment, as well as lifestyle aspirations amid the rising cost of living. The old age support ratio (number of citizens aged 20–64 per citizen aged 65 and above) has declined from 13.5% in 1970 to 3.7% in 2020 (Table 3.2).

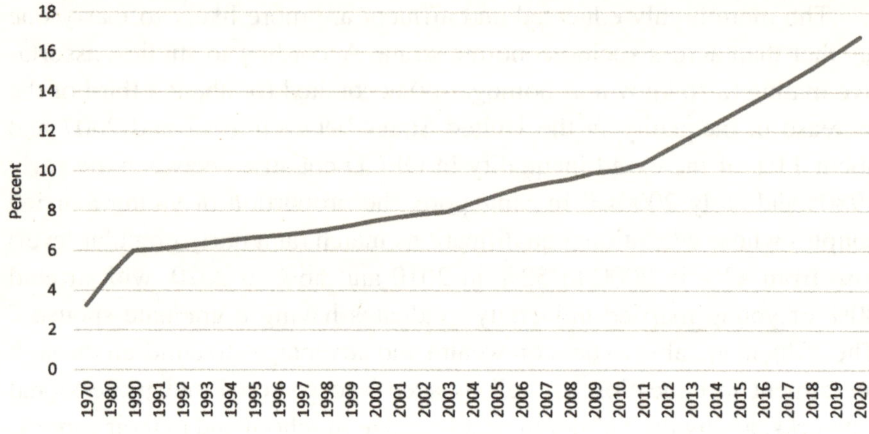

Figure 3.5 Share of Citizen Population Aged 65 and Above

Source: Singapore Department of Statistics.

Table 3.2 Old Age Support Ratio (Number Aged 20–64 per Senior Aged 65 and Above)

	1970	1980	1990	2000	2010	2020
Citizens	13.5	11.4	10.4	8.4	6.4	3.7
Residents	13.5	11.3	10.5	9.0	7.4	4.3

Source: Singapore Department of Statistics.

The average number of children born to female citizens who are or have been married fell from almost 3.5 in 1980 to just over 2.1 in 2020, while average household size has steadily declined.[28]

With more Singaporeans remaining single or having smaller families, a growing number of seniors will not be able to rely on children for income and retirement support, although successive cohorts of seniors would, on average, have higher education levels and more savings to fall back on. Retirement adequacy is a concern for some, particularly those who have earned less during their working years, or who have not set aside sufficient savings.

According to the Ministry of Finance, an elderly person is four times more likely to be admitted to the hospital than a younger person and is likely to stay in the hospital twice as long once admitted.[29] At the same

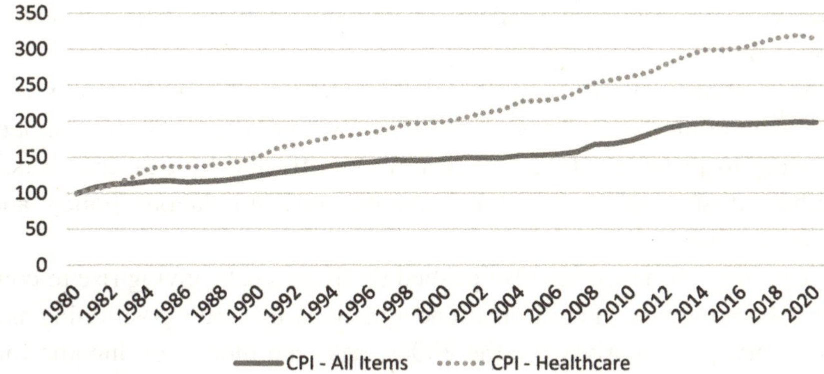

Figure 3.6 Consumer Price Index (CPI)-All Items, Healthcare (1980 = 100)
Source: Singapore Department of Statistics.

time, medical costs are rising quickly due to advances in medical technology, the proliferation of new and more expensive treatments, as well as rising manpower cost. Healthcare prices have more than tripled between 1980 and 2020, compared with a doubling of the general Consumer Price Index (Figure 3.6).

As longevity increases, more seniors are suffering from chronic illnesses such as cardiovascular disease, diabetes, and dementia. Singaporeans are spending more years in ill-health compared with 30 years ago — 10.6 years in 2017, up from nine years in 1990, according to a Ministry of Health study released in 2019.[30] The growing senior population will significantly increase the fiscal and manpower resources required to support and care for seniors. It has become a pressing challenge to ensure that healthcare remains affordable for seniors, while keeping public spending on healthcare sustainable.

Globalisation and Global City Aspirations

Globalisation has put Singaporeans in competition with the growing ranks of engineers, professionals, and skilled workers from China, India, and other emerging economies. In jobs where the supply of skills is abundant, whether due to the influx of foreign workers into Singapore or competition from abroad in exportable sectors, wages have been pegged back. At the same time, tapping into global markets has given outsized rewards to those who possess skills that are in demand globally. This has led to upward pressure on inequality over time.

Dani Rodrik (1998) suggested that economies that are more exposed to global competition have a tendency towards greater government spending to provide safety nets to citizens affected by external risks,[31] another illustration of the link between economic/labour policy and social security.

Growing affluence has also pushed up living costs, giving rise to concerns about income and retirement adequacy. Singapore's positioning as a global city, particularly since the 2000s, has seen more high-income foreigners take up residence in the city state, with a consequent increase in rents and the price of services. The number of non-residents in Singapore more than doubled from 2000 to 2019, rising from 18.7% of the total population in 2000 to 29.4% in 2019 , although it dipped to 28.9% in 2020 due to the COVID-19 pandemic.[32]

Economic Volatility and Contingent Work Arrangements

Globally, heightened economic volatility and a consequent rise in contingent work arrangements such as contract, temporary, or freelance work have led to concerns over employment, income volatility, and consequently, income stability.

In Singapore, there has been a relatively stable share of non-permanent (contract/casual work) as well as "own account" (freelance) work in recent years. The proportion of non-permanent employment has fluctuated between 9.4% and 11.8% over the past decade (Figure 3.7). Likewise, the proportion of own account workers (self-employed persons who run their own trade without employing a paid worker) has hovered between 7.9% and 9.7% (Figure 3.8) in the past 10 years. It has been within this range for 20 years, in fact, despite the growing prominence of gig economy platforms in recent years. However, the COVID-19 outbreak in 2020 saw an uptick in the number and proportion of own account workers, including those who did own account work as their primary job (Figures 3.8, 3.9).

Notwithstanding the relatively stable trends, MPs have over the years raised concerns over the income security and retirement adequacy of

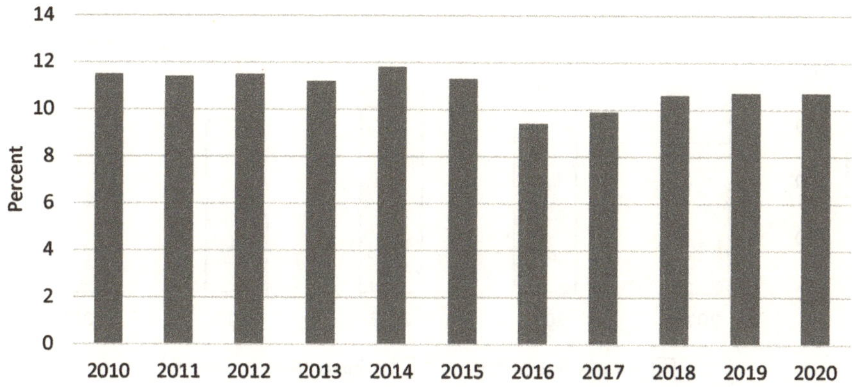

Figure 3.7 Share of Employed Residents in Non-Permanent Employment

Source: Comprehensive Labour Force Survey, Manpower Research and Statistics Department, MOM.

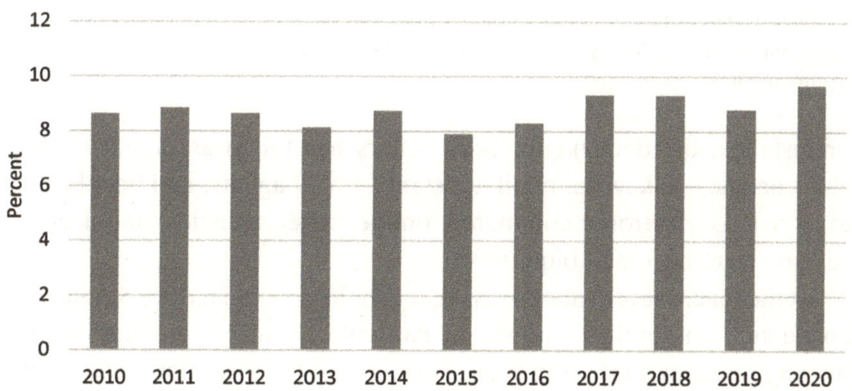

Figure 3.8 Share of Employed Residents Who are Own Account Workers

Source: Comprehensive Labour Force Survey, Manpower Research and Statistics Department, MOM.

self-employed workers, particularly with the increasing visibility of gig work such as private-hire car driving and delivery services.

Technology and Job Displacement

Technology and economic restructuring are transforming jobs and job requirements, displacing some traditional jobs while creating new ones.

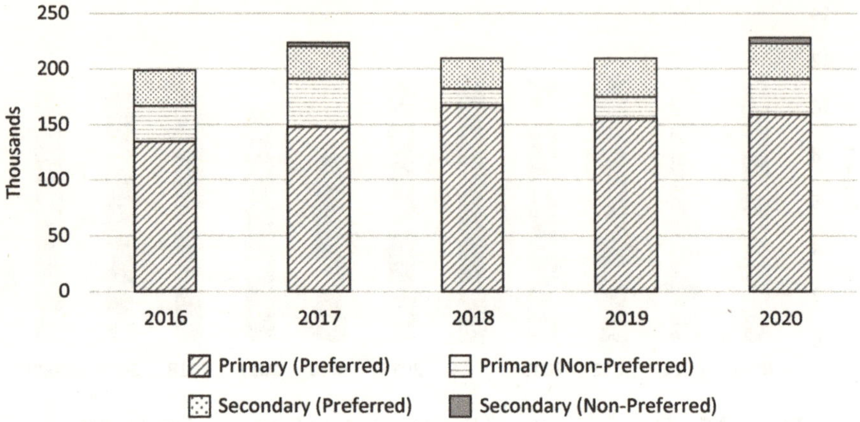

Figure 3.9 Own Account Workers

Note: Data refer to residents engaged in regular own account work in the 12 months ending in June of the year indicated. Primary own account workers are those who engage in own account work as their main job. Preferred refers to those who engage in own account work out of choice rather than necessity.
Source: Supplementary Survey on Own Account Workers, Manpower Research and Statistics Department, MOM.

For instance, the demand for bank tellers has fallen as digital banking gains currency. Likewise, retail assistants, travel agents, and bookkeepers are at risk as electronic commerce, online travel agencies, and accountancy software become ubiquitous.

At the macro level, labour-saving technology could reduce Singapore's dependence on foreign manpower, particularly in low-productivity and low-wage occupations. However, there is also the risk that lower-skilled Singaporeans, including seniors, could be displaced from jobs while lacking the skills to take up the new jobs created.

Job displacement may be an even greater concern for mature workers in professional, manager, executive, and technician (PMET) roles where skills tend to be more specialised and company-specific. Those retrenched may also find it harder to re-enter employment without taking a significant pay cut.

In Singapore, the proportion of PMETs among employed residents has risen from 52.5% in 2010 to 59.9% in 2020.[33] Prior to the COVID-19 outbreak, PMETs have been at slightly higher risk of retrenchment compared with other occupational groups, forming over 60% of retrenched workers

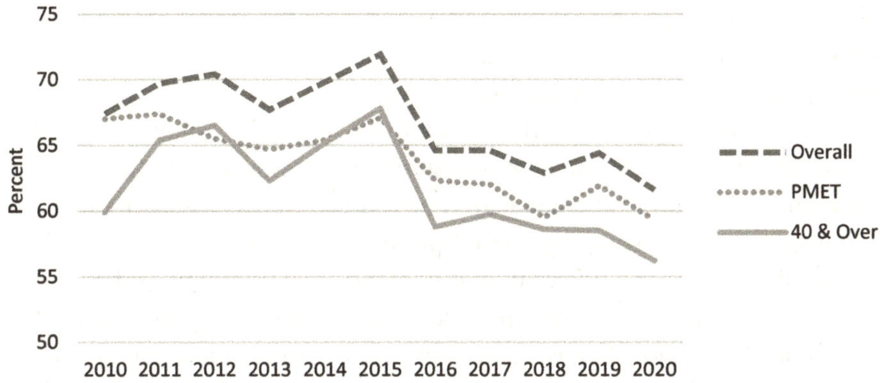

Figure 3.10 6-Month Re-entry Rate into Employment of Retrenched Residents
Source: Manpower Research and Statistics Department, Ministry of Manpower.

in 2018 and 2019. The rate of re-entry into employment of retrenched PMETs is also lower, especially among mature workers (Figure 3.10).

Although the labour market has remained fairly tight up to the onset of the COVID-19 pandemic (Figure 2.4), there is a risk of structural unemployment rising in the medium term as the number of mature PMETs with high reservation wages (i.e. the lowest wage at which a worker would be willing to accept a job) grows. This would affect income security and could widen income inequality unless displaced workers can be quickly eased back into employment at good salaries. Otherwise they may need more robust unemployment benefits, at the risk of undermining the incentive to return to work.

Climate Change and Sustainability

With increasing global awareness of the threat of climate change and the urgency of reducing carbon emissions, Singapore's economic and social strategies will have to take greater cognisance of carbon constraints and sustainability.

In 2015, Singapore committed to a target of reducing emissions intensity by 36% from 2005 levels by 2030, and to peak around 2030. In 2020, the government announced its intent to enhance Singapore's climate pledge by setting an absolute emissions cap, with the aim of halving emissions from the 2030 peak by 2050. This will necessitate changes to Singapore's economic strategies, transportation mix, and infrastructure development, among other efforts under the Singapore Green Plan 2030. Fiscal space could become more constrained as funds have to be set aside for climate mitigation and adaptation measures, such as research on green technologies and developing coastal protection against rising sea levels.

At the same time, international demand for sustainable urban solutions and climate resilience present new economic opportunities for Singapore firms and citizens, such as in green infrastructure, green financing, and renewable energy. Business and investment decisions will need to factor in environmental, social and corporate governance (ESG) considerations, giving an advantage to states and cities best prepared for the green future.

All these will have an impact on incomes, affordability, and other socio-economic outcomes through direct and indirect channels, including jobs and skills requirements, taxes and incentives, and fiscal constraints.

Summary of Emerging Challenges

These emerging challenges, summarised in Table 3.3, have spurred changes to Singapore's socio-economic system in recent years. These challenges relate to the five socio-economic indicators described in Chapter 1:

1. Real income growth
2. Income security/adequacy:
    a. Unemployment (especially structural unemployment) and time-based underemployment
    b. Income volatility, especially for contingent workers
    c. Low/stagnant wages
    d. Retirement adequacy
3. Affordability, especially for healthcare and housing
4. Inequality
5. Social mobility

Table 3.3 Emerging Trends and Challenges

	Trends/Driving Forces	**Presenting Challenges**
Internal	1. Maturing economy	Slowing income growth
	2. Social stratification arising from economic progress	Inequality, social mobility
	3. Ageing population	Retirement adequacy, healthcare affordability
	4. Global city	Cost of living, including housing affordability
External	5. Global competition	Low/stagnant wages, inequality
	6. Economic volatility and contingent work arrangements	Unemployment, income volatility, retirement adequacy
	7. Technological disruption	Structural unemployment, underemployment, inequality
	8. Climate change and sustainability	Incomes, cost of living, fiscal space for social spending

A sixth potential challenge, skills underemployment, may not be (strictly speaking) an issue of income security, but one of structural mismatch, with the economy unable to provide enough jobs of sufficient quality to match the skills, qualifications, or expectations of citizens. As citizens' aspirations rise and the educational profile improves, creating sufficient numbers of quality jobs will become an increasingly pressing need.

Overview of Policy Responses

The government's policy responses to these challenges are multipronged, ranging from upstream education and prevention to downstream transfers and subsidies, along with social insurance, reflecting the complex and often multifaceted nature of the issues faced.

While the basic paradigm of personal effort with collective support remains, the balance between personal effort and collective support has tilted towards the latter over time. The decline in wages among the lower-income and concurrent rise in income inequality in the first half of the 2000s (Figures 2.3, 2.9) prompted soul-searching among Singaporeans. The government committed, at the opening of Parliament in 2006, to "do more to assist lower-income Singaporeans, to help them progress with the rest of society", while reiterating the need to "avoid the mistakes other countries have made in pursuing welfare schemes".[34]

By 2013, the shift in balance towards collective support was evident. As Prime Minister Lee Hsien Loong noted at the 2013 National Day Rally, "Today, the situation has changed. If we rely too heavily on the individual, their efforts alone will not be enough, especially among the vulnerable like the low-income families, like the elderly."[35]

The major socio-economic policy moves since the mid-2000s can be summarised as follows:

1. ***Strengthening fiscal progressivity*** through more progressive income and wealth taxes, and the introduction of the permanent Goods and Services Tax Voucher — addresses inequality
2. ***Augmenting the social security system*** through
   a. Addition of a fourth pillar of social security comprising the Workfare Income Supplement and Silver Support Scheme to supplement wages and retirement income, respectively — addresses low wages, retirement adequacy, and inequality
   b. Risk pooling via CPF Lifelong Income for the Elderly (CPF LIFE) (longevity insurance), MediShield Life (medical insurance), and CareShield Life (long-term care insurance) — addresses retirement adequacy and healthcare affordability
   c. New/enhanced subsidies for housing (Enhanced CPF Housing Grant) and healthcare (particularly the introduction of the Pioneer Generation Package and Merdeka Generation Package) — address housing and healthcare affordability
   d. Supporting housing asset monetisation through the Lease Buyback Scheme and the Silver Housing Bonus — addresses retirement adequacy
3. ***Increasing state investment in preschool education and lifelong learning***, in particular by

a. Raising preschool education standards and subsidies through the setting up of Ministry of Education kindergartens and the Early Childhood Development Agency — addresses social mobility
b. Expanding opportunities for Continuing Education and Training through the SkillsFuture Movement — addresses income growth, underemployment, and social mobility

4. ***Strengthening employment support*** through the Adapt and Grow initiative — addresses income growth and unemployment
5. ***Calibrating foreign worker inflow*** — addresses income growth, underemployment, low wages, and inequality
6. ***Raising incomes and productivity of lower-wage workers*** through the Progressive Wage Model (sector-based minimum wage and wage ladders) — addresses low wages and inequality

With these initiatives, the social security system in 2020 has been significantly augmented (Figure 3.11). The updates to the Singapore System span the entire Socio-Economic Flowchart from upstream to downstream (Figure 3.12).

The chapters that follow will examine, in greater detail, the policy changes in each socio-economic policy domain — unpacking their rationale, design considerations, and implementation, and discussing their efficacy. Beginning with downstream measures such as taxes, transfers, social assistance, and social security, we will thereafter move upstream to

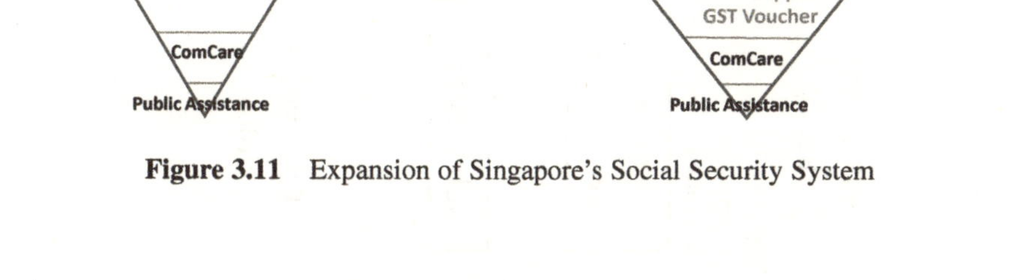

Figure 3.11 Expansion of Singapore's Social Security System

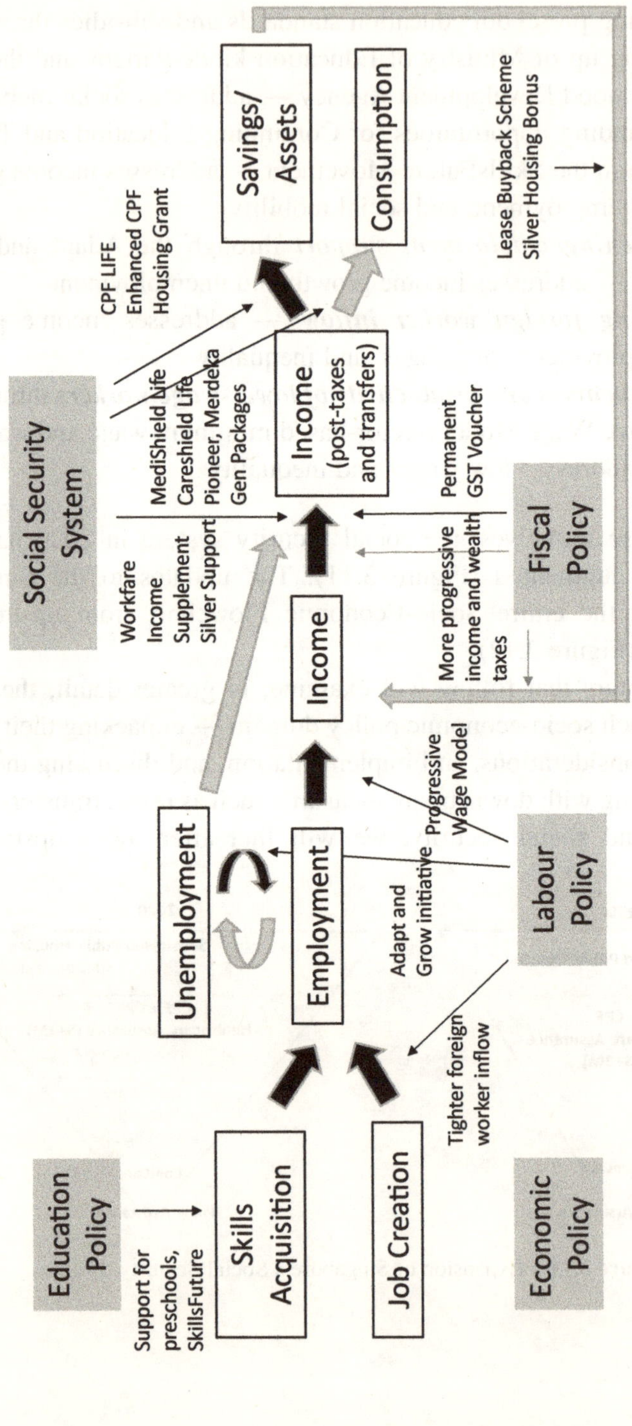

Figure 3.12 Policy Shifts Mapped onto Singapore's Socio-Economic Flowchart

Table 3.4 Socio-Economic Policy Domains and Corresponding Chapters

	Policy Domain	What it Addresses	Chapter
Downstream	Fiscal redistribution	Inequality	4
	Social security system (viz. CPF, public housing, healthcare assurance, Workfare and Silver Support)	Low wages, retirement adequacy, affordability, inequality	5
	Social assistance, targeted and broad-based subsidies	Income security, affordability	6
Upstream	Education and training policy	Income growth, social mobility	7
	Labour market policy	Unemployment, low wages, income growth, inequality	8
	Economic policy	Income growth, income security	9
Constraints and Enablers			
	Fiscal revenue and spending	Financing of socio-economic policies	10
	COVID-19 impact, politics, and the future	Socio-economic outcomes, policy interventions, and policy space	11

consider education, labour, and economic policy before assessing the wider fiscal, economic, and political context (Table 3.4).

This will provide a holistic picture of how Singapore is addressing each of the five emerging socio-economic challenges. We can then consider whether gaps remain, and how the Singapore System can be further updated.

Endnotes

1. Lee Kuan Yew, *From Third World to First: The Singapore Story: 1965–2000* (Singapore: Times Editions, Singapore Press Holdings, 2000), 128.
2. Lee Hsien Loong, Budget Statement, 2005.

3. Christian Aspalter, "The East Asian Welfare Model," *International Journal of Social Welfare* 15 (2006): 290–301.
4. M. Ramesh and Mukul G. Asher, *Welfare Capitalism in Southeast Asia: Social Security, Health and Education Policies* (London: Palgrave Macmillan, 2000).
5. M. Ramesh, *Social Policy in East and Southeast Asia: Education, Health, Housing and Income Maintenance* (London: Routledge-Curzon, 2004).
6. Ron Haskins, "Social Policy in Singapore: A Crucible of Individual Responsibility," *Ethos* 9 (Singapore: Civil Service College, 2011), 79.
7. The notion that expenditure on social welfare in a capitalist state tends to outstrip revenue over time, leading to fiscal crisis, was advanced in James O'Connor, *The Fiscal Crisis of the State* (New York: St Martin's Press, 1973).
8. Lee Hsien Loong, Budget Statement, 2007.
9. Tharman Shanmugaratnam, interview by Stephen Sackur at the 45th St. Gallen Symposium, 2015, https://www.youtube.com/watch?v=hpwPciW74b8.
10. Lee Hsien Loong, National Day Message, 2005, https://www.nas.gov.sg/archivesonline/data/pdfdoc/20050808988.htm.
11. Lim Swee Say, speech at the Ministry of Manpower Committee of Supply Debate, 2018.
12. Chan-ung Park and Dongchul Jung, "The Asian Welfare Regimes Revisited: The Preliminary Typologies Based on Welfare Legislation and Expenditure," paper prepared for the 4th International Conference on Restructuring Care Responsibility. Dynamics of Welfare Mix in East Asia, 20–21 October 2007, University of Tokyo, Japan, http://www.welfareasia.org/4thconference/papers/Park_The%20Asian%20Welfare%20Regimes%20Revisited.pdf.
13. See, for instance, Eugene K. B. Tan, "The Makings of a Social Investment State," *TODAY*, 22 February 2014; Vernon Loke and Michael Sherraden, "Building Assets from Birth: Singapore's Policies," *Asia Pacific Journal of Social Work and Development* 29(1) (2019): 6–19.
14. Tharman Shanmugaratnam, remarks at a virtual discussion organised by the Lee Kuan Yew School of Public Policy entitled "After the Pandemic — The Rebirth of Big Government? State Capacity, Trust and Privacy in the Post-COVID-19 Era," 22 July 2020.
15. Tharman Shanmugaratnam, interview at the 45th St. Gallen Symposium.
16. The 2020 Edelman Trust Barometer found that government, businesses, and non-governmental organisations in Singapore were perceived by the majority of respondents as ethical and competent. Singapore ranked sixth out of 26 economies in terms of trust in the government.
17. See, for example, Lee, *From Third World to First*; Tommy Koh, ed., *Fifty Secrets of Singapore's Success* (Singapore: Straits Times Press, 2020).

18. The Committee on the Future Economy was a high-level committee convened in January 2016 to develop economic strategies for the next decade. It comprised private and public sector leaders and was co-chaired by then-Minister for Finance Heng Swee Keat and then-Minister for Communications and Information S. Iswaran.
19. Vincent Chua, Tan Ern Ser, and Gillian Koh, *A Study on Social Capital in Singapore* (Singapore: Institute of Policy Studies, National University of Singapore, 2017), https://lkyspp.nus.edu.sg/docs/default-source/ips/study-of-social-capital-in-singapore.pdf.
20. Lee Hsien Loong, speech at the Debate on the President's Address, 16 May 2018.
21. Branko Milanovic, *Capitalism Alone: The Future of the System that Rules the World* (Cambridge: Harvard University Press, 2019); Koen Decancq, Andreas Peichl, and Philippe Van Kerm, "Assortative Mating, Joint Labour Supply and Spouses Earnings Correlation: Which Do Matter for Long Term Trends in US Household Earnings Inequality?" paper presented at the 6th ECINEQ conference, Luxembourg, 2015.
22. Singapore Department of Statistics Census of Population 2000, 2010, 2020. Young married couples refer to those below age 35. See Walter Theseira, "Can Singapore Reduce the Frictions of Seeking Help?" *Straits Times*, 30 October 2018.
23. Ministry of Health (MOH), Action Plan for Successful Ageing (Singapore: MOH, 2016), https://sustainabledevelopment.un.org/content/documents/1525 Action_Plan_for_Successful_Aging.pdf.
24. Ibid.
25. United Nations, Department of Economic and Social Affairs, Population Division, *World Population Ageing 2019* (New York: United Nations, 2019).
26. United Nations, Department of Economic and Social Affairs, Population Division, *World Population Ageing 2017* (New York: United Nations, 2017).
27. Source: Singapore Department of Statistics.
28. Source: Singapore Department of Statistics.
29. Ministry of Finance, "Injecting More into Seniors' Healthcare as We Age," accessed 1 May 2021, https://www.mof.gov.sg/singapore-budget/curated-budget-reads. This is similar to the United States, where National Health Expenditure data from the United States Centers for Medicare and Medicaid Services showed that in 2010, per capita personal healthcare spending for those aged 65 and older was about five times that of children and three times that of working-age persons.

30. Janice Lim, "Singaporeans Living Longer but Spending More Time in Ill Health: Study," *TODAY*, 20 June 2019.
31. Dani Rodrik, "Why Do More Open Economies Have Bigger Governments?" *Journal of Political Economy* 106(5) (1998): 997–1032.
32. Source: Singapore Department of Statistics.
33. Source: Manpower Research and Statistics Department, Ministry of Manpower.
34. S. R. Nathan, President's Address at the opening of Parliament, 2 November 2006.
35. Lee Hsien Loong, National Day Rally, 2013.

Chapter 4

Strengthening Fiscal Progressivity

The redistributive impact of taxes and transfers depends not just on the overall size of taxes and transfers but also the mix of taxes, how progressive they are, and how targeted transfers are. An OECD study found that countries with a more unequal distribution of market incomes tend to redistribute more, and that cash transfers reduce income dispersion more than taxes in most OECD economies.[1]

Transfers can take many forms. They could redistribute income across individuals, or over the life cycle via public pensions. They could target the low-income or needy, or specific groups like families with children. They could be in cash, vouchers for specific uses, or in kind through subsidised education, healthcare, housing, etc., whether these services are delivered by the state or private providers. The variety of forms which transfers can take makes cross-country comparisons of redistribution challenging.

The Singapore government uses all these forms of transfers. The state directly provides public education and housing, as well as significant subsidies to highly regulated public healthcare and transport operators. It has institutionalised transfers to lower-income groups through Workfare, Silver Support, and the Goods and Services Tax (GST) Voucher, and targets support to seniors and families with children through healthcare and education subsidies as well as direct cash grants. It also makes frequent use of ad hoc cash payments and Central Provident Fund (CPF) top-ups. Finally, it encourages family and community support through tax reliefs and deductions for those who top up the CPF accounts of family members or donate to Institutions of Public Character, with the state also providing dollar-for-dollar matching grants for donations to charitable causes such as the Community Chest.

While the longstanding priority has been to keep the tax burden low to encourage work and enterprise, recent policy adjustments have been aimed at keeping overall fiscal system progressive (where the tax rate, net of benefits, rises with income) while expanding the revenue base through indirect taxation.

On the Link Between Tax Rates and Tax Revenue

Raising tax rates does not necessarily raise tax revenue or the amount available for redistribution. While countries that levy higher taxes on income or wealth will generally have more revenue available for redistribution, this is not always the case. For instance, revenue may be lost through corruption or inefficient spending on public infrastructure and services.

It is also possible, at least in theory, that lower personal and corporate income tax rates, by encouraging work and economic activity, may raise the total tax collected and enable more transfers to the poor. Lower tax rates could also attract more foreign companies and foreigners whose economic activity could be taxed to boost state coffers.

The Laffer curve, named after economist Arthur Laffer, posits that tax revenue rises with tax rates up to a point (the revenue-maximising tax rate), after which it declines. However, the practical utility of this concept is disputed, given the difficulty in ascertaining the shape of the curve or the revenue-maximising tax rate for any given country. Jacob Lundberg (2017) attempted to estimate the Laffer Curve for 27 OECD economies. He found that the highest income tax rates in most economies (except Austria, Belgium, Denmark, Finland, and Sweden) were below the revenue-maximising rate, which he estimated ranged from 60%–61% to 74%–76%.[2] However, these estimates were based on assumptions about people's willingness to work and did not consider mobility across countries. In Singapore, the use of competitive tax rates to attract foreign investment and talent has been a longstanding feature of economic policy.

Hence, while the progressivity of the tax system is important, fiscal efficacy also depends on the efficiency of government spending and having taxes at levels that attract investment and encourage economic activity. There are, however, limits to the use of competitive tax rates to attract investment. At the time of writing, the US and other Group of Seven (G7) advanced nations are pushing for a global minimum tax rate of at least 15% in order to level the playing field.

Income Taxes in Singapore

Singapore's personal and corporate income tax rates are among the lowest in the world, the aim being to reward work and enterprise and to attract talent.

As at 2021, the top marginal personal income tax rate is 22% for income above S$320,000. The first $20,000 of income do not attract tax, and there are additional reliefs for earned income; contributions to CPF; National Service; life insurance; support for spouse, children, parents, or grandparents; and more. As a result, the effective income tax rate on the median worker is close to zero.[3] About half of Singapore workers pay personal income tax, and among those who do, the top 10% contribute about 80% of personal income tax revenue.[4]

The headline corporate income tax rate is 17% as at 2021. The effective tax rate for most companies is in fact lower due to various tax breaks and incentives. Over half of small and medium-sized enterprises (SMEs) do not pay any corporate tax. Since 2003, Singapore has adopted a single-tier corporate tax system, which means that the tax paid by a company on its income is the final tax, and dividends paid by a company to its shareholders are exempted from further tax. There is no tax on capital gains.

Before 1986, corporate income tax was 40%, and top marginal personal income tax as high as 55% in 1980 (Figure 4.1). Corporate and personal income tax rates have been on a decline since the late 1980s through to the mid-2000s, with a shift towards indirect taxation in the form of GST.

One of the government's key considerations in lowering income taxes was to keep Singapore competitive vis-a-vis other economies. In particular, Hong Kong was viewed as a benchmark given its status as a leading

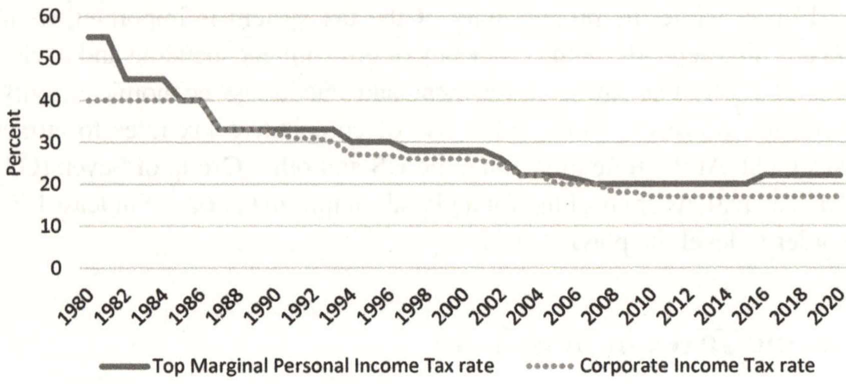

Figure 4.1 Top Marginal Personal and Corporate Income Tax Rates (%)

Source: Lee Kok Fatt, *Singapore's Fiscal Strategies for Growth: A Journey of Self-Reliance* (Singapore: World Scientific, 2017), 84.

Asian financial centre. Tax rates in many jurisdictions have also trended downwards, particularly in the early 2000s.[5]

Corporate tax was reduced from 40% to 33% in 1987, and over the years further brought down to 17% in 2010 where it has since stayed. This is fractionally higher than Hong Kong's headline corporate tax rate of 16.5%. The top marginal personal income tax rate was lowered to 20% in 2007, although it was subsequently raised to 22% in 2016 (Figure 4.1).

Comparative Tax Burden

Compared with most developed countries, Singapore taxes have been kept low, the aim being to reward and encourage work (Tables 4.1, 4.2). This applies not just to top earners but also to the broad middle class, with personal income tax a mere 2% of gross wage earnings for the average worker (Table 4.2) and GST relatively low at 7% at the time of writing.

This, however, means that Singapore has been less aggressive in fiscal redistribution than most other advanced countries, as evinced by the difference in Gini coefficient pre- and post-taxes and transfers (Table 4.3), although this has not factored in implicit government subsidies for public housing.

Table 4.1 Statutory Corporate and Top Marginal Personal Income Tax Rates

	Statutory Corporate Income Tax Rate	**Top Marginal Personal Income Tax Rate**
Australia	30%	47.0%
Canada	15%	53.5%
Denmark	22%	55.9%
Finland	20%	51.1%
France	32.02%	55.4%
Germany	15.83%	47.5%
Japan	23.2%	55.9%
Norway	22%	38.2%
Singapore	**17%**	**22.0%**
South Korea	25%	46.2%
Sweden	21.4%	57.2%
Switzerland	8.5%	41.7%
United Kingdom	19%	45.0%
United States	21%	43.7%

Source: Inland Revenue Authority of Singapore, OECD Tax Database (other countries).

Table 4.2 International Comparison of Tax Burden

	Overall Tax: GDP Ratio (2018)	**Effective Personal Income Tax Rate for Average Worker (2019)***	**Value-Added Tax/ Goods and Services Tax (2019)**
OECD average	**34.6%**	**15.9%**	**19.3%**
France	45.9%	16.0%	20%
Denmark	44.4%	35.6%	25%
Sweden	43.9%	17.7%	25%
Finland	42.4%	20.2%	24%
Norway	39.6%	19.1%	25%
Germany	38.5%	19.2%	19%
Canada	33.2%	15.8%	5%–15% (federal GST + provincial sales tax)

(*Continued*)

Table 4.2 (*Continued*)

	Overall Tax: GDP Ratio (2018)	Effective Personal Income Tax Rate for Average Worker (2019)*	Value-Added Tax/ Goods and Services Tax (2019)
United Kingdom	32.9%	13.9%	20%
Japan	32.0%	7.9%	8%
Australia	28.7%	23.6%	10%
Switzerland	28.1%	11.2%	7.7%
South Korea	26.8%	6.7%	10%
United States	24.4%	16.4%	NA (No federal VAT, range of state and local sales taxes)
Singapore	**13.2%**	**2.0% (2014)**	**7%**

*Personal income tax as percentage of average gross wage earnings for single individual without children.

Source: OECD Tax Database; OECD *Revenue Statistics in Asian and Pacific Economies 2020 —* Singapore; "Income Growth, Inequality and Mobility Trends in Singapore," MOF occasional paper (August 2015).

Table 4.3 Change in Income Gini Coefficient (OECD Square Root Scale) Due to Taxes and Transfers (TT) (From Most Redistributive to Least)

	Pre-TT	Post-TT	Difference	Year
Finland	0.509	0.269	**0.240**	2018
France	0.529	0.301	**0.228**	2018
Germany	0.500	0.289	**0.211**	2017
Denmark	0.446	0.264	**0.182**	2017
Norway	0.429	0.262	**0.167**	2018
Japan	0.504	0.339	**0.165**	2015
Sweden	0.428	0.275	**0.153**	2018
UK	0.513	0.366	**0.147**	2018
Australia	0.454	0.325	**0.129**	2018
Canada	0.427	0.303	**0.124**	2018
US	0.505	0.39	**0.115**	2017
Switzerland	0.386	0.299	**0.087**	2017

Table 4.3 (*Continued*)

	Pre-TT	Post-TT	Difference	Year
Singapore	0.411	0.352	**0.059**	2019
South Korea	0.402	0.345	**0.057**	2018

Note: Singapore's Gini coefficient is based on household income from work among resident employed households, whereas those of OECD economies are based on income from all sources among all resident households.
Source: Singapore Department of Statistics; OECD database, retrieved 8 April 2021 (other countries).

Updates to Singapore Tax Rates Since 2010

The competitive reduction in income tax rates has not continued into the 2010s. Instead, the government has made various adjustments to asset and income tax schedules in the past decade to strengthen the progressivity of the fiscal system.

Increase in Personal Income Tax for High-Income Earners (2012, 2016) and Cap on Personal Reliefs (2016)

The slope of the personal income tax schedule was changed in 2012 to reduce effective taxes for the lower- to middle-income groups while raising rates for high-income earners without changing the top marginal rate of 20%. From year of assessment 2017, the top marginal personal income tax rate was raised to 22%. This was notwithstanding concerns that increasing the gap between personal income tax rates and corporate income tax rates, which remained at 17%, could prompt more high-income earners to incorporate companies in order to pay lower taxes. In 2016, a cap was imposed on personal income tax reliefs, which could previously exceed $80,000 due to generous child relief for working mothers.

Increases in Property Tax (2010, 2013), Vehicle Taxes (2013)

On the wealth front, several moves were also made. These were considered less distortionary than income taxes in regard to their impact on the motivation for work and enterprise.

Prior to 2008, estate duty was payable in Singapore at the rate of 5% for the first $12 million of dutiable assets, and 10% thereafter. An average of about $75 million in estate duty was collected each year. In Budget 2008, the government abolished estate duty, citing the benefits from growing the wealth management industry in Singapore and the desire of Singaporeans to pass on their savings to their families. Another key consideration was that the wealthy could quite easily evade estate duty by transferring their assets abroad, since unmoveable assets such as property overseas were not subject to duty.

However, with the removal of estate duty, and without a capital gains tax, the only significant wealth tax remaining was property tax.

In Budget 2010, the government amended the property tax regime to introduce higher tax rates on owner-occupied properties with higher annual values. Additional tax rate bands were introduced in Budget 2013, along with progressive tax rates for non-owner-occupied residential properties.

Also targeted in Budget 2013 were cars, with higher vehicle taxes imposed on more expensive cars. To curb the growth of the car population in land-scarce Singapore, car taxes were already among the highest in the world. The higher taxes announced in 2013 were aimed at luxury cars, in particular, which saw a 50% increase in Additional Registration Fee payable as a form of wealth tax.

These adjustments to asset and income tax rates, although individually of modest impact, have collectively sharpened fiscal progressivity. Mindful of competition from other jurisdictions, in particular Hong Kong, where the top marginal personal income tax rate has remained at 15%, the government has adopted a gradual approach towards tax changes.

Social Transfers

Ad Hoc Budget Measures

Ad hoc transfers have long been a feature of government budgets as a means of returning fiscal surpluses to citizens, particularly before the end of a government's term where unutilised funds would be locked away in the "past reserves" (more on this in Chapter 10). These transfers have taken the form of tax rebates (Table 4.4), cash handouts, as well as special

Table 4.4 Personal Income Tax Rebates

Year of Assessment	Rebate Quantum	Cap
2008, 2009, 2011	20%	$2,000
2013	30% (< age 60) 50% (≥ age 60)	$1,500
2015	50%	$1,000
2017	20%	$500
2019	50%	$250

shares.[6] There have also been top-ups to CPF and education funds, and rebates on utilities and Housing and Development Board (HDB) service and conservancy charges. Ad hoc transfers have also been made during periods of economic weakness or recession as a means of providing timely support to citizens.

The lowering of personal income tax rebate caps in successive budgets (Table 4.4) reflects the intent in recent years to focus benefits on middle-income taxpayers rather than high-income earners.

Structural Transfers

In terms of permanent transfers, the most notable development in the 2000s was the introduction of the Workfare Income Supplement (WIS) in 2007, a wage supplement for lower-income workers. The GST Voucher (described in the next section) was institutionalised as a structural transfer in 2012 to offset the impact of GST on lower- to middle-income households. In 2015, the government added Silver Support to the suite of permanent transfers. While WIS tops up the income of workers, Silver Support augments cashflow for retirees who have not accumulated substantial savings over their working lives. The next chapter will discuss the role of WIS and Silver Support in the overall social security framework.

In the 2015 Budget Debate Round-Up speech, then-Minister for Finance Tharman Shanmugaratnam noted the increasing importance of permanent transfers relative to ad hoc transfers over the years, indicating that on average, about 90% of annual transfers from 2009 to 2014 were structural transfers under permanent schemes.[7]

Keeping the Overall Fiscal System Progressive

With the shift towards indirect taxation through increases in GST, it has been necessary to take offsetting measures to sustain the overall progressivity of the fiscal system.

As explained in the 2013 Budget Statement, Singapore's system of taxes and benefits is designed to be "fair and progressive", where "everyone contributes something to Singapore, but the bulk of our taxes is paid by the high-income group, and most of the benefits received by the lower-income group".[8] This is depicted in Figure 4.2.

Among the taxes which the government collects, GST is regressive in that it imposes a proportionately larger burden on the lower-income (as a share of their income) than on higher-income earners. When introducing GST at 3% in 1994 and raising it to 5% and 7% in 2003–2004 and 2007, respectively, the government concurrently rolled out GST offset packages comprising cash payouts, utilities, conservancy and rental rebates, and various other subsidies.

The **Budget 1993 GST Offset Package** included cuts in personal and corporate income taxes, higher personal reliefs and rebates for taxpayers,

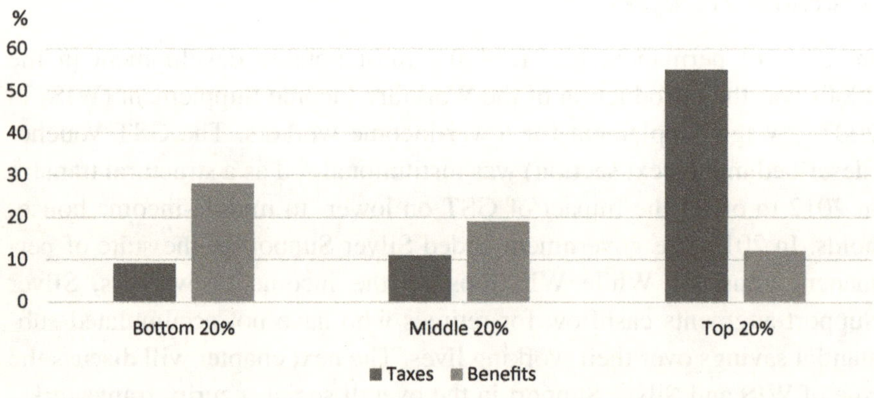

Figure 4.2 Share of Taxes and Benefits per Household Member Across Citizen Household Income Quintiles (2019)

Note: Benefits include all government subsidies, transfers, and rebates. Taxes include direct and indirect taxes.

Source: Ministry of Finance estimates, cited in the 2020 Unity Budget Debate Round-Up Speech.

and help to low-income households. According to the 1993 Budget Statement, the package would be enough to fully offset GST for nearly all households earning at least $1,500 a month.

The pièce de resistance of the $4 billion **Budget 2002 GST Offset Package** was the $3.6 billion Economic Restructuring Shares (ERS) Scheme for Singapore Citizens aged above 21 who had contributed at least $50 into CPF in 2002. Shares worth between $600 and $1,400 (depending on annual home value) were disbursed over a three-year period from January 2003. The ERS could be encashed at any time, but those who did not encash their ERS received bonus shares as dividends. Other components of the package included HDB rental rebates for low-income households, rebates on service and conservancy charges (S&CC), additional subsidies to offset GST charges for healthcare and public education, an increase in the Public Assistance rate and pensioner allowance, and support for lower-income households through grassroots organisations.

The **Budget 2007 GST Offset Package**, also estimated at $4 billion over five years, comprised cash payouts (called GST Credits) of up to $1,250 over four years, depending on income and housing type; a Senior Citizens' Bonus of $250–$1,250 (in cash and MediSave) over four years for lower-income seniors aged 55 and above; utilities, S&CC, and rental rebates over five years for those living in HDB flats; top-ups to Post-Secondary Education Accounts; property tax rebate; and top-ups to the Public Transport Fund for lower-income households, among other forms of assistance.

However, there remained concerns that these GST offsets were ad hoc and time-limited. Hence, the government introduced the **Permanent GST Voucher Scheme** in Budget 2012 as a structural transfer to offset GST expenses for lower- to middle-income households. This provided assurance that the system of taxes and benefits, taken as a whole, would remain fair and progressive. The GST Voucher (GSTV) comprised cash, MediSave top-ups for seniors, and household utility rebates for lower- to middle-income Singaporeans.

According to the Minister for Finance, retiree couples living in smaller flats could expect a GSTV that would more than fully offset their yearly GST expenses. Lower-income households with no elderly person living in three- or four-room HDB flats should receive GSTV covering about half their GST expenses, while middle-income families would receive a GSTV that would partially offset their GST expenses.

In tandem, a GST Voucher Fund was set up to provide certainty of payments regardless of economic circumstances. The naming of this support as a GST Voucher was intended to draw a direct link to GST. This allowed the government to assert that GST, while itself regressive, was part of an overall progressive system of taxes and transfers. In financial year (FY) 2020, the cost of GSTV was about $830 million.

Given the plan to raise GST to 9% sometime between 2022 and 2025, the government announced a $6 billion **Assurance Package** in **Budget 2020** to provide adult Singaporeans with cash payouts of between $700 and $1,600 over five years to offset at least five years of additional GST expenses for most households, and 10 years' worth for those living in one- to three-room flats. The permanent GSTV would also be enhanced in line with the government's commitment to fully offset GST for retiree households in the lower half of the income distribution, significantly offset it for the upper-half of retiree households, and offset about half of GST for lower-income households with no elderly members.

Looking Ahead

Income inequality has stabilised and declined slightly in recent years, as outlined in Chapter 2. Nonetheless, depending on the extent to which structural forces in a post-COVID-19 world, including global competition and asset price appreciation, push up inequality (discussed in Chapter 11), there is a risk that obvious disparities in wealth could fuel envy and discontent in a Gilded Age scenario. There may be a need for further, bolder measures to redistribute wealth in the years ahead.

Higher income and wealth taxes may be one such measure. While raising income taxes for the broad middle could dampen incentives for work and enterprise, it is less clear that higher marginal tax rates on personal income — say at a higher tier of $640,000 (double the current highest income tier threshold) or $1 million — would significantly erode incentives or make Singapore less attractive to talent. Such a move, while having a symbolic impact, would not however yield very much in terms of revenue for redistribution.

Compared with taxes on employment income, taxes on wealth or capital income have the advantage of being less likely to distort work incentives. In fact, in a scenario of property prices outstripping economic or income growth on a sustained basis, wealth taxes may help to prevent the emergence of a rentier state where returns on assets swamp income from employment or enterprise. If there are pressures in this direction, wealth taxes could better support the principle of "Reward for Work, and Work for Reward". As non-work income makes up a larger proportion of household income for the more affluent, taxes on capital income would also make for a more progressive overall tax system.

With the growing number of family offices and influx of foreign funds into Singapore in recent years, Han Fook Kwang (2021) suggested that the government find ways to extract more value from the wealth parked here, whether through taxes or other means.[9]

However, given the aim of keeping Singapore attractive as a talent hub and wealth management centre, any moves to raise income or wealth taxes are likely to be limited and would not be able to fund the bulk of expected increases in expenditure on healthcare and infrastructure. In terms of revenue generation, the heavy lifting is likely to be done by GST as well as investment returns on Singapore's reserves, which will be discussed in Chapter 10.

In the context of Singapore's low tax model, fiscal redistribution will need to be complemented by other levers to keep inequality at bay.

Endnotes

1. Isabelle Joumard, Mauro Pisu, and Debbie Bloch, "Tackling Income Inequality: The Role of Taxes and Transfers," *OECD Journal: Economic Studies* (2012).
2. Jacob Lundberg, "The Laffer Curve for High Incomes," Luxembourg Income Studies Working Paper No. 711, 2017.
3. Ministry of Finance (MOF), "Income Growth, Inequality and Mobility Trends in Singapore," MOF occasional paper, August 2015.
4. Heng Swee Keat, Budget Debate Round-Up Speech, 2018.

5. See, for instance, Elke Asen, "Corporate Tax Rates Around the World, 2020," *Fiscal Fact* No. 735 (Tax Foundation, December 2020), https://files.taxfoundation.org/20201208152358/2020-Corporate-Tax-Rates-around-the-World.pdf.
6. These include the New Singapore Shares (2001), Economic Restructuring Shares (2002–2004), and Growth Dividends (2008).
7. Tharman Shanmugaratnam, Budget Debate Round-Up Speech, 2015.
8. Tharman Shanmugaratnam, Budget Statement, 2013.
9. Han Fook Kwang, "Find Ways to Profit from Safe-Haven Singapore," *Straits Times*, 14 February 2021.

Chapter 5

Expanding Social Security

A Brief Look Back and Around

The International Labour Organization considers social security a "human right which responds to the universal need for protection against certain life risks and social needs."[1] Sir William Beveridge, the architect of the UK's post-war welfare state, referred to social security as denoting "the security of an income to take the place of earnings, when they are interrupted by unemployment, sickness or accident, to provide for retirement through age, to provide loss of support by the death of another person and to meet exceptional expenditure such as those connected with birth, death and marriage."[2]

In fact, social security in one form or another exists in every society, even where formal government structures are lacking.

In the 1800s, Chinese labourers (called coolies) who came to Singapore for work would join clan associations and secret societies on arriving here. Away from their ancestral villages and typically without blood relatives in Singapore, they would seek out those who had come from the same province or who spoke the same dialect. In return for subscriptions, clan associations and secret societies would provide members with financial support when they fell sick and protect their livelihoods. Among the many roles they played, the responsibility for funeral rites was particularly significant to the coolies, given the high risk of premature death from tropical disease, poor nutrition, or work injuries, and the importance they placed on ensuring a smooth passage to the afterlife.

Later, when immigrants had sunk roots in Singapore, large families would help to provide buffer in times of need through informal loans from siblings, uncles, and other relatives, a practice that continued well into Singapore's post-independence years. Even less-educated seniors who had earned little during their working years could retire comfortably with the support of their children who had benefited from Singapore's economic development and entered into the middle class. However, with more remaining single and family sizes shrinking, as described in Chapter 2, Singaporeans today are less likely to be able to rely on children and relatives for social security.

Internationally, social security has emerged in the 20th century as a key responsibility of governments the world over, given growing interdependence among citizens and increasing government regulation over work and almost every aspect of life. Social security and welfare provision expanded significantly in the US and Western Europe following the Great Depression and the Second World War in the forging of a new social compact.

In Singapore, the government has sought to uphold self-reliance and responsibility for one's family as the organising principles for social security, which is built around a system of mandatory savings supplemented by subventions and social transfers. At the same time, the state plays a significant role through direct provision of public amenities and services, the regulation of service providers, and through rules governing the Central Provident Fund (CPF). This approach of collective support for personal effort sees an activist government intervening to support inclusivity while reinforcing individual and community self-responsibility.

The Pillars of Social Security in Singapore

Singapore's system of social security is described as comprising four pillars:

- **Retirement income through CPF**
- **Home ownership**

- **Healthcare assurance**
- **Workfare/Silver Support**

The identification of these four pillars by the government reflects the centrality of income during one's working years and retirement, as well as the affordability of healthcare and housing, these being necessities of life that typically account for a large portion of lifetime expenditure for individuals and households.

Notably, unemployment support is not counted among the pillars, unlike in many other advanced countries. Financial support to tide over periods of unemployment or absence from the labour force comes from one's own savings, family support, or, in the case of retrenched workers, retrenchment benefits paid by employers. The government steps in with temporary support for needy families only as a last resort; otherwise, public support is in the form of training subsidies and wage support to facilitate re-entry into the workforce. This approach has been made possible by the relatively low unemployment rates in Singapore over the years.

Security for income, retirement, housing, and healthcare accrues from:

— **Personal savings**, whose accumulation, returns, and utilisation are regulated by the government through CPF
— **Government transfers, top-ups, and subsidies**
— **Risk pooling/social insurance**

Grants and subsidies under each of these pillars have been continually adjusted and enhanced over the years to address changes in demography, income, wealth distribution, as well as cost of living, as summarised in Chapter 3. The introduction of the Workfare Income Supplement in 2007 and the Silver Support Scheme in 2016 has added a fourth pillar to the system. While retaining a strong emphasis on individual responsibility and self-reliance, there is now greater use of **social insurance** or **risk pooling** with the introduction of CPF Lifelong Income for the Elderly (CPF LIFE), MediShield Life, and CareShield Life to mitigate the vagaries of chance through life. Finally, measures have been taken to **contain**

cost escalation in housing and healthcare, which are critical for affordability and fiscal sustainability.

Collectively, the steps taken since the mid-2000s have made for a stronger and more comprehensive social safety net to address, in particular, retirement adequacy, as well as housing and healthcare affordability.

Central Provident Fund

CPF is the cornerstone of Singapore's social security system. It is a compulsory savings plan for Singapore citizens and permanent residents primarily for retirement, healthcare, and housing. Employers and employees are required to contribute monthly towards an individual's account in defined proportions. CPF is a **defined contribution** scheme in that a CPF member's total benefits are equal to the contributions into the account plus credited interest, unlike a **defined benefit** scheme where a particular stream of benefits is promised. However, unlike most other defined contribution schemes, CPF returns are tied to interest rates (subject to a government-set floor) rather than investment performance. CPF is a **fully funded** system, in contrast to **unfunded (pay-as-you-go)** state pension systems that rely on financing from future pension contributions or general tax revenue.

Looking Around: Pension Systems, Adequacy, and Sustainability

Mandatory savings plans feature in the retirement systems of several countries, including Malaysia, India, and Hong Kong. Others, such as the US, UK, and France, have unfunded state pension schemes that rely on contributions from the working population to pay for the benefits of retirees. Many advanced economies have multi-pillar pensions system comprising a mandatory basic state pension, occupational pensions (which may be voluntary or compulsory), and private pensions (which may be subsidised or attract tax relief).

The two principal concerns in regard to retirement schemes are adequacy and sustainability, with a need to ensure a balance between these objectives.

In 2017, the World Economic Forum warned that the retirement savings gap, which refers to the shortfall between retirement savings and what is needed for an adequate standard of living, would shoot up from US$70 trillion to US$400 trillion in eight countries.[3]

Sustainability is a particular concern for unfunded pension schemes in countries where life expectancy has increased and the share of working age population is declining. Furthermore, the decline in interest rates and bond yields since the 2008–2009 Global Financial Crisis has put pension payouts at risk for millions of retirees. The global pensions crisis, as some have called it, has been exacerbated by the COVID-19 pandemic, which has affected both earnings and savings, with many jobs lost and a number of countries allowing citizens to withdraw more from individual pension accounts to meet immediate needs.

Looking Back: A Brief History of CPF

The basic structure of CPF has been in place since 1955 when it was introduced in Singapore by the British colonial government. However, it has evolved considerably over the years.

According to M. Ramesh (2004), the choice of a mandatory savings plan over a pension plan stemmed from the colonial government's desire not to incur significant public expenditure. A similar provident fund had been established in Malaya in 1951.[4] While the 1957 Committee on Minimum Standards of Livelihood, chaired by Sydney Caine, had recommended that CPF be replaced by a contributory social insurance scheme, CPF was retained by the People's Action Party which took power in 1959 when Singapore was accorded internal self-government. Former Permanent Secretary (Finance) Ngiam Tong Dow (2006) commented that CPF and the Currency Board, measures which the British had imposed on their colonies but not on themselves, turned out to be of considerable advantage to the colonies due to the strict discipline these measures imposed.[5]

In the mid-1960s, when Singapore was embarking on industrialisation, CPF allowed the government to mobilise domestic savings for investment in economic infrastructure at relatively low and stable interest rates rather than rely on foreign borrowing.[6]

In 1968, the scope of CPF was expanded to fund purchases of government-built Housing and Development Board (HDB) flats in support of the government's home ownership policy. Subsequently, in 1981, this was extended to private residential property purchases. The CPF Special Account was introduced in 1977 to ensure that citizens' retirement would be adequately provided for. In 1984, CPF was extended to cover healthcare with the implementation of MediSave.

Initially, the CPF contribution rates of employers and employees were equal. These were increased progressively from 5% each in 1955 to 25% each in 1985. The steep rise in contributions from 1968 to 1985 was made possible by strong wage growth during this period, and helped to mitigate the inflationary impact of rising incomes. The employer contribution rate was reduced to 10% in 1986 to lower costs for businesses as the economy had slid into recession. By 1991, it was restored to 20%. The 1997–1998 Asian Financial Crisis again saw the employer contribution rate cut to 10% to manage business costs, before a gradual restoration to 17%.

The CPF system continues to be fine-tuned in response to changing demographics and socio-economic considerations.

CPF Policy and Recent Updates

Under the CPF Act, Singaporeans and permanent residents, along with their employers, are required to contribute a percentage of their income from work (20% for employees and 17% for employers as at 2021) to their CPF accounts. Contribution rates are lower for older workers aged 55 and above to protect their employability (Table 5.1). Contributions are capped so as to limit the use of CPF as a tax shelter, since CPF contributions are tax-exempt.

CPF comprises:

- The **Ordinary Account (OA)**, which can be used for housing, investment, and education
- The **Special Account (SA)**, which is set aside for retirement
- The **MediSave Account (MA)**, for hospitalisation, medical treatment, and approved medical insurance
- The **Retirement Account (RA)**, which opens upon turning 55 years old and is intended to meet basic retirement needs

Table 5.1 CPF Contribution Rates

Employee's Age	By Employer (% of wage)	By Employee (% of wage)	Total (% of wage)
55 and below	17	20	37
Above 55 to 60	13	13	26
Above 60 to 65	9	7.5	16.5
Above 65	7.5	5	12.5

Note: As at May 2021, for monthly wages ≥$750.

Table 5.2 Allocation of CPF Contribution Rates to OA, SA, and MA

Employee's Age	OA (% of wage)	SA (% of wage)	MA (% of wage)
35 and below	23	6	8
Above 35 to 45	21	7	9
Above 45 to 50	19	8	10
Above 50 to 55	15	11.5	10.5
Above 55 to 60	12	3.5	10.5
Above 60 to 65	3.5	2.5	10.5
Above 65	1	1	10.5

Note: As at May 2021, for monthly wages ≥$750.

The allocation of CPF contributions to the MA ranges from 8% to 10.5% of income, while the SA attracts 1% to 11.5%, depending on age (Table 5.2). The balance of contributions flows to the OA. Self-employed persons are only required to contribute to the MA if they earn more than $6,000 in net trade income in a year, although they may make voluntary CPF contributions to the OA and SA.

CPF balances earn interest, which is pegged to short-term market interest rates (in the case of OA), or the interest rate of 10-year Singapore Government Securities plus one percentage point (for SA and MA) with a guaranteed floor rate. The legislated minimum interest rate on OA balances is 2.5%, while the current floor rate for SA/MA is 4%.

Since 2008, an extra 1% interest has been paid on the first $60,000 of combined balances (with up to $20,000 from the OA), boosting retirement savings while adding a dose of progressivity by increasing the overall rate of return for members who have lower CPF savings. From 2016, a further 1% has been paid on the first $30,000 of combined balances (with up to $20,000 from the OA) for members aged 55 and above.

Members' CPF balances are invested in Special Singapore Government Securities, earning the stipulated interest payments. Given the guarantee by the Singapore government, this is practically a risk-free investment.

At age 55, CPF balances can be withdrawn after setting aside the Full Retirement Sum ($186,000 as at 2021) in the RA for retirement needs; this was formerly known as the CPF Minimum Sum), or the Basic Retirement Sum ($93,500 as at 2021), subject to a pledge to return proceeds from a sale of property to one's CPF account. Members may also choose to set aside a larger retirement sum up to the Enhanced Retirement Sum (set at three times the Basic Retirement Sum) for higher annuity payouts.

In 2009, a compulsory lifelong annuity scheme called **CPF LIFE** was introduced. The intent of CPF LIFE was to ensure that CPF members would not run out of savings, given that life expectancy had increased to 81 years, from below 65 years in the 1950s when the CPF scheme began. CPF members with sufficient savings in the RA may select one of three CPF LIFE plans (Basic, Standard, or Escalating) depending on their preference regarding the size of payouts and whether they need protection against inflation. These plans provide payouts for life from the payout eligibility age (PEA) of 65 onwards, with the option of deferring the PEA up to age 70 in return for higher payouts. The premiums for a member's CPF LIFE plan are paid with his or her CPF savings. The interest earned on premiums is pooled across CPF LIFE members to guarantee payouts for life.

CPF LIFE serves as a form of longevity risk insurance. Members who live longer receive more payouts over their lifetime. Those who pass away before the PEA, or shortly after the PEA, do not forgo any of the premiums they contribute from their CPF savings, which will be paid to their nominated beneficiaries. This approach strikes a balance between allowing CPF members to reap the benefits of risk pooling and moderating the penalty on those who do not live as long as others.

CPF Issues and Concerns: Withdrawal Age/Flexibility, Returns, and Retirement Adequacy

CPF has been acclaimed as a robust and sustainable savings scheme which avoids the tax burden on younger generations that unfunded pension schemes risk. Notable global rankings of pension schemes have placed Singapore top or among the better performers in Asia:

- Mercer CFA Institute Global Pension Index 2020: sixth out of 39 retirement systems; top in Asia (based on adequacy, sustainability, and integrity)
- Allianz SE Global Pension Report 2020: 30th out of 70 pension plans; sixth in Asia (based on demography and fiscal prerequisites, sustainability, and adequacy)

Notwithstanding, the CPF system has also attracted criticism by some members of the public and commentators. Their concerns generally centre on three issues: CPF withdrawal age, CPF returns, and retirement adequacy.

First, some Singaporeans are unhappy that they are no longer able to withdraw half their CPF savings unconditionally at age 55, unlike in years past, and will receive their CPF Life payouts only from age 65. Second, there are those who feel that CPF returns, although guaranteed, are too low. One view is that the returns ought to be inflation-indexed or pegged to the investment returns generated by GIC (Singapore's sovereign wealth fund previously known as the Government of Singapore Investment Corporation), so that CPF members can enjoy the upside when investment returns are strong. Finally, there are concerns that too few people are able to attain the CPF minimum sum upon reaching 55, and hence may not have adequate income in retirement.

CPF Withdrawal Age/Flexibility

The first issue is a visceral one for some Singaporeans. Before 2009, CPF members who turned 55 could withdraw up to half their CPF savings upon turning 55 regardless of whether they were able to set aside the Minimum

Sum. This was progressively phased out from 2009 to 2013 due to increases in life expectancy and the concern that some CPF members had insufficient savings to last their lifetime. The introduction of CPF LIFE, along with the progressive increase in PEA from 60 to 65, added further fuel to the notion of that the goalposts were continually shifting, making it more difficult for them to access their own hard-earned money. Acknowledging this sentiment, the government accepted the recommendation of the CPF Advisory Panel (which had been set up in 2014) to give members the option of withdrawing up to 20% of RA savings in a lump sum at the PEA, even if they have not set aside the Basic Retirement Sum.

The trade-off between pension withdrawal age and retirement adequacy has to be carefully considered. One approach adopted by countries such as Denmark has been to tie the statutory pension age to life expectancy, which also encourages people to extend their working years as life expectancy increases. Such indexing may help to depoliticise revisions to pension withdrawal age made necessary by increased life expectancy. However, such a move itself may not be well-received by CPF members who already feel that the current PEA of 65 is too high.

Given that the government has in the past topped up MediSave balances, and provided additional interest payments on CPF balances, it is in fact arguable whether a CPF member should be entitled to unfettered access to his or her CPF monies. This was a question articulated by former Nominated Member of Parliament (Nominated MP) Chia Yong Yong in the 2015 Budget debate:

> "Is it our money? Our CPF savings are enhanced and forced CPF savings which are accumulated through our own deferred consumption, through co-payment by our employers and through top-ups from public funds. Is it really my private money? Do I have the right to spend it the way I would spend my own salary? I'm not entirely sure."[7]

CPF Returns

The second issue is whether the interest rates on CPF balances are fair to members, and whether they are enough for members to build up adequate retirement savings. Unlike most defined contribution schemes, CPF returns are not dependent on the investment performance of the fund.

Instead, CPF monies are invested in special government bonds issued to the CPF Board by the government.

The proceeds from these bonds are pooled with the rest of the government's funds, such as proceeds from other government securities and land sales, and deposited with the Monetary Authority of Singapore (MAS), which converts them into foreign assets through the foreign exchange market. The majority of these assets are long-term and managed by GIC. CPF returns are delinked from the actual investment performance of GIC.

There have been suggestions for CPF returns to be pegged to the investment returns generated by GIC, or for the CPF interest rate to be pegged to inflation. Responding to criticisms that CPF is a source of cheap funds for the state, which profits from the difference between the returns earned on the savings of CPF members and the interest paid to CPF members, the government has pointed out that the state can in fact borrow from the market at lower rates. It has also highlighted that GIC's higher returns are the consequence of it taking on higher risks, whereas CPF members are insulated from market risk by the floor interest rates earned on CPF balances.

A study by Christopher Gee, Peter Ryan-Kane, Mark Whatley, and Will Rainey (2014) concluded that CPF returns were broadly equivalent to a portfolio invested 60:40 in global equities and bonds but with a much lower downside risk given Singapore's strong sovereign credit rating.[8] This made CPF, in their view, a more attractive proposition than other investment opportunities. Compared with the individual CPF member, the government is better placed to bear the downside risk of investments due to its resources and long time horizon. Gee et al. also found that since 1993, CPF OA and SA/MA interest rates had exceeded inflation except in three periods (1994, 2008, and 2011–2012).

Many Singaporeans have taken advantage of the stable returns on CPF accounts to grow their savings significantly by transferring savings from the OA to SA and topping up the SA with cash. Self-styled CPF guru Loo Cheng Chuan has run seminars and webinars to educate the public on how they can become "CPF millionaires" by accumulating $1 million, or even up to $4 million, in their CPF accounts by age 65.

Some, however, have compared Singapore's CPF with savings or pension schemes in other jurisdictions, such as Hong Kong's Mandatory

Provident Fund, Malaysia's Employees' Provident Fund, and Australia's voluntary MySuper fund, noting that nominal returns on these funds are variable and, in some years, have significantly exceeded 2.5%. However, real returns depend on the inflation rate in these economies.

While it is conceivable that higher interest rates could be paid to CPF members in years of strong investment returns, this would likely come at the cost of lower guaranteed interest rates, which may not be in the interest of the majority of CPF members who rely on stable returns for their retirement.

Rather, it would seem more appropriate to offer higher risk/return options to CPF members, especially those who are younger or have higher incomes or more savings and hence can afford to take on greater risk. Since 1986, members have been allowed to invest part of their OA balances to seek higher returns. Under the **CPF Investment Scheme (CPFIS)**, members can choose among various instruments such as insurance products, funds, bonds, and shares.[9] However, then-DPM Tharman Shanmugaratnam highlighted in 2016 that a significant proportion of members who invested in CPFIS in the preceding 10 years would have been better off leaving their money in the OA.[10] This, he explained, could be attributed to high management fees for investment funds as well as investors' tendency to buy when the market is euphoric and sell when prices are depressed. In 2016, the CPF Advisory Panel recommended introducing the **Lifetime Retirement Investment Scheme (LRIS)**, aimed at providing a simple, low-cost, aggregated investment option suitable for the majority of CPF members. LRIS would simplify decision making by offering a small number of well-diversified, passively managed funds for members to choose from. To lower investment fees under CPFIS, the government reduced the sales charge cap from 3% to 1.5% in 2018, and removed the sales charge entirely from October 2020.

Joelle Fong, Olivia Mitchell, and Benedict Koh (2011) assessed that CPF LIFE offered good value for money to annuitants based on the "money's worth ratio" (MWR), which is the expected present discounted value of the annuity payments to the initial premium. They estimated MWRs ranging from 1.24 to 1.32 for males and 1.26 to 1.34 for females, compared with MWRs of below 1 for annuities provided by private life insurers.[11]

CPF and Retirement Adequacy

Regarding the third issue of contention, viz. the adequacy of retirement savings, the proportion of active CPF members attaining the required retirement sum (which is adjusted for inflation) by age 55 climbed from 52% in 2012 to 61% in 2019 (Figure 5.1). This upward trend has been aided by the Workfare Income Supplement (WIS) for lower-income workers (from 2007) and the payment of an extra 1% interest for the first $60,000 in CPF savings (from 2008).

Recognising the need to build up members' savings for retirement, the government restored the employer's CPF contribution to 16% over 2010–2011 (it had been cut to 13% in 2003) and gradually raised employer and employee CPF contributions for older Singaporeans. The employer's contribution towards the MA was raised by a further one percentage point from 2015, bringing the total employer CPF contribution to 17%.

The 2019 Report of the Tripartite Workgroup on Older Workers recommended increasing CPF contribution rates for older workers aged 55 to 70 in order to strengthen older workers' retirement adequacy, in tandem with increases in the Retirement and Re-employment Age (details in Chapter 8, Table 8.6). In particular, the panel proposed step-by-step

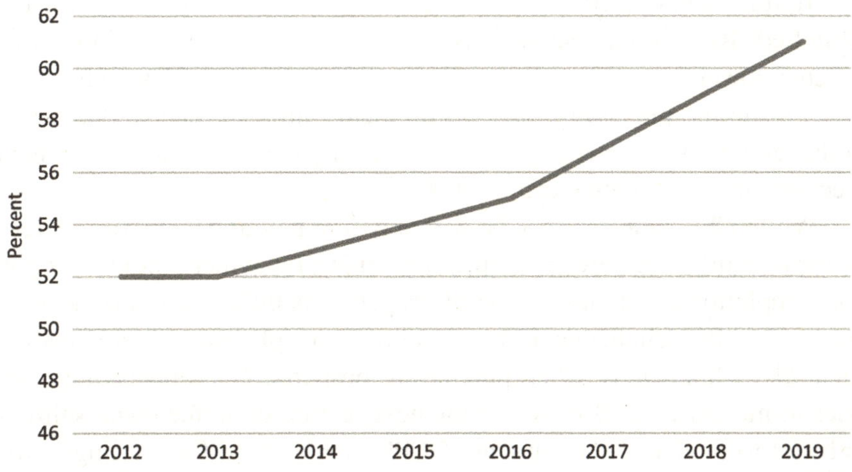

Figure 5.1 Share of Active CPF Members Able to Meet the Retirement Sum at Age 55

Note: Data for 2018 not available.

Source: Public Sector Outcomes Review (2016, 2018, 2020), Ministry of Finance.

increases in both employer and employee contribution rates, with the aim of having those aged 55 to 60 reach the full CPF contribution rate of 37%. Those aged 60 to 70 years should have "smaller but meaningful" increases in CPF contribution rates, while those aged above 70 should not see changes to their CPF contributions, which could otherwise affect their employability as employers have no obligation to re-employ workers beyond 70. However, the government deferred the first step of the planned increase from 1 January 2021 to 1 January 2022 to help employers manage costs amid the COVID-19 pandemic.

While cuts to CPF contribution rates had been used as a countercyclical demand management tool to lower business costs in past downturns in 1986, 1998, and 2003, the government did not cut rates during the Global Financial Crisis in 2008–2009. The increasing adoption of a flexible wage policy gave firms more options to adjust wages in response to economic conditions. Responding to an MP's suggestion to consider CPF rate cuts in response to the COVID-19 pandemic, then-Minister for Manpower Josephine Teo noted that such a move would have to be considered very carefully as it could impair workers' ability to save for retirement, although she indicated that the government would monitor the situation and consider if CPF rates needed to be adjusted in the future.[12]

To further boost retirement savings, the government is introducing the **Matched Retirement Savings Scheme** from 2021–2023. Under this scheme, lower- to middle-income Singaporeans aged 55–70 who have yet to set aside the prevailing Basic Retirement Sum can receive dollar-for-dollar government matching for cash top-ups made to their Retirement Account, up to an annual cap of $600.

While CPF balances may be withdrawn to pay university tuition fees or for housing, there are strict rules governing repayment into CPF upon the completion of studies or sale of property, including return of accrued interest. A key challenge is to discourage people from overextending themselves financially when purchasing property. Notwithstanding avenues to monetise HDB flats (see the next section on home ownership), it is better to moderate the amount of CPF monies used for housing in the first instance. Following the recommendations of the 2003 Economic Review Committee, there was a progressive tightening of limits on the withdrawal of CPF for housing financed with bank loans. In 2013, as part of property cooling measures, limits were set on the use of CPF for public housing with leases of less than 60 years.

Financial education is an often overlooked but critical upstream intervention to address income security. Many of the financial difficulties citizens find themselves in as a result of interruptions to employment or earnings could be averted through prudential savings and more modest consumption habits. Living below one's means, or not taking continuous employment with ever-growing wages as a given, can increase financial resilience for individuals and households and avoid a transference of risk to the state. **MoneySense**, a joint initiative by the Ministry of Manpower and MAS, was started in 2003 as a national financial education programme to help Singaporeans make sound financial decisions. Partners include institutes of higher learning, community organisations, and financial industry associations, all of which play key roles in improving financial literacy and decision-making.

Home Ownership

Home ownership is another pillar of Singapore's social security and a distinctive feature of the Singapore socio-economic system. Sociologist Chua Beng Huat (2017) identified the national housing programme as one of four "institutionalised political and economic practices grounded in social democracy", alongside ideological anti-liberalism, state capitalism, and multiracialism.[13] About nine in 10 resident households own their homes, an asset which is hedged against inflation and has the potential to appreciate over time, besides providing security for retirement.

Looking Back: Public Housing Since the 1960s

HDB was formed in 1960 to address the housing shortage by providing low-cost housing for those living in slums and squatter settlements. In the five years from 1960, HDB built over 54,000 housing units in apartment blocks. In 1964, the Home Ownership for the People Scheme was introduced to help Singaporeans own rather than rent their flats. This had the purpose of giving Singaporeans a tangible stake in the success of the country with the potential for their housing assets to appreciate in value in tandem with Singapore's development. It was thought that this would also contribute to rootedness and a stronger will to defend the country.

Founding Prime Minister Lee Kuan Yew explained, "My primary preoccupation was to give every citizen a stake in the country and its future. I wanted a home-owning society… I believed this sense of ownership was vital for our new society which had no deep roots in a common historical experience."[14]

HDB flats are generally sold on 99-year leases, after which the land is returned to the government to be recycled for new uses.

The 1966 Land Acquisition Act allowed the state to acquire land for any public purpose, including public housing. An amendment passed in 1973 allowed the state to set payments independent of the land's purchase price or prevailing market prices, facilitating the construction of HDB estates and new towns. State ownership of land grew from 44% in 1960 to 76% by 1985.[15] HDB's housing stock increased from 120,138 units in 1970 to 574,443 units in 1990, housing 87% of the resident population.[16] Demand for new flats picked up as CPF savings could be used for HDB flat down payment and mortgage payments from 1968. The steady increase in CPF contribution rates from 1968 facilitated the purchase of HDB flats even as flat prices rose.

Unlike public housing in many countries, Singapore's HDB flats cater to the majority of the population, not just the lower income. At its peak in the late 1980s, nearly 90% of Singapore residents lived in HDB flats, although this proportion has since come down to 80% in 2019/2020[17] with growing affluence spurring more to upgrade to private property. The rate of home ownership for resident households increased from 29% in 1970 to 59% in 1980, and 88% in 1990, and has remained in the ballpark of 90% since then.[18]

In the 1990s, the focus of public housing was on quality and asset enhancement. Older HDB flats benefited from heavily subsidised upgrading programmes, and a wider range of flats with better finishings was made available. Privately developed executive condominiums were introduced in 1997 for those who could afford more than an HDB flat but found private property to be out of reach. The run-up in property prices (both HDB and private) in the 1990s came to an abrupt halt with the Asian Financial Crisis in 1997, which triggered a sharp price correction.

Property owners who had bought their homes near the market peak suffered significant asset price falls by the end of 1998. HDB resale prices declined by 27% from their peak in 1996, while private residential property prices fell by about 45% (Figures 3.3, 3.4).

The market correction led to a significant supply overhang of some 31,000 unsold HDB flats, which eventually took more than five years to sell.[19] This experience led to the introduction of the Build-To-Order (BTO) system in April 2001 where new flats would only be built when there was sufficient actual demand, with applicants required to make a down payment.

Conversely, in the decade that followed, housing stock did not keep pace with population growth. A resurgence in HDB resale prices from 2008 led to surging demand for BTO flats. There were long waits for new units as flats took three to five years to construct. Prices of new BTO flats, which took reference from the market prices of comparable resale flats, also rose, although the increase was moderated through higher government subsidies from 2011–2013.

How It Works: HDB Grants and Sale Conditions

To ensure housing affordability, HDB sells new flats at subsidised prices and offers grants and loans to eligible buyers of both new and resale flats. The **Enhanced CPF Housing Grant** (which replaced the former Additional CPF Housing Grant and Special CPF Housing Grant in 2019) provides first-time buyers purchasing new or resale flats with subsidies of up to $80,000 depending on their household income.

In addition, families purchasing a resale flat for the first time may receive the:

— **Family Grant** of up to $50,000
— **Proximity Housing Grant** of $20,000 to $30,000 for those living with or near their parents or children

Altogether, first-time resale flat buyers may receive up to $160,000 in grants, putting home ownership within reach of even the bottom 10% of wage earners.

In 2012, then-DPM Tharman caused a stir when he said in Parliament that a family earning $1,000 a month could afford to purchase a $100,000 two-room HDB flat with the monthly mortgage payments paid entirely from their CPF contributions. Many Singaporeans found it hard to believe that it was possible to own an HDB flat with such a low income. In fact, among the lowest 20% of households by income, 85% own their homes.[20]

Second-time applicants purchasing new or resale three-room flats in non-mature estates may also receive a $15,000 **Step-Up CPF Housing Grant** to offset the cost of their purchase.

Given the sizeable government subsidies for public housing, eligibility rules and other conditions are imposed on the purchase and ownership of HDB flats. Generally, a new or BTO flat can only be purchased by a citizen with an eligible family unit comprising at least another citizen or permanent resident. There is a monthly household income ceiling, which has been revised upwards over the years and, in 2021, stands at $14,000 for families buying new HDB flats (four-room or larger), or $21,000 if purchasing as an extended or multi-generation family.[21] The income ceiling of $14,000 allows more than eight in 10 citizen households to purchase new HDB flats.

To buy a new or resale HDB flat with CPF Housing Grants, private property owners are required to dispose of their property 30 months prior to making an application. Purchase of a resale HDB flat without CPF Housing Grants requires the owner to dispose of any other residential property owned within six months. Upon purchase of an HDB flat, there is a Minimum Occupation Period of five years, during which the flat owner is not permitted to purchase other properties in Singapore or abroad. In addition, the flat cannot be sold or leased out in entirety during this period, although rooms can be rented out with HDB's approval.

HDB rules also reflect the government's social objectives including ethnic integration and the promotion of marriage and parenthood.

The Ethnic Integration Policy, introduced in 1989, ensures that each HDB block and neighbourhood is occupied by a racial mix not too different from the national average. Once the quota for a particular ethnic group has been reached, buyers from that ethnic group can only purchase a flat from sellers of the same ethnic group. In 2010, HDB also introduced the Singapore Permanent Resident Quota, which caps the number of permanent resident households per block to 8% and per neighbourhood to 5% (Malaysian permanent residents excluded).

It was only in 1991 that singles were allowed to purchase resale HDB flats on their own; still, they had to be at least 35 years of age and were initially restricted to three-room flats in selected locations. In 2013, the purchase of new flats from HDB (limited to two-room flats in non-mature estates) was opened to single Singaporeans aged 35 and above with an average monthly income of not more than $5,000, as well as Singaporean-foreigner couples. The income ceiling has since been raised to $7,000, and singles may receive the Enhanced CPF Housing Grant depending on their income. Singles buying resale flats may be eligible for the Singles Grant, Enhanced CPF Housing Grant, and Proximity Housing Grant but at lower support levels compared with families.

Housing Equity Versus Retirement Cashflow

The HDB flat has become an integral part of the life story of Singaporeans. It is said, only partly in jest, that the typical Singapore marriage proposal is not "Will you marry me?" but "Shall we apply for an HDB flat?" By working hard and moving up in one's career, one can aspire to upgrade to a larger HDB flat or even private property. Indeed, property typically forms a sizeable part of a Singaporean family's wealth.

Singapore's rapid economic development was accompanied by a sharp appreciation in the price of HDB flats, giving flat owners considerable housing equity. As Prime Minister Lee Hsien Loong pointed out in 2012, "Households in the lowest income quintile have on average more than $200,000 of equity in their HDB flat."[22]

While this is impressive, the question is whether too much of the average Singaporean's net worth is tied up in housing equity. Residential property assets formed 44% of total household assets in 2018,[23] which although lower than in 2012 (50%),[24] remains higher than countries such as the US and UK.[25]

This has led to concerns that asset-rich but cash-poor Singaporeans may not have sufficient retirement cashflow. These may include not just HDB flat dwellers, but also retirees or low-income earners living in old private landed properties, which today are worth a considerable sum due to the value of the land.

The government has sought to address this in various ways, including tightening limits on the use of CPF savings for home purchases (described in the section on CPF) and helping homeowners monetise their housing assets.

One option to monetise housing is to rent out spare bedrooms. To provide a further option for seniors aged 65 and above to monetise their flats, the government introduced the **Lease Buyback Scheme** in 2009. The idea behind this is that if the remaining lease on one's flat is longer than one expects to live, the excess lease (subject to a minimum of 20 years) can be sold back to HDB. This has the advantage of allowing seniors to age in place — to continue living in familiar surroundings instead of having to move to a smaller flat which may be in a different estate. As a further sweetener, those who sell the excess lease back to HDB and use the net proceeds to top up their CPF Retirement Account will receive a cash bonus. From 2019, the scheme was extended to all flat types, including five-room and larger flats, bringing the total number of eligible households to about 130,000.

In 2013, the **Silver Housing Bonus** was introduced to encourage "empty nesters" (those whose children have grown up and moved out) to downsize to smaller flats. Currently, under this scheme, elderly households may receive a cash bonus of up to $30,000 (up from $20,000 in 2013) when they sell their property, buy a three-room or smaller flat, channel part of the proceeds to their CPF Retirement Account, and join CPF LIFE. Since 2020, seniors may apply for the Silver Housing Bonus when purchasing a three-room or smaller HDB flat, even if they have not downsized from a larger flat.

While these are useful options, the take-up of the Lease Buyback Scheme and Silver Housing Bonus has not been strong as many older Singaporeans prefer to age in place as well as leave their property as an inheritance. In October 2018, the Ministry of National Development reported in Parliament that about 3,100 households had taken up the Lease Buyback Scheme since its introduction in March 2009.

In a 2019 working paper, the Workers' Party proposed an alternative Universal Sale and Lease Back Scheme which would cover all HDB property types and would be open to all HDB leases after the Minimum

Occupation Period and with at least 80% of the loan repaid. Compensation would be determined by a published formula based on expected rental receivables over the remaining lease period.[26] Under the proposal, the government could use flats bought under this scheme to offer shorter-term rental, creating a market for shorter leases. However, depending on the take-up of the scheme and the demand for such leases, the government could be exposed to the financial risks from guaranteeing lease purchases under the scheme, which is significantly broader than the existing Lease Buyback Scheme.

Another possibility to consider is whether new flats could be sold with shorter leases, given that a 99-year lease would exceed the remaining life expectancy of purchasers. Flats sold with a 70-year lease, for instance, would be more affordable and require lower government subsidies. This would focus private and public resources on the provision of needs during the flat buyer's lifetime, rather than have a significant portion channelled to bequests.

Housing Appreciation Versus Housing Affordability

Notwithstanding the sizeable government grants to defray the cost of purchasing HDB flats, the rapid appreciation of HDB flat prices contributed to a perception that housing prices were getting beyond the reach of ordinary Singaporeans, especially in the years following the 2008–2009 Global Financial Crisis. Prices in the HDB resale market were determined by the market along with private property prices, with no barrier separating the two markets save for rules governing the resale of HDB flats. While HDB set the prices of new BTO flats, these too were informed by market prices of comparable resale flats. Consequently, there was a slight dip in home ownership rates and a rise in debt servicing ratios for first-time buyers purchasing HDB flats in non-mature estates from 2007 to 2011.[27]

With low interest rates that accompanied quantitative easing arising from the 2008–2009 crisis, asset prices in many parts of the world surged. The HDB Resale Price Index rose by nearly 37% between 2008 and 2011 against growth in median household income from work of about 15% during this period (Figure 3.4). Even well-off property owners, who had benefited from the growth in their property values, expressed anxiety that property was becoming out of reach for their children. Contributing to this perception were some eye-catching HDB resale transaction prices: upwards of a million dollars for flats in prime locations or with unique features. Consequently, there were calls for the price of new HDB flats to be pegged to median household incomes rather than to resale market prices.

Between 2010 and 2013, the government responded with multiple rounds of property cooling measures that included the introduction of **Seller's Stamp Duty**, **Additional Buyer's Stamp Duty**, and reduction in loan limits for mortgages. The Minimum Occupation Period for non-subsidised resale HDB flats was raised to five years in 2010. In 2013, the **Total Debt Servicing Ratio** was introduced for housing loans granted by financial institutions whereby the percentage of borrowers' gross income used to service all loan obligations including mortgages, car loans, and credit card debt is limited to no more than 60%. Such macroprudential measures have since become a staple in the government's toolkit to prevent property prices from running ahead of fundamentals, which could have serious implications for household balances sheets and the financial system.

In early 2013, former Minister for National Development Khaw Boon Wan said that the government had delinked the prices of BTO flats from resale prices since he took on the housing portfolio in 2011. This allowed BTO prices to climb more modestly even as resale prices chalked up robust gains from 2009 to 2013. Khaw added that he aimed to bring down BTO prices from about 5.5 times applicant households' annual income to 4 times their median annual income.[28]

The difficulty of a complete delinking of new HDB flat prices from resale HDB and private property market is that some HDB flat purchasers would stand to make windfall gains in the resale market once the Minimum Occupation Period is over. There would be an issue of parity, since those who are fortunate enough in balloting to secure a prime-location HDB flat would enjoy significantly higher gains when reselling their flat in the future. At the time of writing, the Ministry of National Development is studying options for future housing projects in prime locations, such as having shorter leases, a longer Minimum Occupation Period, resale levies to recover additional housing subsidies, or the imposition of other conditions on resale.

In a bid to keep HDB flat prices affordable while avoiding the inequity of windfall gains, some have argued for a complete withdrawal of HDB flats from the open market — that is, HDB flats can only be sold back to HDB at predetermined prices rather than to private buyers. Others, including the Singapore Democratic Party in 2012, have argued for a two-track HDB system with the option for Singaporeans to purchase a lower-cost BTO flat on the condition that it can only be sold back to HDB while concurrently permitting flats under the current system to be sold in the open resale market.

However, these proposals present challenges. First, significant fiscal resources would have to be set aside for the repurchase of HDB flats. Second, as Phang Sock Yong, David Lee, Alan Cheong, Phoon Kok Fai, and Karol Wee (2013) pointed out, the predetermined prices at which flats may be sold back to HDB may not reflect prevailing market prices and variations in market demand.[29] In the case of the two-track system, those who are committed to sell their flats back to HDB at predetermined prices may bear significant gains or losses relative to those on the open market scheme depending on market conditions. Should market prices exceed the predetermined sale price, those who sell their flats back to HDB would not be able to fully benefit from asset appreciation and may find themselves priced out of the private property market. Either proposal would make upgrading from an HDB flat to private property less seamless. In essence, the separation of HDB and private property markets would fundamentally alter the narrative of home ownership as a means of giving Singaporeans a share in Singapore's economic growth.

Home Ownership Versus Liquidity, Risk, and Choice

Over the years, the home ownership policy itself has been questioned. Some have argued that over-allocation of resources to housing has crowded out consumption and investment. For instance, Phang Sock Yong (2004) found no evidence that property price increases had boosted aggregate consumption through wealth effects.[30] Manu Bhaskaran (2003) suggested that the low percentage of disposable income had hurt the development of Singapore's retail sector.[31]

Others have pointed to the risks to individuals and households of tying up a large proportion of lifetime wealth in housing. One concern is the impact on homeowners during property price downturns. The fall in resale HDB flat prices during the Asian Financial Crisis resulted in a spike in non-performing loans. Having a large mortgage could also discourage risk-taking and entrepreneurship. It has also been argued that high housing prices may be causing Singaporeans to delay marriage and parenthood till they have built up their careers and accumulated wealth. If so, giving Singaporeans more options for rental could boost the marriage and fertility rate.

In the early years of Singapore's housing development programme, HDB developed significant numbers of one- to three-room HDB rental flats. However, with the strong push for home ownership, the Public Rental Scheme in recent decades has been limited to the very low-income, with a small number of one- and two-room flats which are heavily subsidised. The income ceiling for rental housing eligibility, at $1,500 a month, has been unchanged since 2003, although HDB will review whether applicants have other housing options and may exercise flexibility based on circumstances such as medical expenses. Each rental tenancy is for two years, after which financially able tenants are encouraged to buy a flat with the help of significant government subsidies. Under the Tenants' Priority Scheme, a portion of two-room Flexi and three-room flats offered under BTO or Sale of Balance Flats exercises are set aside for rental tenants buying a flat. At the National Day Rally 2015, Prime Minister Lee announced the Fresh Start Housing Scheme to help those with young children who have purchased an HDB flat before but are currently in rental housing to own a flat again. The scheme provides a housing grant of $35,000, with the option of purchasing shorter-lease (45 to 65 years) two-room Flexi flats which are more affordable.

While public rental housing is limited to the low-income, other rental options include private property and HDB flats beyond the Minimum Occupation Period. One group who may find it advantageous to rent rather than take on a mortgage to purchase property are freelancers with irregular income streams. Another would be entrepreneurs who need capital for their business and whose earnings may be uncertain before their business takes off. With greater income volatility and employment uncertainty going forward, even regular wage earners may prefer rental or shorter-lease options.

For now, however, the home ownership paradigm remains one of the key pillars of the social security system.

Housing as Appreciating Asset Versus Lease Rundown

On the fate of HDB flats upon lease expiry, the government has been consistent in its position over the years. In 1989, former Minister for National Development S. Dhanabalan explained, in response to suggestions to extend the lease of HDB flats slated for upgrading, that doing so would raise the cost of redeveloping the country. Replying to a Parliamentary Question in 2014, then-Minister Khaw reiterated that "like all leasehold properties, HDB flats will revert to HDB, the landowner, upon expiry of their leases. HDB will in turn surrender the land to the State."[32]

More recently, in 2017, then-Minister for National Development Lawrence Wong cautioned home buyers not to assume that all old HDB flats would be automatically eligible for the Selective En Bloc Redevelopment Scheme (SERS), a scheme under which the government acquires HDB flats en bloc for redevelopment, provides compensation, and facilitates relocation to a new flat in a designated replacement site on a fresh 99-year lease.

He wrote, "In fact for the vast majority of HDB flats, the leases will eventually run out, and the flats will be returned to the HDB, who will in turn have to surrender the land to the State. As the leases run down, especially towards the tail-end, the flat prices will come down correspondingly."[33]

While nothing Wong stated was actually new, his statement elicited considerable public consternation, perhaps because of the ingrained notion of HDB flats as an appreciating asset. This also led to a debate on the technicality of whether HDB buyers were property owners, as the government maintained, or mere tenants, as suggested by the Workers' Party.[34]

There were also concerns about the future prices of ageing flats in view of the steady supply of new BTO flats against the backdrop of a rapidly ageing population. Even if flat owners were willing and able to monetise their assets by selling their flats, they might not fetch a good price in the market, particularly if many older homeowners chose to sell their flats at around the same time.

The government's response came in the 2018 National Day Rally, where the forthcoming **Voluntary Early Redevelopment Scheme (VERS)** was announced. Under this scheme, flat owners aged 70 years or older in selected precincts may vote for the government to repurchase their homes before their leases expire. This would allow the government to pace the redevelopment of older HDB towns over two to three decades rather than within the space of four to five years, as a number of older estates had been built within a short span of time in the 1970s and 1980s to address a housing shortage. VERS would give more Singaporeans the chance to benefit from redevelopment, since only an estimated 5% of flats would have been eligible for SERS. Unlike SERS, VERS would be put to a vote. However, Prime Minister Lee indicated that compensation under VERS would be less generous compared with SERS, given the more limited financial upside, as sites with higher redevelopment potential would have been selected for SERS. He noted that VERS would not be implemented for another 20 years, given the current age of older flats. Meanwhile, the government would work out how to select the precincts, the specific terms of offer, and how to finance the scheme over the long term.

Besides VERS, it was announced that the Home Improvement Programme would be extended to include flats built up to 1997, and that there would be a new programme to provide all flats with a second round of upgrading when they turn 60 or 70 years old. These were intended to keep flats safe and liveable, and also help them retain their value as their leases run down.

Healthcare Assurance: The S + 3M Framework

Singapore's public healthcare has been lauded as among the world's most cost-effective. In 2019, Bloomberg ranked Singapore the world's eighth healthiest country in the world, and second in Asia (after Japan), according to international data on health outcomes and health risk factors. Singapore was also ranked second in the world (after Japan) for healthcare outcomes by the Economist Intelligence Unit in 2014. This has been achieved with lower healthcare spending compared with other OECD economies (Table 5.3).[35] Over the years, investment in sanitation, nutrition, disease vector control, infant vaccinations, smoking curbs, and other public health measures have contributed significantly to improving health outcomes in the population, beyond expenditure on healthcare per se.

In Bloomberg's Health-Efficiency Index, which compares life expectancy with healthcare expenditure, Singapore consistently placed second in the world in the years before the COVID-19 outbreak. Adjustments to the ranking formula to account for the impact of COVID-19 saw Singapore leapfrog Hong Kong to take the top spot in 2020.

Table 5.3 Healthcare Expenditure and Outcomes

	Singapore	Japan	United Kingdom	United States	Sweden
Total health expenditure (% of GDP) (2018)	4.5	11.0	10.0	16.9	10.9
Government health expenditure (% of GDP) (2018)	2.2	9.2	7.9	8.5	9.3
Life expectancy at birth (years) (2019)	83.5	84.4	81.2	78.8	83.0
Infant mortality rate (< 1 year of age, per 1,000 live births) (2019)	2.1	1.8	3.7	5.6	2.1

Source: World Bank, World Development Indicators, last updated 21 May 2021.

Whether or not Singapore's demographic profile (no longer relatively youthful) is taken into account, Singapore's healthcare efficiency is high. However, as one of the world's fastest ageing countries, healthcare spending in Singapore is expected to accelerate sharply.

Already, national health expenditure has risen from $10.5 billion in 2010 to $20.7 billion in 2018, and it is expected to reach $59.1 billion in 2030.[36] Total government expenditure on health rose from $3.6 billion in FY2009 (1.2% of GDP) to $11.5 billion in FY2019 (2.3% of GDP), and overtook education spending in FY2020. It will become increasingly challenging to keep healthcare financing sustainable, as many other developed countries have found.

Singapore's Healthcare Sector

In Singapore, primary care is delivered through 20 government polyclinics and around 1,700 private general practitioner (GP) clinics that range from solo practices and partnerships to large corporate groups. Private clinics address about 80% of primary care demand, with the polyclinic share at 20%.

The government's role is largest in the acute hospital segment, where it can influence the supply of hospital beds, the introduction of new equipment and technology, and the cost of treatment. There are eight public acute care hospitals (called restructured hospitals) comprising six general hospitals, a women's and children's hospital, and a psychiatry hospital. General hospitals provide multidisciplinary inpatient and specialist outpatient services, as well as emergency services. In addition, there are six public specialty centres providing cancer, cardiac, eye, skin, neuroscience, and dental treatment. In 2020, public hospitals and specialty centres accounted for over 80% of acute care hospital beds (excluding psychiatric hospitals).[37] Public hospitals and specialty centres have been restructured to run as private entities wholly owned by the government. They have autonomy over recruitment and management and are subject to competition for market discipline. However, they receive an annual government subvention and are managed as not-for-profit organisations subject to the policy guidance of the Ministry of Health (MOH). They are grouped into three regional clusters and work with other healthcare providers within the clusters to deliver integrated care to their patients.

Acute hospitals are complemented by intermediate and long-term care facilities and services. Step-down care is provided by eight community hospitals, of which four are publicly run, and four are run by not-for-profit/voluntary welfare organisations, with an approximately equal split of beds between the two groups. There are also public, private, and not-for-profit nursing homes and hospices. A network of eldercare centres provides day care and rehabilitation services for seniors, while home-based services such as home nursing and personal care are also available.

The ageing population has put pressure on Singapore's healthcare capacity, with concerns raised from time to time about the availability of public hospital beds and long waiting times for admission.[38] The total number of hospital beds (in public, private, and non-profit institutions including psychiatric hospitals) rose by 6.6% between 2006 and 2013, against an increase in total population of 22.7%. Over the past 15 years, the government has embarked on an aggressive expansion programme, building new public hospitals while also tapping on the capacity of private hospitals. Khoo Teck Puat Hospital began operations in 2010, while the 700-bed Ng Teng Fong General Hospital, 400-bed Jurong Community Hospital, and 428-bed Yishun Community came onstream in 2015. They were joined by the 1,000-bed Sengkang General Hospital and 400-bed Sengkang Community Hospital in 2018. The government has announced that by 2030, a new integrated hospital will be built, while 12 new polyclinics will be added to the current 20.

Looking Around: Healthcare Financing Models

Most countries adopt a hybrid of the following financing models, although one form of financing is typically dominant:

— **Self-financed**: e.g. China, where a significant proportion of healthcare is paid for out of private savings, as public financing or insurance remains underdeveloped
— **Tax-financed**: e.g. Canada (Medicare) and the UK (National Health Service), where universal healthcare is financed mainly by general tax revenue, and most basic health services are free at the point of delivery
— **Social insurance**: e.g. Germany, the Netherlands, and Japan, where universal health coverage is funded through compulsory social insurance (national or private) and supplemented by government subsidies and out-of-pocket expenditure
— **Private insurance**: e.g. US, where private insurance (mainly employer-based) plays a significant role, although government-funded insurance programmes (e.g. Medicare, Medicaid) account for over half of US healthcare spending

Healthcare services may be delivered by the government (e.g. the UK), private providers (e.g. Canada), or both. A social health insurer could employ healthcare providers or purchase services from providers. In the latter case, payment methods could include fee for service, capitation payments (where providers are paid a set amount for each enrolled person or resident in an area), or performance-related payments. Some health insurance systems sign contracts with preferred providers while others are required to work with all medical care providers.

Healthcare Financing in Singapore

Singapore adopts a multi-payer, hybrid healthcare financing approach with mandatory savings, tax-financed government subventions, social insurance, private insurance, and out-of-pocket expenditure all playing a significant role. Singapore is unusual in having mandatory individual health savings accounts on a national scale through the CPF system. As

Jeremy Lim (2017) highlighted, a relatively high proportion of overall healthcare expenditure in Singapore comes from non-government sources (Table 5.3) including personal savings, private insurance, family support, and philanthropy.[39] Self-financing continues to be a key feature of the system, notwithstanding increasing government funding[40] and a larger role for social insurance in recent years.

Healthcare financing in Singapore is underpinned by the S+3M framework comprising:

— **Subsidies** for medical care, especially for hospitalisation and chronic conditions
— **MediSave** (a mandatory savings scheme for medical expenses)
— **MediShield Life** (a compulsory insurance scheme for hospitalisation and costly outpatient treatment)
— **MediFund** (a government endowment fund to help needy Singaporean who are unable to cover their medical expenses through MediSave or MediShield Life)

The government provides direct subsidies of up to 80% of the total bill for inpatient treatment in acute public hospitals for Singaporeans and permanent residents in subsidised wards (these account for around 80% of public hospital beds), as well as varying subsidies for treatment at community hospitals, other intermediate and long-term care facilities, polyclinics, specialist outpatient clinics, and medications. Under the **Community Health Assist Scheme (CHAS)**,[41] Singaporeans receive subsidies for medical and dental care at participating GP and dental clinics. The subsidies and caps vary according to the citizen's household income and home value, apart from older citizens in the Pioneer and Merdeka Generations (described later in this chapter) who receive the highest subsidy tier regardless of income or home value.

MediSave, which is part of the CPF system, had its roots in the 1983 National Health Plan. The idea was for individuals to take responsibility for their healthcare needs through their own savings, in contrast to the pay-as-you-go systems common elsewhere. This would also avoid intergenerational transfers from the young to the old, which could become increasingly burdensome on the working-age population as the number of seniors they support grows. However, non-employed persons, such as homemakers, do not receive MediSave contributions from employment and would have to rely on their spouse or family members to cover their healthcare expenses or make voluntary contributions to their MediSave accounts. The use of MediSave has been slowly but progressively liberalised. MediSave can now be used for hospitalisation costs, certain outpatient treatments like dialysis and chemotherapy, as well as treatment of chronic conditions such as diabetes and hypertension. It can also be used to pay premiums for insurance plans (i.e. MediShield Life, Integrated Shield Plans, and CareShield Life, which will be described below).

In time, it became evident that reliance on personal savings and government subsidies for hospital treatment would not suffice. In 1990, MediShield was introduced as a basic, low-cost insurance scheme to offer financial protection against catastrophic illnesses, in recognition that MediSave would not be adequate to cover large hospital bills. However, MediShield was not compulsory and excluded those above 65 years old (the cut-off age was subsequently raised, in steps, to 90 years) and those with pre-existing medical conditions. Consequently, MediShield enrolled fewer than half the citizen population at inception.[42]

To provide universal coverage and reap the full benefits of risk pooling, the government replaced MediShield with MediShield Life in November 2015. A mandatory scheme, MediShield Life offers lifelong protection for all citizens and permanent residents. No one is excluded, although those with serious pre-existing conditions have to pay additional premiums. Coverage benefits were also enhanced, with higher caps and lower co-insurance rates. However, claim limits and deductibles remain in place to keep premiums affordable and focus coverage on larger hospital bills. MediShield Life is the base plan on which private insurers can offer additional coverage through Integrated Shield Plans, for example, to cover the cost of treatment at private hospitals. In 2020, the government announced a major enhancement to MediShield Life to increase claim limits and remove exclusions, with a concurrent rise in premiums.

MediFund is an endowment fund set up in 1993 to provide a safety net for citizens who have difficult paying for medical expenses even after government subsidies and drawing on MediShield Life, MediSave, and their own savings. Initially meant to cover hospital bills, MediFund has been extended over the years to cover primary care, dental services, as well as antenatal and delivery services. Applications for MediFund assistance are based on a holistic assessment of the applicant's financial, health, and social circumstances, including family means. MediFund Silver and MediFund Junior were introduced in 2007 and 2013, respectively, to provide more targeted assistance to the needy elderly and young. MediFund (inclusive of MediFund Silver) disbursed a total of $159.1 million in FY2019, with average support of $900 per inpatient treatment and $90 per outpatient treatment.[43] As at end-FY2019, $4.64 billion remained in the fund.

Containing Healthcare Cost

It is well recognised that in healthcare markets, supply tends to generate its own demand.[44] One reason is that healthcare is perceived as a necessity; ethical questions arise if the most effective treatment is withheld from any patient, regardless of his ability to pay. Another is that there is typically an asymmetry of information between a medical professional and patient, where the former knows more about the patient's condition than the patient himself. This makes cost containment difficult, especially when the cost is borne by a third party such as the government or insurance companies.[45]

Healthcare financing is therefore a major challenge in most countries. Singapore faces a further demographic hurdle with the ratio of working adults to seniors rapidly shrinking (Table 3.2). Moreover, growth in healthcare costs has outstripped general price inflation. Healthcare inflation was 30.6% in the 10 years from 2005 to 2015, compared with a 21.7% increase in the general price level proxied by MAS core inflation.[46]

In Singapore, the government wields considerable influence over healthcare delivery and costs through the public healthcare system, national health insurance, and healthcare subvention policies. Various strategies have been adopted to keep healthcare affordable, appropriate, and cost-effective.

The **control of medical manpower supply** has been one way to guard against supply-induced demand.[47] The government controls the number of places in undergraduate medical schools in Singapore. Through

Table 5.4 Doctor and Nurse Densities

	Singapore	Japan	US	UK	Sweden
Doctors per 1,000 population	2.3 (2016)	2.4 (2016)	2.6 (2017)	2.8 (2018)	4.0 (2016)
Nurses and midwives per 1,000 population	6.2 (2017)	12.2 (2018)	14.5 (2017)	8.2 (2018)	11.8 (2017)

Source: World Bank, World Development Indicators, last updated 19 March 2021.

Table 5.5 Government Subsidies for Different Ward Classes in Restructured Hospitals

Ward Class	Government Subsidy
A [Single-bed, air-conditioned, TV]	0%
B1 [4 beds, air-conditioned, TV]	20%
B2 [6 beds, self-ventilated, no TV]	50%–65%*
C [8–10 beds, self-ventilated, no TV]	65%–80%*

*To be streamlined to 50%–80% (highest income to lowest income) from mid-2022.

the Singapore Medical Council, it regulates the accreditation of foreign-trained specialists who wish to practise in Singapore. The government also sets the specialist-to-generalist ratio to prevent over-specialisation, which fragments care delivery and increases costs. As a result, Singapore has one of the lowest doctor and nurse densities among developed countries (Table 5.4).

Prior to the introduction of **means testing**, government subsidies for inpatient treatment in public hospitals depended only on the class of ward and not on the patient's income. There are four main ward classes (A, B1, B2, and C) with differentiated physical amenities and number of beds per room. This is intended to induce more affluent patients to opt for the higher ward classes with lower subsidies. While this had succeeded to an extent, there was still a significant take-up of Class B2/C wards by patients who could afford unsubsidised rates. Hence, means testing was introduced in restructured hospitals in 2009 to target subsidies at patients with greater need. Subsidies are scaled according to income, in addition to ward class (Table 5.5).

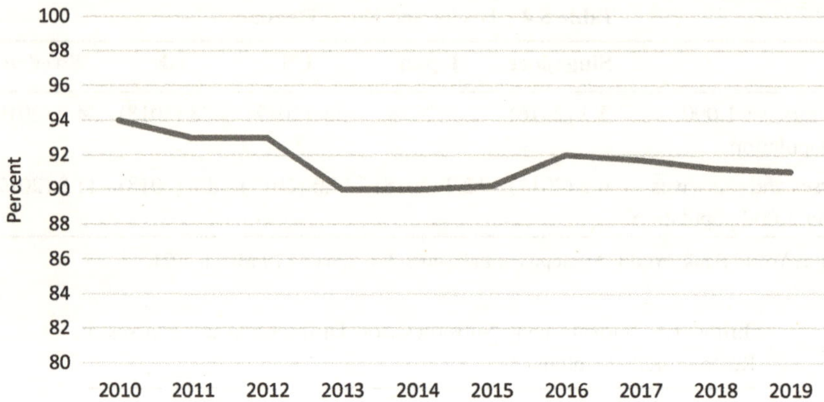

Figure 5.2 Average Coverage of Class B2/C Bills by MediSave and MediShield Life

Source: Revenue and Expenditure Estimates for the Ministry of Health, FY2012–FY2021, Ministry of Finance.

Advances in medical technology have made available more expensive drugs and therapies, driving up costs (Figure 3.6). Notwithstanding support through the S+3M framework, there remain concerns over high out-of-pocket costs for medical treatment due to MediSave claim limits and co-payment requirements for those on the basic MediShield Life plan. While out-of-pocket expenditure as a percentage of Singapore's health expenditure had declined from 56% in 2001 to 31% in 2018, according to the World Bank, it remained higher than the OECD average of 14% in 2017.[48] Post-2010, medical affordability as proxied by the average coverage of hospital bills by MediSave/MediShield Life has dipped slightly (Figure 5.2).

Insurance reform is central to efforts to contain healthcare costs. In February 2016, an industry-led Health Insurance Task Force was set up to look into ways to manage the escalating costs of health insurance, given rapidly rising claims under Integrated Shield Plans (IPs) offered by private insurers, which augment Medishield Life by covering treatment in class A/B1 public hospital wards or private hospitals.[49] A 2015 study by the Life Insurance Association found that IP policyholders with premium riders had bills about 20%–25% larger than those with the same plan but without riders. Between 2012 and 2014, private hospital bill sizes increased by 8.7% per year, compared with a 0.6% per year increase in public hospital bills.

One of the recommendations of the Task Force was to set up panels of approved healthcare providers.[50] Another was to do away with the practice of insurance premium riders that allow the insured to be treated without co-payment or deductibles, which leads to the buffet syndrome of healthcare consumption. Accordingly, MOH imposed a requirement for all IP riders to incorporate co-payment of at least 5% (with a minimum co-payment cap of $3,000) in plans sold from 1 April 2019. While this requirement does not apply to the approximately 1.1 million people who already have full riders, leading insurer National Trades Union Congress (NTUC) Income has introduced co-payment of at least 5% for policy renewals from 1 April 2021. This would apply to about 160,000 policyholders on full-rider plans, including those purchased before the MOH announcement. Other insurers are reviewing their policies at the time of writing.[51]

To further encourage policyholders to stay healthy, insurers could consider giving premium discounts, or even no-claims bonuses, to those who practise healthy living or perform well in health checks. However, some have argued that claims-based premiums may deter policyholders from seeking necessary treatment, and would unfairly penalise those who fall ill through no fault of their own.

Although the basic MediShield Life (as of 2020) covers only 35% of private hospital bills, a smaller proportion than for subsidised public wards, private hospital bills are typically much higher. Hence, the amount paid out from MediShield Life is often greater for treatment at private hospitals than at public hospitals. In effect, those with private hospital IPs are being subsidised by those without such IPs. The MediShield Life Council, in recommending enhancements to MediShield Life, has therefore proposed that the pro-ration factor for private hospital bills be reduced from 35% to 25%. This will raise costs for private insurers and lead to higher IP premiums.

With MediShield Life premiums set to rise in 2021 in tandem with enhanced coverage, some have questioned why premiums collected from 2016 to 2019 ($7.6 billion) were more than double what was paid out in claims ($3.5 billion) over the four years. According to MOH, premiums collected are needed to meet both current claims as well as future commitments. On this basis, there was in fact a slight shortfall in MediShield Life premiums collected, with the incurred loss ratio for the fund at an average of 104% for 2016–2019.[52]

"Three Beyonds"

Sustaining an affordable and cost-effective healthcare system requires a holistic approach. The overall distribution of resources across acute care, long-term care, and home care, between prevention and treatment, and across the public, private, and community sector, are vital pieces of the puzzle. These are encapsulated in the "Three Beyonds" articulated by MOH in 2016:

— Beyond Quality to Value
— Beyond Hospital to Community
— Beyond Healthcare to Health

Beyond Quality to Value: Ensuring Value for Money

Efforts have been made to keep treatment and drugs cost-effective without compromising quality.

In 2018, MOH introduced **fee benchmarks** for over 200 common surgical procedures. This followed the removal, in 2007, of the Singapore Medical Association's (SMA's) fee guidelines, which had been deemed anti-competitive by the Competition Commission of Singapore. While the SMA fee guidelines had been set by a professional association with no direct contribution from organisations representing patients' interest, the MOH fee benchmarks are set by a government ministry and hence exempted from the prohibitions of the Competition Act.[53] Jointly determined by hospitals and stakeholders, the fee benchmarks serve as a guide for doctors as well as insurers and patients, making it easier to detect overcharging and inflated claims.

Containment of drug cost is also critical. The government subsidises up to 75% of the cost of standard drugs on the MOH-approved list for Singaporeans at polyclinics and subsidised specialist outpatient clinics. Those in the Pioneer Generation receive a further 50% off subsidised medication. Invariably, there will be pressure for the government to expand the list of standard drugs or to provide subsidies for non-standard drugs. The list is reviewed annually by the Drug Advisory Committee, which considers advances in medical science and clinical practice.

The **Agency for Care Effectiveness** was set up by MOH in 2015 to evaluate health technologies such as drugs, devices, and medical services for clinical effectiveness and value for money. The agency's findings provide guidance to healthcare institutions, doctors, and patients, as well as inform government subsidies on healthcare treatments. MOH reported in 2021 that the agency had saved the government over $300 million since 2016, and benefited over 375,000 patients.[54]

Beyond Hospital to Community: Rebalancing Resources for Appropriate, Cost-Effective Healthcare

In planning for services along the care continuum, the intent is to deliver care by the most appropriate service provider in a cost-effective setting. There is a need for a gradual shift from subsidies that are tied to hospitalisation in acute care settings to greater support for intermediate and long-term care (ILTC), such as step-down facilities in community hospitals. Otherwise, there would be an incentive for patients to stay longer in the acute hospitals, which are more resource-intensive than step-down facilities. Given the needs of the rapidly ageing population, it is also vital to strengthen home care support so as to avoid a hospital bed crunch.

In any rebalancing, it is easier to step up support for the less well-funded area than to cut back support for the area that is already heavily subsidised. In Budget 2012, a series of measures was introduced to make ILTC more affordable and to strengthen support for "ageing in place". Subsidies for ILTC were stepped up and extended to cover about two-thirds of Singaporean households. Other measures included the absorption of Goods and Services Tax by MOH for all subsidised ILTC patients, a foreign domestic worker grant for the frail elderly, as well as higher cash payouts for the elderly under the Interim Disability Assistance Programme for the Elderly. From October 2019, the means-tested Home Caregiving Grant replaced the Foreign Domestic Worker Grant, providing a monthly $200 cash payout to support family members with at least moderate permanent disability.

Insurance for long-term care has been strengthened with the transformation of ElderShield into **CareShield Life** from 2020. The enhanced long-term care insurance scheme, compulsory for all Singaporeans born from 1980, provides lifetime payouts upon severe disability and extends universal coverage to those with pre-existing disabilities. Older Singaporeans are also encouraged to join, with the government providing participation incentives. There are permanent means-tested subsidies for lower- to middle-income Singaporeans, with up to two-thirds of households eligible. From October 2020, MediSave may be withdrawn for long-term care needs, up to a monthly cap.

As part of the suite of changes to MediShield Life announced in 2020, the deductible for day surgery has been lowered for patients above 80 years of age so that they would not have an incentive to choose a hospital stay in lieu of day surgery.

Support has also been stepped up for outpatient treatment. With the introduction of **Flexi-MediSave** in 2015, seniors are allowed to use MediSave for outpatient treatment at polyclinics, private GP clinics under CHAS, as well as specialist outpatient clinics.

In 2019, the **CHAS green card** was introduced, extending subsidies for chronic conditions under GP care to all Singaporeans regardless of income. Making this benefit universal was intended to encourage the management of chronic conditions in the community, outside acute care settings, particularly as the population ages.

Beyond Healthcare to Health: Encouraging Healthy Living and Preventive Healthcare

A holistic approach to health goes beyond medical care. Singapore's Health Promotion Board was set up to 2001 to promote healthy living and disease prevention. A "war on diabetes" was declared in the 2016 National Day Rally to tackle a disease that cost the country over $1 billion a year to manage. Diabetes had affected over 400,000 people and is expected to affect nearly a million people in Singapore by 2050. Initiatives to improve diets and encourage exercise included Healthier Choice labels for packaged food and a National Steps Challenge that rewarded participants who met daily walking targets with grocery vouchers and lucky draw prizes.

Under the **Screen for Life programme**, Singaporeans pay between nothing and $5 for a list of recommended health screenings according to their age and gender. In January 2018, the government rolled out **Project Silver Screen**, a national screening programme to detect functional decline in vision, hearing, and oral health among seniors and to provide timely follow-up and affordable assistive devices. The programme aims to screen 45,000 seniors aged 60 and above by 2023. MediSave withdrawal limits were increased from $400 to $500 in 2018 for chronic conditions as well as preventive care such as vaccinations and health screenings (mammograms and selected tests for newborns). In 2020, subsidies for recommended child and adult vaccinations were enhanced.

Healthcare Affordability for Seniors: The Pioneer Generation and Merdeka Generation Packages

The **Pioneer Generation Package (PGP)**, introduced in 2014, was an unusual departure from the principle of means testing for healthcare subsidies. In introducing this package of healthcare subsidies for some 450,000 members of Singapore's pioneer generation (i.e. those aged 16 and above in 1965, the year of Singapore's independence, and who obtained citizenship in 1986 or earlier), the government declared that it was meant to honour and thank this generation for their hard work and dedication in building up the nation. Hence the special dispensation for what amounted to a universal package of benefits regardless of income or wealth.

Under the PGP, pioneers receive additional subsidies for subsidised outpatient care at specialist outpatient clinics, polyclinics, as well as private clinics participating in CHAS. They also enjoy annual MediSave top-ups for life and subsidies of between 40% and 60% for MediShield Life premiums. In addition, those with disabilities can receive up to $1,200 per year for their cash expenses.

To fund the package, $8 billion was set aside in the government's FY2014 budget, which together with accumulated interest was expected to meet its full projected cost of $9 billion over the remaining lifetime of the pioneers. This provided assurance that support under this package would not depend on Singapore's future economic performance or government revenue.

Of note, the government made clear that this generous package of healthcare assistance would not be an entitlement for all seniors going forward; it was meant only for the Pioneer Generation, in view that many did not have high incomes during their working years and may not have set aside money for healthcare in the pre-MediSave years. Furthermore, the nation owed this generation a debt of gratitude for their efforts in building up an independent Singapore.

PGP has contributed towards improving intergenerational equity by supporting seniors who, for the most part, had significantly lower incomes and savings compared with their children's generation and whose contributions helped Singapore to build up its financial reserves.

Without the package, the government might well have had to step in to help needy seniors in any case. PGP would also relieve the financial burden on working-age children supporting their aged parents, thus providing an indirect benefit to a significant number of families.

The Pioneer Generation Office was set up in August 2014 to train volunteers who would visit seniors in their homes to explain the benefits of PGP. This office was subsequently renamed the Silver Generation Office and became part of the Agency for Integrated Care, a statutory board under MOH.

For those who missed out on the PGP largesse, Budget 2014 provided MediSave top-ups to a wider group of seniors, namely non-pioneers aged 55 and above. In addition, higher subsidies were given to lower- and middle-income Singaporeans seeking treatment at specialist outpatient clinics.

The $6.1 billion **Merdeka Generation Package** followed in 2018, this time for about 500,000 Singaporeans born between 1950 and 1959 and who had become citizens by 1996.

Similar to PGP, the Merdeka Generation receives additional subsidies for subsidised outpatient care at specialist outpatient clinics, polyclinics, as well as private clinics participating in CHAS, but at lower rates than the Pioneer Generation. They also enjoy annual MediSave top-ups for five years and lifelong subsidies of between 5% and 10% for MediShield Life premiums. In addition, they receive an additional participation incentive to join CareShield Life.

This prompted speculation of a Majulah Generation next, with some expecting similar packages to be given to future generations of seniors, albeit with smaller benefits, in view of the rise in incomes and savings in successive generations.

With Singapore's total healthcare spending expected to surge in the years ahead, the balance across personal savings, social insurance, and tax-funded subsidies will have to be continually reviewed and recalibrated to ensure healthcare affordability and equity.

Workfare and Silver Support

Workfare, introduced in 2007, is perhaps the most significant addition to Singapore's social security system since the turn of the century. It comprises the **Workfare Income Supplement** that tops up the incomes of the bottom 20% of wage earners, and the **Workfare Skills Support** Scheme (**WSS**, previously known as Workfare Training Support) that provides additional training subsidies for lower-wage workers. Ad hoc **Workfare Special Payments** have also been given in 2008, 2009, and 2020 in response to economic conditions.

WIS has become a permanent feature of Singapore's social security system since its launch in 2007, replacing the one-off Workfare Bonus Scheme introduced in 2006. Its aim is to encourage lower-wage workers aged 35 and above to remain in employment so as to build up their CPF for retirement, housing, and healthcare needs. WIS is targeted at those whose earnings are in the bottom 20%, with some support for those slightly above.

Over the years, WIS has been repeatedly enhanced, with the qualifying wage ceiling and maximum annual payout (for those aged 60 and above) raised to $2,300 and $4,000, respectively, in 2020, following increases in 2010, 2013, and 2017. WIS payouts depend on age and income. 40% of payouts are in cash, up from the initial 30% when the scheme was launched, with the remainder channelled equally to the CPF MediSave and Special Accounts. This can amount to as much as 30% of an older worker's income. Self-employed persons are also eligible for WIS if they make CPF contributions. However, they receive two-thirds the payouts of employees and only 10% of their payouts in cash.

WIS benefits close to 440,000 workers at an annual cost of about $1 billion based on 2020 eligibility criteria and rates announced in Budget 2019.

WSS complements WIS by equipping lower-wage workers with skills needed to progress in their jobs. It provides a training allowance to low-wage employees and the self-employed who undertake skills training that is relevant to their work, on top of other grants under SkillsFuture or Adapt and Grow (see Chapters 7 and 8 for details of SkillsFuture and Adapt and Grow, respectively). A training commitment award is given to encourage workers to undertake sustained training over a period of time. Employers also receive absentee payroll for their employees who undergo training.

Looking Back: Motivation for Workfare

Considering the Singapore government's longstanding aversion to social dependency, the introduction of WIS could be viewed as a policy breakthrough — an implicit recognition by the government that the lower-income group required structural support for wage and retirement adequacy, and not just temporary support through ComCare or ad hoc transfers. This was a sizeable group too — at 20% of the workforce — and not just a residual of the lowest income earners who could not keep pace with the rest of society. As a wage supplement that boosts the pay and savings of lower-income Singaporeans, WIS also helps to stave off widening inequality, although this is not its stated objective. WIS payments are not earned income, hence they only affect the Gini coefficient after taxes and transfers.

The motivation for Workfare was explained by then-Ministry of Finance Director (Special Duties) Jacqueline Poh in 2007:

> *It only became obvious that the problem of the working poor was a structural and not cyclical problem when the economy started to recover in late 2004. While the media focused on a Gini coefficient that had risen from 0.442 in 2000 to 0.468 in 2005, growing income inequality was not in itself to be feared... The worrying phenomenon was real wage stagnation and structural unemployment. Wages at the low-end failed to keep pace for the first time since 1965. Despite a buoyant job market from 2004 to 2006, real wages of the lowest 30% of workers (i.e. those earning wages up to S$1,500) in Singapore fell by 0.5% per annum.*[55]

The government recognised that globalisation, especially the opening up of China and India, and technological change were driving wage dispersion and real wage stagnation across developed countries. Rather than try to insulate Singaporeans from these forces by protecting jobs or imposing a minimum wage, the government sought a structural solution with the aim of preventing a rise in applications for state assistance. ComCare, introduced in 2005, had a needs-based focus. It was necessary to have a parallel scheme that reinforced the principle of "Reward for Work, and Work for Reward".

Inspiration was found in the welfare reforms instituted in the US state of Wisconsin in the 1990s. The Wisconsin Works programme imposed strict employment and behavioural conditions on welfare recipients, with close supervision by case managers, but also generous benefits in the form of wage supplements, as well as healthcare, childcare, transport, and family support. The idea was to "make work pay" or make work a more attractive proposition than welfare. Work-based welfare or "Workfare" thus came under serious consideration for Singapore policymakers.[56]

Design of WIS

WIS shares similarities with the US Earned Income Tax Credit (EITC), a refundable tax credit for low- to middle-income earners that was introduced in 1975 and significantly expanded over the years. EITC has been credited with lifting 5.4 million Americans above the poverty line in 2010, according to data from the US Census Bureau.[57] It contributed towards the US work-based welfare or "Workfare" approach to push welfare recipients into jobs, which had been introduced by the Clinton administration in 1996.[58]

Unlike a pure negative income tax[59] which gives people a percentage of the difference between their income and an income cut-off (the level at which they start paying income tax), WIS and EITC only kick in on employment and are designed to encourage people to put in more hours of work. The amount of money received under WIS and EITC rises, or "phases in", with income, up to a point. Support then plateaus before "phasing out" when income rises above a certain threshold. This ensures that payouts are not cut off abruptly as one's income rises, which could otherwise deter work and career progression, particularly as other means-tested subsidies may also be withdrawn as wages rise.

WIS could also be seen as an alternative to a minimum wage in raising low-wage workers' incomes, with the government footing the bill instead of employers. WIS is more targeted as it excludes youth below 35 years old (apart from those with disabilities), who could have high earning potential or come from wealthy families, and excludes those with high spousal income or high property value. However, it comes at a significant fiscal cost of about $1 billion a year.

Workfare was complemented by the Special Employment Credit, which provided a wage subsidy to employers to encourage employment of older workers, along with lower CPF contributions for older workers (see Chapter 8).

Impact of Wage Subsidy: Evidence from WIS

The impact of a wage subsidy on labour supply or employment, as well as wages, is an empirical one that depends on the elasticity of labour demand as well as supply. The introduction of WIS ought to have induced more workers to enter the labour market, enabling employers to lower wages and capture part of the WIS subsidy.

The more elastic labour supply is, the more workers enter the market for a given wage subsidy, allowing employers to capture a larger share of the subsidy. This results in a larger increase in employment and a larger fall in wages.

The impact of WIS was investigated in a 2014 study by economists from the Ministry of Trade and Industry (MTI).[60] The study found that WIS was effective in increasing the employment rate of less-educated Singaporeans, particularly those in the older age group who were more likely to enter and stay in the workforce. A subsequent study by Tiago Freire (2018), using Hong Kong as a control group, estimated that WIS had increased labour force participation for women aged 60–64 by 3.1–5.5 percentage points, but had no significant impact for men.[61]

The MTI study also found that WIS had led to a slower rate of wage growth among WIS-eligible workers compared to those ineligible for WIS. This could be due to workers choosing to work fewer hours or a sharing of the WIS subsidy between employers and workers. However, WIS appeared to have a lower incidence on employers (i.e. the share of subsidy captured by employers), which was up to 25%, compared with that for the US EITC, which Jesse Rothstein (2008) estimated to be at least 72%.[62]

Silver Support Scheme

While WIS tops up the wages of low-income working Singaporeans, it does not address the needs of those in retirement. To plug this gap, the Silver Support Scheme was introduced in 2016 to supplement the incomes of the bottom 20% of retiree households. Along with Workfare, it is regarded as the fourth pillar of Singapore's social security system.

By considering lifetime income (proxied by total CPF contributions by age 55) in determining eligibility, Silver Support addresses lifetime inequality rather than just inequality at a point in time. Support is aimed at the bottom 20% of Singaporeans aged 65 and above who have had low lifetime incomes and who currently have little or no family support. These households automatically receive quarterly cash payouts without having to apply for support.

While most commentators welcomed the introduction of WIS and Silver Support, some have argued for higher support levels. In 2015, economist Yeoh Lam Keong suggested that to meet the needs of the elderly and working poor, WIS should be raised to $500–$600 per month and given largely in cash, while Silver Support should be trebled from the then-average payout of $200 per month.[63] It should be noted that raising the quantum of support under WIS or Silver Support would also require the pool of beneficiaries to be expanded in order to preserve the incentive gradient or relativities (i.e. to minimise the likelihood that those who do not qualify for the scheme end up worse-off than those who qualify).

In Budget 2020, the government announced a significant enhancement to Silver Support, broadening eligibility to about 250,000 seniors (up from 150,000 previously) by increasing the eligibility thresholds for lifetime wages as well as household income. Benefits under Silver Support would also increase by 20% to between $720 and $3,600 a year (paid out quarterly) from January 2021. This would double government expenditure on Silver Support from S$330 million to around S$620 million in 2021.

Taking Social Security Further: Gaps, Opportunities, and Possibilities

Taken together, the various programmes introduced and enhanced by the government in the past 15 years have amounted to a significant upgrade of Singapore's social security system. The main interventions can be broadly classified as (a) subsidies/grants, (b) risk pooling, (c) cost containment, and (d) prevention/public education. This framework shows where gaps have been plugged through the introduction of new initiatives and enhancements (indicated in bold), making the overall system more comprehensive (Table 5.6). Also indicated in parentheses are potential features of social security that have been proposed by analysts and will be discussed later in the book.

Table 5.6 Enhancements to Singapore's Social Security System

	Subsidies/Grants				
	For Majority/Middle-Income, With or Without Progressive Features	**For Lower Income**	**Risk Pooling**	**Cost Containment**	**Prevention/Education**
Retirement-Adequacy	**Extra interest on first $60,000 CPF balances (2008), extra 1% for seniors (2016)**	**Workfare Income Supplement (2007)** (bottom 20%–30%) **Silver Support (2016) (bottom 20%)** **Lease Buyback Scheme (2009)** **Silver Housing Bonus (2013)**	**CPF LIFE (2009)**	Cost containment efforts for healthcare, housing, and general cost of living	MoneySense (national financial education programme)
Housing Affordability	Subsidised new flats (universal, up to income ceiling) **Enhanced CPF Housing Grant (2019)** (tiered by income)	Subsidised rental housing	NA	**Seller's Stamp Duty (2010)** **Additional Buyer's Stamp Duty (2011)**	Mortgage Servicing Ratio **Total Debt Servicing Ratio (2013)**
Healthcare Affordability	Subsidised hospital treatment/ward charges (means tested) **Pioneer, Merdeka Generation Packages (2014, 2018)** (dependent on age; independent of means) **Community Health Assist Scheme** (tiered according to means)	MediFund	**MediShield Life (2015)** **CareShield Life (2020)**	**Insurance reform** **Drug cost containment** **Surgical fee benchmarks**	Health Promotion Board campaigns **Screen for Life** **Project Silver Screen (2018)**

Table 5.6 (*Continued*)

	Subsidies/Grants				
	For Majority/Middle-Income, With or Without Progressive Features	**For Lower Income**	**Risk Pooling**	**Cost Containment**	**Prevention/Education**
Income Adequacy	Low taxes (part of progressive fiscal system)	**Workfare Income Supplement (2007)** (bottom 20%–30%)	NA	NA	Education and skills upgrading **Progressive Wage Model*** [Minimum wage?]
Employment and Income Security	**Adapt and Grow* employment/training support** (dependent on age, length of unemployment, type of training programme)	**ComCare*** [Top-ups to unemployment savings?]	[Unemployment/ wage loss insurance?]	NA	**SkillsFuture* (national continuing education programme)** **Adapt and Grow redeployment programmes***

*To be covered in subsequent chapters.

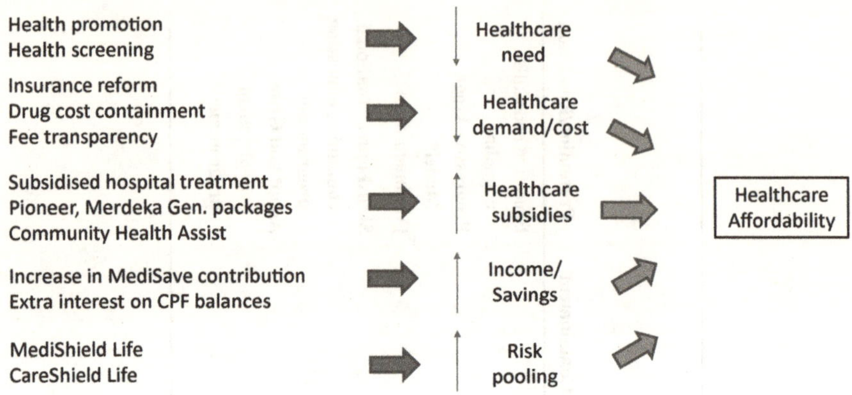

Figure 5.3 Interventions to Boost Healthcare Affordability

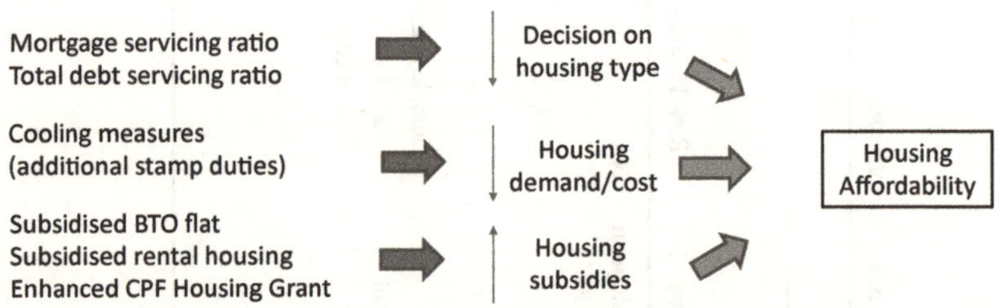

Figure 5.4 Interventions Affecting Housing Affordability

The Socio-Economic Flowchart (Figure 3.12) captures the interventions for retirement adequacy, income adequacy, and employment/income security. The drivers of healthcare and housing affordability can be unpacked further (Figures 5.3, 5.4) to illustrate the multipronged approach taken.

Notwithstanding the many initiatives that have fortified social security in recent years, the system must continue evolving in tandem with the social compact. In particular, the balance between self-responsibility and collectivism, whether in the form of risk pooling or government transfers and subsidies, will need to be continually recalibrated as Singapore seeks new ways to address emerging socio-economic challenges.

In this context, it is worth asking whether there are further gaps to be plugged in Singapore's social security toolkit. Two issues that have been prominent in public discourse are (a) the adequacy of work and retirement incomes and (b) income security for displaced contingent workers.

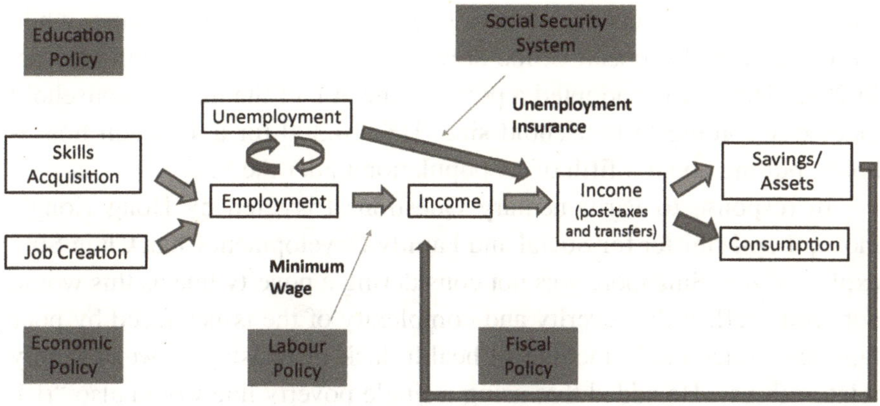

Figure 5.5 How Minimum Wage and Unemployment Insurance Fit in the Socio-Economic Flowchart

Of the proposals that have surfaced over the years, two stand out for their recurrent appeal — **minimum wage** (to address income adequacy) and **unemployment insurance** (to address income security from unemployment) (Figure 5.5). These are also policies that feature in the socio-economic systems or welfare models of many advanced countries.

Discussion on the minimum wage will be deferred to Chapter 8 on labour market policy to give a more holistic picture of the range of policy tools used to address the challenge of low and stagnant wages. Nonetheless, a brief comment on the issue of income adequacy is useful here.

Income Adequacy: Poverty Line and Household Budgets

Most countries have established an official poverty threshold or poverty line in order to set poverty alleviation targets and track progress towards their achievement. This could be an absolute sum based on what is needed to meet basic living needs or a relative measure of poverty expressed as a proportion of the median income.

The World Bank's international poverty line, which represents a global absolute minimum, has been set at US$1.90 (in 2011 purchasing power parity) per day since October 2015. The United Nations has adopted this as an extreme poverty threshold in its Sustainable Development

Goals. The OECD sets the poverty line at 50% of median income, while the UK and the European Union draw the line at 60% of median income. In 2013, Hong Kong adopted a poverty line at half the median household income according to household size (HK$14,300 for a 4-person household), putting about a fifth of its population under the line.

In response to Parliamentary Questions triggered by Hong Kong's move, then-Minister for Social and Family Development Chan Chun Sing explained that Singapore was not considering a poverty line as this would not "fully reflect the severity and complexity of the issues faced by poor families, which could include ill health, lack of housing or weak family relationships". He added that using a single poverty line would also "risk a 'cliff effect,' where those below the poverty line receive all forms of assistance, while other genuinely needy citizens outside the poverty line are excluded".[64]

Indeed, means-tested income criteria vary across government support programmes so as to avoid a cliff effect. While it would be unwise to set a single threshold to qualify for assistance, others have argued that an official poverty line need not mean that all efforts to help the lower-income must be directed at those below the line.

Irene Ng (2020) estimated absolute poverty in Singapore to be 12% in 2019, taking into consideration basic needs and subsidies.[65] Her estimate of relative poverty was 24% for working households, using half of median household income from work as the poverty threshold. She also found that relative poverty had been increasing since 2000, albeit at a slower rate since 2010.

Amartya Sen has advocated a capability approach to understanding poverty where poverty reflects the inability to fully function in society.[66] This has spurred the development of non-monetary measures of poverty such as the Multi-Dimensional Poverty Index by the Oxford Poverty and Human Development Initiative, which features in the UNDP's Human Development Reports.

To factor in social inclusion and social acceptability in the measurement of poverty, an approach pioneered in the UK (known as the Minimum Income Standard), involves members of the public participating in discussions with the aim of reaching a consensus on what an adequate household budget should be. Adopting this approach to study the needs of elderly households, Ng Kok Hoe et al. (2019) conducted focus group discussions with over a hundred participants from a wide range of backgrounds. According to the study, participants felt that "budgets should enable older adults to thrive rather than just stay alive."[67] The minimum household budgets arrived at were $1,379 for single elderly households, $2,351 for couples, and $1,721 for singles aged 55 to 64. This could give an indication of the top-up to market incomes for low-wage occupations, or top-up to CPF LIFE payouts needed from state, community, and family support.

Unemployment Insurance

Unemployment insurance (UI) or unemployment benefits of some form exist in most countries. Benefits are tax-funded in countries such as the UK, Australia, and New Zealand. Others require employer or employee contributions with an element of risk pooling or insurance, such as Canada, France, Japan, the Netherlands, and Sweden. In many of these countries, participation is compulsory; in some, like Sweden, a voluntary scheme providing higher payments sits alongside a comprehensive, compulsory scheme. In Southeast Asia, Thailand and Malaysia adopted UI schemes in 2004 and 2018, respectively.

One argument for UI is that with rapid technological cycles and changes in the way work is organised, people are likely to have more frequent and longer spells of unemployment during their working years. They may need financial support to tide them over these spells and could benefit from risk pooling. This is especially if they have major financial commitments such as housing, car, or education loans to service. Some have argued that with suitable protection, retrenched workers need not take up the first job that comes along, allowing them more time to wait for a job that is a better fit in the long run. On the other hand, those sceptical of UI are concerned about its impact on the willingness to work as it could potentially blunt the incentive to get back into employment.

In Singapore today, most retrenched workers receive retrenchment benefits from their employer. About two in three employees who were laid off over a six-month period in 2020 were eligible for retrenchment benefits as they had worked for their employer for at least two years, and of these, nine in 10 received a payout.[68] According to the Tripartite Advisory on Managing Excess Manpower and Responsible Retrenchment, the prevailing norm is a payout of between two weeks' and one month's salary per year of service, allowing the retrenched worker some time to find another job. Many also rely on their savings to tide them over. With greater economic volatility, however, some may not be able to stay long enough in a job to be entitled to a significant quantum of retrenchment benefits. It has also been suggested that retrenchment benefits tied to an employee's length of service adds unnecessary rigidity to the employment market.

Amid elevated retrenchments in 2016, the Workers' Party reiterated its 2011 proposal for redundancy insurance,[69] a form of UI for retrenched workers. This was the topic of an adjournment motion in Parliament in May 2017. The party renewed its call for redundancy insurance in its 2020 general election manifesto.

While broadly supporting Singapore's approach to economic transformation, the International Monetary Fund (IMF), in concluding its Article IV consultations with Singapore in 2017, suggested "scope to strengthen Singapore's permanent social insurance arrangements, including by introducing time-bound unemployment insurance". This, the IMF felt, was needed to help address uncertainty arising from economic transformation, shorter product life cycles and job tenures, and greater labour churn.[70]

Within Singapore's context of low unemployment, high savings and home ownership, and employer-sponsored retrenchment benefits, the government's focus has been on training and employment facilitation to help displaced workers bounce back as quickly as possible. To this end, the **Adapt and Grow initiative** under Workforce Singapore was launched in 2016 and its various constituent programmes strengthened since then (details in Chapter 9). A Retrenchment Taskforce has also stepped in to provide timely help to retrenched workers, aided by the implementation of **mandatory retrenchment notifications** since 2017.

In explaining to Parliament in 2017 why the government preferred wage support and training subsidies to help jobseekers instead of UI, then-Second Minister for Manpower Josephine Teo cited studies that suggested the unemployed in Denmark tended to wait till just before their benefits expired to take up jobs.[71] Such moral hazard could be an issue even if UI is time-limited and made contingent on reasonable effort to find employment.

Another challenge is "adverse selection", where only workers most at risk of unemployment choose to take up insurance, driving up premiums. To avoid such self-selection, a UI scheme would either have to be mandatory or made sufficiently attractive to bring on board enough members of varying risk profiles. However, the willingness of employers and workers to pay UI premiums may be limited given the generally low unemployment rates in Singapore. While the government could step in with co-funding of premiums, this could necessitate higher taxes or reduced spending in other areas.

The introduction of UI would also likely upend the current norm of companies paying retrenchment benefits to workers. As many workers would have built up retrenchment benefit entitlements from their companies after years of service, any transition to a UI system would have to be carefully managed and may take a long time to complete.

Eligibility for UI would also have to be carefully considered. In the US, state-run UI systems have tended to exclude new labour force entrants, those who have not been consistently in full-time employment (e.g. gig workers), or those whose income falls below minimum thresholds, leaving these groups of workers inadequately protected.[72]

While UI can mitigate the risk of job losses in normal times, its efficacy in times of severe economic downturn and widespread layoffs may be limited without additional government support. In such times, enhanced UI payouts would have to be funded from significantly higher premiums or tax revenue. During the COVID-19 pandemic, for instance, the US Congress enacted relief bills to greatly enhance UI benefits and expand coverage to vulnerable groups.

Although then-Manpower Minister Josephine Teo reiterated the government's stance on UI in the 2020 Budget Debate, she indicated that the government would "keep an open mind" on UI.[73] In April 2021, NTUC Secretary-General Ng Chee Meng revealed that NTUC was looking at designing a UI scheme through its insurance arm, further indication that Singapore's approach to social security continues to evolve in response to changing circumstances.

Options to Help the Unemployed: CPF Withdrawal, Unemployment Savings, and Wage Loss Insurance

To help workers tide over periodic bouts of unemployment without the moral hazard of UI or state-funded unemployment benefits, one possibility would be to tap on the worker's own savings. For instance, flexibility could be given to workers to **withdraw CPF balances** in their Ordinary Account either for pre-specified uses such as servicing mortgage, car or student loans, or for general living expenses. However, such withdrawals could compromise retirement adequacy, a key objective of CPF, unless members are required to restore withdrawn CPF balances with interest upon re-employment.

Another suggestion is to set up an **unemployment savings** programme so that workers set aside their own money for use during periods of unemployment (Low, 2014).[74] This would be consistent with individual responsibility, without taking advantage of risk pooling. For this to be feasible, the government would need to contribute the bulk of savings for lower-income workers.

A way of operationalising this would be to ride on the CPF system with workers and employers contributing to a CPF income replacement account. To minimise the additional outlay for workers and employers, part of current Ordinary Account contributions could be diverted to this account while low-wage workers could receive top-ups via Workfare. Even without such a savings scheme, workers (especially the middle- or higher-income) may already be setting aside precautionary savings on their own. Introducing a mandatory saving scheme would instil greater financial discipline across the board at the cost of a reduction in take-home pay and flexibility. Alternatively, a voluntary scheme may be considered, with sufficient incentives such as tax deductions and top-ups to encourage saving.

If the concern is about difficulty servicing mortgages and loans during a period of temporary unemployment, this can be addressed without the need for a new scheme. HDB already allows for deferment or rescheduling of housing loan instalments for those with insufficient CPF contributions. During the COVID-19 pandemic in 2020, MAS and the Association of Banks in Singapore rolled out a package of temporary financial relief measures including **deferment of repayments** to banks for loans on property, education, renovation, and motor vehicles.

Finally, a less common alternative to UI is wage insurance, also known as **wage loss insurance**, which compensates workers if they are forced to move into a job with lower salary. In the US, this has taken the form of the Alternative Trade Adjustment Assistance for Older Workers, which gives retrenched workers over the age of 50 a wage supplement of half the difference between the worker's old and new wages. France and Japan also have wage loss insurance programmes that cover a limited group of workers.[75]

In advocating for wage loss insurance to be implemented along with unemployment savings, Donald Low (2014) noted that unlike UI, payouts from wage loss insurance would kick in on re-employment, giving workers an incentive to find a new job, even if it is lower-paying, rather than to remain unemployed.[76] This would encourage displaced workers to broaden their job search to new sectors and occupations and smooth over their income loss while they gain skills and experience in their new job. Like UI, wage loss insurance would also be funded by employers and workers rather than the government and would make retrenchment benefits portable rather than tied to one's employer.

Again, the willingness of firms and workers to participate in a mandatory wage loss insurance scheme must be assessed, given that wage loss is generally not perceived to be as debilitating as unemployment and total income loss. Care must also be taken in the design of wage loss insurance to avoid supporting workers who voluntarily step down to less demanding roles or who switch sectors out of interest rather than necessity. It can also be argued that company retrenchment benefits and WIS already perform a role similar to that of wage loss insurance.

Social Security and the Gig Economy

The emergence of the gig economy, enabled by online platforms and intermediaries such as Grab, UpWork, and Deliveroo, poses new questions for policymakers. These online intermediaries connect service buyers with workers who undertake short-term, piecemeal jobs mostly as freelancers.

Freelancing itself is not new. Freelance tutors, sports coaches, plumbers, cleaners, real estate agents, taxi drivers, photographers, and web designers have been plying their trades for many years. The proportion of "own account workers" who freelance regularly has stayed roughly constant at between 8% and 10% of employed residents over the past decade and beyond (Figure 3.8).

Technology, however, has thrust the gig economy into greater prominence of late. For instance, private-hire cars have already disrupted the taxi industry in Singapore — taxi trips fell to 353,000 a day in 2019, below that of private-hire trips (419,000 a day), and 65% lower than the 1,020,000 taxi trips per day in 2014.[77] They have also prompted taxi companies to review their fare and rental policies.

Apart from the convenience and choice afforded by the gig economy to customers, gig platforms have also provided more opportunities to freelancers, including those in regular employment who freelance to supplement incomes. More young people are also choosing gig work over regular employment as they are attracted by the flexible working conditions or other perks of the job, such as having a car for their own use. The polytechnics' Graduate Employment Survey found that 4.1% of polytechnic graduates were in freelance work six months after graduation in 2019, roughly similar to the proportion in 2017 and 2018, but higher than the 2.9% in 2016. While the number of young Singaporeans who have chosen freelance careers is not large, MPs and members of the public have expressed concern regarding these freelancers' long-term prospects and welfare.

Concerns for gig workers include the following:

1. Do gig workers **invest sufficiently in their training** and professional development? What are their longer-term career prospects?
2. Are gig workers **adequately protected** on the job? Do they have sufficient recourse to help if they are not paid or are subject to dangerous or adverse working conditions?
3. Are gig workers **saving enough for retirement**, given the irregularity of their income streams and no requirement for them to contribute to CPF apart from MediSave?

Of the above, the third is arguably the most vexing, given that Singapore's social security system is premised on regular CPF contributions and a steadily rising income that supports home ownership and home upgrading over time.

To address the challenges facing gig workers, a tripartite workgroup was set up in 2017 to look into the issues and come up with workable solutions. The workgroup recommended a **Contribute-As-You-Earn (CAYE)** model where a MediSave contribution is required as and when a service fee is earned. Under this model, intermediaries (platform providers) and corporate service buyers who contract self-employed persons (SEPs) would be required to make MediSave contributions to the SEPs' MediSave accounts.

The government has taken the lead in piloting CAYE from 2020, making MediSave contributions easier and hassle-free for SEPs. It is also matching CAYE contributions made by self-employed persons in 2020–2021 up to a cap of $600.

However, this is only the first step in addressing the issue of savings and retirement adequacy for freelancers. For work that does not go through platform intermediaries, the responsibility for making CPF contributions would have to be placed either on freelancers themselves or service buyers. Each has its challenges. The current process of self-declaration of income by self-employed persons is susceptible to non-declaration or under-declaration, whether intentional or otherwise. Collection from service buyers is also challenging if freelance jobs are small and piecemeal. New infrastructure for CPF contributions may have to be set up, and the transaction costs may be high relative to the value of the work done. Small service buyers like households may have to be exempted.

Another challenge facing freelancers is income volatility, for which new social safety mechanisms may need to be devised. The COVID-19 pandemic has brought into focus the vulnerability of gig workers to work and income disruptions. One possibility, as discussed earlier, is to set up a CPF savings account for income replacement during periods of unemployment or significant earnings loss. This could be a voluntary scheme with government top-ups or matching contributions as an incentive to participate in return for constraints on the use or withdrawal of these funds.

In 2021, the UK Supreme Court ruled that Uber drivers were "workers" — a legal status distinct from employees and the self-employed that provides for rights such as minimum wage, pensions, and holiday pay, as well as protection from unfair dismissal. While the concern is that creating a third category of workers in Singapore could prompt some employers to seek to reclassify existing employees, there is scope to review the responsibilities of service buyers and intermediaries such as digital platforms, so as to ensure a fairer and more balanced relationship.

The National Trades Union Congress has set up a Freelancers and Self-Employed Unit to strengthen income security and skills mastery through access to insurance, training grants, and seminars. The government has signalled openness to reviewing current legislation that prevents union representation of freelancers for collective bargaining and grievance handling.

This is a space that should be closely watched as work arrangements evolve, given the potential consequences on income protection, social security, and society at large.

Concluding Remarks on Social Security

Singapore's social security system has come far in recent decades. In particular, personal savings for the lower-income have been augmented by WIS and Silver Support, while the introduction of longevity, healthcare, and long-term care insurance in the form of CPF LIFE, MediShield Life, and CareShield Life have unlocked collective benefits from risk. Still, more can be done — to better equip workers to ride out job disruptions and income volatility, and to strengthen social security for freelancers. As needs change over time, social security will require continual upgrading to provide Singaporeans with peace of mind during their working years and in retirement.

Endnotes

1. International Labour Organization (ILO), "International Labour Standards on Social Security," ILO, https://www.ilo.org/global/standards/subjects-covered-by-international-labour-standards/social-security/lang--en/index.htm.
2. William Beveridge, *Social Insurance and Allied Services,* report presented to the UK Parliament, December 1942, 120.
3. World Economic Forum (WEF), *We'll Live to 100 — How Can We Afford It?*, WEF white paper, May 2017.

4. M. Ramesh, *Social Policy in East and Southeast Asia: Education, Health, Housing and Income Maintenance* (London: Routledge-Curzon, 2004).
5. Ngiam Tong Dow, *A Mandarin and the Making of Public Policy: Reflections by Ngiam Tong Dow* (Singapore: NUS Press, 2006), 44.
6. Kok Fatt Lee, *Singapore's Fiscal Strategies for Growth: A Journey of Self-reliance* (Singapore: World Scientific, 2017), 16.
7. Chia Yong Yong, speech at the Budget Debate, 2015.
8. Christopher Gee, Peter Ryan-Kane, Mark Whatley, and Will Rainey, "The Investment Risks in Singapore's Retirement Financing System," IPS Working Paper No. 24, December 2014.
9. According to the Central Provident Fund (CPF) Board Annual Report 2019, about $21.8 billion in CPF savings (from the Ordinary and Special Accounts) were invested by members under the CPF Investment Scheme (CPFIS) as of 31 December 2019. This is a modest sum compared with total CPF balances of $425.1 billion in 2019.
10. Tharman Shanmugaratnam, speech at the Economic Society of Singapore Dinner, 13 September 2016.
11. Joelle Fong, Olivia Mitchell, and Benedict Koh, "Longevity Risk Management in Singapore's National Pension System," *Journal of Risk and Insurance* 78(4) (2011): 961–981.
12. Toh Wen Li, "No Plans to Reduce Rates for CPF Contributions," *Straits Times*, 5 June 2020.
13. Chua Beng Huat, *Liberalism Disavowed: Communitarianism and State Capitalism in Singapore* (Singapore: NUS Press, 2017).
14. Lee Kuan Yew, *From Third World to First: The Singapore Story: 1965–2000* (Singapore: Times Editions, Singapore Press Holdings, 2000), 116–117.
15. Sock-Yong Phang and Kyunghwan Kim, "Singapore's Housing Policies: 1960–2013," *Frontiers in Development Policy: Innovative Development Case Studies* (Workshop in Seoul, 21–22 November 2013), 123–153, https://ink.library.smu.edu.sg/soe_research/1544/.
16. Ibid.
17. Housing and Development Board (HDB), "Key Statistics," *HDB Annual Report 2019/2020,* https://services2.hdb.gov.sg/ebook/AR2020-keystats/html5/index.html?&locale=ENG&pn=9.
18. Sources: Singapore Department of Statistics; Sock-Yong Phang, "The Singapore Model of Housing and the Welfare State," in Rick Groves, Alan Murie, and C. J. Watson, eds., *Housing and the New Welfare State: Perspectives from East Asia and Europe* (Aldershot: Ashgate, 2007), 15–44.

19. Mah Bow Tan, *Reflections on Housing a Nation: A Collection of Commentaries* (Singapore: Ministry of National Development, 2011), 29–31.
20. Singapore Department of Statistics (DOS), *Report on the Household Expenditure Survey 2017/18* (Singapore: DOS, July 2019).
21. The income ceiling for executive condominiums is $16,000 as at 2020.
22. Lee Hsien Loong, speech at the Economic Society of Singapore Dinner, 8 June 2012, https://www.pmo.gov.sg/Newsroom/speech-prime-minister-lee-hsien-loong-economic-society-singapore-annual-dinner.
23. Singapore Department of Statistics, *Singapore in Figures 2019*, https://www.singstat.gov.sg/-/media/files/publications/reference/sif2019.pdf.
24. Singapore Department of Statistics, *Singapore in Figures 2018*, https://www.singstat.gov.sg/-/media/files/publications/reference/sif2018.pdf.
25. Net property wealth accounted for about 35% of UK household wealth from April 2016–March 2018 (Source: Office for National Statistics, Wealth and Assets Survey). Non-financial wealth, of which real estate forms the bulk, accounted for about 28% of US household wealth in 2018 (Source: Federal Reserve Board, Balance Sheet of Households, Financial Accounts of the United States). For data on other countries, see OECD/Eurostat, "The Value of Land and its Contribution to Wealth," *Eurostat/OECD Compilation Guide on Land Estimation* (Luxembourg: Eurostat, 2015).
26. The Workers' Party, "Counting Down to Zero: Are There Alternatives to VERS?" working paper, November 2019, https://wpsg.s3-ap-southeast-1.amazonaws.com/perspectives/WP-Working-Paper-on-HDB-Resale-Prices.pdf.
27. The home ownership rate among resident households in HDB dwellings fell from 91.8% in 2007 to 90.0% in 2011 while the debt-servicing ratio for first-time applicants buying new flats in non-mature estates rose from 18% to 24% over this period. See Ministry of Finance, *Singapore Public Sector Outcomes Review (SPOR) 2012, SPOR 2014, SPOR 2016.*
28. Janice Heng, "New HDB Flats More Affordable Now," *Straits Times*, 17 November 2014.
29. Sock-Yong Phang, David Lee, Alan Cheong, Phoon Kok Fai, and Karol Wee, "Perils of Having a Non-market Housing Segment," *Straits Times*, 17 August 2013.
30. Sock-Yong Phang, "House Prices and Aggregate Consumption: Do They Move Together? Evidence from Singapore," *Journal of Housing Economics* 13(2) (2004): 101–119.
31. Manu Bhaskaran, *Re-inventing the Asian Model: The Case of Singapore*, (Singapore: Eastern Universities Press, 2003).

32. Khaw Boon Wan, written answer to Parliamentary Question by Non-constituency MP Gerald Giam, 20 January 2014.
33. Lawrence Wong, blog post, March 2017.
34. The Workers' Party, "Counting Down to Zero."
35. It should be noted, however, that low expenditure on healthcare as a proportion of GDP in part reflects Singapore's high GDP base (to which corporate profits contribute significantly).
36. Ong Ye Kung, speech at the Ministry of Health Work Plan Seminar, 25 May 2021.
37. "Beds in Inpatient Facilities and Places in Non-residential Long-term Care Facilities," Ministry of Health, accessed 1 May 2021, https://www.moh.gov.sg/resources-statistics/singapore-health-facts/beds-in-inpatient-facilities-and-places-in-non-residential-long-term-care-facilities.
38. Claire Huang, "Hospital Bed Crunch a Cumulative Problem," *Business Times*, 17 July 2014.
39. Jeremy Lim, "Sustainable Health Care Financing: The Singapore Experience," *Global Policy* 8(2) (2017): 103–109.
40. Government healthcare spending has risen from 40% of national health expenditure in 2013 to 46% in 2018 (source: Gan Kim Yong, Ministry of Health Committee of Supply speech, 5 March 2021).
41. Formerly known as the Primary Care Partnership Scheme, which was introduced in 2000 for the low-income elderly. The scheme was upgraded to CHAS in 2012, with qualifying age and income criteria relaxed to allow more Singaporeans to benefit.
42. Jeremy Lim, *Myth or Magic: The Singapore Healthcare System* (Singapore: Select Publishing, 1993), 67.
43. Ministry of Health, *Medical Endowment Scheme Annual Report 2019/2020*, Singapore: MOH (2020).
44. See, for instance, Frank A. Sloan and Roger Feldman, "Competition Amongst Physicians," in Warren Greenberg, ed., *Competition in the Health Care Sector: Past, Present and Future*, (Washington DC: Federal Trade Commission, 1978), 57–131; Cam Donaldson and Karen Gerard, *Economics of Health Care Financing: The Visible Hand* (New York: St. Martin's Press, 1993).
45. To address divergent interests, some have advocated replacing the "fee-for-service" model with an integrated care model such as the Geisinger Health System and Kaiser Permanente in the US, where healthcare provider and payer are integrated, and doctors receive a flat salary with bonuses based on patient health outcomes.

46. Health Insurance Task Force Singapore, *Managing the Cost of Health Insurance in Singapore*, October 2016. Cited in Salma Khalik, "What the Health Insurance Task Force Recommends," *Straits Times*, 7 March 2018.
47. Described in the government's 1993 White Paper on Affordable Health Care.
48. World Bank, "Out-of-Pocket Expenditure (% of Current Health Expenditure)," World Development Indicators, last updated March 19, 2021, https://data.worldbank.org/indicator/SH.XPD.OOPC.CH.ZS?locations=OE. Data originates from the World Health Organization Global Health Expenditure database (https://apps.who.int/nha/database).
49. According to the Life Insurance Association Singapore, about 2.81 lives (about 69% of residents) were covered by Integrated Shield Plans and riders as at 30 September 2020 (https://www.lia.org.sg/news-room/industry-performance/2020/life-insurance-industry-sees-increase-in-new-business-in-3q-2020-compared-to-2q-2020/).
50. In 2021, the size of approved doctor panels became a bone of contention between the Life Assurance Association Singapore and the Singapore Medical Council, with the latter calling for inclusion of more private doctors.
51. Jessie Lim and Prisca Ang, "Insurers Moving Away from Covering Hospital Bills in Full," *Straits Times*, 11 February 2021.
52. Linette Lai, "Delaying MediShield Life Premium Increase Will Mean Larger Hike Later: Koh Poh Koon," *Straits Times*, 19 October 2020.
53. Kala Anandarajah and Joshua Seet, "Medical Fee Guidelines — A Case of Full Circle?" *Straits Times*, 15 December 2017.
54. Gan Kim Yong, speech at the Ministry of Health Committee of Supply debate, 2020.
55. Jacqueline Poh, "Workfare: The Fourth Pillar of Social Security in Singapore," *Ethos* 3 (Singapore: Civil Service College, 2007): 48–55.
56. For a less sanguine view of workfare-type programmes, see Jamie Peck, "The Rise of the Workfare State," *Kurswechsel* 3 (2003).
57. Robert Greenstein, "Government Programs Kept Millions Out of Poverty in 2010," Center on Budget and Policy Priorities blog, 13 September 2011, https://www.cbpp.org/blog/government-programs-kept-millions-out-of-poverty-in-2010.
58. "From Welfare to Workfare," *Economist*, 29 July 2006.
59. Milton Friedman, *Capitalism and Freedom* (Chicago: University of Chicago Press, 1962).
60. Leong Chi Hoong, Ong Pinchuan, Tan Di Song, and Kuhan Harichandra, "The Impact of the Workfare Income Supplement Scheme on Individuals'

Labour Outcomes," *Economic Survey of Singapore Second Quarter 2014* (Singapore: MTI, 2014), 27–36.

61. Tiago Freire, "Wage Subsidies and the Labor Supply of Older People: Evidence from Singapore's Workfare Income Supplement Scheme," *Singapore Economic Review* 63(5) (2018): 1101–1139.
62. Jesse Rothstein, "The Unintended Consequences of Encouraging Work: Tax Incidence and the EITC," Center for Economic Policy Studies, Economics Department, Princeton University, Working Paper No. 1049, 2018.
63. Jeanette Tan, "Ex-GIC Chief Economist Yeoh Lam Keong Issues Badass Reply to DPM Tharman's Now-Viral Speech," *Mothership*, 8 September 2015.
64. Robin Chan, "Why Setting a Poverty Line May Not Be Helpful: Minister Chan Chun Sing," *Straits Times*, 23 October 2013.
65. Irene Y. H. Ng, "Definitions and Measures of Poverty 2020," *SSR Snippet* 4 (2020): 2–9.
66. See, for instance Amartya Sen, "Development as Capability Expansion," *Journal of Development Planning* 19 (1989): 41–58.
67. Ng Kok Hoe, Teo You Yenn, Neo Yu Wei, Ad Maulod, and Ting Yi Ting, "What Older People Need in Singapore: A Household Budgets Study," May 2019, https://whatsenoughsg.files.wordpress.com/2019/05/what-older-people-need-in-singapore-a-household-budgets-study-full-report.pdf.
68. Josephine Teo, oral answer to Parliamentary Question by MP Louis Chua, 6 October 2020.
69. The Workers' Party, "Redundancy Insurance: The Workers' Party Proposal for a Resilient 21st Century Workforce," policy paper, November 2016, https://wpsg.s3-ap-southeast-1.amazonaws.com/perspectives/WP-Redundancy-Insurance-FINAL-30112016.pdf.
70. International Monetary Fund, "IMF Executive Board Concludes 2017 Article IV Consultation with Singapore," press release, 28 July 2017, https://www.imf.org/en/News/Articles/2017/07/28/pr17306-imf-executive-board-concludes-2017-article-iv-consultation-with-singapore.
71. Liz Alderman, "Why Denmark is Shrinking Its Social Safety Net," *New York Times*, 16 August 2010.
72. Annelies Goger, Tracy Hadden Loh, and Caroline George, "Unemployment Insurance Is Failing Workers During COVID-19. Here's How to Strengthen it," *Brookings Metro's COVID-19 Analysis*, 6 April 2020.
73. Josephine Teo, speech at the Budget Debate, 2020.
74. Donald Low, "New Options in Social Security," in Donald Low and Sudhir Thomas Vadaketh, eds., *Hard Choices: Challenging the Singapore Consensus* (Singapore: NUS Press, 2014), 125.

75. See Pierre Cahuc, "Wage Insurance, Part-Time Unemployment Insurance and Short-Time Work in the XXI Century," IZA Discussion Paper No. 12045, December 2018.
76. Low, "New Options in Social Security," in Low and Vadaketh, eds., *Hard Choices*, 126.
77. Christopher Tan, "Public Transport Ridership Hits New High Except Taxis," *New Paper*, 13 February 2020; "Average Public Transport Ridership (2005 to 2014)," Land Transport Authority, https://www.lta.gov.sg/content/ltagov/en/who_we_are/statistics_and_publications/statistics.html.

Chapter 6

Keeping Singapore Affordable for All — Social Assistance and Beyond

Guiding Principles

In the Singapore System, social assistance for the needy is positioned as outside the ambit of the mainstream social security system, since it is applicable only to the minority of households and individuals who are unable to provide for their own needs. With the exception of Public Assistance, it is temporary and conditional support with recipients obliged to undertake training, seek employment, or manage their finances in order to attain self-reliance. It is also intended to be a last resort after all other sources of help have been exhausted or found lacking, so as not to encourage reliance on the state unless absolutely necessary.

The then-Ministry of Community Development, Youth and Sports (MCYS) Committee of Supply speech in 2005 set out three principles that continue to guide the provision of social assistance in Singapore:

— **Self-reliance**
— **Family as the first line of defence/support**
— **Many helping hands**

Former MCYS policy officer Lim Xiuhui (2007) summed up this approach:

> *Put together, these three principles are actually part of a single overarching principle — that government help must be the last resort. If we do not uphold this principle, people will modify their behaviour to become more reliant on the state than would otherwise be the case. This would reduce the incentive for the low-income group to provide for themselves and improve their lot.*[1]

Put another way, these principles have a twofold aim: to prevent a drain on fiscal resources, given that social spending has proved hard to keep in check in many advanced democracies, and to promote the values of individual, family, and community self-help which are deemed essential to economic dynamism and social resilience.

This chapter describes how social assistance is delivered in Singapore, outlining efforts to strengthen support and improve implementation, as well as discussing further ways to achieve affordable living for all citizens, whether through means-tested or universal subsidies, cost management, or novel approaches such as a universal basic income or a social dividend.

Public Assistance and Community Care (ComCare)

The **Public Assistance Scheme**, also known today as **ComCare Long-Term Assistance**, pre-dates Singapore's independence and continues to serve as the safety net of last resort for the elderly poor and disabled with little or no savings, assets, or family support to rely on for their daily needs. The number of households assisted under this scheme has risen from 2,700 in December 2004 to over 4,000 since 2015 (Figure 6.1),[2] but remained below 0.5% of the 1.37 million resident households in 2019.

Public Assistance rates are updated every two to three years as the cost of living rises. While there is no formula based on a poverty threshold or peg to inflation, the Public Assistance rate for a single-person household has more than doubled from $290 per month in 2007 to $600 in 2019 (Figure 6.2), compared with a 28% increase in the CPI for the bottom quintile of households (and 26% increase in general CPI) over this period.

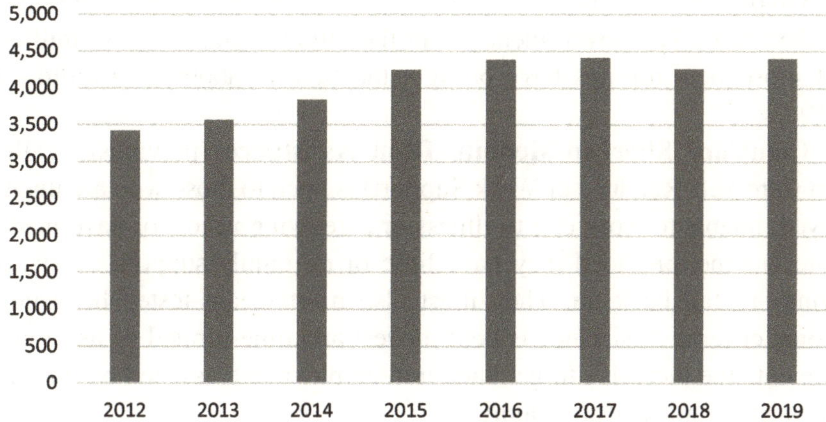

Figure 6.1 Number of Households on Public Assistance

Source: ComCare Annual Reports, Ministry of Social and Family Development.

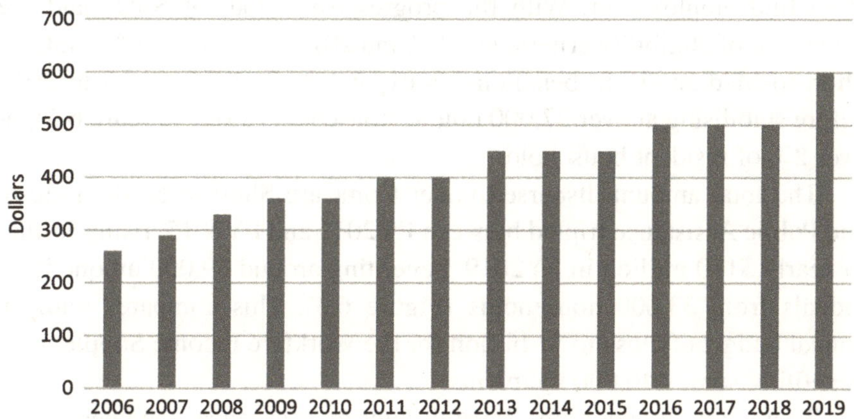

Figure 6.2 Monthly Public Assistance Rate (1-Person Household)

Public Assistance recipients may also receive Silver Support and the Goods and Services Tax (GST) Voucher. Most of their medical fees are covered by MediFund and other subsidies and they have access to rental housing if they so require. They also receive additional support from voluntary welfare organisations (VWOs, now called social service agencies) such as free food and home help.

The Community Care (ComCare) Endowment Fund was set up in 2005 to provide a sustainable source of funding for assistance programmes for the needy. The government put in the initial capital of $250 million, and subsequent top-ups have brought the fund to about $1.9 billion in 2019.[3]

ComCare Short-to-Medium-Term Assistance (previously called ComCare Self-Reliance or Work Support) is open to those who are unemployed, unable to work due to illness or caregiving needs, or have inadequate income, provided they have little or no family support, assets, or savings to fall back on. They must also meet means-tested household income criteria. Assistance is kept modest and time-limited so as to give recipients the incentive to get back into employment, assisted by training grants and employment support.

ComCare funding today is disbursed by 24 Social Service Offices (SSOs) whose staff assess eligibility and work with their beneficiaries (called clients) to place them in employment or in suitable training to help them find employment. With the progressive rollout of SSOs and the expansion of eligibility criteria in 2012 and 2014, the number of ComCare Short-to-Medium-Term beneficiaries expanded significantly up to 2015 before stabilising at over 27,000 unique households a year (Figure 6.3), or over 2% of resident households.

The total amount disbursed under ComCare Short-to-Medium-Term and Public Assistance tripled between FY2011 and FY2015, rising further to nearly $130 million in FY2019, benefiting around 69,000 unique individuals from 33,000 households (Figure 6.3). This compares with an annual budget of close to $1 billion for the Workfare Income Supplement, benefiting some 440,000 recipients.

There are, in addition, several interim assistance schemes under ComCare which provide immediate financial assistance to individuals and families who require urgent and temporary financial relief. These are administered by SSOs, Citizens' Consultative Committees (a type of grassroots organisation), Family Service Centres (a type of social service agency), and the Community Justice Centre. In FY2019, a total of $1.75 million was disbursed through interim schemes to over 7,700 unique individuals.

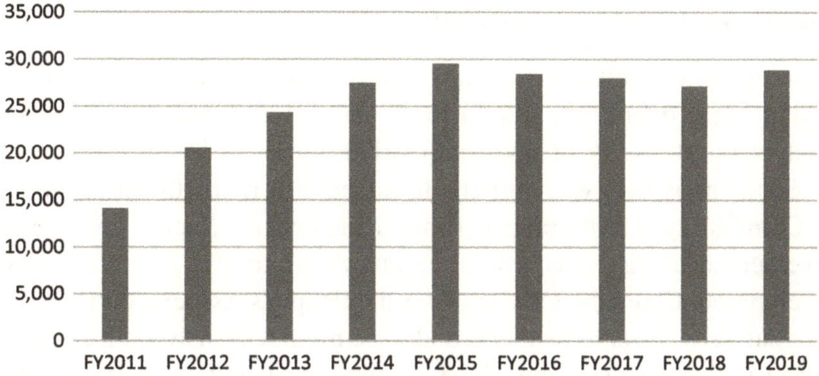

Figure 6.3 Number of Households on ComCare Short-to-Medium-Term Assistance

Source: ComCare Annual Reports, Ministry of Social and Family Development.

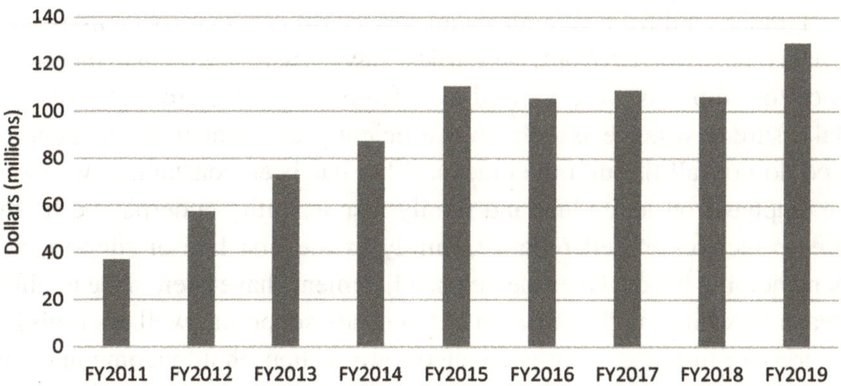

Figure 6.4 Amount Disbursed Under ComCare Short-to-Medium-Term and Public Assistance

Source: ComCare Annual Reports, Ministry of Social and Family Development.

Another set of social assistance schemes focuses on the needs of children from needy families. Previously branded collectively as ComCare Grow, these schemes provide financial assistance for childcare, kindergarten, and student care for children from low-income families.

Social Assistance Implementation

The principles of self-reliance and "family as the first line of support" are evident in the qualifying criteria for ComCare: there must be little or no family support, assets, or savings to fall back on.

Social assistance was initially disbursed directly by the then-Ministry of Community Development (now Ministry of Social and Family Development).[4] Assistance was decentralised to the five Community Development Councils (CDCs) under the People's Association in 2001 to bring services closer to residents and to be more responsive to local needs. During my stint as General Manager of South East CDC between 2007 and 2009, the CDCs were responsible for disbursing ComCare support and coordinating with social service agencies within their respective districts to support needy families. These roles were subsequently transferred to the newly formed SSOs in 2013.

I understand from veteran social service officers that social assistance delivery has evolved from the earliest days when stigma and inconvenience to recipients were viewed as a feature, to a system that strives to make sure assistance is delivered efficiently and that those in genuine need do not fall through the cracks. What has been constant, however, is the emphasis on individual and family responsibility underpinned by the three principles of self-reliance, family as the first line of support, and many helping hands. Over the years, adjustments have been made to allow greater flexibility in the duration of ComCare support as well as eligibility criteria, for instance, what is counted towards household income in determining if someone is eligible for ComCare support.

ComCare Call, a toll-free number, was set up in January 2008 to provide an accessible touch point for those in need to seek help, as well as for others in the community to refer needy residents for help.

In assessing eligibility for ComCare support, the social service officer first interviews the applicant to understand his or her circumstances and needs, and then combs through the applicant's financial records to ascertain that he or she has little or no savings to fall back on.[5] Clients are also expected to explore if they can monetise their assets, such as renting out a room in their HDB flat or downsizing their property.

Next, the social service officer checks the finances of children and other members of the applicant's household. ComCare eligibility is now based on defined household income thresholds which, as at 2021, are $1,900 or below in total household income or $650 or below in per capita household income, although the Ministry of Social and Family Development (MSF) has highlighted that these are not hard thresholds.

"Family as first line of support" finds tangible expression in the **Maintenance of Parents Act**, which was passed in 1995 arising from a private member's bill introduced by former Nominated MP Walter Woon. The act allows needy Singapore residents aged 60 and above to claim financial support from their children. It also imposes legal liability on the child to support his or her financially dependent aged parent. While this may appear an oddity to Western observers, the Confucian emphasis on filial piety makes it less of an eyebrow-raiser in Singapore. A needy senior may receive ComCare Short-to-Medium-Term Assistance but is expected to seek support from his or her children and, if necessary, file for a Maintenance Order against the children via the Maintenance of Parents Tribunal for longer-term support. However, if the senior's children are ascertained to be low-income, the senior may receive Public Assistance.

Implementation Challenges

While self-reliance is a worthy goal, I learnt at South East CDC how difficult it is for some families to sustain it. Our social service officers were trained to help clients identify and overcome barriers to self-reliance, such as suggesting ways to trim expenditure, better manage household budgets and monetise assets, or by getting homemakers into the workforce or breadwinners to take on additional part-time jobs to supplement incomes. We also referred clients for employment assistance based on their skills, work experience, and aspirations.

Even when we succeeded in weaning families off ComCare dependence, a significant proportion would return for help some months down the road. For many, it was a case of "three steps forward, two steps backward" in a cycle of progress and regress. The inability to sustain self-reliance was in some cases down to poor habits or personal choices such as gambling or overspending. However, chronic illness afflicting one family member could also put an entire household under strain by obliging other work-capable members to take on caregiving roles. Sometimes, more than one family member may be stricken by mental illness. Other common challenges included incarceration of the breadwinner, large numbers of dependents, and teenagers falling afoul of the law. Some of these challenges were correlated, making self-reliance even more difficult to attain or sustain. Our officers worked closely with partners in the community, such as Family Service Centres and other social service agencies (SSAs) to address clients' needs more holistically, with case management provided to families with multiple challenges.

I also realised that the implementation of "family as the first line of support" was not straightforward and could sometimes lead to policy conundrums and suboptimal outcomes.

While officers provide short-term assistance and encourage seniors to seek longer-term help from their working children or file a Maintenance Order, there were seniors who, despite their financial difficulties, opted to forgo further assistance, either because they did not wish to burden their offspring or found it humiliating to do so. This was the case even for parents who were not on good terms with their children. In one instance, a senior only qualified for longer-term ComCare support as he had been deemed ineligible for support from his children, having been derelict in his parental duties previously.

The requirement to consider support from other family members living under the same roof could have the perverse effect of prompting seniors to stay apart from their relatives. As social service officers also considered regular contributions from relatives and support from SSAs as part of the senior's income when assessing ComCare applications, there was also incentive for seniors not to accept or disclose such support, which undermined the aim of family and community help.

Like other means-tested support schemes, a rise in household income could render a client ineligible. I recall the case of a ComCare recipient whose household income tipped over the threshold when her son's full-time National Service allowance was raised. Today, greater leeway has been given to social service officers in determining whether community support received by a household should be taken into account, while bearing in mind the need for broad consistency in assessing eligibility.

Many Helping Hands

There has been a long tradition of community self-help in Singapore. When Singapore was a British colony, inadequate state provision of social infrastructure and services spurred business leaders and philanthropists to step in to fill the gaps. The likes of Tan Kim Seng, Tan Tock Seng, and Tan Kah Kee sponsored the building of public waterworks, hospitals, schools, and universities. Subsequently, the government took over the provision of public amenities and services, staking its reputation on efficient provision and delivery. Even where hospitals and universities have been corporatised, the government retains close regulatory supervision.

Social support is an area where the government has held back from assuming full control, in keeping with the philosophy of community self-help. The aim has been to support rather than supplant the plethora of faith-based as well as secular SSAs. If organisations or individuals consider it their religious duty or otherwise feel moved to help the less fortunate in society, it would make sense to tap their resources and efforts rather than have the government supplant them. The trade-off, however, has been a social service landscape that is not fully streamlined.

To encourage community giving, the government granted 250% tax deduction for donations to approved Institutions of Public Character (charities that serve the needs of the community Singapore as a whole rather than confined to specific racial or religious groups) from 2009 to 2014. This was stepped up to 300% in 2015 to commemorate Singapore's jubilee year, before reverting to 250% for 2016–2021. Tax-deductible donations averaged $1.1 billion a year from 2014–2018, topping $1 billion in most years. Singapore's volunteerism rate (among residents and foreigners) has fluctuated between 18% and 35% since 2010, according to surveys conducted by the National Volunteerism and Philanthropy Centre. Under the SG Cares Movement, the government has partnered community groups to set up Volunteer Centres for volunteer matching, deployment, and training in several HDB towns.

Much of the government's support for social assistance is indirect in the form of subventions for SSAs, which are also expected to raise funds from the public. In return for funding, the SSAs are held to certain targets and standards to ensure consistent delivery of quality services. There is both national and local planning to try to optimise the distribution of social services and facilities in each town and constituency. However, the inclinations of the SSAs running these services still hold considerable sway. For instance, more than one SSA may wish to provide similar services in a particular residential neighbourhood or precinct, whereas other areas may be underserved. Standards and efficiency may also be less than optimal from a public planning standpoint.

In 2006, the CDCs set up nine ComCare Local Networks across Singapore to coordinate financial support and social services for needy and vulnerable families across schools, government agencies, SSAs, and grassroots organisations in each area.

However, service delivery remained somewhat fragmented. Braema Mathi and Sharifah Mohamed (2011) found that the many helping hands approach was "short-changed by issues of complexity, overlaps, resource constraints and piecemeal intervention". Notwithstanding a ComCare database for information sharing and case coordination meetings across organisations, they noted that those seeking assistance often had to repeat their story to various agencies while interventions tended to be "band aid" rather than transformative.[6]

In recent years, there have been renewed efforts to improve service delivery. There is now better coordination across SSOs, government agencies, Family Service Centres, SSAs and grassroots organisations, with SSOs given responsibility for the planning of resources in their respective areas. SSAs seeking to run social services at subsidised rental charges are also subject to MSF's assessment of need. MSF and partner agencies are developing capability among officers to identify client needs more comprehensively and connect families with relevant support. There are protocols and processes to facilitate case coordination, supported by system enablers that provide officers with a comprehensive view of clients' circumstances and assistance. SG Cares Community Networks have been set up in every HDB town to foster community partnerships and co-develop solutions to meet ground needs.

To support families with children living in rental housing, MSF launched Community Link (ComLink) in 2019. The programme provides proactive, collaborative, and community-driven support to empower families to achieve sustained stability and social mobility. Led by the SSOs, ComLink also serves as a platform for SSOs to coordinate other national programmes and initiatives (such as KidSTART and UPLIFT, which support disadvantaged families with children) to ensure family-centric service delivery.

These efforts have made the delivery of social assistance more streamlined, saving clients the trouble of having to apply separately to multiple agencies. They have also facilitated integrated case management to more holistically address the multifaceted difficulties some families face.

Challenges Arising from Tensions Between Policy Objectives

Some of the downstream challenges in social assistance derive from upstream tensions in policy objectives.

One is the longstanding tension between the objective of promoting parenthood in the context of marriage (as a social norm the government wishes to uphold) and meeting the needs of single parents, especially those who are lower-income. For instance, single parents are not eligible for automatic benefits such as the Baby Bonus Cash Gift and parenthood tax rebate and face restrictions in the types of HDB flats (new or resale) and housing grants they can apply for.

Over the years, there has been a gradual extension of benefits that support the child's development or caregiving needs of single parents. In 2013, paid childcare leave was extended to single parents. As announced in 2016, maternity leave for single mothers was increased from 8 to 16 weeks to be on par with that for married mothers, and their children became eligible for benefits through the Child Development Account, a government-supported savings scheme for children. The government also indicated that it would exercise greater flexibility in assisting single parents with their housing needs, depending on their individual circumstances.[7] This was in recognition that many single parents may need support for child-rearing, and to avoid jeopardising opportunities for their children to do well in life. Still, there remain some benefits reserved exclusively for married parents so as to encourage parenthood within marriage in line with the prevailing social norm.

Another source of policy tension pertains to benefits for foreign spouses of Singaporeans, among whom are foreign women married to lower-income Singaporean men. There is, for instance, a differentiation in HDB housing grants between households under the Public Scheme and Non-Citizen Spouse Scheme. While there is understandably an intent to tilt support towards citizens, this accentuates the financial vulnerability of less well-off households comprising citizen-foreigner couples without citizen/permanent resident (PR) children. Less well-educated foreign spouses may be particularly vulnerable should they become separated or divorced as they are not automatically entitled to work in Singapore, and may lack social networks or extended family support in Singapore. Nonetheless, low-income Singaporean families with foreign spouses, as well as divorced foreign spouses with a Singaporean/PR child, may be eligible for ComCare assistance.

Social Assistance Design

Challenges to the Self-Reliance and Social Assistance Paradigm

Teo You Yenn (2017) directed a fundamental critique at Singapore's social assistance paradigm:

> *...(these programmes) are clearly earmarked as targeting a specific and small group of Singaporeans rather than part of broad, universal citizenship rights to social security... What is at stake here is not only that the low-income may not be receiving sufficient support, but that this way of framing support creates indignity for 'recipients' through marking qualification as exceptional and for the most 'needy'.*[8]

Elsewhere she wrote:

> *When a low-income person goes to the Social Service Office and is asked numerous personal questions about their family lives or how $40 appeared on their bank account statement, or why don't they just get a better-paying job, this adds to their sense of themselves as inferior, unworthy or excluded.*[9]

This is a critique that resonates, to some extent, with my experience overseeing social assistance delivery at South East CDC. The inability of a family to be self-reliant may be due to factors ranging from poor choices and attitudes to circumstances beyond the family's control. It is necessary to recognise the role of chance through life in determining economic outcomes, and that the cognitive stress or "bandwidth tax" from worrying about how to make ends meet can impair executive function and decision-making, perpetuating a vicious cycle.[10] At the same time, incentives are important in spurring effort towards self-reliance; there is something to be said for a culture that upholds responsibility for self and family. As a senior social service officer put it to me, there is always something that needy individuals or families can do to improve their financial situation.

It should be evident that Teo's critique of the Singapore System is fundamental and cannot be fully addressed by merely adding more programmes or layers of support. The point in question is the **residual model** of social welfare, which sees the government's role in social assistance as a last resort, in contrast to the **institutional model**, where state social support is seen as a right to be enjoyed by all citizens in the normal course of living.

The institutional model is consistent with welfare "universalism", which Teo advocates. However, a full-fledged embrace of universalism would require the entire edifice of Singapore's social security and socio-economic policy to shift from one that is centred on self-reliance to one where universal benefits are pervasive, necessitating significantly higher taxes and transfers.

Whether Singapore can or should adopt the Nordic model is a question of the values that society holds in regard to self-reliance versus mutual obligation. There is also no easy pathway from the current socio-economic system to one that is so different, given the suite of interlocking economic, manpower, and social policies that stand behind each system.

Could there be, notwithstanding, a middle ground between targeted help and universalism, a blend of approaches that would take the edge off the indignity of the current system without abandoning the cherished principle of self-reliance, or requiring a significantly higher tax wedge? We will explore this possibility in the sections that follow.

Different Forms of State Assistance

Social support can be provided by the government in different ways, including:

— Direct subsidies for public amenities and services (such as subsidised housing and education), which could be universal or tiered according to means
— Higher interest paid on Central Provident Fund (CPF) balances
— Automatic structural transfers (such as Workfare Income Supplement, Silver Support, and GST Voucher)
— Ad hoc transfers (such as CPF top-ups or the Solidarity Payment during the COVID-19 pandemic)
— Application-based assistance (such as ComCare and Public Assistance)

It is well recognised that direct subsidies run the risk of mispricing public amenities and services. For instance, fuel subsidies in some countries have led to overconsumption, straining fiscal resources, and proving politically difficult to unwind. In the case of merit goods such as education and vaccinations, where public benefits exceed the consumer's private benefit, overconsumption is less of a concern and the case for implicit subsidies is stronger.

In the early 2000s, there was a push within the public sector to shift from implicit to explicit subsidies. The idea was that every public good and service should first be correctly priced for full cost recovery, with help subsequently extended to those who need it. This help could take the form of means-tested direct subsidies or through general transfers or application-based social assistance.

It is important, however, to avoid expanding the need for application-based social assistance. Consider housing, where rental flats for the lower-income are highly subsidised. A question that arose was whether subsidised rents ought to be raised closer to market rates; if so, those who could not afford the new rents could approach the CDCs for assistance.

However, this would have pushed a significant number of lower-income households to apply for social assistance from the government, making it harder for them to attain self-reliance (as defined in the system), and adding considerable uncertainty to their finances as ComCare support is meant to be temporary. It would also affect their dignity in a system and society that esteems self-reliance. If all direct subsidies and transfers were removed, it is entirely conceivable that over half the population would require such support.

How the government provides help to the needy can impinge on self-worth. In fact, many Singaporeans who qualify for social assistance do not apply for it. While some are unaware of the support available, others prefer to get by without seeking state assistance, albeit with the help of implicit subsidies and transfers. It is important to retain various channels of automatic redistribution that do not entail queuing up for the dole or having to fill in forms, particularly as the high cost of living is a product of Singapore's status as a global city and high median incomes. Placing a person on explicit welfare support may reinforce feelings of dependency and even resentment at the system. Even those who view welfare stigmatisation as a feature rather than a bug would find their position untenable if the majority of citizens had no alternative but to apply for social assistance.

Means-Tested Versus Universal Benefits

Government subsidies and transfers are the principal means of supporting a broader segment of Singaporeans beyond the narrow base of ComCare recipients.

Means-tested benefits, which depend on a person's income, household income, or wealth, are more targeted and less costly than universal benefits that are provided equally to all citizens. For instance, with the introduction of means testing in public hospitals in 2009, patients with lower incomes receive higher subsidies for Class B2 and C wards than those with higher incomes.

Means testing allows the government, within a given budget, to provide greater support to the needy by targeting support to those who need it most. This enables greater redistribution from the tax revenue collected. Hence, means-tested benefits play an important role in a sustainable fiscal system.

At the same time, there are several drawbacks and limitations to means testing which policymakers have to try to mitigate.

The first is the implicit **marginal tax on work** (or on saving, if means testing is based on wealth) as benefits drop off as one's income increases, which could lead to work disincentives.[11]

This will grow as a concern with more widespread means testing, both in the provision of public amenities as well as in the tiering of structural and ad hoc transfers. It is difficult to track the collective effect on all subsidies and transfers as household income rises, particularly as consumption baskets differ across households. In some instances, a person may experience a loss in income net of benefits as her wages from employment increase.

In 2010, the UK government introduced Universal Credit for working-age people by merging six benefit schemes into one. Besides making it easier to claim benefits, a key motivation was to better control the rate of withdrawal of benefits as income increases.

Another way to avoid cliff effects is to use a variety of qualifying criteria and income or wealth thresholds for different schemes. In Singapore, given the multiplicity of means-tested and targeted benefits, this is an area the government ought to carefully monitor.

A second issue pertains to the **accuracy of means tests in identifying the truly needy**. Personal income or wages do not take into account a household's resources and needs. However, reliance on household income or per capita household income presupposes that members of a household share their resources equitably. Incomes measured at a point in time do not reflect accumulated savings or wealth. They may also fluctuate from month to month for gig workers and others who are self-employed. Yet, without readily available measures of a household's wealth, the Singapore government typically uses housing type as a proxy indicator, which supposes that housing assets can be monetised to meet living expenses.

A possible way of means testing is to take a worker's average monthly income over a period of time, even years. This would address the issue of self-employed workers' income, provided wages are regularly reported or otherwise accurately captured. A smoothened income basis would also avoid having welfare benefits drop off suddenly when a worker receives a pay raise, which could pose incentive problems.

A third drawback of means testing, which is related to the first two, is the **administrative cost and the potential for gaming**. The more finely calibrated the means-testing framework is, in order to achieve fairness or incentive compatibility, the greater the complexity and cost of administration. It also becomes more difficult to communicate the criteria in a way that the public can easily understand. On the other hand, a less finely graded system has sharper fall-offs and is likely to be challenged by those who find themselves just below the cut-off of each tier of benefit eligibility.

At South East CDC, I often reflected on how much more financial support we could provide to the needy with the savings on administrative costs, inclusive of rents and wages, if we did not have to go through the laborious process of checking financial documents and ascertaining family support.

A fourth and potentially the most challenging aspect of means testing is the **psychological impact** on both the recipients of support and those who are excluded. Those who receive means-tested benefits are reminded that they are poorer than the majority of the population and may therefore feel entitled to the benefits, while also feeling unhappy at their relative position on the socio-economic ladder.

While most people can accept, at least intellectually, the principle that the most help should be given to those who need it most, there will be some among those who do not qualify for means-tested benefits who feel unfairly excluded, especially when confronted with rising food prices, medical bills, or water tariffs. For instance, a retiree living in a condominium may see inflation eat into her retirement savings and feel aggrieved that she is excluded from help based on the value of her property, which she may not think is an accurate reflection of her disposable wealth.

Comparisons and envy invariably surface: why is my neighbour getting more from the government when she is in fact better off, has more savings, or has wealthy children who can support her, etc. Ironically, the more finely tuned the means-testing framework is to ensure fairness, for instance, taking into account both income and wealth measures, the greater the potential for misunderstanding when comparisons are made by members of the public.

Along with targeted, means-tested benefits, a case can be made for more inclusive or even universal benefits to be retained in the portfolio of social support. Citing research by Bo Rothstein and Eric Uslaner (2005), Donald Low and Yeoh Lam Keong (2011) suggested that countries with universal social programmes enjoyed higher levels of social trust than countries without such programmes.[12]

Inclusive benefits, on the other hand, generate a sense of solidarity, which helps to legitimise the tax and redistribution system for those who contribute the most to it. The affluent are well aware that they are contributing more to the pool than they are taking from it, but it helps that the pool is a shared one from which they, or their loved ones, derive benefit from time to time.

In Singapore, universal benefits for citizens include highly subsidised school fees, free entry to museums, and nominal fees for the use of public gyms and swimming pools. More recent additions are the Pioneer and Merdeka Generation Packages, described in Chapter 5, albeit restricted by year of birth. During the COVID-19 pandemic in 2020, a Solidarity Payment was given to all adult Singaporeans, along with a Solidarity Utilities Credit (details in Chapter 11).

Sometimes, even small gestures may have a large salutary impact. The Finnish practice of giving every expectant mother a baby box, with essentials for mother and baby, has become a powerful symbol of national identity and belonging for all Finnish families. It was likely the inspiration for Singapore's Jubilee Baby Gift, which alas was limited to those born in 2015.

Mitigating the Welfare Trilemma: Progressive Universalism, Self-Selection, and Moral Suasion

At the heart of welfare provision is a trilemma where at most two of the objectives of adequacy, cost, and inclusivity can be achieved (Figure 6.5).

Means-tested social programmes can adequately provide for the needy at a manageable fiscal cost, but at the expense of inclusivity, and potentially weakening incentives to increase income through the implicit marginal tax on work. Universal programmes, on the other hand, do well

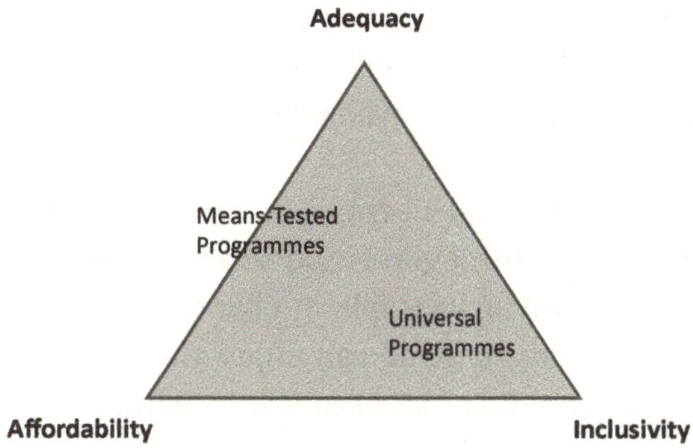

Figure 6.5 The Welfare Trilemma

on inclusivity and incentive-alignment, but typically face a trade-off between adequately meeting needs and containing fiscal cost.

In some instances, **progressive universalism**[13] may provide a reasonable balance between these objectives by having a basic subsidy tier accessible to all while providing higher tiers of subsidies according to income or wealth. This has been the case for government hospital subsidies since the introduction of means testing in 2009. Patients who are well-off still receive subsidies in public hospitals but receive less than those who are within the lower income or wealth bracket.

These principles can also be applied to ad hoc transfers. For instance, the recent cash handouts in response to the COVID-19 pandemic gave a base $600 (called the Solidarity Payment) to all adult citizens, with the middle- and lower-income receiving $300 and $600 more, respectively. While some well-off Singaporeans questioned why the state was expending resources to provide them with cash they did not need, others welcomed the universal support.

Another way to keep universal benefits affordable is to take advantage of **self-selection**, whereby the less well-off would be more likely to take up the subsidies. Again, ward charges at public hospitals provide an illustration. Notwithstanding means testing, wealthy patients may still opt for class C wards and enjoy subsidies; however, they are more likely to prefer the privacy and amenities of the higher-class wards. This self-sorting approach, where workable, has the advantage of inclusivity.

Social enterprises, too, may adopt a similar approach. For instance, NTUC Foodfare prepares affordable, nutritious meals with the lower-income in mind but makes these available to the general public at similar prices.

Moral suasion and **social norms** can also be effective in managing the consumption of subsidised goods and services. Taking a leaf from the non-profit sector, we find an example in charity kitchens run by temples and religious associations: anyone can enjoy free meals, but there is an unspoken moral onus on the rich not to abuse such provisions.

Managing Costs for Affordability

As outlined in Chapter 1, affordability is a key outcome that a country's socio-economic system must deliver.

Keeping the cost of living affordable can reduce the need for means-tested social assistance with its attendant challenges. Cost of living is also related to the impact of inequality, which is most keenly felt where rising affluence drives up the cost of living for lower- and lower-middle-income families, thus directly affecting their welfare.

Living costs are a determinant of absolute social mobility — whether one can aspire to do better than one's parents. Every generation hopes that the next will enjoy a higher standard of living. While purchasing power has generally increased over time in Singapore, some parents lament that their children may have to downsize to smaller homes as property prices rise.

Finally, living costs are particularly pertinent to retiree households. Rising costs reduce the purchasing power of retiree households, even if real incomes are rising for employed households, unless pensions are size-able and indexed to inflation.

To address affordability, the state could provide targeted transfers or subsidies to those in need. This is more efficient than holding down the prices of public services and amenities as it provides greater transparency and is less likely to result in overconsumption.

However, a system of targeted social transfers also runs up against psychological challenges, particularly during times of strong inflation. Behavioural economics suggests that periodic or one-off transfers tend to have a smaller impact than the daily observation of escalating prices and bills. One way to mitigate this is to make transfers "sticky" in the minds of recipients, such as by spreading out the benefits over the year or presenting these benefits visibly and clearly.

Whether transfers are means-tested, there is another inherent challenge: any given transfer or subsidy appears smaller to a middle-income household, as a percentage of their expenditure, than to a low-income household. Hence, it will always be an uphill battle for the government to win over the broad middle class through transfers of any size. Middle-income Singaporeans unhappy with their own situation may be among those most vocal in claiming that the government is not doing enough for the poor.

It is worth recognising that there are in fact various ways in which the government can endeavour to hold down costs without necessarily mispricing services or introducing market distortions. The state wields various levers, including control of land and housing supply and regulation of public service providers (Figure 6.6).

First, the government can influence prices through the **supply of land**, whether for housing, commercial, or industrial use, subject to Singapore's overall land constraints and long-term development plans. By providing a steady supply of land adequate for residential and business needs, it can avoid supply crunches driving up prices and, where necessary, take steps to rein in speculation.

While general inflation is driven by cyclical demand, the ability to control or influence supply (for instance, the supply of public housing) is

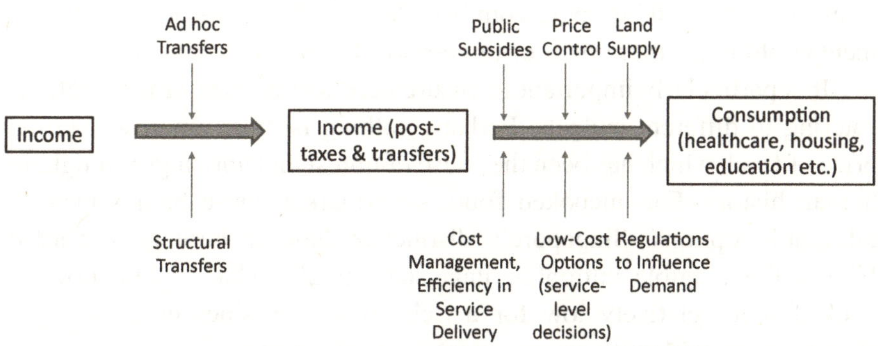

Figure 6.6 Policy Levers Influencing Incomes and Affordability

a critical lever the government can employ to manage costs. This can have a significant impact on price without necessitating distortive downstream interventions.

Second, the government can keep a close eye on the **cost of delivering public goods and services**. There are good reasons for these goods and services to be priced for cost recovery, fiscal sustainability, and to prevent overconsumption. Notwithstanding, the cost of production or delivery itself can be managed to avoid transferring an excessive burden to the public. Public services, even those provided by corporatised outfits, may not be subject to the full rigour of market competition, particularly if they are natural monopolies. Hence, careful attention should be paid to the cost of infrastructure and operations, including manpower. Innovation, too, can help to cut costs. Public agencies have many examples of well-designed systems and processes that have led to significant savings that can be passed on to members of the public.

Third, government agencies' **decisions on service levels** and public amenities directly affect costs to the public. Given income disparities in Singapore, it is important to provide the public with a range of choices, including low-cost options. Without compromising safety and security, not all public services have to be premium services. For instance, we may not need the fancier trappings and amenities in our buses, train stations, and hospitals if these translate into higher costs for the public. The government may not be able to do away with some degree of creature comforts in public transport if its priority is to encourage greater public transport usage, but it could look at ways to make lower-cost options such as cycling and walking more comfortable. In public housing, the government could make more two- or three-room HDB flats available.

It is particularly important to ensure access to a range of food options catering to different budgets. Perhaps nothing is more emotive than the price of food, which has been the cause of unrest and uprisings throughout human history. For uncooked food, supermarket house brands provide affordable options. Singapore's distinctive hawker heritage (awarded UNESCO intangible cultural heritage status in 2020) has kept the price of cooked food relatively low for a rich country, besides engendering a shared culinary identity across socio-economic strata.

There had been a 26-year hiatus in the development of new hawker centres leading up to 2011, when the government announced that 10 new hawker centres would be built over 10 years, amid concerns about affordable dining-out options. A Public Consultation Panel on Hawker Centres, formed in the same year, recommended that new hawker centres be operated on a not-for-profit basis by social enterprises or cooperatives. In 2012, the subletting of hawker stalls (which had previously driven up rentals) was disallowed, and the minimum reserve rent requirement for tender of vacant stalls was removed. With the government announcing the addition of more social enterprise hawker centres from 2020, steps have been taken to address hawker feedback on the social enterprise model, including high rents and onerous contract terms.[14] One of the key challenges today in sustaining Singapore's hawker heritage is being able to attract enough young people into the business, given the spread of more attractive career options.[15]

Fourth, we have seen in Chapter 5 that the government can influence market pricing and affordability through various **upstream means to influence demand**, such as macroprudential cooling measures (in the case of housing) and insurance reform (in the case of healthcare).

Finally, the government could take a sensible **approach to market pricing, especially of land**. Market pricing should not be carried to extremes where it would drive higher prices across the board for vulnerable segments of the population. Unlike larger countries, Singapore has no rural areas or boondocks for the less well-off to escape the high cost of living in a global city with a high concentration of wealth. One can only imagine what the price of drinking water would be if the government were to strictly "market price" the land used for water catchment and transfer the cost to the consumer. Market pricing is important for fiscal discipline and economic efficiency but should not be overextended at the expense of non-market considerations including the public's notion of fairness.

The cherished principle of cost recovery should also be sensibly applied to the pricing of public services. While marginal cost pricing provides for economic efficiency, the revenue generated may be insufficient to cover fixed costs, in which case the government has to carefully consider whether to recover the full cost from consumers or, for broader reasons of equity, from general taxation instead.

In times of income volatility, conditional assistance and ad hoc transfers do not provide as much assurance to the public compared with affordable necessities, whether food, healthcare, housing, or public services. Hence, the commitment by NTUC FairPrice supermarkets to keep the prices of a range of house brand items unchanged till the end of 2020 helped to reassure consumers during the COVID-19 pandemic.

Universal Basic Income

Universal benefits may take the form of free or subsidised public services and amenities or universal income transfers to households.

The concept of a basic income or **universal basic income** (UBI), whereby all citizens receive from the state an income sufficient to meet their basic needs without a means test or requirement to look for work, is one that has appealed to thinkers across the political spectrum over time.

Unlike a **guaranteed minimum income**, which raises household incomes to a guaranteed minimum, or a **negative income tax**, which partly offsets any income shortfall from a guaranteed minimum, UBI payments are independent of income from other sources. Unlike a wage supplement like Workfare, there is also no requirement for recipients to be committed to job search or skills training.

What accounts for the appeal of UBI? It can impart financial peace of mind, providing a safeguard against people falling through the cracks due to lack of awareness or inability to access other forms of state aid — addressing the concerns of the Left. It can significantly reduce the cost and complexity of administering a large number of overlapping welfare schemes — addressing the concerns of the Right. Compared with means-tested benefits which are withdrawn as one's income increases, there is also less risk of incentive distortion with UBI. Some proponents of UBI cite its potential to liberate people from drudgery by affording them more flexibility in their choice of work and facilitating human capital investment, thereby unlocking their potential for the benefit of society.[16] Less desirable jobs will have to be redesigned with better pay and working conditions in order to attract workers in receipt of UBI. Unlike wage supplements or negative income tax, UBI does not disregard the value of non-market work such as caregiving and it can free people from the stigma of state assistance, in line with the institutional model of social welfare provision.[17]

Even in Singapore, from time to time, we hear of families who fall through the cracks or slip through the social safety net. Application-based ComCare support through SSOs incurs substantial administrative costs in terms of manpower, office space, and overheads. While the government has taken care not to distort incentives when introducing means-tested benefits, a point may be reached where some people would be better off shunning a pay raise in order to retain state benefits.

With economic growth increasingly dependent on innovation and enterprise, governments may find that focusing on value creation moves the needle more than making sure that every citizen pulls weight through gainful employment. UBI could also be an efficient social safety net if jobs are scarce or the rewards from economic growth unevenly distributed, such as in a scenario where automation eliminates jobs while enlarging profits for owners of capital and technology.

Looking Around: UBI Experiments

Notwithstanding the theoretical appeal of UBI, it has yet to be fully implemented on a nationwide basis by any country. A proposal to implement UBI in Switzerland (amounting to 2,400 Swiss francs a month for adults) was soundly defeated in a 2016 referendum with 77% voting against it. However, there have been several basic income-related experiments and pilots over the years.

In the Manitoba Basic Annual Income Experiment (Mincome) that took place in Canada in the 1970s, lower-income households were given a guaranteed minimum income with payouts scaled down for every dollar they earned by working. The results showed only a small decline in hours worked, except among new mothers and working teenagers.[18]

In 2017, Finland's centre-right government conducted a nationwide basic income experiment involving 2,000 randomly selected unemployed persons who had received unemployment support in 2016 to see whether the provision of unconditional support (i.e. regardless of employment/income status or efforts to find employment) would activate greater employment. As it turned out, basic income recipients did not have more workdays or higher incomes than those in the control group. However, in subjective evaluations, they reported significantly fewer problems relating to health and stress and also had a more positive view of their future.[19] In any case, these findings do not speak to whether UBI would reduce work incentives among those in employment.

Ontario, Canada, also implemented a basic income experiment in 2017 where 4,000 participants were guaranteed a minimum basic income, with 50 cents deducted for every dollar they earned through employment. This was intended to test whether a basic income would "reduce poverty more effectively, encourage work, reduce stigmatisation, and produce better health outcomes and better life chances for recipients". While the experiment was prematurely terminated after 17 months upon a change in government, researchers at McMaster University and Ryerson University who surveyed 217 participants reported improvements in physical and mental well-being, housing stability, and social relationships. Participants interviewed also suggested that they felt empowered to find better jobs.[20]

With technological disruption appearing to threaten jobs on a large scale, UBI is often looked to as a solution.[21] It formed the signature policy proposal of US presidential aspirant Andrew Yang's campaign for the 2020 Democratic Party's nomination. Citing the risk of mass layoffs arising from automation, Yang proposed a "Freedom Dividend" of $1,000 per month for every American aged 18 and above. Yang did not clinch the Democratic nomination, but he stayed in the race longer than many had expected, and generated considerable discussion on the efficacy and feasibility of UBI. Various surveys found a significant increase in support for UBI among Americans following the outbreak of COVID-19.[22] In Germany, a privately funded UBI experiment kicked off in 2020 where 120 people will receive €1,200 a month (just above Germany's poverty line) for three years, and their experiences compared with those of a control group.[23]

In Singapore, economists Walter Theseira and Ong Qiyan proposed a "Majulah UBI" in response to the economic fallout from COVID-19. This would be a time-limited payout of $110 per week for 12 weeks for all Singaporeans, including children, intended to provide assurance amid widespread job and income losses. The estimated cost of $4.62 billion would be funded by a temporary increase in personal income tax, which would be paid in 2021 when the economy was expected to have improved.

The chief concern regarding UBI is fiscal cost. The Finnish version where everyone receives the same payout regardless of their income is expensive and would have to be funded from fairly high taxes. The German Parliament, in a debate on UBI in 2013, identified financing as a major obstacle, among others, to the realisation of a basic income in Germany. To address cost, basic income could be tapered (or phased out) as earned income rises. This could be effected through a progressive tax schedule that starts from the first dollar of earned income.[24] While this would lower cost, the incentive to move up the income ladder would not be as strong.

Luke Martinelli (2020) expressed this as a UBI trilemma across affordability, adequacy, and the "advantages of radically simplified welfare" (advantages arising from the elimination of means testing and conditionality), which shares similarities with the trilemma depicted in Figure 6.5. Nonetheless, he contended that "it is possible to design an affordable and adequate 'partial' BI scheme".[25]

Besides affordability, several other caveats about UBI are worth noting. First, there would be pressure to increase it over time, much like the pressure to increase Public Assistance rates or, in other countries, the pressure to continually revise the minimum wage, unless it is indexed to inflation in the first place.

Second, some families beset with physical/mental disabilities or chronic illnesses may require more than a basic income to get by, hence active screening and assessment of needs for additional assistance would still be required even with UBI.

Third, some families and individuals need more than just financial assistance to turn their lives around. The work of the SSOs is more than just financial aid — it involves active help and intervention, in partnership with SSAs, to help families escape from the poverty trap. This must continue even with a basic income.

If, like in many other advanced democratic economies, social assistance schemes continue to proliferate and expand over time, we may reach a point where a basic income becomes a credible alternative to the prevailing system of welfare benefits. A rise in job losses or income volatility, whether precipitated by automation or economic uncertainty, may necessitate either stronger employment protection or stronger income protection through interventions such as UI or UBI.

Social Dividend: An Option for Singapore?

A concept related to UBI, but distinct from it, is the social dividend. This term originally referred to the return on capital and natural resources owned by society in a socialist economy. In market socialism, it is a dividend paid to each citizen from the property income generated by publicly owned enterprises. Some refer to this as a universal basic dividend to distinguish it from UBI.

As part of his envisaged system of liberal socialism, British economist and Nobel laureate James Meade proposed that the government should have ownership but not control of state enterprises, with income accruing to the government as shareholder used to finance a social dividend for citizens.

Since 1982, the state-owned Alaska Permanent Fund (established using oil revenue) has paid an annual dividend that is based on the price of oil and other budgetary considerations to every adult and child living in the state.[26] The dividend was US$1,606 per person in 2019. Several studies have reported a positive impact: Matthew Berman and Random Reamey (2016) estimated that about 25% more people would have fallen below the poverty threshold in the absence of the dividend.[27] Damon Jones and Ioana Marinescu (2018) found that the dividend did not deter work, but in fact increased part-time work.[28] Nishant Yonzan, Laxman Timilsina, and Inas Kelly (2019) found that the dividend increased fertility in Alaska by over 13%.[29]

Such a concept, in Singapore's context, could serve three aims:

— Giving citizens a further shared stake in the nation's progress
— Mitigating the impact of inequality and rising costs in a global city
— Strengthening social security amid restructuring and economic volatility

From time to time, the Singapore government has given ad hoc bonuses such as the Growth Dividend in 2011 to return budget surpluses to citizens. New Singapore Shares were disbursed in 2001 to adult

Singaporeans, Economic Restructuring Shares were distributed from 2003–2005 as part of a package to offset GST, while the SG Bonus was handed out in FY2018. A more regular, systematic sharing of budget surpluses could be effected through a social dividend.

Another possibility is to fund a social dividend from the returns on Singapore Inc., the stable of Temasek-linked companies where the government is a major shareholder. Following the privatisation of Singapore Telecoms, the government offered discounted Singtel shares in 1993 and 1996 with the intent to share the nation's wealth and broaden the base of equity-owning Singaporeans.

It may be timely to revive this concept, not necessarily by distributing actual shares in Temasek-linked companies to Singaporeans but by funding a social dividend from the returns, or long-term expected returns, of the state's investments. Progressive universalism could be applied, whereby all adult citizens receive a dividend, tiered based on wealth (ideally), with a bonus for older citizens or parents of young children. This could be given in the form of cash as well as CPF to build up retirement and healthcare savings.

Thus far, public housing has been the means by which the government has sought to give Singaporeans a stake in the nation's progress. As home prices are unlikely to appreciate as quickly as before, and the leases on older flats are running down, a social dividend could be a further means by which Singaporeans are given a share in the nation's economic prosperity.

A social dividend could also help to offset the cost to less well-off citizens from living in a global city where high median incomes and purchasing power bid up the cost of land and services. It would mitigate the traditional tension between labour and capital by allowing citizens to derive income both from the personal labour they supply as well as the collective economic capital of the nation. It is possible to frame a social dividend as supporting national solidarity and social cohesion rather than as an explicit form of welfare or social support.

Sustainability would be assured if the dividend is tied to the state's investment returns, with Singapore in a stronger position than most countries to implement a social dividend or UBI. While a social dividend could be funded from any stream of public revenue, linking it with investment returns (or alternatively GDP growth) has the advantage of making tangible the notion of shared prosperity, potentially engendering support for policies that promote growth and keep the economy open.

A more ambitious positioning for the social dividend would be to have it take on a key role in providing social security. With job and income security at greater risk from economic restructuring and the potential lingering impact of COVID-19, it is recognised that Singapore's social safety nets need strengthening. Compared with unemployment insurance or stronger unemployment benefits, a social dividend is less likely to distort incentives to work.

A social dividend of a meaningful size for this role would incur a substantial fiscal cost. Its feasibility depends on the extent to which it can be rationalised with other components of the social security and social assistance system so as to reduce complexity and administrative burden and mitigate the psychosocial downsides of a residual system of welfare provision. For instance, the GST Voucher, Silver Support, and ComCare Medium/Long-Term Assistance schemes could be folded into the social dividend while WIS could be retained to encourage work, albeit with lower payouts. However, replacing any of these schemes would require the social dividend to provide a guaranteed baseline support regardless of investment return or GDP growth in any given year. Even with rationalisation of schemes, the government would likely need to extract more from the state's investment income or capital receipts to balance the budget, or consider raising taxes.

To keep the fiscal cost manageable, progressive features are necessary. If payout tiers are based on income, there is a risk of blunting incentives to move up the income ladder. Given that housing remains an imperfect proxy for wealth, one possibility is to also look at cumulative CPF contributions (similar to Silver Support) or smoothened income over several years to minimise this risk.

While affluent Singaporeans would still receive a modest dividend, this could be offset by increasing progressive income or wealth taxes. In addition, those who are better-off should be encouraged to donate their social dividend to charitable causes of their choosing. Behavioural nudges could be applied, such as by making it easy to donate to a drop-down list of charities or Institutions of Public Character, with donation to the

Community Chest the default option. However, those who fall into difficult circumstances can opt out and fall back on the social dividend.

As part of the social security system, a social dividend could give Singaporeans more psychological assurance, notwithstanding the myriad assistance schemes and subsidies already in place today. Such assurance may have a bearing on the all-important fertility rate. Moreover, if a social dividend can mitigate cognitive stress, improve social cohesion, and empower more citizens to pursue their passion, whether in entrepreneurship or creative pursuits, it could fuel the engine of innovation so important for the future economy and potentially pay for itself.

In tackling the challenges of economic precarity and inequality, there are many ways to skin a cat. The Socio-Economic Flowchart (Figure 1.3) shows that various interventions can be taken upstream or downstream. It is possible to add to the patchwork of support schemes, widen the coverage of existing schemes such as WIS and Silver Support, or step up support through these schemes in order to keep income volatility and inequality at bay.

A social dividend is by no means the only solution, nor is it a complete solution in itself. In weighing a social dividend or UBI against other social forms of social support, the key trade-offs to consider are:

1) Fiscal cost savings from targeting/means testing versus benefits of universalism/progressive universalism (e.g. streamlined administration, no one falling through the cracks, feeling of social inclusion and avoidance of stigma for welfare applicants)
2) Risk of free-riding and erosion of work incentives versus income security and flexibility to choose one's work

The balance of risks must be carefully considered. Is it possible to shore up the existing system, or do we risk stretching it to breaking point? Conversely, can we retain a dynamic and motivated workforce with a generous social dividend, or do we risk undermining the foundations of Singapore's success?

The challenges to the Singapore System will only intensify in the years ahead, and we may be just a major innovation or mindset shift away from a fair and durable solution.

Endnotes

1. Lim Xiuhui, "Security with Self-Reliance: The Argument for the Singapore Model," *Ethos* 3 (Singapore: Civil Service College, 2007): 36.
2. Vivian Balakrishnan, speech at the Ministry of Community Development, Youth and Sport Committee of Supply Debate, 2005.
3. Ministry of Social and Family Development (MSF), *Community Care Endowment Fund Annual Report for Financial Year 2019* (Singapore: MSF, 2020).
4. The Ministry of Community Development, in existence from 1985–2000, was reorganised and renamed the Ministry of Community Development and Sports (2000–2004). This became the Ministry of Community Development, Youth and Sports (2004–2012), before being restructured into the Ministry of Social and Family Development (2012 to date).
5. I was told by long-serving colleagues that the savings threshold had in years past been pegged to the cost of Taoist funeral rites, the most expensive among the last rites of all the official religions in Singapore.
6. Braema Mathi and Sharifah Mohamed, "Unmet Social Needs in Singapore — Singapore's Social Structures and Policies, and Their Impact on Six Vulnerable Communities," *Social Insight Research Series* (Singapore: Lien Centre for Social Innovation, 2011).
7. Lawrence Wong, speech at the Ministry of National Development Committee of Supply Debate, 2020.
8. Teo You Yenn, *This Is What Inequality Looks Like,* new edition (Singapore: Ethos Books, 2019), 169–170.
9. Ibid., 40–41.
10. Anandi Mani, Sendhil Mullainathan, Eldar Shafir, and Jiaying Zhao, "Poverty Impedes Cognitive Function," *Science* 341(6149) (2013): 976–980; Frank Schilbach, Heather Schofield, and Sendhil Mullainathan, "The Psychological Lives of the Poor," *American Economic Review* 106(5) (2016): 435–440.
11. Jonathan Bradshaw, "The Case for Family Benefits," *Children and Youth Services Review* 34(3) (2012): 590–596.
12. Donald Low and Yeoh Lam Keong, "Beware the Inequality Trap," *Straits Times*, 14 December 2011. See also Bo Rothstein and Eric M. Uslaner, "All for All: Equality, Corruption and Social Trust," *World Politics* 58(1) (2005): 41–72.

13. Also known as proportionate universalism or targeted universalism, this term had its origins in healthcare but has gained currency in other areas of social work. The ethos behind this concept, although not the term, was articulated in Richard Titmuss, "Welfare State and Welfare Society," lecture at the British National Conference on Social Welfare, 1967. See also Michael Marmot et al., *Fair Society, Healthy Lives: The Marmot Review: Strategic Review of Health Inequalities in England Post-2010* (2010); Florence Francis-Oliviero, Linda Cambon, Jérôme Wittwer, and Michael G. Marmot, "Theoretical and Practical Challenges of Proportionate Universalism: A Review," *Revista Panamericana de Salud Publica* 44(1) (2020).
14. Cheryl Tay, "Lower Rents for Hawkers at Social Enterprise Hawker Centres; 13 More to Open by 2027," *Straits Times*, 26 August 2019.
15. To this end, a Work-Study Certificate in Hawkerpreneurship has been launched to prepare recent polytechnic and Institute of Technical Education (ITE) graduates for a career as a hawker. The National Environment Agency is also piloting a Hawkers Succession Scheme that matches retiring hawkers with new entrants, and provides financial support for retiring hawkers to train their successors.
16. See, for instance, Philippe van Parijs and Yannick Vanderborght, *Basic Income: A Radical Proposal for a Free Society and a Sane Economy* (Cambridge: Harvard University Press, 2017).
17. Nathan Schneider, "Why the Tech Elite is Getting Behind Universal Basic Income," *Vice*, 6 January 2015.
18. Vivian Belik, "A Town Without Poverty? Canada's only Experiment in Guaranteed Income Finally Gets Reckoning," *Dominion*, 5 September 2011.
19. Heikki Hiilamo, "Disappointing Results from the Finnish Basic Income Experiment," *Nordic Welfare News*, 8 February 2019.
20. Rich Haridy, "Canada's Cancelled Basic Income Trial Produces Positive Results," *New Atlas*, 12 March 2020.
21. See, for instance, Andy Stern, *Raising the Floor: How a Universal Basic Income Can Renew Our Economy and Rebuild the American Dream* (New York: Public Affairs, 2016).
22. Catherine Thomas, David Kalkstein, and Gregory Walton, "How the Coronavirus Is Opening Doors to Universal Social Policies in the US," *Time*, 17 June 2020; "Support Grows for Government-run Healthcare, Universal Basic Income," *Rasmussen Reports*, 3 April 2020.

23. Organised by the German Institute of Economic Research, or DIW Berlin, a non-profit academic institution.
24. In developing countries where there is substantial casual or non-market labour, it may not be feasible to tax back universal transfers over a significant part of the income distribution. This tilts the argument in favour of targeted transfers in developing countries, as highlighted by Rema Hanna and Benjamin Olken, "Universal Basic Incomes Versus Targeted Transfers: Anti-Poverty Programmes in Developing Countries," *Journal of Economic Perspectives* 32(4) (2018): 201–206.
25. Luke Martinelli, "A Basic Income Trilemma: Affordability, Adequacy, and the Advantages of Radically Simplified Welfare," *Journal of Social Policy* 49(3) (2020): 461–482.
26. Dylan Matthews, "Americans Have Fewer Kids than They Say They Want. Alaska Has a Solution," *Vox*, 7 February 2020.
27. Matthew Berman and Random Reamey, "Permanent Fund Dividends and Poverty in Alaska," presentation given to Anchorage Population and Economic Data Workshop on 18 October 2016, https://iseralaska.org/static/legacy_publication_links/presentations/2016_10_18-AlaskaPFDPoverty.pdf.
28. Damon Jones and Ioana Marinescu, "The Labor Market Impacts of Universal and Permanent Cash Transfers: Evidence from the Alaska Permanent Fund," NBER Working Paper No. 24312, February 2018.
29. Nishant Yonzan, Laxman Timilsina, and Inas Rashad Kelly, "Economic Incentives Surrounding Fertility: Evidence from Alaska's Permanent Fund Dividend," NBER Working Paper No. 26712, January 2020.

Chapter 7

Improving Education: Access, Quality, and Future Readiness

Education has been the lynchpin of the Singapore System, a cornerstone of the social investment state. It is the foundation for skills acquisition and employability, enabling **good incomes** and self-reliance for citizens while keeping the economy competitive and attractive to investment.

It is also the principal means by which **social mobility** has been sustained in Singapore. A high-quality, affordable public education, made possible by heavy state investment and universal subsidies, has enabled each generation to do better than the one before, helping to level the playing field for children from less well-off families to climb the socio-economic ladder.

Of course, the aims of education go beyond the economic, encompassing character formation and skills equipping for effective participation in society as well as opportunities for self-actualisation.

With Singapore students excelling in international tests such as the Programme for International Student Assessment (PISA), Singapore's education system is much admired worldwide.

The two pressing challenges facing Singapore's education system are to **prepare citizens for the future economy**, so as to enable good employment outcomes, including income growth, and to **sustain social mobility**, which is expected to become increasingly difficult as wealth accumulates and society stratifies.

Broadly, the government's response to the first has been to (i) **revamp education in schools** to foster independent learning and support innovation, Asia readiness, and digitalisation, and (ii) support lifelong learning via the **SkillsFuture movement**. The response to the second challenge has been to (i) enhance **state support for early childhood education**, to level the playing field, and (ii) **step up assistance to children from disadvantaged and dysfunctional families** while providing opportunities for all to excel.

Indeed, the extension of support down into the preschool years, and up into the working years (by rebalancing resources between pre-employment education and continuing education/training) are among the most significant moves in education policy since the turn of the century.

Concerns over income inequality, wage stagnation, and social mobility call for a **downstream response** in the form of **redistribution and stronger social safety nets**, and an **upstream response** in the form of **increasing investment in education**, particularly for the less well-off or more vulnerable. The latter sits more comfortably within Singapore's socio-economic paradigm of personal effort and responsibility, and hence is the natural first recourse — a no-regret move notwithstanding its fiscal cost. As discussed in Chapters 4–6, a concomitant downstream response may also be needed.

Quality Education as an Enabler of Income Growth and Social Mobility

Substantial broad-based public investment in education has helped to give every child the opportunity to move up in life. In FY2019, the Ministry of Education (MOE) spent close to $13 billion, amounting to over 16% of annual government expenditure, or about 2.5% of GDP. This exceeded expenditure of all other ministries besides Defence. Although education spending has come down from 20% of government expenditure and 2.9% of GDP in FY2014, this was due to smaller student cohort sizes as well as rising expenditure in other areas such as healthcare.

Compared with other countries, Singapore's spending on education as a percentage of GDP appears low, but as a share of total government expenditure, it is relatively high.

Table 7.1 Public Spending on Education in Selected Economies (2017)

	Public Spending as % of GDP	**Public Spending as % of Budget**
Finland	5.4	9.9
United Kingdom	5.1	12.1
United States	4.7	12.1
South Korea	3.9	13.0
Japan	3.1	7.8
Singapore	**2.6**	**17.3**
OECD Average	4.4	10.7

Source: Ministry of Finance (Singapore); OECD database, retrieved 8 April 2021 (other countries).

As at 2021, school fees (inclusive of miscellaneous fees) were up to $13 a month at primary level (Grades 1–6) and up to $25 a month at secondary level (Grades 7–10/11), nominal sums considering government subsidies of over $11,000 a year for each Singaporean primary school student and some $15,000 a year for each secondary school student. Those in post-secondary education receive $15,000 to $22,000 for every year in the Institute of Technical Education (ITE), junior college, polytechnic, or university.[1] This amounts to subsidies of around 75% for university education, 85% for polytechnic education, and well over 90% for ITE education. Further support is available to those from lower-income families through bursaries (covering up to 75% and 95% of subsidised tuition fees for undergraduates and polytechnic students, respectively) and subsidised student loans.

Considerable resources are also invested in the recruitment and professional development of teachers, with pre-deployment and in-service training provided by the National Institute of Education (NIE).

Compulsory primary school education ensures that all children have the opportunity to participate in the national education system. Under the Compulsory Education Act enacted in 2000, all Singapore citizens born from 1996 must attend a national primary school. Even for the few exemptions from the system granted for home schooling or religious education, educational standards are enforced through a national examination, the Primary School Leaving Examination (PSLE).

"Every School, a Good School"

In keeping with its slogan, "Every school, a good school", MOE ensures that all schools are well-resourced. In fact, per capita funding is higher for schools with a higher proportion of students from less well-off families. At the secondary level, the greatest resources are given to students in the specialised secondary schools (Northlight, Assumption Pathway, Crest, and Spectra), followed by those in the Normal (Technical) and Normal (Academic) streams, all of whom receive higher per capita funding than the secondary school baseline.[2]

Besides ensuring consistently high standards of teaching, the ministry regularly rotates some of the best teachers and principals across different types of schools, including "neighbourhood schools". Notwithstanding, many Singaporean parents put in considerable effort to get their children into the better-known, "brand name" primary schools, such as by serving as parent volunteers or even taking up residence near the school in order to boost their children's chances of admission.

Giving Every Child Opportunities

To ensure that no child gets left behind, the **Learning Support Programme** is available in all primary schools for Primary 1 and 2 students without adequate English literacy or numeracy skills. Schools use a common screening test to identify students for additional support under this programme.

Northlight School was set up in 2007 to cater to the needs of students facing difficulties with the mainstream curriculum, in particular those who have failed the PSLE twice. Along with Assumption Pathway School, another specialised school with similar objectives, Northlight provides a nurturing environment with an emphasis on experiential learning to help students stay in education and enhance their employability.

At the post-secondary level, the government has invested considerable resources in all educational institutions, including the polytechnics and ITE. Expanded and improved education pathways cater to students with varied aptitude and interests, and widen opportunities for those who come into their strengths, or discover their interests, when they are older. In

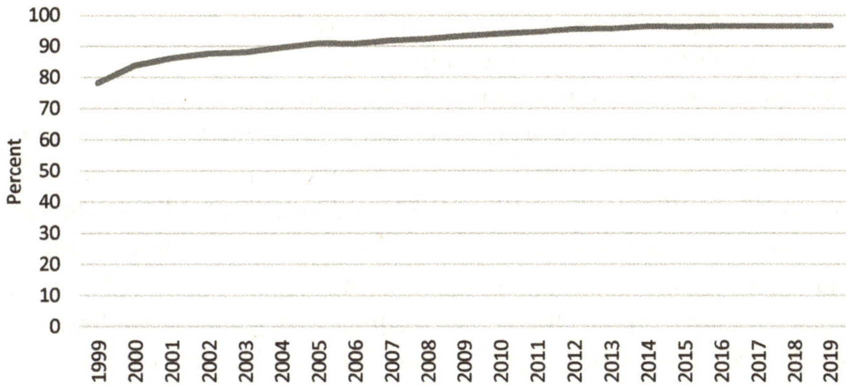

Figure 7.1 Share of Primary One Cohort that Progressed to Post-Secondary Education*

*Year marked on the horizontal axis refers to the typical year in which a student in the cohort progresses to post-secondary education (10 years after Primary One). Figures for 2015–2019 are preliminary.

Source: Ministry of Education.

2019, about 97% of each primary one cohort progressed to post-secondary education (universities, polytechnics, ITE and other equivalent institutions, in Singapore or abroad), up from 78% in 1999 (Figure 7.1).

Outcomes and Mobility

Singapore's focus on providing a high-quality education across all schools has resulted in high averages in terms of educational outcomes, with even weaker students performing relatively well by international standards.

In the 2018 PISA test conducted by the OECD to evaluate quality, equity, and efficiency across 79 school systems, Singapore 15-year-olds came in second in reading, mathematics, and science, finishing only behind China (represented by Beijing, Shanghai, Jiangsu, and Zhejiang) in each domain.[3] In the previous test in 2015, Singapore had topped each of these domains while also performing best among 52 economies in collaborative problem-solving.

The 2018 PISA study also found that Singapore students in the bottom 25% of socio-economic status (SES) homes performed better than the OECD average (across all income levels) in each of the three domains.[4]

47% of Singapore's lower-SES students were "core-skills resilient", i.e. attained at least proficiency level 3 in all three domains, up from 43% in 2015, and about double that of the OECD average (23%). 53% of lower-SES students in Singapore were "internationally resilient", placing in the top quarter (in terms of reading) of students from all economies after accounting for SES, compared with 33% of lower-SES OECD students. In terms of "national resilience", however, only one in 10 lower-SES students in Singapore had reading scores in the top 25% nationally, similar to other countries in the OECD. The reading score gap between lower and higher-SES students in Singapore was 104, a shade down from 108 in 2015. By comparison, the OECD average score gap was 89.

Notwithstanding, students from lower-income households still have a good chance of doing well in school. In 2011, about half of students from the bottom one-third by socio-economic background obtained PSLE scores within the top two-thirds of their cohort. This was a lower proportion than the two-thirds that would have been expected under perfect social mobility, but still considerable. One in six from this group scored within the top one-third, a figure that had remained stable over about a decade.[5]

Improving Early Childhood Education Access and Quality

While a strong national education system does much to level opportunities, compulsory education in Singapore only begins in the year a child turns seven. In the formative years of early childhood and preschool, where the foundations for intellectual and social development are laid, there could be significant disparities in the educational experience of children from different socio-economic strata. At one end there are preschools that charge thousands of dollars per term and give children the opportunity to learn everything from coding to foreign languages. While it is arguable whether such expensive enrichment programmes are necessary, the concern is that at the other end, some children from disadvantaged backgrounds are less likely to attend preschool on a regular basis. Even if these children are enrolled in a preschool, the likelihood of absenteeism may be high due to various family circumstances.

Up to the 2000s, the government had been understandably cautious about nationalising preschool — this would be a costly undertaking and would disrupt an already well-established private market in preschool education. Furthermore, bringing forward the start of formal education could trigger the education "arms race" among parents earlier and increase stress for all without necessarily producing better outcomes in the long run.

Yet, there was evidence that early childhood education had a significant impact on cognitive and behavioural development in the schooling years and beyond.[6] Studies in other countries, such as Lynn Karoly and James Bigelow (2005),[7] found a high rate of social returns from public investment in high-quality early childhood education programmes, particularly for vulnerable children. In Singapore, middle-class and wealthier parents were already investing considerably in their preschoolers' education. While preschool participation by age six had been at 99% for some years, absentee rates among those from lower-income families could still be high.[8]

With concerns over inequality and social mobility rising, it was recognised that more had to be done to improve preschool education access and quality. The government decided to progressively step up its involvement and investment in preschool education without full-scale nationalisation.

To this end, the **Early Childhood Development Agency** (jointly overseen by the Ministry of Social and Family Development (MSF) and MOE) was set up in 2013 to catalyse improvements in the preschool sector. Concurrently, it was announced that MOE would set up a few of its own kindergartens to pilot and showcase best practices in early childhood education.

Efforts were also made to make preschools more affordable. Under the **Anchor Operator Scheme**, which was started in 2009 and enhanced in 2014, selected preschool operators receive government subsidies in return for keeping to a monthly fee cap and raising the quality of childcare and education. A complementary **Partner Operator Scheme** commenced in 2016 with partner operators also committed to improving quality and supporting the development of early childhood professionals, but allowed higher fee caps compared with anchor operators. As at 2020, there are five major preschool chains under the Anchor Operator Scheme, and 23 operators running some 250 centres under the Partner Operator Scheme.

Support under the Kindergarten Fee Assistance Scheme (KiFAS) was enhanced and extended to middle-income families from 2015, while preschool subsidies and coverage (Child Care Additional Subsidy and KiFAS) were further raised in 2020. Full-day preschool capacity has doubled from 90,000 in 2012 to almost 180,000 in 2019, with plans to grow this to over 200,000 over the next few years. The extension of the Partner Operator Scheme to more childcare centres, along with the expansion of Anchor Operators and MOE kindergartens, will enable 80% of preschoolers to have a place in a government-supported preschool, up from just over 50% in 2019. With these plans to enhance preschool affordability, accessibility, and quality, annual government expenditure on early childhood education is expected to more than double over the next few years from about $1 billion in 2019.

In 2019, the **National Institute of Early Childhood Development (NIEC)** was formed to bring together various existing preschool teacher training programmes and provide more unified foundational training. The NIEC offers both certificate and diploma-level training courses in early childhood education for post-secondary students as well as professional development courses for mid-career professionals and teachers already in service.

Reforming Education in Schools and Tertiary Institutions

Looking Back

NIE has identified four phases in the development of the education system in Singapore[9]:

In the **survival-driven** phase (1965–1978) the focus was to ramp up the building of schools and recruitment of teachers to meet basic education needs. A **bilingual policy** was adopted, with English as the first language and Mother Tongue as the second language for the majority of students. There was a strong focus on science and mathematics to support the needs of the economy. The **Institute of Education** was set up in 1973 to raise the standards of teacher training.

In the **efficiency-driven** phase (1979–1997), "**streaming**" was introduced to address high student attrition and low literacy achievement, by allowing students of different abilities to learn at their own pace. In the 1980s, students were streamed at the end of Primary 3 into normal bilingual, extended bilingual, or monolingual streams (later called EM1, EM2, and EM3, respectively). Secondary school students were divided according to their academic ability into Special, Express, and Normal streams. The Normal stream was split into Normal (Academic) and Normal (Technical) in 1994. Selected schools were given greater autonomy in curriculum planning and school programmes with the formation of **independent and autonomous schools** in 1987 and 1991, respectively. ITE was formed in 1992 as a post-secondary institution to raise the quality and standing of vocational and technical education and improve the employability of vocational trainees. With the addition of two new polytechnics, the polytechnic cohort participation rate rose from 5% of the cohort in 1980 to over 35% in 1996.

In the **ability-based, aspiration-driven** phase (1997–2011), **specialised independent schools** were set up to develop students with particular aptitude for mathematics, science, technology, arts, and sports. In 2004, the **Integrated Programme** was introduced in a handful of top schools, allowing students to skip the General Certificate of Education Ordinary Level (GCE O-Level) exams at the end of Secondary 4 and proceed directly to the General Certificate of Education Advanced Level (GCE A-Level) exams or International Baccalaureate. In the same year, **Direct School Admission** was introduced, allowing secondary schools and junior colleges to select a portion of their students based on specific domain talents and achievements independent of results in national examinations. The intent of these moves was to broaden the concept of meritocracy and discover, recognise, and develop a range of abilities within and across individuals.[10] The EM1 and EM2 streams were merged in 2004, and EM3 stream scrapped in 2008, removing streaming at primary school level.

In the **values-based, student-centric** phase (2011 onwards), emphasis is placed on values through character and citizenship education. There has been continued shift away from a fixation on academic performance towards a more holistic education that seeks to equip students with the interest and skills to learn through life. **Subject-based banding** has been introduced in secondary school and will replace streaming by 2024. Changes to the PSLE scoring system will also be implemented from 2021.

Primary and Secondary Education Reform

While Singapore's education system has produced strong educational outcomes and won international acclaim, there are longstanding challenges associated with a highly competitive, exam-oriented system.

Chief among them is the stress imposed on students, parents, and even teachers. The OECD's 2018 PISA survey found that Singapore students experienced greater anxiety regarding failure than their peers in most OECD economies. A survey of 1,050 children aged between 10 and 15 by a charity (Focus on the Family) found that 70% of children polled felt negatively about upcoming exams, with more than 60% feeling "worried".[11] Content-heavy curriculum and high expectations have resulted in a heavy workload for students, exacerbated by a $1.4 billion tuition industry,[12] as parents seek external help for their children to cope or to give their children a leg-up to get further ahead.

Streaming at an early age has also been charged with "pigeonholing" children according to a narrow measure of academic ability and keeping them in pre-set pathways. This has resulted in some students feeling stigmatised or demoralised and unable to realise their full potential in life, whether through lack of opportunities or self-limiting mindsets.

Over the years, MOE has taken steps to reduce stress, emphasise holistic development, and foster positive attitudes towards learning. This has entailed:

(a) Reducing curriculum to free up time for independent learning
(b) Shifting away from a focus on examinations and academic results towards greater emphasis on good learning habits and skills and engendering greater joy in learning
(c) Expanding education pathways and programmes catering to different skills and aptitudes while replacing streaming with subject-based banding

These correspond to three of the four trade-offs articulated by former Minister for Education Ong Ye Kung in a speech at the 2018 Schools Work Plan Seminar:

> The first is the balance between **rigour and joy** — how much robustness we want in the system and hard work we require from students, versus making learning fun and nurturing the joy of learning in our students. We know that many of us realise education in schools is at risk of becoming too stressful and maybe some unwinding is in order.
>
> The second is **sharpening versus blurring of academic differentiation** — how finely differentiated we want examination results to be as a tool for placement and admission, versus blunting the distinction of results between students so that we can gauge learning outcomes without encouraging an overly competitive culture in our schools. The **reform of the PSLE scoring system**, effective in 2021, is a decisive step to reduce unnecessary competition.
>
> The third trade-off is **customisation versus stigmatisation** — how our curriculum caters to students of different learning paces and learning needs, versus inadvertently stigmatising certain groups of students who are less academically inclined. I know many educators feel strongly about this, and we should explore how to further leverage **subject-based banding** to optimise this trade-off. (emphasis in boldface added)[13]

Curriculum Reduction

In 1997, the ‘Thinking Schools, Learning Nation’ vision was developed with the aim of strengthening thinking and inquiry among students. The following year, curriculum content was reduced by about 30%. In 2005, the “Teach Less, Learn More” movement was launched to help teachers better engage students and develop their critical faculties through real-life learning experiences. Curriculum was further reduced by 20% to create time and space for more active and independent learning. Minister Ong indicated at the 2018 Schools Work Plan Seminar that even with these cuts, Singapore’s curriculum size at all levels was comparable to other education systems. However, he said that any further reduction would risk under-teaching.[14]

Examination and Assessment Reform

Examinations and assessments serve several important functions in almost every education system. They (a) measure a student's progress and understanding of concepts, identifying any gaps that need to be plugged, (b) motivate students to study and master content, (c) determine if a student has sufficient mastery to progress to the next level, (d) differentiate among students as selection criteria for institutions and courses, and (e) serve as a signal of ability or skill for potential employers. However, an excessive focus on examinations and academic competition may detract from learning objectives and impose undue stress on students, parents, and teachers.

In Singapore, the PSLE is a major, high-stakes national examination at the end of primary school that determines a student's subsequent education pathways, including secondary school stream. The student's aggregate or "T-score" also determines which schools he or she can enter, depending on whether the score exceeds the school's cut-off point for admission. The PSLE has been a major source of stress for parents and students alike. It is not uncommon for parents to take leave from work to help their children prepare for the PSLE; a major local bank even saw fit to launch a PSLE Leave Scheme for its employees.[15]

Several steps have been taken to reduce stress and avoid an unhealthy focus on academic grades, particularly in regard to the PSLE. In 2012, MOE ended the longstanding tradition of the media profiling top scorers in national examinations such as the PSLE or O-Level. The following year, MOE ceased the practice of showing the highest and lowest score achieved by pupils in the cohort on PSLE result slips. Since then, MOE has been working towards replacing the PSLE T-score with grade bands (in eight achievement levels), which will take effect from 2021. For students at all levels of school, their position in class and at the cohort level will also no longer be reflected in their report books so as to signal that learning is not a competition.

In a Parliamentary debate on education for the future in 2018, several MPs suggested scrapping the PSLE entirely. While then-Education Minister Ong Ye Kung admitted that the PSLE added stress and was far from a perfect system, he contended that it was also "the most meritocratic, and probably the most fair of all imperfect systems". He added that alternative systems such as those in Switzerland and Hong Kong, which did not have a PSLE-equivalent, had led to a thriving private school sector that benefited the rich. With Malaysia replacing its primary school national examination (called the UPSR) with school-based assessments from 2021, the relevance of PSLE has again been called into question.[16]

Another suggestion has been to defer the high-stakes examination, currently taken by 11- or 12-year-olds, to age 15 or later to allow children more time to discover their interests and develop their strengths, and not to disadvantage "late bloomers". Education professors Linda Darling-Hammond and Pasi Sahlberg both noted during a 2013 visit to Singapore that a "high-stakes sorting examination" at age 12 was rare in most school systems, which typically held such exams at age 15 or 16.[17]

The PSLE aside, there has been a reduction in other school-based assessments to free up curriculum time and allow more space for students to find joy in learning. From 2019, there have been no exams for the first two levels of primary school. More schools are also doing away with mid-year examinations at other primary and secondary grade levels.

While many parents welcome the reduction in curriculum content as well as the number of assessments, other parents are worried if their children are being adequately prepared for major examinations such as the PSLE, and look to tuition to top up what they perceive may be lacking in school. The government, on its part, has indicated that it has no intention of banning tuition.

Changes to Progression and Admissions Policy

The **Direct School Admission (DSA)** scheme was introduced in 2004 to allow selected secondary schools to take in a number of students based on discretionary criteria including non-academic achievements, such as in the sports and arts, rather than results in national examinations. This was to recognise the importance of achievements in other spheres, beyond academic results.

From 2018, DSA has been extended to all secondary schools in Singapore, which can take in up to 20% of their students through the scheme. Under the enhanced scheme, schools may no longer use tests of general academic ability to assess applicants. Instead, students' strengths in areas such as sports, arts, language, maths, science, or leadership will be considered.

For universities, the **Discretionary Admission Scheme** was introduced in 2004 to allow public universities to admit 10% of students based on criteria besides academic grades. This was increased to 15% in 2017. It was announced in January 2020 that in a few years' time, up to 50% of the undergraduate intake in the National University of Singapore (NUS), Nanyang Technological University (NTU), and Singapore Management University (SMU) may be selected based on aptitude and interest rather than grades or academic cut-off points.

Subject-Based Banding to Replace Streaming

Besides Singapore, countries such as Germany, the Netherlands, Finland, and Switzerland also practise "streaming", more commonly known as "tracking", separating students into academic and technical or vocational tracks according to ability. This can take place as early as 10 years of age (in Germany) or, more commonly, at age 15 or 16 (e.g. Denmark). Ludger Wößmann (2009) reviewed various international studies on the impact of tracking on educational outcomes, as measured by international student achievement tests such as PISA.[18] The general finding was that the dispersion of educational performance increased considerably more between primary and lower-secondary school in systems that practised tracking compared with those that remained comprehensive. Further, later tracking was associated with a smaller impact of family socio-economic background on student performance. According to Wößmann, tracking was also not found to have improved student performance even among higher-ability students. A study of the Finnish comprehensive school reform in the 1970s, which shifted the sorting of students to academic and vocational tracks from age 11 to 16, suggested that the reform reduced intergenerational income elasticity (i.e. increased social mobility) by 23%.[19]

Irene Ng and Hyekyung Choo (2021) found that educational stream played a key role in mediating the effect of parents' education on youth's educational aspirations in Singapore.[20] Specifically, children of parents with lower educational qualifications were more likely to be in the technical stream, which in turn led to lower educational aspirations. Conversely, children of parents with higher educational qualifications were more likely to be in the Integrated Programme or International Baccalaureate, which in turn led to higher educational aspirations (Ng & Senin, 2018).[21]

While streaming at primary school was removed in 2008, students continue to be streamed at the secondary level. Recognising that students may have uneven strengths across the different subjects they study, MOE has gradually pivoted towards subject-based banding. This allows teaching to be further customised to students' aptitude at the subject level while avoiding the stigma associated with the Normal stream.

In 2014, subject-based banding was introduced in 12 secondary schools to allow Normal (Academic) and Normal (Technical) students to take subjects at the Express level. Subject-based banding was made available in all secondary schools in 2018. By 2024, full subject-based banding will be implemented across all secondary schools, with students no longer grouped in classes according to their stream.

Expanding Education Pathways

The range of education pathways has been expanded with the establishment of the Singapore Sports School, School of the Arts, NUS High School of Mathematics and Science, and School of Science and Technology between 2004 and 2010. More choices have been given to students in top schools with the establishment of the Integrated Programme, which allows students to skip the GCE O-Level exams, as well as the introduction of the International Baccalaureate as an alternative to the GCE A-Level exams. For Normal (Technical) students, two specialised secondary schools, Crest and Spectra, were set up in 2013–2014 to offer a customised curriculum that integrates academic learning and vocational training, adopting practice-oriented teaching methods.

More opportunities were given to ITE graduates to enter polytechnics, while the number of places for polytechnic graduates in publicly funded universities was greatly expanded with the setting up of the Singapore University of Technology and Design and the Singapore Institute of Technology in 2009, and the designation of the Singapore University of Social Sciences (formerly UniSIM) as Singapore's sixth autonomous university in 2017. Since 2014, one in four ITE graduates have progressed to polytechnics, up from one in five previously. In 2011, just one in seven polytechnic graduates had a publicly funded place in the local universities. By 2015, this had jumped to one in five, with polytechnic graduates making up a third of students admitted to the local universities.

To enable more porosity across pathways, MOE announced in January 2020 that A-Level students enrolling in polytechnics would enjoy more course exemptions and a shorter pathway to graduation. From 2021, admission to full-time polytechnic courses will be extended to those with part-time Workforce Skills Qualifications or ITE qualifications (if they possess relevant working experience), while working adults may also take up technical diplomas at ITE.

Singapore will also have its first university of the arts, a state-supported private university to be formed from an alliance between LASALLE College of the Arts and Nanyang Academy of Fine Arts.

Admissions, Examinations, and Their Impact on Social Mobility

Given its role in building up skills and human capital, education has been, over time and across countries, a key means by which individuals and families climb the socio-economic ladder.

The education system and institutions of learning play a huge role in mediating social mobility by determining access to various opportunities at each level of schooling. These include the choice of primary school, the type of secondary school programme, as well as the selection of post-secondary institution and course, with the last having a direct bearing on an individual's occupation as well as income trajectory.

While the Singapore education system has been enormously successful over the years in enabling citizens to take up good jobs with strong income growth, serving as an engine of social mobility, it has also been faulted for locking individuals into pre-set pathways from an early age. Critics charge that the system pigeonholes people based on a narrow definition of merit, i.e. academic performance, which may not always relate to skills needed on the job, particularly in the future economy. An excessive focus on exams and academic competition also detracts from instilling positive attitudes towards learning, which is a foundational skill and habit that must be carried on through life. Changes to the education system in the past two decades — curriculum reduction, assessment reform, changes to progression and admissions policy, subject-based banding, and expansion of education pathways — are all helpful and important in this regard.

However, it is worth examining the impact of existing rules and policy changes on social mixing and social mobility, in particular, as there could be tension between various educational objectives and the aims of social integration and social mobility.

Primary School Admission

Notwithstanding efforts to make every school a good school, many parents remain anxious about getting their children into particular "brand name" primary schools, whether because of secondary school affiliation (which makes it easier for their children to subsequently progress to secondary schools of choice) or the perceived rigour or academic standards of the school. Hence, popular primary schools may receive many more applicants than they have places for.

The primary school admissions exercise accords priority first to children with a sibling studying in the school of choice (Phase 1), then to children of alumni, member of school management committee, or staff (Phase 2A), then to children who have served as a parent volunteer or with clan or church affiliation to the school (Phase 2B), and then to others (Phase 2C). For Phase 2B and 2C, priority is given to those living within one kilometre of the school, followed by those within a two-kilometre radius. Where there are more applicants than places in each phase, a ballot is conducted to assign the places.

The admissions criteria reflect practical considerations (siblings, distance from school) as well as a desire to build familial and community links, which contribute to a school's culture. However, this could come at the cost of diversity and social mixing, given that many popular primary schools have well-to-do alumni and are located in private residential districts with expensive housing.

Since 2012, 40 places in each school are reserved and split between Phase 2B and Phase 2C to prevent children with affiliation from taking up all the places within a school. Nonetheless, it is worth considering if this is sufficient to promote diversity in student intake. A more varied mix of students would help foster interaction among children across the socio-economic spectrum. This is particularly important at the primary level before ability-based sorting of students takes place at the secondary level and above. It is therefore heartening that MOE has announced in March 2021 that it is reviewing the primary school registration system to see how it can increase the number of places in Phase 2C.

Integrated Programme

The Integrated Programme (IP), which gives students who have done well in the PSLE the opportunity to skip the O-Level via a through-train programme from Secondary 1 (7th grade) to the A-Level or International Baccalaureate (12th grade), has become one of the most highly sought, competitive programme for top students. It frees up time for students to focus on learning rather than having to prepare for a major national examination, which has little bearing on these students' ability to progress in the system.

From a pedagogical standpoint, this has clear advantages. However, the IP raises the stakes in the PSLE, which determines entry into the IP, and reduces opportunities for late bloomers to enter the best schools and programmes. Although there are students who are admitted mid-stream, locking in a group of elite students after the PSLE limits the scope for subsequent mixing. This is pertinent to social mobility as differences in school readiness linked to socio-economic status are likely to be accentuated at the primary school level.

Broader Criteria for Admissions

DSA into secondary schools and junior colleges and discretionary (or "aptitude-based") intake into universities broaden assessment of merit to non-academic areas of excellence, providing balance to a system that has traditionally focused excessively on examinations and grades. Interviews, portfolios, and co-curricular activities may provide a better gauge of aptitude and interest and be a better predictor of fit for and success in a course than academic grades.

Notwithstanding, there could be inadvertent effects on social mobility, depending on how discretion is applied in the admissions process.

It is often said that affluent parents can give their children a major advantage in exams and academic performance through expensive tuition, calling into question the legitimacy of an "exam-based meritocracy". However, it may well be that examinations are a more effective social leveller than other forms of selection into educational institutions and programmes such as co-curricular pursuits, interviews, and internship experiences.

Children from better-off families are more likely to have exposure to extracurricular pursuits from an early age, besides having better spoken language and interview skills. Some parents are also able to give their children access to internships though their business and professional networks.

This point is well-made in Chua Mui Hoong's (2012) commentary:

> ...qualitative assessments like project work or interviews can supplement tests and exams. But they are also areas where social and cultural capital give children of more educated and wealthier parents an advantage. They can become means to entrench the privilege that children from better-off homes already enjoy in school... The greatest disservice we can do to working-class children today is to tweak the examination system in such a way that their hard work in mastering the syllabus to sit an exam is undervalued, and they are instead assessed in areas where they have a native handicap, long before they can hope to overcome it.[22]

In moving from a more objective (grade-based) to a more subjective (holistic) evaluation of students for admission to institutions and programmes, much depends on how institutions and interviewers assess applicants. Some may pay greater heed to personal obstacles a candidate from a disadvantaged background has faced while others may not. There may thus be unevenness in implementation, which could have repercussions on social mobility. This is an area that merits further research.

Ideally, a pivot away from exams and academic achievement should alleviate stress for students and free up more time for other areas of development. In practice, a challenge is that excelling in co-curricular activities and non-academic pursuits becomes perceived as a requirement on top of academic excellence. Children from more affluent families would generally have more time and family resources to pursue both academic and non-academic excellence. For children from disadvantaged homes, doing well in just one area is already an achievement.

It is reassuring that with the significant resources schools have been endowed with, they can back students from lower-income families who show exceptional talent in areas such as music and sport to go as far as they can. However, the financial risks of non-mainstream pursuits in one's choice of career are always greater for those from less well-off families. In China, a student's decision to study archaeology at university in 2020 sparked a major online debate as some felt that being the daughter of poor migrant workers, she ought to have picked a more lucrative field which her grades allowed for, whereas others felt that she was right to pursue her passion for archaeology.[23]

Beyond the exceptionally talented, the question is whether the majority of children from less well-off families would find it easier to do well — both relative to what they would otherwise have achieved and relative to children from middle-class or affluent families — in a system that is less focused on academics and examinations, and if not, what offsetting assistance or consideration can be given to them. In this regard, the retention of the PSLE and other national examinations may still be needed for balance and should continue to play a part in the progression and sorting of students.

Regardless of assessment metric, there will continue to be intense competition to get ahead in the educational race as long as the economic rewards tied to performance in the education system are perceived to be vastly disparate. The finger is often pointed at parents for being overly competitive and heaping stress on children by putting them through tuition. However, it is natural for parents across socio-economic strata to want the best for their children. A holistic response to excessive competition in schools must go beyond curriculum and assessment reform to address occupational wage disparities and the fear of being unable to lead a comfortable life in a high-cost city. Possible labour market interventions will be discussed in Chapter 8.

Stepping Up Help for Disadvantaged Children

The key to preventing the emergence of a permanent underclass is to ensure that education is an uplifting force even for those from disadvantaged families. This remains the principal upstream means to address inequality, poverty, and social mobility.

The stepping-up of government support for preschool education is a major plank in this effort; the other is support for children from disadvantaged families, where the efforts of MOE dovetail with those of MSF and the network of Family Service Centres and community organisations.

KidSTART exemplifies the integrated approach in supporting children from lower-income families. It was launched in 2016 as a pilot programme to help children from low-income families have a good start in life. KidSTART supports parents with child development, coordinates and strengthens holistic support for families where needed, and monitors the developmental progress of children from birth such as through home visitations by health or social service professionals. The programme aims to build an ecosystem of support where multidisciplinary professionals and the community work together with parents to support the child's development in his immediate settings such as home and preschool, and respond to both the child's and family's needs. Following the pilot phase which supported some 1,000 children in selected neighbourhoods, the Early Childhood Development Agency announced in 2019 that KidSTART would be expanded to other parts of Singapore to reach another 5,000 children over the next three years.

The **MOE Financial Assistance Scheme (FAS)** is a fairly broad scheme that provides financial assistance to primary, secondary, and pre-university students from lower-income families. This includes full waiver of school and miscellaneous fees, free uniforms and textbooks, transport subsidies, and (for pre-university students) cash bursaries. Students may apply if their household income (gross or per capita) falls within the eligibility threshold. In 2018, FAS benefits were enhanced and the qualifying criteria relaxed, bringing the total number of eligible students to around 90,000.

The **Uplifting Pupils in Life and Inspiring Families Taskforce (UPLIFT)** was set up in 2018 to strengthen support for students from disadvantaged families. The UPLIFT scholarship provides a cash award to students from lower income families who are admitted into independent schools to help offset their out-of-pocket expenses so that students will not be deterred from applying to these schools.

Adopting a holistic approach that integrates support for children through the school system with community help for families is particularly important for children from dysfunctional or at-risk families. Notwithstanding the amount of time spent at school, the influence of family on a child's attitude towards school and life is often substantial. Children from families where one or both of their parents are incarcerated or absent may suffer from a lack of parental attention. Even where parents are present, poor parenting can lead to children imbibing unhelpful attitudes and values towards family, work, and spending. Social service agencies (SSAs) can fill the breach by providing after-school care, tuition, and mentoring programmes.

With every primary school equipped with a school-based student care centre (SCC) from 2020, the next step is to increase enrolment of students who could benefit from student care. Through UPLIFT, MOE is strengthening after-school care and support through SCCs in primary schools and after-school programmes in secondary schools, with plans to expand capacity and enrolment and partner the community to enhance programming. The ministry will set up an UPLIFT Programme Office for better coordination of community resources, including citizen volunteers, ethnic Self-Help Groups, and the MSF network of SSAs to strengthen support for disadvantaged students and families at the local level.

Preparing Students for the Future Economy

Impact of Technology and Global Competition on Future Jobs and Skills

In preparing the young for the future economy, two driving forces stand out: advances in technology and automation; and global competition.

A 2016 World Economic Forum Report on the Future of Jobs cited an estimate that 65% of children entering primary school would, in the future, find themselves working in new job types that did not presently exist.[24]

According to American economist David Autor, many routine "middle-skill" jobs in the US and developed countries have been made redundant by technology, with employment growth largely concentrated at the upper and lower ends of the skills distribution, a phenomenon known as "job polarisation".[25]

While artificial intelligence (AI) has caught up with and surpassed human beings in well-defined games such as chess and weiqi, it is still difficult to get robots to perform what is easy for a human being, such as navigating around a room and recognising common objects. Hence, lower-skill jobs such as cleaning are less at risk of being displaced by automation. At the other end of the skills spectrum, jobs that require creative, open-ended decision-making, such as running a company or crafting public policy, are also relatively secure. It is middle-skill, routine jobs such as bookkeeping that are thought to be most at risk from obsolescence.

In a seminal study, Carl Benedikt Frey and Michael Osborne (2013) concluded that as many as 47% of US jobs had at least a 70% probability of being taken over by machine learning or mobile robotics.[26] As a guide to the future, this picture is perhaps too pessimistic. Taking into account that occupations typically comprise a bundle of tasks, not all of which are easily automatable, another study by Melanie Arntz, Terry Gregory, and Ulrich Zierahn (2016) arrived at considerably more sanguine conclusions about the potential for technology to displace entire occupations.[27] For instance, they found that only 9% of US jobs were at risk instead of the 47% estimated by Frey and Osborne. Furthermore, labour-saving technologies could improve productivity and raise incomes, in turn spurring demand for labour.[28] Notwithstanding, technological advances and shortening tech cycles are expected to result in rapidly evolving job requirements, requiring frequent reskilling.

Technology aside, global competition may also drive down wages or put middle-skill jobs in Singapore at risk. This is especially if such jobs do not have to be physically located in Singapore.

The education system must therefore deliver on the following counts:

— Cultivating a **positive mindset towards learning** which students must carry through life
— Equipping students with **foundational concepts and skills** they can build on
— Developing students' curiosity and capacity for **creativity and innovation**

— Preparing students for a future where there is a premium on interpersonal ("**high touch**") skills over routine skills which may be rendered redundant by automation, and where nearly everyone will have to utilise technology ("**high tech**") in the course of their work
— Providing opportunities and support for **reskilling and continual learning** through life

We have already looked at the various efforts to promote the joy of learning and healthy learning attitudes in the section on education system reform earlier in this chapter.

Foundational Concepts and Skills

Given that the jobs of the future may require specific skills that are hard to anticipate today, it is all the more important to develop students' foundational concepts and skills in literacy, communications, numeracy, and reasoning as a base from which they can acquire specific skill sets subsequently.

Since the early days of Singapore's industrialisation, the government has made it a priority to equip Singaporeans with skills in demand by industry to optimise scarce manpower for economic growth. To assure multinational corporations that they would have access to a pool of manpower trained with skills relevant to industry, joint training institutes were set up with the help of the French, German, and Japanese governments in the late 1970s and early 1980s. For decades, there has been systematic manpower planning for current and future skills needs under the auspices of the National Manpower Council, which sets intake sizes for university, polytechnic, and ITE course clusters in consultation with economic agencies.

The utility of manpower planning, however, may be diminishing given how rapidly industry evolves and how quickly industry demands change. For instance, those trained in the life sciences or chemical engineering may find job opportunities limited in the event of industry downturns or structural shifts in demand. There is also attrition to contend with, as evinced by the large number of trained engineers taking up alternative jobs in public policy, business, and finance.

A reason to train more people in mathematics and science is that those well-versed in these domains find it easier to move into other fields, whereas it is harder for those trained in the humanities or social sciences to cross over to scientific or technical fields. This remains a compelling argument, particularly in the current context where Singapore needs to rebuild its traditional strengths in engineering both for future industry as well as for the maintenance of existing infrastructure.

The speed of product cycles and technological obsolescence reinforces the case for strong foundational skills and knowledge. A computer science student may find it worthwhile to learn the latest, most industry-relevant programming language to be job-ready, but she would still be vulnerable to changes in industry requirements unless she has a strong foundation in programming that makes it easier to pick up new languages.

There is no suggestion, however, that educators should eschew applied learning pedagogies in favour of traditional, abstract learning or academic-oriented pedagogies as foundational skills can also be imparted through applied learning.

Over the past decade, there has been a shift towards making learning more relevant through the introduction of project work and applied learning pedagogies. For instance, Republic Polytechnic, which began operating in 2003, introduced the problem-based learning approach in all its diploma programmes. More generally, polytechnic education, with its focus on applied learning, has been attracting increasing numbers of students who qualify for junior college. Since 2017, all secondary schools have offered **Applied Learning Programmes (ALPs)** that emphasise the application of thinking skills and connecting knowledge around subject disciplines. There are plans for all primary schools to establish ALPs by 2023.

It is well recognised that students have different learning styles. For many students, it is difficult to absorb abstract concepts in the absence of real-world applications. The shift in emphasis towards application-based learning has the potential to get more students engaged and also foster interdisciplinary thinking and solutioning.

As more applied learning routes, or curricula that are "closer to market", are opened up, it is worth remembering that applied learning is a means to an end. The end goal must be development of fundamental skill sets, for these are the skills most resilient to automation-induced obsolescence, and will enable young Singaporeans to capitalise most from the relentless advance of technology.

Creativity, Innovation, and Interdisciplinary Education

Nurturing innovation has long been a goal of curriculum and pedagogy. Opportunities for experiential learning throughout the curriculum allow students to situate and apply their knowledge and skills in real-world contexts, so that learning comes alive.

An annual **Innovation Programme** provides participating schools with a launch package comprising activities, videos, and lesson resources to introduce student to the concept of innovation. Students are given the opportunity to think critically about existing problems, generate possible solutions and develop prototypes to test their ideas. They are assigned innovation mentors from tertiary institutions and other organisations to guide them in this process. Selected innovation projects are showcased at the Young Innovators' Fair.

In 2011, **Yale-NUS College** was set up to provide the option of a liberal arts education in Singapore. Liberal arts provide a broad training of the mind in contrast to programmes that focus on deepening expertise in a particular area. Given the emphasis on skills deepening for job readiness today, the utility of a liberal education is sometimes questioned. At face value, subjects such as classics or philosophy do not appear to lend themselves readily to immediate application in the workplace. However, they expose students to different thought traditions and analytical rigour. It has been said that innovation often takes place at the intersection of disciplines, with exposure to a range of different subjects helpful in generating ideas and approaching problems from multiple angles. If creativity and the synthesis of ideas from different fields are among the greatest advantages people will have over machines, there will still be a place for liberal arts in the education landscape.

Even mainstream universities are heading in the direction of interdisciplinary education. NUS has merged its science faculty with the arts and social sciences faculty to form a new interdisciplinary college. From 2021, NTU undergraduates will go through a common core curriculum that will help them form connections across disciplines.

High Touch and High Tech — Interpersonal Skills, Asia-Readiness, and Digital Strategies

Even a typical university education — three or four years of full-time education at a residential college — may seem a rather costly and inefficient way of acquiring knowledge and skills. After all, in lieu of a finance or accountancy degree, one can acquire the requisite skills in finance or accountancy through the Chartered Financial Analyst programme or a chartered accountancy programme. Such professional programmes and qualifications are gaining currency in other fields as well.

Proponents of the traditional university model contend that a university education is not just about hard skills but also about soft skills picked up in the classroom, the opportunity to work collaboratively on projects, and the camaraderie and friendships forged in college.

Given that soft skills may be less easily replicated by machines and AI, there will in all likelihood continue to be demand for traditional university education. Perhaps the way learning is organised will be transformed and made more efficient, for example, through e-learning and video recordings of best-in-class instructors, supplemented by classroom sessions, so as to cut costs and speed up learning. The experience of e-learning and virtual meetings during the COVID-19 pandemic may add impetus to this.

The future will likely see a greater role for professional skills programmes as part of an increasingly diverse mix of programmes and pedagogies to suit different learning styles, different learning objectives, as well as differences in time and financial commitment across learners.

A key aspect of interpersonal engagement at work is being familiar with the culture and language of one's business associates, clients, or co-workers. With Southeast Asia one of the few bright spots in the world in terms of economic growth, it has been a priority to help

Singapore students better understand Asia, particularly Southeast Asia, so as to engage Singapore's Association of Southeast Asian Nations (ASEAN) neighbours and participate in the region's economic growth. Among the key recommendations of the 2010 Economic Strategies Committee was to anchor Singapore as a "Global-Asia hub". The 2017 Report of the Committee on the Future Economy affirmed the "strong market potential in many Asian markets" which Singapore is well-poised to tap.

An enhanced secondary and pre-university humanities curriculum, to be rolled out from 2021–2023, will have a deeper focus on ASEAN. MOE will also provide schools with planning and curriculum resources to help them design overseas learning experiences in ASEAN countries. More students will be given the opportunity to learn conversational Chinese or Malay, in addition to their own mother tongue languages.

Institutes of Higher Learning (IHL) already provide overseas exposure programmes such as trips, exchanges, and internships for about one in two students. In the past, students have tended to pick cities in Europe and North America for their exchange programmes and internships. However, in recent years, tertiary institutions have been encouraging students to explore internships within Asia and Southeast Asia. MOE has set a target for 70% of local IHL students to have the opportunity to participate in overseas exposure programmes, with 70% of these students gaining exposure in ASEAN, China, or India.

The future will also be digital. Digital technologies will become more pervasive, transforming sectors ranging from finance to manufacturing. Data will drive decision-making in business and government, requiring capabilities in data analytics and cybersecurity, among other data-related skills. While not every worker will need to be a programmer or data science expert, many more will be required to work with technology and data in the course of their work.

To give students a foundation in digital literacy, all primary students will participate in a "Code for Fun" enrichment programme from 2020. Beginning in 2023, some primary schools will offer ALPs in technology-related areas such as health science, robotics, and coding.

All secondary students will have their own personal learning device, which they can use in tandem with the Singapore Student Learning Space to personalise and enhance their learning. More schools will offer O-Level and A-Level computing subjects. The secondary mathematics and science curriculum will be updated to deepen computational thinking as well as help students acquire a better understanding of AI and emerging technologies. From 2020, all ITE students are required to take a module on the basics of AI in their first year of study.

Baseline digital competencies such as computational thinking, data analysis, and quantitative reasoning will be enhanced across IHLs, along with the deepening of digital competencies such as AI in selected courses such as in finance, manufacturing, and logistics.

While it is difficult, perhaps even futile, to try to predict the specific skills the labour market may demand in five to 10 years' time, there is good reason to believe that digital skills, an understanding of Asia, and the capacity to innovate will be important. The future economy, in all likelihood, will be high tech and high touch; many jobs will require people to work with technology and engage with people, even with automation taking over routine tasks performed by people today.

SkillsFuture: Towards a Culture of Lifelong Learning

Given rapidly advancing technology and the shortening of product cycles, what a person learns in school and university is unlikely to carry her through working life without a periodic renewal of skills and knowledge. Today, many more people expect to change career or vocation in the course of their lives compared with a generation ago. Not only will the proportion of company "lifers" decrease, those remaining in the same company will be expected to pick up new skills as job requirements change. The education system must respond to these driving forces to ensure that learning is supported through life.

Looking Back: Skills Renewal and the Paper Chase

Over the years, Singapore has built up a strong system of pre-employment training (PET), enabling Singapore students to excel in international tests of literacy and numeracy.

Likewise, Singapore laid the foundations for continuing education and training (CET) early. The Skills Development Fund (SDF) was set up in 1979 to support employee training, retrain retrenched workers, and upgrade business operations and technology. All employers contributed to the fund via a Skills Development Levy imposed by law. Programmes funded by the SDF included Basic Education for Skills Training (BEST), Work Improvement through Secondary Education (WISE), and Modular Skills Training (MOST), which helped workers with little or no formal education to attain basic proficiency in English, mathematics, and technical skills. These programmes were subsequently replaced by the Singapore Employability Skills System, a part of the Workforce Skills Qualifications (WSQ) system. Launched in 2005, WSQ is a CET system based on industry-agreed competency standards that provides training for skills upgrading as well as certification of workers' existing skills. WSQ courses are delivered by CET centres as well as approved training providers, with course fee subsidies for both employer-sponsored and self-sponsored trainees.

Yet between PET and CET, significantly more resources have been invested in PET. Given the critical importance of learning through life, a case has been building for a rebalancing towards CET. In fact, PET ought to blend into CET seamlessly given that learning must continue through life.

At the same time, there has been concern that an excessive focus on paper qualifications would fail to optimise outcomes for individuals as well as the economy. Like the Japanese, Koreans, and other Asians, Singaporeans have traditionally placed considerable emphasis on educational attainment. Putting a child through university is not only seen as a ticket to a good job and high income but is also a source of pride for many Singaporean families. This has been reinforced by a national narrative of academic upgrading where ITE students aspire to a polytechnic diploma, and diploma holders aspire to a university degree, all in the quest to build a better future for self and family.

Concerned about over-education and underemployment of graduates, the government has kept a tighter leash on the number of publicly funded university places in Singapore compared with countries like the UK or South Korea. Even so, the university cohort participation rate (i.e. the proportion of each cohort that can be accommodated in Singapore's publicly funded universities) has grown from 5% in 1980 to 26% in 2010, and exceeded the target of 40% in 2020.[29] This has been achieved not just through the expansion of places in existing universities but also through the creation of new institutions (the Singapore Institute of Technology or SIT and the Singapore University of Technology and Design or SUTD), and through the government funding of places in UniSIM, a private university which has been restructured and renamed the Singapore University of Social Sciences (SUSS). With six publicly funded universities, there are now places for nearly one in three polytechnic diploma holders from each cohort.

In fact, the proportion of polytechnic diploma holders obtaining a degree has been higher for some time now. Many have pursued private degrees through tie-ups between education providers in Singapore and foreign universities. Consequently, the proportion of degree holders among residents has jumped from 12% in 2000 to 33% in 2020 (Figure 7.2).

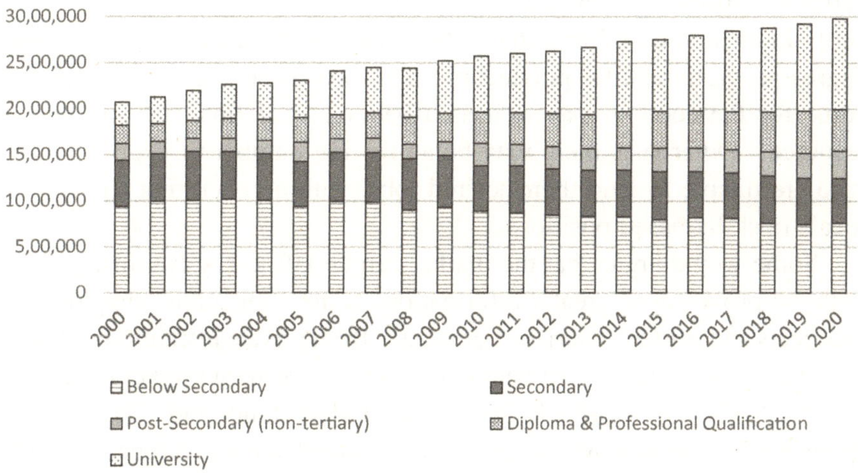

Figure 7.2 Singapore Residents Aged 25 and Over by Highest Qualification Attained

Source: Singapore Department of Statistics.

Although employers often differentiate between the degrees awarded by local universities and those awarded by universities of lower standing, the private university degree is still considered by many polytechnic students to be their ticket to a coveted management track position. Of further concern is that many are taking generic business or management degrees rather than choosing to deepen the skills they have acquired at polytechnic, such as engineering or technical skills. For those who do continue in their area of study, the rigour of the polytechnic education means that, more often than not, they derive limited further educational value from the degree-awarding private institution, which nonetheless charges them a hefty sum to convert their diploma into the all-important degree.

In sum, the paper chase may have become more of a costly signalling exercise rather than one that adds to knowledge or skills in a substantive way. Pursuing a private degree may still be a rational choice on the part of the student given that private degree holders, on average, earn higher starting salaries than polytechnic diploma holders without a degree, but this could merely reflect the role of a degree as a signal of ability, or even a lack of sophistication in recruitment practices. On the other hand, it is widely acknowledged that skills are the currency of the future; it would be better for polytechnic graduates to gain work experience and build deep skills in their area of training rather than jump straight into a private degree programme after polytechnic. This would be a more optimal outcome for the economy, as well as a better use of financial and human resources. Otherwise, there may be a growing number of degree holders who are unable to land their desired jobs, with a concurrent shortfall of locals in skills-based positions.

Some would argue that the market can be left to resolve this, perhaps with the provision of greater information on the comparative employment prospects and starting salaries of graduates from private institutions. Others, however, look to the government to correct the apparent market failure.

In 2013, the Applied Studies in Polytechnic and ITE Review (ASPIRE) committee was set up to recommend ways to strengthen pathways and opportunities for polytechnic and ITE students. Among other things, ASPIRE proposed ways to strengthen education and career guidance, enhance polytechnic and ITE education, and help students deepen their skills after entering the workforce. This generated considerable public interest, with the recommendations debated at length in Parliament.

Concurrently, a major review of CET was carried out under the CET 2020 Masterplan, with three areas of focus: to build deep expertise in the workforce, with employers playing a role in developing and recognising skills; to enable individuals to make informed learning and career choices; and to develop a vibrant CET ecosystem with high-quality training providers.

These workstreams would come together in a major revamp and rebranding of CET under the SkillsFuture movement.

Learning Through Life: The SkillsFuture Reboot

In a 2014 speech, then-DPM Tharman Shanmugaratnam introduced SkillsFuture as a "new phase in our development in education, and as a nation". The intent, he said, was to "build a first-rate system of continuing education and training" that will "intertwine education and the world of work in ways that strengthen and enrich both".[30]

From the outset, SkillsFuture was intended to encompass not just traditional CET but learning throughout life. Hence, it was elevated to a national movement whose target was all Singaporeans, whether schooling, working or retired. The movement needed a name that would stick in people's minds. SkillsFuture was selected to reflect the emphasis on building skills for the future.

The SkillsFuture Council, comprising tripartite representatives and chaired by then-DPM Tharman, was formed in November 2014. Subsequently, in Budget 2015, a suite of SkillsFuture initiatives was launched. This would increase government spending on CET from an average of $600 million per year in the five preceding years to an average of over $1 billion per year from 2015 to 2020. The key initiatives included:

— **Career counselling** in schools and IHLs
— **Enhanced internships** in IHLs with clear learning outcomes, better mentoring, and, where appropriate, extended internship duration
— **Individual Learning Portfolios**: an online education, training, and career guidance resource for each Singaporean from Primary 5 onwards (this has since become the MySkillsFuture portal)
— **SkillsFuture Credit**: an initial credit of $500 given to all Singaporeans aged 25 and above for a broad range of education and training courses supported by government agencies

— **SkillsFuture Earn and Learn Programme**: structured on-the-job training for polytechnic and ITE graduates leading to industry-recognised qualifications with government support for both trainees and employees
— **SkillsFuture Mid-Career Enhanced Subsidy** (90% course fee funding support) for Singaporeans aged 40 and above pursuing education/ training, in addition to multiple subsidies for modular courses for all Singaporeans regardless of age
— **SkillsFuture Study Awards and Fellowships** for building deep, industry-relevant skills and skills mastery
— **SkillsFuture Leadership Development Initiative**: collaboration with companies to develop a pipeline of Singaporeans to take on corporate leadership roles
— **Sectoral Manpower Plans**: collaboration among training institutions, unions, trade associations, and employers to develop manpower plans for all key sectors
— **SkillsFuture SME Mentors**: a pool of trained mentors with industry experience attached to SMEs to help them implement measures to deepen workforce skills and upgrade training capability.

Budget 2020 took stock of the progress of SkillsFuture five years on, introducing the "Next Bound of SkillFuture" with three themes to support Singaporeans in the workforce: enabling the individual, enhancing the role of enterprises in developing staff, and helping mid-career workers. These themes reflected the desire to focus the SkillsFuture movement on addressing the major concern of job readiness and relevance in a time of rapid change and restructuring, and particularly to enable skills refreshing and career transitions for mature mid-career Singaporeans who were vulnerable to job losses. A significant new initiative was launched — a $10,000 Enterprise Credit to encourage employers to embark on transforming both their business and their workforce.

Individual Learning Accounts and SkillsFuture Credit

Of the various SkillsFuture initiatives introduced in 2015, **SkillsFuture Credit** was not among the recommendations of ASPIRE or CET 2020, but the concept had been long discussed. Between 2008 and 2010, then-MPs Ahmad Magad, Penny Low, Halimah Yacob, Teo Ho Pin, and Ho Geok Choo mooted in Parliament various forms of the idea, whether called "individual learning accounts", "individual skills accounts", or "lifelong learning accounts", to empower Singaporeans to take control of their own learning and upgrading needs.

Individual learning accounts have been tried in various parts of the world, including the UK, Ireland, Italy, and the US. Of these, the UK's experiment with individual learning accounts from 2000–2002 is perhaps closest in form to SkillsFuture Credit. According to the UK's National Audit Office, the scheme was implemented too quickly without adequate planning: there was a lack of quality assurance for courses and a failure to monitor the escalating demand for accounts, resulting in budget overruns.[31] However, subsequent programmes in Scotland and Wales, which were targeted at the lower-income and less-educated, reported some success in increasing access to lifelong learning.[32]

While the increase in training participation arising from the introduction of individual learning accounts in some countries could be due to the paucity of prior training support, course fee subsidies were already high in Singapore prior to the launch of SkillsFuture Credit.

That said, a national movement like SkillsFuture required nothing less than a change in mindset and culture. A scheme such as SkillsFuture Credit, by empowering the individual to take responsibility for learning, was seen as a culture-building tool. The value of SkillsFuture credits in the first tranche amounted to some $1.3 billion, though actual utilisation in the initial years was much lower.

The challenge for such a broad-based scheme has been to ensure that the credit is utilised for high-quality, work-relevant programmes while minimising abuse and deadweight funding. In practice, it is difficult to distinguish between learning for interest and learning with a future job in mind. For instance, one could study a foreign language to boost employability, or simply for enjoyment and love of the culture. As all skills can potentially be built upon for future employability, it may not be practicable to try to weed out learning for personal interest from support under SkillsFuture Credit. Some expenditure of this nature may be unavoidable to achieve the broader goal of individual empowerment and shift in mindset towards learning through life.

In 2020, a one-off SkillsFuture Credit top-up was given to all Singapore citizens aged 25 and over, with the credit expiring in 2025. A further $500 credit was given to Singaporeans aged 40 to 60 to be used only for career transition programmes at CET centres. This was part of focused efforts to support mature mid-career workers under the "Next Bound of SkillsFuture" announced in Budget 2020.

From Apprenticeships to "Earn and Learn"

The **SkillsFuture Earn and Learn Programme (ELP)** is at the heart of what the movement hopes to address: the socially inefficient paper chase and, conversely, the need for skills deepening and mastery over time.

In decades past, when there were few places in university or even polytechnics, those leaving school with a general certificate in education would typically join companies and learn their trade on the job. After some years in employment, a number would seek educational upgrading through the government's BEST and WISE programmes or through part-time courses, whether self-funded or sponsored by their employers.

Over time, however, the expansion in the number of government-funded university and polytechnic places has facilitated immediate academic progression. ITE students with good results may enter polytechnics upon graduation, while more polytechnic graduates go straight on to university. Those unable to secure places in local universities may apply to any of a multitude of private degree programmes run by training providers through tie-ups with foreign universities. This has made immediate academic upgrading more attractive than joining the workforce upon leaving ITE or polytechnic.

The ELP aims to redress this by encouraging those fresh out of ITE and polytechnic to join a firm to gain income and work experience straightaway, while concurrently taking formal lessons in an institution of higher learning that could lead to an industry-relevant or industry-recognised degree. To give this a push, significant government support is available to both employers as well as their employees in the programme. A study by the Ministry of Trade and Industry (MTI) found that ELP graduates enjoyed a wage premium over polytechnic graduates, which stabilised at around 10% 19 months after ELP graduation.[33]

Since its introduction, the ELP has been rebranded as a **Work Study Programme**, and the work-study modality has been extended to cover diploma, post-diploma, and degree programmes. MOE has announced plans to grow Work-Study Programmes into a mainstream education pathway by 2025 with the number of places in such programmes expanding from 1,600 (about 3% of each cohort) in 2020 to 5,000 (12% of each cohort) in 2025.

Supporting Self-Sponsored and Employer-Sponsored Training

The SkillsFuture movement aims for a blend of self-directed training and employer-initiated training. The former encourages autonomy and self-responsibility for learning and is important for individuals who wish to consider job roles beyond their existing firm or sector. The latter requires companies to take responsibility for their workforce development. This would ensure that a sizeable portion of SkillsFuture expenditure is directed towards industry needs, and enhances workers' employability by keeping their skills job relevant.

Both self-sponsored and employer-sponsored training are supported via course fee funding of between 50% and 90% (depending on type of course, age of trainee, and whether PMET or non-PMET) for courses offered by SkillsFuture Singapore (SSG)-appointed CET centres and certifiable courses approved by SSG. Employers also receive an Absentee Payroll that offsets the cost of man-hours forgone due to training. They may also claim support for non-certifiable courses approved by SSG as well as approved in-house training, whether certifiable or otherwise.

Singapore citizens aged 40 and above are eligible for the **SkillsFuture Mid-Career Enhanced Subsidy** which provides higher course fee grants of up to 90%.

SMEs are eligible for the **Enhanced Training Support for SMEs** which provides higher course fee grants of up to 90% when they sponsor employees to attend courses supported by SSG. They may also claim Absentee Payroll funding of 80% of basic hourly salary (at a higher cap than for non-SMEs until end-2021).

The Next Bound of SkillsFuture introduced the employer counterpart to the SkillsFuture Credit for individuals — a one-off **SkillsFuture**

Enterprise Credit of $10,000 for employers to defray 90% of out-of-pocket costs (i.e. costs net of other business grants and SkillsFuture support) for business and workforce transformation inclusive of job redesign and skills training. Part of this sum is reserved for workforce transformation programmes to encourage employers to upgrade and develop their workers in tandem with business transformation.

Notwithstanding the panoply of training support schemes under SkillsFuture, the question is whether there needs to be an even greater push to encourage mid-career Singaporeans to make significant, periodic investments in skills. To make further progress may require considerably larger subsidies or incentives — whether to individuals or employers — to offset the opportunity cost of time away from work, but could pay dividends in terms of a more highly skilled and productive workforce.

Mindset Shift: "A Meritocracy of Skills, Not a Hierarchy of Grades"

SkillsFuture is not intended to dissuade Singaporeans from the pursuit of graduate or postgraduate qualifications. Its message is that people should not chase qualifications for the sake of qualifications; for someone who has spent some years in industry, a relevant degree or higher qualification may be a natural step for skills deepening in his chosen area, and this is not inconsistent with the aims of the Work-Study Programmes.

More fundamentally, SkillsFuture recognises that education must not stop early in life and that it should not be a mere exercise in signalling intellect or ability. While more pathways have been introduced in the schooling years to enable those taking the technical education route to advance to university, obtaining a good honours degree ought not to define success in life. It would be detrimental to workplace motivation, sense of fairness, and upward mobility if one's lot in life were fixed by one's class of degree or grades obtained in school. As then-DPM Tharman put it in the 2015 Budget speech, "Singapore must become a meritocracy of skills, not a hierarchy of grades earned early in life."[34] In short, there must be multiple pathways to career and personal success, and opportunities for late bloomers who take a more circuitous path to success.

For this vision to be realised, employers have a critical role to play. Much depends on the extent to which recruitment decisions are based on academic qualifications, and whether it is possible for someone without a university degree to progress to the most senior roles within an organisation. Skills-based hiring and career development are facilitated by sectoral **Skills Frameworks**, which have been developed by tripartite stakeholders to provide a common skills language for individuals, employers, and training providers. The Public Service, as the largest employer in Singapore, can help to shape norms through its own recruitment and promotion practices. For the information and communications technology sector, the government has launched a "TechSkills Accelerator" initiative that works with anchor employers to commit to hiring based on certified skills proficiency rather than academic qualifications alone.

A robust and responsive education system from childhood into adulthood is foundational for the Singapore socio-economic system, centred as it is around individual self-reliance through employment. The renewed focus on support for early childhood education and SkillsFuture through the working years is vital to sustain employment, keep incomes growing, mitigate inequality, and provide for continued social mobility.

Endnotes

1. Heng Swee Keat, Budget Debate Round-Up Speech, 2019.
2. Indranee Rajah, "Helping All Succeed Regardless of Background," *Straits Times*, 25 March 2019.
3. Andreas Schleicher, *PISA 2018: Insights and Interpretations* (OECD, 2019). In 2018, Singapore students also performed best among 27 countries in PISA's assessment of "global competence" — the ability to examine significant issues, appreciate other perspectives, engage in effective interactions across cultures, and take action for collective well-being and sustainable development.
4. Organisation for Economic Co-operation and Development (OECD), *PISA 2018 Results (Volume II): Where All Students Can Succeed* (OECD, 2019). Data cited in Jolene Ang, "Pisa 2018: Students from Lower-Income Homes in Singapore Do Better than Students Overseas," *Straits Times*, 3 November 2019.

5. Figures cited by then-Minister for Education Ng Eng Hen, reported in Reico Wong, "Why Education is Key Leveller in Singapore," *mypaper*, 8 March 2011.
6. Lawrence J. Schweinhart and David P. Weikart, "Why Curriculum Matters in Early Childhood Education," *Educational Leadership* 55(6) (1998): 57–60; Donald B. Bailey, "Are Critical Periods Critical for Early Childhood Education? The Role of Timing in Early Childhood Pedagogy," *Early Childhood Research Quarterly* 17(3) (2002): 281–294. See also Kathy Sylva, Edward Melhuish, Pam Sammons, Iram Siraj-Blatchford, and Brenda Taggart, *Early Childhood Matters: Evidence from the Effective Pre-school and Primary Education Project* (London: Routledge, 2010).
7. Lynn A. Karoly and James H. Bigelow, *The Economics of Investing in Universal Preschool Education in California* (Santa Monica: RAND Corporation, 2005).
8. "The Big Read: Educators Flag Absentee Rates of Children of Low-Income Families as a Concern," *TODAY*, 1 August 2015.
9. National Institute of Education, "Presentation to the International Congress for School Effectiveness and Improvement on Singapore's Education System," 10 January 2017, https://nie.edu.sg/docs/default-source/oer/presentation-to-icsei-on-singapore-39-s-education-system5e0005ffdeb0605693ab4b9265f5641c.pdf?sfvrsn=cbb065b5_0. See also OECD Country Note on Singapore, https://www.oecd.org/pisa/PISA-2015-singapore.pdf.
10. Loh Chee Kong, "Pragmatic Parting Advice from Tharman," *TODAY*, 31 March 2008.
11. Jolene Ang, "Survey: Kids More Anxious about Exams than Covid-19," *Straits Times*, 19 September 2020.
12. Based on data from the Household Expenditure Survey 2017/18.
13. Ong Ye Kung, speech at the Schools Work Plan Seminar, 28 September 2018.
14. Ibid.
15. OCBC Group, "More than 7,000 Staff Benefit from New Three-Month Career Break and PSLE Leave Schemes," press release, 22 October 2012, https://www.ocbc.com/group/media/release/2012/hr-3-months-career-break-and-psle-leave.html.
16. Peter Heng Teck Wee, "Time to Reconsider Whether PSLE Serves Singapore's Goals," *Straits Times* forum letter, 4 May 2021.
17. Sandra Davie, "One in Four Thinks PSLE Is Redundant," *Straits Times*, 21 April 2014.
18. Ludger Wößmann, "International Evidence on School Tracking: A Review," ifo Institute — Leibniz Institute for Economic Research at the University of Munich *ifo DICE Report*, 7(1) (2009): 26–34.

19. Tuomas Pekkarinen, Roope Uusitalo, and Sari Kerr, "School Tracking and Intergenerational Income Mobility: Evidence from the Finnish Comprehensive School Reform," *Journal of Public Economics* 93(7–8) (2009): 965–973.
20. Irene Y. H. Ng and Hyekyung Choo, "Parental Education and Youth Educational Aspiration in Singapore: A Path Analysis in Institutional and Psychological Context," *Asia Pacific Journal of Education* (2021) 41(1): 55–69.
21. Irene Y. H. Ng and Nursila Senin, "Educational Pathways, Youth Wellbeing and Outlook," in National Youth Council, *YOUTH.sg: The State of Youth in Singapore 2018* (2018), 72–91.
22. Chua Mui Hoong, "A Place for Exams as Social Leveller," *Straits Times*, 30 September 2012.
23. Phoebe Zhang, "Class Debate in China over High-Achieving 'Left-Behind Child' Who Chooses to Study Archaeology at University," *South China Morning Post*, 4 August 2020.
24. World Economic Forum, *The Future of Jobs: Employment, Skills and Workforce Strategy for the Fourth Industrial Revolution*. (WEF, January 2016), http://www3.weforum.org/docs/WEF_Future_of_Jobs.pdf.
25. David H. Autor and David Dorn, "The Growth of Low-Skill Service Jobs and the Polarization of the US Labor Market," *American Economic Review* 103(5) (2013): 1553–1597.
26. Carl Benedikt Frey and Michael A. Osborne, "The Future of Employment: How Susceptible Are Jobs to Computerisation?" *Technological Forecasting and Social Change* 114 (2017): 254–280.
27. Melanie Arntz, Terry Gregory, and Ulrich Zierahn, "The Risk of Automation for Jobs in OECD Countries: A Comparative Analysis," OECD Social, Employment and Migration Working Paper No. 189, 2016.
28. See, for example, Georg Graetz and Guy Michaels, "Robots at Work," *Review of Economics and Statistics* 100(5) (2018): 753–768.
29. In view of the COVID-19 pandemic in 2020, the local universities offered additional places to students, pushing the cohort participation rate to 42%.
30. Tharman Shanmugaratnam, speech at the official opening of the Lifelong Learning Institute, 17 September 2014, https://www.mof.gov.sg/newsroom/speeches/Speech-by-Mr-Tharman-Shanmugaratnam-Deputy-Prime-Minister-and-Minister-for-Finance-at-the-Official-Opening-of-the-Lifelong-Learning-Institute.
31. National Audit Office, *Individual Learning Accounts*, Report by the Comptroller and Auditor General, HC 1235 Session 2001–2002, 25 October 2002.

32. Hazel Rutherford, "ILA Scotland: Practical Case Study of Demand-Led Funding for Adult Learning," and Simon Gugh, "Individual Learning Accounts in Wales," in European Centre for the Development of Vocational Training (Cedefop), *Individual Learning Accounts*, Cedefop Panorama Series 163 (Luxembourg: Office for Official Publications of the European Communities, 2009), 44–51.
33. Afiqah Suhaiemi and Ong Swee Joo, "Evaluation of the SkillsFuture Earn and Learn Programme (ELP), *Quarterly Economic Survey of Singapore Second Quarter 2019* (2019), 40–48.
34. Tharman Shanmugaratnam, Budget Statement, 2015.

Chapter 8

Regulating the Labour Market

The labour market is a key upstream driver of income security, income growth, and inequality, as evident in the Socio-Economic Flowchart (Figure 1.3). The better the outcomes from the labour market, such as employment stability and income growth across workforce segments, the less the need for downstream intervention through social support and redistribution.

Business-friendly employment laws and industrial harmony, along with ready access to skilled manpower, both local and foreign, have made Singapore an attractive location for investment and business. This has helped to keep Singapore's unemployment rates consistently low over the years (Figures 2.4, 2.5), and provided the foundation for real income growth.

In the Singapore System, full employment is the principal guarantor of social security, with Central Provident Fund (CPF) accumulation and home ownership dependent on continuous, stable employment.

However, the assumptions that underpin this model are being tested. Structural unemployment is emerging as a concern with technology, automation, and economic transformation rendering a number of job roles redundant. The future may bring heightened volatility in employment and incomes as business cycles shorten and contingent work arrangements become more prevalent. In addition, the forces of global competition are threatening to widen occupational wage dispersion and income inequality while fuelling concerns over income and retirement adequacy.

These have translated into four priorities for the government over the past decade:

- — Calibrating foreign worker inflow to support economic growth while managing job competition with locals
- — Raising the wages of lower-income workers
- — Extending "productive longevity" by helping older workers to remain employed
- — Facilitating employment and career transition

This chapter will examine each of these in turn. To achieve these objectives, the government has employed four principal sets of manpower policy levers:

- — Foreign workforce policy
- — Employment laws and tripartite guidelines/advisories
- — Financial incentives and public recognition
- — Employment facilitation (job search assistance, reskilling, and hiring incentives)

Foreign workforce policy has an outsized impact on labour market outcomes in Singapore since foreign workers comprise around a third of the workforce. The relative ease of hiring foreign workers, whether higher-skilled or lower-skilled, contributes to Singapore's economic competitiveness and attractiveness to foreign investment. However, the inflow of foreign workers must be calibrated to safeguard employment outcomes for locals. Given many firms' heavy reliance on foreign manpower, foreign workforce policy gives the government an effective administrative lever to influence firm behaviour beyond what the law provides for.

Employment laws determine the flexibility of the labour market as well as employment protection for workers. The Employment Act gives employers the freedom to hire and fire workers while giving workers recourse to the Ministry of Manpower (MOM) in cases of unfair dismissal. Retirement and re-employment laws have enabled older workers to stay longer in employment if they wish to, increasing the labour supply while boosting retirement adequacy as life expectancy increases.

Tripartite guidelines, based on mutually agreed positions among the government, the Singapore National Employers' Federation, and the

National Trades Union Congress, supplement the law. MOM can act against firms that do not comply with these guidelines. **Tripartite advisories** outline progressive workplace practices but are non-mandatory. The National Wages Council (described later in this chapter) issues wage guidelines that guide wage bargaining for unionised firms and serve as a benchmark for non-unionised firms.

Wage offsets are provided to encourage the employment of seniors and disabled persons. The government has also encouraged firms to raise workers' pay in line with productivity growth by co-funding wage increases for Singaporean employees from 2013 to 2020. **Tripartite standards** help employers with good practices to distinguish themselves from their competitors.

Employment facilitation, delivered through a range of career services and support programmes (inclusive of job matching, reskilling, and wage subsidies), is vitally important in a system that is premised on getting displaced workers back into employment as quickly as possible.

Labour market interventions ought to be considered in conjunction with fiscal transfers and social support in addressing the key challenges of income growth, income security, and inequality.

Tripartism

Any discussion of Singapore's labour market would be incomplete without a mention of "tripartism", the secret sauce behind Singapore's harmonious industrial relations.[1] This refers to the institutionalised collaboration among the government, trade unions, and employers (known as tripartite partners) in addressing a wide range of labour issues such as the wage system, workforce training, job redesign, and fair employment practices.

The trust built up among tripartite partners has facilitated wage moderation during economic downturns to preserve jobs, the sharing of gains when economic growth is strong, as well as commitment on the part of both employers and workers to invest in training to raise productivity.

Before introducing major manpower legislation, MOM typically convenes a tripartite committee to study the issues so as to take in the views of employers and unions and work out a consensus. Examples include the Tripartite Committee on Employability of Older Workers (set up in 2005), the Tripartite Committee for Low Wage Workers and Inclusive Growth (2007), and the Tripartite Committee on Work-Life Strategy (2000).

Tripartite organisations include the Tripartite Alliance for Fair and Progressive Employment Practices, the Tripartite Alliance for Dispute Management, and the Workplace Safety and Health Council.

Calibrating Foreign Worker Inflow

Role of the Foreign Workforce

To understand Singapore's labour market and its part in Singapore's socio-economic system, it is vital to have an appreciation of the size and role of the foreign workforce here.

As at December 2019, prior to the COVID-19 outbreak, Singapore's foreign workforce stood at 1.43 million, or about 38% of the employed workforce. Excluding the 260,000 foreign domestic workers (FDWs), there were about 1.17 million foreign workers, or about 33% of the employed workforce less FDWs.

By comparison, Australia and Switzerland have a foreign-born population share close to 30%, the highest among OECD economies;[2] the percentage of foreign nationals in the employed workforce in these countries is likely to be lower. However, cosmopolitan cities may have a higher foreign-born population. For instance, 36.7% of London's population in 2011 was foreign-born.[3] The Gulf states also have a higher estimated share of foreigners in the employed population, ranging from 57%–95% in 2015.[4]

Singapore's foreign workers span the skills spectrum in three major pass types:

- **Work Permit holders** (lower-skilled), no minimum salary
- **S Pass holders** (mid-skilled), incomes $2,500 and above at the time of writing in 2021
- **Employment Pass holders** (higher-skilled), incomes $4,500 and above ($5,000 and above for financial services sector)

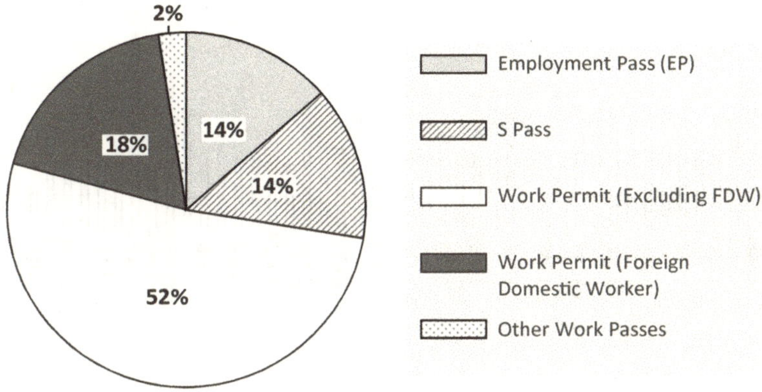

Figure 8.1 Breakdown of Foreign Workforce (as of December 2019)
Source: Ministry of Manpower.

Each group plays a major role in Singapore's economy.

— Work Permit holders perform many essential jobs that not enough Singaporeans wish to take up in areas such as construction, marine shipyard and process industries, along with general manufacturing and a range of services sectors
— S Pass holders fill numerous roles across the manufacturing and services sectors, including retail and food and beverage
— Employment Pass holders take up a range of skilled jobs, especially in services sectors such as finance and information and communications technology (ICT)

Collectively, foreign workers enable a significantly larger and more diversified economy than would be otherwise possible. This adds to Singapore's economic heft, as well as resilience through economic diversification, which also increases the variety of jobs available here.

Work pass holders do not have an automatic path to permanent residence or citizenship in Singapore, unlike in some countries. With the exception of a small number of Personalised Employment Pass holders, all other foreign workers may only remain in Singapore if they are employed. Hence, citizen and resident unemployment rates are always higher than the overall unemployment rate in Singapore.

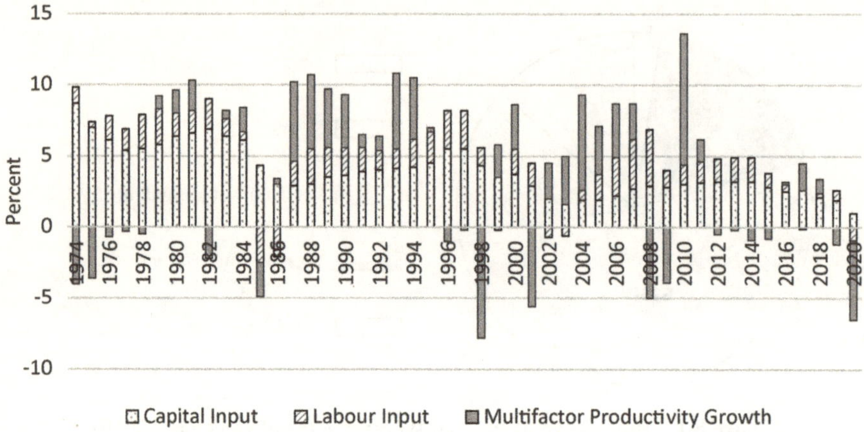

Figure 8.2 Breakdown of Real GDP Growth

Source: Singapore Department of Statistics.

In the 1990s and 2000s, foreign worker growth contributed to nearly half of Singapore's total workforce growth, which in turn contributed significantly to Singapore's GDP growth (Figure 8.2).

The foreign workforce is intended to complement the local workforce by filling shortfalls in numbers, skills, or availability — "the number gap, skills gap and timing gap", in the words of former Minister for Manpower Lim Swee Say.[5] They may serve as a buffer during economic downturns if they are first in line to be shed from companies that need to downsize. This has appeared to be the case in the downturns in 2001–2003, 2009, and 2020, when foreign manpower declined while local employment continued to grow (Figure 8.3).

In practice, foreign workers also compete with Singaporeans for jobs at all skill levels, even if collectively they increase the net demand for local workers by enabling increased economic activity. The steady growth in the share of professionals, managers, executives, and technicians (PMETs) in the local workforce has accentuated competition with Employment Pass holders, particularly in sectors such as ICT and finance where foreigners occupy many well-paying jobs. Foreign manpower has been a contentious issue in successive elections especially since 2011. It was again in focus in the run-up to the 2020 general election with

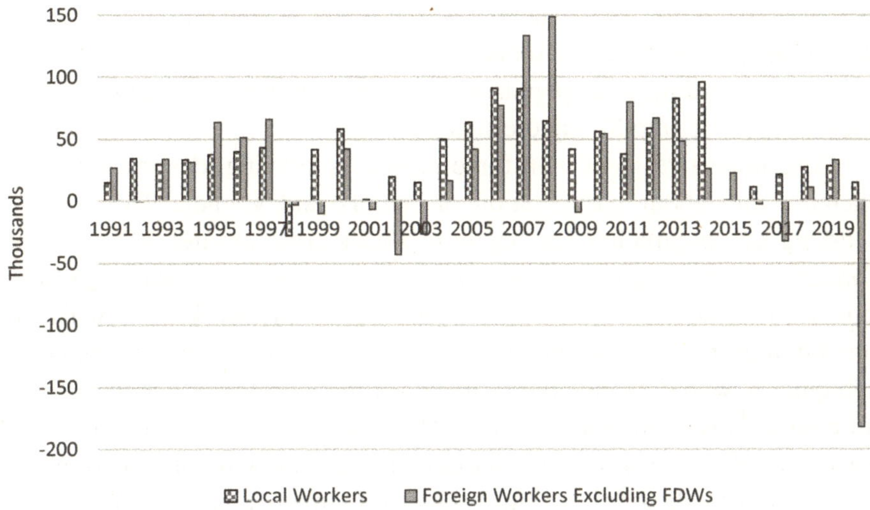

Figure 8.3 Local and Foreign Workforce Growth

Source: Manpower Research and Statistics Department, MOM.

detractors taking aim, in particular, at the India-Singapore Comprehensive Economic Cooperation Agreement (CECA), which facilitates skilled manpower flow between Singapore and India.

Growth of the Foreign Workforce and Its Impact

Looking over the past three decades, foreign employment growth has, on average, kept pace with local employment growth, keeping the foreign share of employment largely unchanged since 1991 (Figure 8.3). Foreign employment growth exceeded local employment growth in the late 2000s while it fell below local employment growth in the early 2000s and from 2013 onwards.

A key priority for the government is to calibrate the growth and quality of the foreign workforce, for several reasons.

The influx of foreign workers over the past two decades, particularly between 2006 and 2012, contributed to Singapore's population growth exceeding infrastructure capacity, leading to crowding in trains, which was an issue in the 2011 general election. Besides land and infrastructure constraints, there is also a social acceptability constraint given citizens' concerns regarding total population size, the number of foreigners, and their integration into Singapore society.

Singapore's resident workforce growth is slowing, despite efforts to increase the labour participation of seniors and women. The resident working age population has begun to shrink from around 2020.[6] While foreign workforce growth could help to offset slowing local workforce growth, it would increase the foreign share of the workforce, which is already high by international standards. Diluting the "Singaporean core" too quickly would change the character of the workforce, which may not sit comfortably with many citizens. There is also the risk of overdependence on foreign workers, particularly in sectors with high nationality concentration. The border controls erected by many countries in response to COVID-19 underscore the risks of foreign worker reliance.

The quality of the foreign workforce is also of concern. Low-wage, low-skilled foreign workers are thought to depress productivity and wages in sectors such as construction and domestic services. Reliance on such workers hampers adoption of automation and technology, resulting in weak productivity growth. At the same time, the ready supply of low-wage foreigners tends to hold back job redesign and wage growth in a number of sectors and job roles, resulting in a large occupational wage disparity between high- and low-skilled occupations (Table 8.1). For instance, the median gross monthly income of clerical support workers in Singapore is about 30% of that of the top-earning group, managers, and administrators, and about 65% of the median gross monthly income of all workers. In the UK, those in the equivalent group (administrative and secretarial occupations) earn about 52% of those in the top-earning managers, directors, and senior officials group, and about 77% of the median gross annual earnings of all workers.

At the S Pass level, mid-skilled foreign workers compete with local polytechnic and Institute of Technical Education (ITE) graduates for jobs, some in services sectors such as hospitality and food services that have greater potential to attract locals.

At the Employment Pass (EP) level, the competition is with local university graduates as well as mid-career or mature PMETs. In finance

Table 8.1 Relative Pay of Major Occupation Groups in Singapore and UK (2019)

Singapore	**Median Gross Monthly Income (SGD)***	**% of Top Occupation (% of All)**	**United Kingdom**	**Median Gross Monthly Earnings (GBP)****	**% of Top Occupation (% of All)**
All	4,563		All	2,532	
Managers & Administrators (including working proprietors)	9.961	100 (218)	Managers, directors & senior officials	3,731	100 (147)
Professionals	7,069	71 (155)	Professional occupations	3,284	88 (124)
Associate Professionals & Technicians	4,437	45 (97)	Associate professional & technical occupations	2,756	74 (109)
Craftsmen & Related Trades Workers	3,042	31 (67)	Skilled trades occupations	2,356	63 (93)
Clerical Support Workers	**2,979**	**30 (65)**	**Administrative & secretarial occupations**	1,957	**52 (77)**
Service & Sales Workers	2,535	25 (56)	Sales and customer svc occupations	1,701	46 (67)
			Caring, leisure & other svc occupations	1,616	43 (64)
Plant & Machine Operators & Assemblers	2,310	23 (51)	Process, plant & machine operatives	2,145	57 (85)
Cleaners, Labourers & Related Workers	1,582	16 (35)	Elementary occupations	1,713	46 (68)

*Full-time employed residents (income includes employer CPF)

**Full-time employees

Sources: Occupational Wage Survey, Manpower Research and Statistics Department, MOM (Singapore); Annual Survey of Hours and Earnings, Office for National Statistics (UK).

and ICT, where the concentration of foreigners is high, there have been complaints about discrimination against locals both in hiring as well as promotion to senior positions. Some believe that foreigners here are not necessarily more qualified than locals or possess skills that locals lack, and that they may not understand the local context well. Foreign executives, it has been said, prefer to hire people from their own country rather than Singaporeans. Foreign manpower and unfair employment practices received a thorough airing in the debate on the President's Address at the opening of the 14th Parliament in 2020.

Foreign Workforce Policy Levers

The government does not directly set limits on the number of work passes granted but calibrates the inflow of foreign workers through the following levers:

- **Minimum salary requirements**
- **Foreign worker levies**
- **Dependency ratio ceilings** (DRCs) (maximum proportion of S Pass and Work Permit holders a company can employ)

In addition, there are **source controls** for Work Permit holders which specify which countries they may come from, depending on sector. This is intended to avoid the undercutting of locals by workers from low-income countries.

The minimum salary requirements for EP and S Pass holders take into account the worker's age and qualifications, with older, more experienced workers required to have a higher salary (at approximately twice the

Table 8.2 Work Pass Controls

	Minimum Salary	Levies	DRC	Source Control
Employment Pass	Yes	No	No	No
S Pass	Yes	Yes	Yes	No
Work Permit	No	Yes	Yes	Yes

minimum). These salary thresholds are periodically updated as local salaries grow so that locals are not priced out of jobs. In particular, the salary requirement is the only lever to control EP inflow, although firms that have a workforce profile skewed towards foreigners and are suspected of discriminatory hiring may be put on the Fair Consideration Framework Watchlist for closer scrutiny.

Foreign worker levies are used to calibrate the cost of hiring Work Permit and S Pass holders so that local workers are not unduly disadvantaged due to cost, especially in view that employers have to make CPF contributions for local workers. The levies range from a few hundred dollars to nearly a thousand dollars depending on the sector, the skills profile of the workers, and the proportion of work pass holders hired by the firm. Levies are also reviewed and raised periodically.

The DRCs are not absolute numerical caps but refer to the maximum ratio of Work Permit and S Pass holders to total workforce (less EP holders) that a company in a particular sector may hire. As at 2021, they range from 35% for the services sector to 87.5% for the construction and process sectors. There is a sub-DRC for S Pass holders, which is a subset of the overall DRC. The DRCs have been periodically tightened, forcing firms that are at the DRC to hire more locals or shed work pass holders. The DRCs also cap the ability of other firms to take in new Work Permit or S Pass holders.

The **Local Qualifying Salary** (LQS; previously known as the full-time equivalent salary) determines the number of local workers that can be used to calculate an employer's DRC entitlement. This is to ensure that locals are employed meaningfully rather than on token salaries just to allow the employer access to foreign workers. The LQS is revised periodically and is $1,400 as at 2021. This means that a local employee earning at least $1,400 a month is deemed as one local headcount for the purpose of DRC computation while a local employee earning between $700 to below $1,400 is deemed as half a headcount.

For the construction sector, which employs about 300,000 Work Permit holders, there is an additional lever called the **man-year entitlement** which is based on the value of the construction project. Firms which hire above their man-year entitlement are subjected to higher Work Permit levies of up to $950 a month.

Some have questioned the need for both foreign worker levies and DRCs — price and quantity controls — to calibrate Work Permit and S Pass numbers. DRCs give more certainty over the maximum number of foreigners who can come in compared with levies whose effectiveness depends on the elasticities of demand and supply of foreign workers. However, as many firms are not yet at their dependency ceilings, removing the price lever could result in a potential surge in foreign worker numbers. An alternative to levies would be to set a minimum wage for Work Permit holders. However, this would amount to a significant transfer from the government to Work Permit holders and is unlikely to be considered in the absence of a general minimum wage for both local and foreign workers.

Given the strong demand for Work Permit and S Pass holders, the DRCs help to boost hiring demand for locals, including seniors and marginal workers, keeping the labour market tight. The low unemployment rate in Singapore over many years may owe much to the DRCs, in addition to robust job creation, skills training, and lack of statutory unemployment benefits.

The many firms that hire Work Permit and S Pass holders have a strong incentive to keep local worker salaries at or above the LQS, which thus serves as an effective wage floor for local workers.

Looking Back: Foreign Workforce Tightening Measures Since 2010

The rapid growth in population in the second half of the 2000s (Figure 8.4) posed several difficulties for Singapore, which became evident on hindsight. First, investment in public infrastructure had not kept pace with population growth, resulting in overcrowded trains and an undersupply of housing. Second, ready access to low-skilled foreign workers blunted the impetus for investment in capital and productivity. Finally, the sheer growth in foreign workers numbers was unsustainable from the standpoint of population planning and social acceptability. These made necessary a sharp deceleration in foreign worker growth post-2010.

That said, it is important to remember the context in the mid-2000s. The economy had been in the doldrums for the first half of the decade

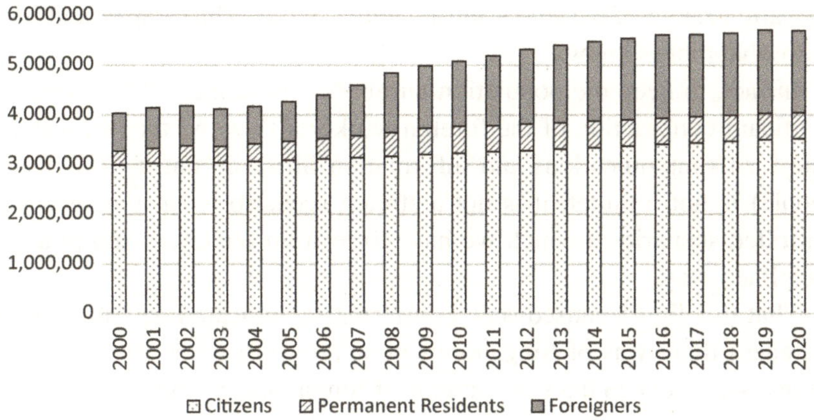

Figure 8.4 Singapore's Population

Source: Singapore Department of Statistics.

following the bursting of the dot-com bubble, the downturn in the global electronics cycle, and SARS. With the pickup in external demand from 2005, the government was keen to allow firms the manpower they needed to nurture the first green shoots of growth. The influx of foreigners, whose numbers increased by 57% in the four years between 2005 and 2009, did not lead to a rise in resident unemployment, which was in fact significantly lower between 2006 and 2010 (barring the recession in 2009) compared with 2001–2005 (Figure 2.4). Household incomes, including those of lower-income households, grew faster over the second half of the 2000s compared with the first half of the decade.

It became clear, however, that the growth in population could not be sustained at these rates. If the total population had been allowed to expand from 2009 at the same rate as it had in the preceding four years (4.0% in compound annual terms), it would have reached a whopping 11.3 million by 2030.

The Population White Paper released in 2013 was an attempt to rein in foreign workforce growth and draw out the implications of constrained population growth on Singapore's economy and society. Many Singaporeans were, however, taken aback by the potential 2030 population range of 6.5 to 6.9 million cited in the White Paper, and made their unhappiness known.

In fact, to keep the population within 6.9 million by 2030 required a significant constriction of the foreign worker inflow. As then-Minister of State for Communications and Information Sim Ann put it, "6.9 million (people) is not a target, it is not a stretch scenario — it is a very, very controlled scenario in which we have to restrain ourselves and in a very disciplined way."[7]

That this figure caused such consternation indicated how little public awareness there was of Singapore's population trajectory and how large the gap was between the expectations of Singaporeans and the actual situation. Subsequently, the government clarified that 6.9 million was a planning parameter and that the 2030 population was expected to come in below this figure.

The turning point for labour force policy had come a few years earlier with the release of the 2010 Economic Strategies Committee (ESC) report. The ESC recognised that Singapore's population could not continue expanding at previous rates and that ultimately, economic growth had to be powered by productivity. Of the 3%–5% real growth per annum envisaged by the ESC over the decade, the aim was for productivity growth to contribute 2–3 percentage points and labour force growth 1–2 percentage points.

2010 marked the beginning of measures to tighten the inflow of foreign workers. Work Permit levies were increased every year from July 2010 to July 2013 and Work Permit DRCs were cut yearly between 2012 and 2015. Likewise, beginning in 2011, S Pass levies were raised, DRCs cut, and qualifying income thresholds raised. For the construction sector, the man-year entitlements were reduced by 45% between 2010 and 2013. The qualifying income threshold for EP was repeatedly raised beginning in January 2011.

The tightening measures were phased in gradually to give firms time to adjust. Given the robust demand for labour, foreign worker inflow continued to be strong. In fact, the net increase in foreign workers (excluding foreign domestic workers) rose from 54,400 in 2010 to 79,800 in 2011 before tapering to 67,100 in 2012, 48,400 in 2013, and finally 26,000 in 2014.

For many firms, DRC constraints did not bite immediately as they were able to employ more local workers, including many older workers, which allowed them to hire correspondingly more foreign workers. Nonetheless, manpower availability and cost were among the top business concerns in annual surveys conducted during this period.

Restructuring and Transition Support (2013–2015)

The government recognised that it would take time for firms to restructure by lowering reliance on foreign manpower and concurrently raising labour productivity. To help firms make the transition, a three-year, $5.35 billion Transition Support Package was introduced in Budget 2013, comprising (i) a 30% corporate income tax rebate capped at $30,000 per annum, (ii) a Productivity and Innovation Credit (PIC) Bonus providing matching funding for investments in productivity under the PIC scheme (this was intended to encourage take-up of the PIC), and (iii) the Wage Credit Scheme (WCS) where the government would co-fund 40% of qualifying wage increases for Singaporean employees of firms.

The WCS was by far the largest component of the Transition Support Package and eventually disbursed to employers a total of $3.9 billion for wage increases given from FY2013 to FY2015. The premise of the WCS was that wages would climb as the inflow of foreign workers slowed and the labour market tightened. The WCS would help firms cope with rising wages, allowing them to "free up resources to invest in productivity, and share their productivity gains with their employees".[8] This support would only be provided for Singaporean employees, thus further driving a wedge between the attractiveness of employing foreigners and citizens. WCS was extended to 2020, but with co-funding support tapered.

Further Calibration (2016–2020)

Since 2016, numerous steps have been taken to further contain the foreign worker inflow (Table 8.3).

These measures have helped moderate the growth in foreign workforce. The number of EP and S Pass holders grew by fewer than 9,000 a year on average between 2014 and 2019, down from a yearly average of

Table 8.3 Foreign Workforce Measures Since 2016

	EP	S Pass	Work Permit	Local Qualifying Salary
2016		S Pass levies (all sectors) raised from 1 July 2016	— Services and construction basic-skilled levies raised from 1 July 2016 — Marine shipyard DRC reduced from 1:5 to 1:4.5 from 1 January 2016	
2017	Minimum salary raised to $3,600 from 1 January 2017		Construction basic-skilled levies raised from 1 July 2017	LQS raised from $1,000 to $1,100 from 1 July 2017
2018	—		Marine shipyard DRC reduced from 1:4.5 (81.8%) to 1:3.5 (77.8%) from 1 January 2018	LQS raised to $1,200 from 1 July 2018
2019	—	Minimum salary raised to $2,300 from 1 January 2019		LQS raised to $1,300 from 1 July 2019
2020 and beyond	Minimum salary raised to $3,900 from 1 May 2020, and further raised to $4,500 from 1 September 2020 ($5,000 for financial services sector from 1 December 2020)	— Minimum salary raised to $2,400 from 1 January 2020, and $2,500 from 1 October 2020 — Services sub-DRC reduced from 15% to 13% from 1 January 2020 and to 10% from 1 January 2021. Other sectors' sub-DRC reduced from 20% to 18% from 1 January 2020/21 and to 15% from 1 January 2023.	Services sector DRC reduced from 40% to 38% from 1 January 2020, and to 35% from 1 January 2021	LQS raised to $1,400 from 1 July 2020

Table 8.4 Number of Foreign Workers by Work Pass Type

Pass Type	Dec 2014	Dec 2015	Dec 2016	Dec 2017	Dec 2018	Dec 2019	CAGR (%)*
Employment Pass (EP)	178,900	187,900	192,300	187,700	185,800	193,700	1.60
S Pass	170,100	178,600	179,700	184,400	195,500	200,000	3.29
Work Permit (Total)	991,300	997,100	992,700	965,200	972,600	999,000	0.15
Work Permit (Excluding FDW)	768,800	765,600	753,000	718,400	718,800	737,200	–0.84
Work Permit (FDW)	222,500	231,500	239,700	246,800	253,800	261,800	3.31
Other work passes	15,400	23,600	28,300	30,700	32,100	34,700	17.64
Total	**1,355,700**	**1,387,300**	**1,393,000**	**1,368,000**	**1,386,000**	**1,427,500**	**1.04**

*Compound Annual Growth Rate

Source: Ministry of Manpower.

30,400 between 2009 and 2014.[9] EP growth dipped for the first time in many years in 2017–2018 following the raising of the EP minimum salary, although it resumed its upward trajectory in 2019 (Table 8.4). S Pass has been the fastest growing major pass type over the past five years, with the total number of S Pass holders exceeding EP holders in 2018 and 2019. However, the DRC tightening in 2021 and 2023 is expected to constrain S Pass growth in the coming years.

Foreign employment (excluding foreign domestic workers) plunged by 181,500 in 2020 (16,700 EP holders, 26,000 S Pass holders, and the remainder work permit and other work pass holders) due to the COVID-19 pandemic and imposition of travel restrictions.

In August 2020, with concerns about job prospects mounting amid the COVID-19 pandemic, MOM announced, at the opening of the 14th Parliament, significant EP and S Pass tightening measures. This was an unusual move, coming so soon after previously announced changes. The EP minimum salary, which had already been raised from $3,600 to $3,900 earlier in the year, was further raised to $4,500, with qualifying salaries for older candidates raised correspondingly. For the first time, higher qualifying salaries were set for a specific sector — financial services — in view of the higher wages earned by professionals in this sector. The S Pass qualifying salary was also raised to $2,500, and S Pass jobs were subjected to the Fair Consideration Framework Advertising requirement.

Quality and Experience of Work Permit Holders

Some have argued that raising Work Permit levies has the effect of lowering worker quality as employers resort to hiring even less-skilled, lower-wage foreigners to reduce their manpower outlay. With business costs a concern, there has been a hiatus in levy raises in the past few years with tightening being effected instead through DRC cuts or increases in the Local Qualifying Salary for Work Permit and S Pass holders.

Concerns have been raised regarding the quality and experience of Work Permit holders. Rising incomes in source countries such as China have reduced the attractiveness of Singapore as a place for work while the high churn of foreign workers in sectors such as construction has seen fewer experienced workers retained in Singapore. In response, MOM has taken steps to raise quality and help employers retain their better Work Permit holders so as raise overall workforce productivity.

Since January 2017, all construction firms are required to have at least 10% of their Work Permit holders qualified as higher-skilled (R1) workers. From June 2017, Work Permit holders in the process sector have been allowed to change employer at the end of their Work Permit term.

The Market-Based Skills Recognition Framework (MBF) provides an additional pathway for employers to improve the quality of their Work Permit holders. Besides skills certification, Work Permit holders who are more experienced with higher pay can also be upgraded from basic skilled to higher skilled, attracting lower foreign worker levies. The MBF was first introduced in the services sector in 2013, followed by construction and process, and in 2018 it was extended to manufacturing and marine shipyard.

In 2018, MOM extended the maximum period of employment for all Work Permit holders by four years for all sectors to allow employers to retain their experienced workers for longer.

Control of Foreign Worker Inflow

Without hard caps, the government is not able to directly control the number of work pass holders coming into Singapore. Even after several rounds of foreign workforce tightening through levy increases and DRC cuts beginning in 2010, foreign inflow remained strong from 2011–2013 before finally being brought to heel from 2014 onwards.

However, strict quotas would have to rely on forecasts of business conditions and would not be as responsive to the needs of industry. There is also the question of how the quota would be allocated. A first-come, first-served basis would be untenable for businesses, as is a bidding system, which would add much uncertainty for business planning and skew the flow of manpower towards sectors that can pay the most. Another possibility is a points-based system, which is used in countries such as the UK, Canada, and Australia to determine who is allowed to enter the country for work.

Access to Talent

For EPs, the only policy lever today is the minimum salary criterion, which takes into consideration the age of the EP applicant and his or her qualifications. The salary threshold serves as a fairly objective, market-based test for EP quality that until 2020 applied equally across all sectors and occupations. Some have suggested that the salary bar be raised for sectors such as finance, ICT, and professional services, given the high prevailing wages in these sectors. It may also be argued that continually raising the EP minimum salary across the board to manage EP growth could price out foreigners with rare or niche skills that are lacking in the local workforce, even if their jobs do not command very high salaries.

Even as EP salary thresholds are raised, the government recognises that it is important to allow companies access to skills that they require.

MOM has indicated that economic agencies may exercise flexibility in allowing companies to bring in EP holders below the minimum salary threshold, provided the companies practise fair consideration of local workers and demonstrate a need for talent with skills that are in demand globally but not available locally.[10]

In July 2019, the Economic Development Board and Enterprise Singapore introduced Tech@SG, a pilot scheme that provides flexibility in EP qualifying criteria for participating companies,[11] although it was not clear that tech talent would require such flexibility given their high wages. As an extension to this programme, a new work pass (called Tech.Pass) was launched in January 2021 for highly skilled technology professionals (limited to 500 places at launch) to perform a range of activities in Singapore such as starting a business, serving as a director of Singapore-based companies, or investing in companies here.

The salary threshold may be effective in slowing the growth of EPs, but it is a blunt instrument that does not discriminate by job attributes (such as skills requirements) or firm characteristics (such as foreign worker dependence, nationality concentration, etc.). A points-based system would allow consideration of a variety of factors, but at the cost of greater administrative complexity and less certainty for companies.

In the Parliamentary Debate on the President's Address in August 2020, then-Minister for Manpower Josephine Teo said that imposing quotas and levies on EP holders to regulate their numbers, as some had suggested, was "not unthinkable" but "unwise", as it could result in a loss of investments and jobs to other countries.[12] She noted that raising minimum salaries had been effective in pushing EP holders on lower salaries into the S Pass category, where they are subject to quotas. As to concerns that employers may falsely declare salaries to clear the higher bar, she said that the solution was to strengthen enforcement.

Fair Consideration

A major complaint among a segment of the local PMET workforce is that employers, particularly foreign human resource and line managers, are discriminating against locals in hiring and promotion for skilled job roles.[13]

Without source and levy controls over EP hiring, the government felt it necessary to establish the **Fair Consideration Framework (FCF)** in 2014. This was a cautious first step, with care taken not to roil businesses and foreign investors. The FCF is not positioned as a "labour market test" whereby companies must prove a shortage of suitably qualified local candidates before they can hire a foreigner, as practised in Australia and the UK for certain classes of work visas. Companies are only required to give fair consideration to local candidates before selecting an employee based on merit. Under the FCF, companies were required to advertise on a national jobs portal called the National Jobs Bank (later revamped and rebranded as MyCareersFuture.gov.sg.) for 14 days before they could make an EP application. To avoid imposing a burden on smaller companies, only companies with 25 or more employees were required to advertise. Candidates earning more than $12,000 were also exempted from the **FCF advertising requirement**. The government stressed that Singapore continued to welcome skilled foreign manpower.

As it turned out, the FCF advertising requirement did not cause too much disquiet among the business community as many multinationals were used to operating in countries with more stringent work visa controls.

Further steps were taken subsequently. In August 2016, the FCF Watchlist was introduced. Companies suspected of discriminatory hiring, for instance those that were outliers in their industry in terms of EP dependency, were placed on a watchlist for closer scrutiny with a longer processing time for their EP applications (three months instead of up to three weeks). The government emphasised that the watchlist was targeted at the minority of unfair employers. MOM and the Tripartite Alliance for Fair and Progressive Employment Practices (TAFEP) would work with companies on the watchlist to help them improve their human resource processes so they could eventually exit the watchlist. Unresponsive companies could be renewed on the watchlist or have their work pass privileges curtailed entirely, meaning they would not be permitted to hire new foreign workers or to renew existing ones.

In 2018, the FCF advertising requirement was strengthened, lowering the exemption thresholds to companies with fewer than 10 employees and positions paying above $15,000. 2020 saw significant tightening moves, with the income threshold for advertising further raised to $20,000, and the period of advertisement doubled from 14 to 28 days. For the first time, S Pass positions were also subjected to the FCF advertising requirement.

From January 2020, administrative penalties for discriminatory hiring were raised — the minimum period of debarment from hiring foreign workers was raised from six months to 12 months, with serious offenders debarred for 24 months. For the many firms that depend heavily on foreign workers, these penalties have the potential to put them out of business. MOM has also announced that from October 2020, licensing conditions would be imposed on employment agencies to ensure that they do not, in any way, abet discriminatory hiring by their clients.

Looking Ahead: Trade-Offs at the Heart of Foreign Workforce Policy

Singapore's approach to foreign workers intake in the years ahead will profoundly affect its international competitiveness and socio-economic outcomes.

Some have argued that since Singaporeans do not aspire to many of the blue-collar jobs held by Work Permit holders, efforts to reclaim jobs for locals should focus on those held by EP holders while keeping the tap open for Work Permit holders.

However, as discussed earlier in this chapter, an abundance of low-wage, low-skilled Work Permit holders is likely to hold back the adoption of automation and manpower-saving technology, posing a drag on productivity growth. It may also hold down local wages, raising occupational wage dispersion and giving employers little impetus to redesign jobs to attract more locals. A heavy dependence on foreigners works against national resilience in the event of labour supply disruptions such as border closures. Furthermore, as traditional source countries develop economically, it may become more difficult to hire Work Permit holders at the same wages. Finally, a large number of Work Permit holders adds to Singapore's total population and puts a strain on land and infrastructure. As the COVID-19 experience has shown, it is not simply a matter of housing foreign workers in large, purpose-built dormitories where they are less likely to cross paths with locals and impose social disamenities. Consideration of workers' welfare and health will require lower-density, more expensive housing.

It will certainly be challenging to wean local firms off heavy reliance on low-skilled foreign workers, particularly in the construction, process, and marine shipyard sectors. However, the direction seems clear — a sustained effort must be made to reduce manpower intensity through automation and, to the extent possible, redesign and reclaim some of the jobs for locals. This is particularly important for the career prospects of

Singaporeans at the lower end of the skills and income spectrum, with implications for inequality and the socio-economic compact.

At the same time, Singapore cannot realistically scale back the number of Work Permit holders beyond a point in the near future without jettisoning entire industries such as marine shipyard and process. In the case of manufacturing, some of the cost increase from downsizing the foreign workforce will impinge on business competitiveness although labour costs, for the most part, are smaller than capital and land costs. In the case of domestic services, some of the cost increase will be passed on to consumers, but this can be mitigated by changes in customer behaviour (e.g. more "do-it-yourself" or self-service), changes in business processes, as well as potential adjustment in rents and non-labour costs of businesses.

At the other end of the skills spectrum, it is harder to determine how many skilled foreigners Singapore should aim to admit, much less to actually achieve a given target. On the one hand, many foreigners compete with locals for good jobs even though a large proportion cannot, by any stretch of the imagination, be considered exceptional talents possessing skills that Singaporeans lack. On the other hand, the ease of bringing in foreigners (exceptional or otherwise) to Singapore through the EP route is core to Singapore's attractiveness to foreign businesses deciding where to locate their global or regional headquarters. Moving too aggressively to restrict the inflow of EP holders could spook foreign investment, inflicting a blow to Singapore's attractiveness and competitiveness from which it would be hard to recover. Yet if too little is done, local resentment against foreigners may spill over (it is already a political hot potato) and there may be insufficient effort on the part of businesses to develop local talent. The employment outcomes of university and polytechnic graduates may also be compromised.

One approach is for the government to impose strict qualifying conditions for EP holders such as a high minimum salary, and give economic agencies the flexibility to waive the requirements for meritorious cases. While this is already practised to an extent, there are limits to how far this approach can be taken. Stringent upfront conditions could deter some companies from even considering moving to or investing in Singapore. The lack of upfront clarity and certainty could also be off-putting to some firms. Furthermore, not every business has a clear-cut champion agency, particularly in emerging areas that are not yet well-established.

A points-based system for EP admission could help but is also not a panacea. Much would depend on the design details and implementation of such a system, for instance, how transparent such a system would be, how effective it is in distinguishing between foreigners who are complementary and those who are substitutive vis-à-vis the local workforce, and whether there would be strict caps or otherwise on the total number of EPs allowed into Singapore.

On discrimination against locals, there have been enough complaints about unfair hiring practices to conclude that these are not isolated instances. The FCF penalty framework has been enhanced, but considerable effort is still required to investigate and establish wrongdoing on the part of the firm. There is also a need for upfront policies to minimise the opportunity for such discrimination to take place, and to nudge employers to shift from a "plug-and-play" approach to one that invests in building up a sustainable workforce with a local core. However, moves to increase the selectivity of EP holders will reduce employers' access to skilled foreign manpower, with consequent impact on Singapore's attractiveness to foreign investment.

Even harder to discern than unfair hiring is discrimination in opportunities for career progression. Singaporeans in financial institutions and multinationals have complained about being bypassed for promotion by foreign bosses more inclined to give opportunities to their own compatriots. On the other hand, employers have cited Singaporeans' lack of international experience or relevant skills as reasons for their inability to take on senior roles.

The government will have to feel its way forward on fair consideration, testing the waters as it slowly pushes the boundaries while taking care not to sink the ship.

Regarding the impact of EP tightening and fair consideration measures on Singapore's attractiveness to global business and investment, it is worth bearing in mind that perceptions may matter more than substance. The rhetoric that accompanies policy moves, amplified and sometimes distorted by consultancy firms in their advisories to business clients, may give the impression that Singapore is less open to global talent than is in fact the case. The communications challenge is how to simultaneously reassure the business community and local workers without putting out messages that appear to contradict.

Raising the Wages of Lower-Income Workers

While there are many upstream and downstream measures that can be taken to boost the take-home income of lower-wage workers, public debate has often circled back to discussions on whether to introduce a minimum wage.

The Minimum Wage Debate

Minimum wages are wage floors that can be set by legislation, regulation, or legally binding collective agreements.

In a competitive labour market, economic theory suggests that a minimum wage could lead to a reduction in employment or hours worked if the minimum wage is set at a level not commensurate with the productivity of some workers. The reduction in employment would depend on the elasticity of demand for labour, i.e. how much labour demand falls for a given increase in labour cost. On the other hand, in labour markets that are more monopsonistic (single employer or employers with market power), employment may even increase with a minimum wage.

Many advanced and developing economies have implemented a statutory minimum wage including Malaysia (since 2012), Hong Kong (since 2011), South Korea, the US, UK, and Japan. As at 2021, Luxembourg has the world's highest minimum wage, followed by Australia and New Zealand. Notably, Sweden and Denmark have not enacted statutory minimum wages, in keeping with their model of flexible labour markets, while Norway has set minimum rates of pay only in certain sectors. Switzerland saw a minimum wage proposal in 2014 defeated in a referendum; certain Swiss cantons have, however, implemented minimum wages. In countries without minimum wages, wages are typically set through collective bargaining agreements in various sectors.

The empirical evidence on minimum wage has divided opinions among economists. Earlier studies, such as David Card and Alan Krueger (1994), reported minimal or non-existent negative employment effects of minimum wage increases.[14] Others, like David Neumark and William Wascher (1992), reached the opposite conclusion that minimum wage increases have had a dampening impact on employment or employment growth.[15] Over time, however, the proportion of economists concerned about the employment impact of minimum wages appears to have declined.[16]

Meta-studies that summarise the findings of a large number of individual studies have generally reported little or no negative employment effects on overall employment.[17] However, Neumark (2017) questioned the utility of averaging estimates across studies that cover different populations and vary in empirical rigour, arguing that it was more important to understand why results differed across studies.[18] Echoing these sentiments, Jeffrey Clemens (2019) suggested that a more careful reading of the minimum wage literature, particularly research from Europe, did not lend weight to a sanguine view of minimum wage increases.[19] He also noted that a minimum wage increase may lead to non-wage adjustments to employment terms that affect workers, as well as decisions on capital investment that would reduce employment in the longer-term.

While there is no longer a presumption that minimum wages lead to significant aggregate job losses, the employment impact on certain groups may be stronger depending on the level at which the minimum wage is set, i.e. how much "bite" it has. For instance, the OECD (2015) found that youth employment was likely to be negatively affected,[20] while Doruk Cengiz, Arindrajit Dube, Attila Lindner, and Ben Zipperer (2019) found evidence of reduced employment in tradeable sectors.[21] In attempting to reconcile empirical findings with theory, economists have pointed to the following factors in determining employment impact for specific economies, sectors, firms, and jobs:

— Labour market structure, i.e. whether more competitive or monopsonistic
— Firm production structure, i.e. whether firms are able to substitute machinery for labour

— Product market structure, i.e. whether firms are able to pass on costs to consumers
— Macroeconomic conditions, i.e. whether economic growth is robust

José Azar et al. (2019) found that employment may rise in more concentrated (and hence more monopsonistic) labour markets with a higher Herfindahl-Hirschman Index (HHI), as predicted by theory.[22] Peter Harasztosi and Attila Lindner (2019) and Christian Dustmann et al. (2019) suggested that firm profitability, as well as employment, is less likely to fall in the non-tradeable sector where firms are better able to pass prices on to consumers.[23] Dara Lee Luca and Michael Luca (2019) and Dustmann et al. (2019) found that minimum wages can shift production and workers to higher-quality firms through churn and reallocation.[24] John Addison, McKinley Blackburn, and Chad Cotti (2013), and Jeffrey Clemens and Michael Wither (2019) showed that the negative effects of minimum wages on employment, firms, and consumers are more pronounced in recessionary environments as firms and consumers are less able to absorb minimum wage increases.[25]

In a February 2021 report, the non-partisan US Congressional Budget Office estimated that increasing the US federal minimum wage from US$7.25 to US$15 an hour by 2025 would directly raise the wages of 17 million workers (about 10% of the labour force), and could also benefit another 10 million workers earning slightly above the wage floor.[26] This would lift an estimated 0.9 million people out of poverty, at the cost of a 0.9% reduction in employment (1.4 million workers), with young, less educated people accounting for a disproportionate share of potential job losses.

Over the years, there have been calls for Singapore to implement a minimum wage in line with the practice in most other advanced economies. The enactment of a minimum wage in Hong Kong in 2011 sparked discussions in the mainstream media on whether Singapore needed a minimum wage to tackle growing inequality. A motion on inclusive growth in Parliament in January 2011 ("That this House affirms its commitment to inclusive economic growth, and calls on the Government to continue doing more to support low-skilled and low-wage workers, so that all Singaporeans may share the fruits of our prosperity through better skills, better jobs and better incomes") saw a robust debate on the minimum wage. The Workers' Party and Singapore Democratic Party advocated for a minimum wage in their 2015 and 2020 election manifestos, while the Progress Singapore Party called for the introduction of a living wage in 2020. Public intellectuals including Ambassador-at-Large Tommy Koh have also spoken up in favour of a minimum wage.

In considering a minimum wage, it is important to take into account the composition of Singapore's workforce.

There is still a significant number of lower-educated/low-skilled seniors in the workforce whose employment may be at risk from a minimum wage.[27] Older people in Singapore, particularly 55- to 65-year-olds, had among the lowest scores in literacy and numeracy among countries that participated in the Survey of Adult Skills, a product of the OECD Programme for the International Assessment of Adult Competencies (PIAAC).[28] A key factor is whether these older workers are willing and able to raise productivity and skills through retraining in order to stay employed. Notwithstanding, some employers may find it necessary to hold on to such workers to earn their quota for Work Permit or S Pass holders.

The high proportion of foreigners in the workforce adds another significant complication. If the minimum wage includes Work Permit holders, this will push up the price of foreign manpower considerably and may require a significant cutback in levies. In essence, this will be a transfer of billions of dollars annually from the state to foreign workers. If the minimum wage excludes foreigners, it could drive a wedge between the cost of hiring foreigners and locals and risk pricing out Singaporeans or necessitating a sizeable increase in foreign worker levies.

The limitations and risks of a minimum wage are also worth noting. A minimum wage is less targeted than a wage supplement with qualifying criteria as it could end up boosting the wages of students from well-to-do families on part-time or short-term employment, in addition to those who are less well-off. It would also not help the low-income self-employed. During a downturn, employees earning a minimum wage may risk retrenchment if employers do not have the flexibility to adjust salaries downwards — there is a risk of firms cutting jobs to save costs rather than cutting costs to save jobs.

The government has sought to address the issue of low-wage workers through two principal means — Workfare, introduced in in 2007, and the Progressive Wage Model, introduced in 2012. In addition, foreign worker policy measures, in particular the raising of the Local Qualifying Salary, have helped to push up wages at the lower end of the skills and income distribution. The Wage Credit Scheme (2013–2020) incentivised firms to give wage increments to employees, while the Inclusive Growth Programme (2010–2020) provided funding support to companies to embark on productivity improvement projects that were accompanied by wage increases for lower-income workers. Finally, the National Wages Council provides annual wage recommendations, which for several years have included quantitative recommendations on wage increases for lower-income workers (Figure 8.5).

Workfare

Workfare, as described in Chapter 5, comprises the Workfare Income Supplement (WIS) as well as Workfare Skills Support. WIS is more targeted than a minimum wage as it takes into account spousal income and property value while excluding those under age 35. A study by the

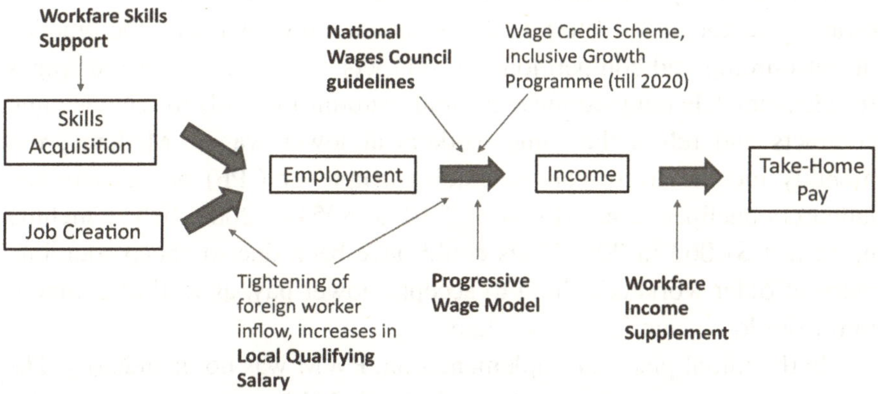

Figure 8.5 Interventions to Help Low-Wage Workers

Ministry of Trade and Industry found that most of the WIS subsidy accrues to workers rather than employers, which suggests that labour demand is elastic relative to supply at these wage levels, conditions that favour a wage subsidy over a minimum wage.[29] As the government bears the cost of WIS, it does not push up costs for businesses which could be passed on to consumers in price increases. Under Workfare, there is also support for training to help low-wage workers upskill and upgrade to better-paying jobs. However, Workfare does not guarantee the take-home pay of workers as this still depends on what employers are willing to pay.

Progressive Wage Model

The Progressive Wage Model (PWM) stipulates wage structures for local workers (citizens and permanent residents only) in selected sectors and occupations, effectively setting a minimum wage in sectors where it is mandatory. It can be considered a sectoral minimum wage but goes beyond a minimum wage by also establishing wage ladders (or progression pathways) corresponding to different levels of skill and responsibility. While mandatory in certain sectors including cleaning, security, and landscaping, PWM has been effected in other sectors through government procurement or subvention for some occupations in the public transport and healthcare sectors (e.g. bus captains). There are now plans to extend mandatory PWM to all sectors in time.

Pioneered by the Labour Movement, PWM was introduced in the cleaning sector in 2012 to tackle "cheap sourcing" whereby the practice of outsourcing and competition for contracts had led to depressed wages for cleaners. Cleaning companies would submit low bids to win cleaning contracts and rehire the same workers at lower wages. Median gross monthly income from work (including employer CPF) of cleaners and labourers declined from $1,044 in 2001 to $954 in 2007, before inching up to just $1,063 in 2011. This could have been due to cheap sourcing, entry of older workers willing to accept a lower pay, as well as competition from low-wage foreign workers.

In the initial phase of implementation, PWM was not mandatory. The government announced that from 1 April 2013, government agencies would only engage cleaning companies with the National Environment

Agency's Enhanced Clean Mark Accreditation, which required the adoption of PWM. From 1 September 2015, PWM adoption became a requirement for all licensed cleaning companies.

PWM was subsequently mandated in the security and landscaping sectors in 2016, these being sectors that were also prone to market failure from cheap sourcing.

The wage ladders are revised yearly, with the lowest wage floor for cleaners increasing from $1,120 in 2018 and $1,200 in 2019 to $1,236 in 2020. Plans have been announced to nearly double the wage floor to $2,420 by 2028.

At the time PWM was introduced, I was concerned that setting a wage ladder (beyond a simple wage floor) could be overly prescriptive or market-distortive, even if it were possible to obtain tripartite consensus. A simpler alternative, in my view, would have been to calibrate the supply of foreign manpower in sectors vulnerable to low wages so that market wages would adjust accordingly.

However, the PWM has been smoothly implemented in the three mandatory sectors — cleaning, security, and landscape — raising the real median wages of around 80,000 local workers (40,000 cleaners, 36,000 security guards, and 3,000 landscape maintenance workers) by a cumulative 30% between 2014 and 2019, higher than the 21% increase at the median for all sectors.[30]

While all local workers in PWM sectors have gained from the yearly increases in wage floors, it may be more difficult for older, less skilled workers to move up the wage rungs. As Linda Lim (2020) pointed out, employers are likely to take the easier route of assigning higher-level job roles to younger foreign workers than to invest in training older local workers for these roles.[31]

In 2018, the government accepted the recommendations of the Lift and Escalator Sectoral Tripartite Committee to introduce PWM for the lift and escalator industry. This was significant as lift technicians had considerably higher wages than most workers in the cleaning, security, and landscaping sectors. From 2019, government agencies took the lead by only awarding lift maintenance tenders to firms that had adopted the PWM. The government will mandate PWM for the lift industry in 2022 and extend PWM to escalator maintenance technicians as well.

Notwithstanding, there remains a significant number of low-wage workers not covered by PWM in occupations such as retail assistants, kitchen assistants, and office clerks. It was previously thought difficult to extend PWM to sectors and occupations where there are many employers and the government is not a major buyer (e.g. food services) or where there are no existing licensing requirements (e.g. retail assistants and clerical staff). Another challenge is to ensure that the stipulated wage ladder is appropriate, taking into account the potential variety in job and wage structure (e.g. commission-based pay) and roles across different firms, even within the same sector and occupation. It is also important to recognise that tying wages strictly to productivity is not always feasible as scope for productivity improvement may be limited in some job roles or run into diminishing returns over time.[32]

If these challenges can be overcome, PWM could serve as a coordination mechanism, along with tightening of foreign worker inflows, to spur job redesign, higher wages, and productivity. This could help to lower occupational wage disparities and attract more locals to join sectors and occupations that are highly dependent on low-skilled foreign manpower. Obtaining tripartite consensus on wage increases would minimise the risk of job losses, although this also means it may take significantly longer to implement PWM than a minimum wage.

In 2020, the government announced its intent to identify more sectors where PWM can be implemented, and eventually extend PWM to all sectors. There are plans to extend PWM to up to 3,000 local workers in the waste management sector, a further 50,000 in-house cleaners, security, and landscape maintenance workers, and up to 80,000 local workers in food services and retail.[33]

National Wages Council

The National Wages Council (NWC) is a tripartite committee comprising representatives from the employers' federation, trade unions, and the government. Formed in 1972, its role is to formulate annual recommendations to guide employers and unions in making wage adjustments, taking into account factors such as productivity growth, employment, as well as international competitiveness. While employers and unions use the NWC's guidelines as a framework for wage negotiations, some non-unionised companies also take reference from the guidelines in determining wage increments for their workers.

Following the 1985–1986 recession, the NWC shifted from issuing quantitative guidelines to qualitative guidelines to allow more flexibility in wage negotiations. However since 2012 it has re-introduced quantitative guidelines for low-wage workers, specifying a quantum or range of wage increases for this group of workers. The basic wage threshold for coverage under these quantitative guidelines has been periodically raised, from an initial $1,000 in 2012/2013 to $1,400 in 2019/2020 as incomes continued to rise. The NWC has, in recent years, also recommended giving low-wage workers earning above the basic wage threshold a reasonable wage increase and/or one-off lump sum based on skills and productivity so that all lower-wage workers enjoy a higher percentage built-in wage increase compared with other workers.

The proportion of private sector establishments with low-wage workers below the quantitative guidelines threshold that adopted the recommended wage increase for their low-wage workers has fluctuated in recent years from a low of 18.5% in 2015 to a high of 60.1% in 2019.

Looking Ahead: Understanding the Profile of Lower-Income Workers

As outlined in Chapter 2, there has been significant progress in the past decade in raising incomes at the lower end and even closing the relative gap to the median. However, given that social norms and expectations in regard to daily expenses are changing, lower-income individuals may not feel that their purchasing power has increased or that social inclusion is improving.

It is worth taking a closer look at the number and proportion of lower-wage workers.

The proportion of full-time resident employees earning a basic monthly wage (excluding employer CPF) of up to $1,000 in nominal terms is estimated to have fallen considerably, from 10.6% in 2011[34] to 4.7% in 2016. Even the proportion of those earning up to $1,300 is estimated to have declined from 9.2% in 2017 to 7.9% in 2018.[35]

In a Facebook post following the 2020 general election, Workers' Party MP Jamus Lim noted that there were still an estimated 100,000 locals who earned a salary below his party's proposed minimum take-home pay of $1,300 a month. It was subsequently clarified in Parliament that while about 100,000 workers earned below $1,300 a month, a smaller number of resident workers, about 56,000, earned less than $1,300 a month after factoring in WIS and employer CPF contributions.[36]

Of the approximately 52,000 Singapore citizens (30,000 full-time employees and 22,000 self-employed workers) earning below $,1300 a month, more than a third were aged 50 and over and about a third were aged between 15 and 24, comprising youth in vacation jobs.[37] About half lived in households with household income per capita of more than $1,300, suggesting that they were not primary breadwinners for their families.

While some of today's seniors who are less well-educated or without formal schooling may be able to retrain and reskill for higher productivity, others may find it difficult to do so. For the latter group, it may not be in their best interest to pursue increases in their market wages too aggressively lest they be priced out of the market. Rather, the government can top up their incomes through WIS and continue supporting their employment through the Senior Employment Credit (discussed in the next section), as well as top up their retirement savings through Silver Support.

However, it would be a concern if younger workers, having been through the education system with the vast majority at post-secondary level, remained in low-wage jobs through their prime working years. This would necessitate firmer intervention, whether through foreign workforce policy, job redesign, progressive wages, or a combination of policy levers.

Productive Longevity: Helping Older Workers Remain Employed

Increasing labour force participation and employment among older workers has the twin socio-economic objectives of boosting retirement adequacy as life expectancy increases, as well as tempering the decline in local workforce growth. From the perspective of the older individual, engagement through work or volunteering can provide meaning and identity and slow physical and cognitive decline.

This is a priority given that the citizen population aged 65 and above is expected to increase from about 590,000 in 2020 to 900,000 by 2030, with around half a million citizens turning 65 over the decade.[38]

The share of older workers among employed residents has already grown significantly over the past decade. In 2020, there were about 570,000 employed residents aged 55 and above, accounting for 26% of all employed residents, up from 17% in 2010. This was due to the ageing resident population as well as the rise in employment rate among older workers.

The employment rate of 55- to 64-year-old residents has climbed from 59.0% in 2010 to 67.5% in 2020 (Figure 8.6). This puts Singapore well above the OECD average of 62% in 2019, although behind about a dozen OECD economies including Sweden, Japan, and Germany.

The employment rate of residents 65 years and above has nearly doubled in the past decade from 17.1% in 2010 to 28.5% in 2020 (Figure 8.7). This puts Singapore ahead of all OECD economies except Iceland and South Korea (Table 8.5).

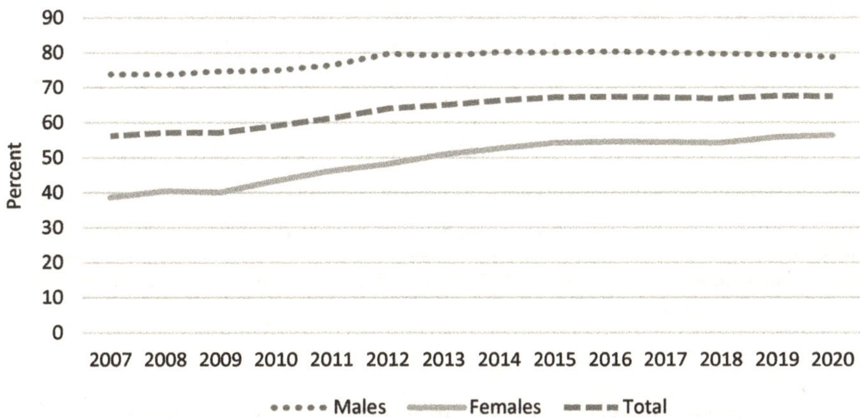

Figure 8.6 Employment Rates of Residents Aged 55 to 64

Source: Comprehensive Labour Force Survey, Manpower Research and Statistics Department, MOM.

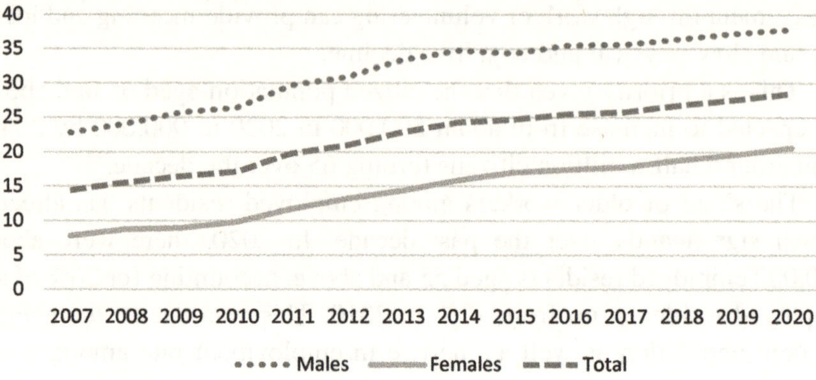

Figure 8.7 Employment Rates of Residents Aged 65 and Over (%)

Source: Comprehensive Labour Force Survey, Manpower Research and Statistics Department, MOM.

Table 8.5 Employment Rate — Age 65 and Above (%)

	Singapore	France	Germany	UK	Sweden	US	Japan	S. Korea	Iceland
2010	17.1	1.5	4.0	8.1	13.3	16.2	19.5	29.0	34.9
2011	19.8	2.0	4.6	8.4	13.4	16.7	19.3	29.1	32.7
2012	21.0	2.3	4.9	8.9	14.9	17.3	19.5	30.0	32.8
2013	22.9	2.2	5.4	9.6	14.6	17.7	20.1	30.7	34.2
2014	24.3	2.3	5.8	10.0	16.5	17.7	20.8	31.1	36.2
2015	24.7	2.6	6.1	10.3	16.4	18.2	21.7	30.4	38.7
2016	25.5	2.9	6.6	10.4	15.8	18.6	22.3	30.6	40.4
2017	25.8	3.0	7.0	10.2	17.0	18.6	23.0	30.6	38.2
2018	26.8	3.0	7.4	10.5	16.9	18.9	24.3	31.3	37.4
2019	**27.6**	**3.3**	**7.8**	**10.7**	**17.5**	**19.6**	**24.9**	**32.9**	**34.8**

Source: Comprehensive Labour Force Survey, Manpower Research and Statistics Department, MOM; national statistical agencies; OECD.

The increase in older worker employment rates over the years could be due to various factors affecting both supply and demand for older workers: a more educated workforce in job roles that enable them to contribute for longer, concerns over retirement adequacy as life expectancy increases, a tight labour market, DRC controls which require firms to have sufficient local employees to qualify to hire foreigners, as well as a suite of policies that support hiring and retention of older workers.

Retirement and Re-employment Act

Singapore's statutory retirement age is sometimes misunderstood as the age at which workers have to retire. To the contrary, it is the age up to which local workers are legally protected from termination on the grounds of age. In the 1980s, workers typically retired at age 55 in the absence of a statutory retirement age. In 1988, the government encouraged employers and unions to voluntarily raise the retirement age in their companies to 60 years, but only about 10% did so.[39] When the Retirement Age Act was introduced in 1993, the statutory retirement age was 60, and this was subsequently raised to 62 in 1999.

With the population ageing, the natural question that arose was whether to raise the retirement age further to support productive longevity and enable older workers to accumulate more savings for their retirement. The countervailing concern was that this would have an adverse impact on business costs and productivity given that many companies continued to practise seniority-based pay, and could be deterred from hiring older workers in the first place. According to former Minister for Manpower Lim Swee Say, younger workers were also opposed to a further increase as they did not want their senior colleagues to stand in the way of their career progression.[40]

Japan provided the inspiration for a middle way. Its re-employment model obliged companies to offer older workers re-employment but with adjustments to job scope and pay permitted. The Singapore government set out its plans for re-employment in 2007, giving employers and workers ample time to prepare ahead of the introduction of the Retirement and Re-employment Act (RRA) in 2012. The Act retained the retirement age at 62 but required firms to offer re-employment to eligible employees up to age 65, with the flexibility to adjust job scope and pay based on reasonable factors such as new duties or responsibilities. An employer that is unable to offer re-employment can transfer the obligation to another employer with the agreement of the employee. Otherwise, the employer would have to make an Employment Assistance Payment of up to 3.5 months' salary, subject to a minimum quantum and a cap. The re-employment age was raised from 65 to 67 on 1 July 2017.

The experience of older workers with re-employment has been mixed. While some have welcomed the opportunity to work longer, others have complained about being asked by their employers to shoulder the same workload for reduced pay or benefits, prompting resignation in some instances.[41] The Public Service did away with wage adjustments for re-employed public officers from 1 July 2017, eliminating a significant grouse among older employees regarding the terms of re-employment.

A 2017 study by economists from MOM found that the RRA had raised the employment rate of the target group aged 62 to 65 by an average of 1.6 percentage points per annum since its implementation.[42] This was primarily through the supply-side channel of social norms among older workers as 65 years became the new "mental anchor" for them. Given that the re-employment age is not linked to the CPF payout eligibility age, there is no financial incentive arising from RRA legislation for older workers to continue working beyond the retirement age of 62. According to the MOM study, among private sector local employees offered re-employment at age 62, the percentage who accepted the offer increased from 94.8% in 2011 to 98.1% in 2016.

On the demand side, the impact of RRA is likely to have been limited. In 2011, prior to the RRA coming into force, private sector firms were already offering re-employment to a large majority (97.9%) of workers who turned 62 and wished to continue working. This proportion increased marginally to 98.6% in 2016. Moreover, over 95% of the re-employed workers in 2011 did not experience a cut in their basic wages, suggesting that demand by firms for these workers was high.

In 2019, the government accepted the recommendation of the Tripartite Workgroup on Older Workers to raise the retirement and re-employment ages by three years, to 65 and 70 respectively, by 2030.[43] This was in consideration that Singapore's health-adjusted life expectancy had risen by three years since 1999, when the retirement age had been raised to 62. The retirement age will first increase from 62 to 63, and the re-employment age from 67 to 68, from 1 July 2022.

Curiously, the retirement age and re-employment age are misnomers — the former is actually the age when a worker must be offered re-employment, and the latter the age when a company is legally permitted to retire a worker. However, the labels have stuck and swapping them now may cause confusion.

In addition to legislation on retirement and re-employment, there are various policy measures to encourage the hiring of older workers: lower CPF contribution rates, wage offsets, and grants for job redesign.

Lower CPF Contribution Rates for Older Workers

To boost the employability of older workers, CPF contribution rates for workers above age 55 are set below the full contribution rate of 37%, tapering by age band to 12.5% for those 65 and above.

Prior to 1 September 2012, lower rates applied from age 50. However, with concerns over retirement adequacy, and as employment rates among older workers had shown marked improvement, the full CPF contribution rate was restored for those aged 50 to 55, with smaller increments for those aged 55 to 65.

Besides changes to the retirement and re-employment ages, the 2019 Tripartite Workgroup on Older Workers also recommended further raising the CPF contributions of older workers. A target was set to raise CPF contributions to the full 37% for those aged 55 to 60 over the next 10 years or so. Those aged 60 to 70 would also see rates increase by smaller but meaningful amounts over the next decade, according to Table 8.6.

Table 8.6 Planned Increases in Older Worker CPF Contribution Rates

Age Band	2020	From 1 Jan 2022*	Long-Term Target
≤55		37%	
>55 to 60	26%	28%	37% (+10% pt)
>60 to 65	16.5%	18.5%	26% (+9.5% pt)
>65 to70	12.5%	14%	16.5% (+4% pt)
>70		12.5%	

*In Budget 2020, the government announced that in view of the impact of COVID-19 on businesses, the scheduled rise in CPF contribution rates for older workers would be deferred from 1 January 2021 to 1 January 2022.

Senior Worker Support Package

To ease the transition to a higher retirement and re-employment age, as well as higher CPF contributions for older workers, a Senior Worker Support Package was announced at the 2020 Unity Budget. This comprises:

— **Senior Employment Credit** (1 January 2021–31 December 2022), which provides wage offsets ranging from 1%–8% to employers hiring Singaporean workers aged 55 and above and earning up to $4,000 a month. This has replaced the Special Employment Credit (SEC) (2011–2020) which provided wage offsets to raise the employability of older workers, and the Additional SEC (2015–2020) which was an additional 3% wage offset to encourage employers to voluntarily re-employ Singaporeans above the re-employment age.
— **Senior Worker Early Adopter Grant** (1 July 2020–30 June 2023): a grant of up to $250,000 for progressive companies willing and able to implement a higher internal retirement age and re-employment age than the statutory minimum.
— **Part-Time Re-employment Grant** (1 July 2020–30 June 2023), a grant of up to $125,000 for companies that commit to offering part-time re-employment to eligible older workers who request for it.
— **CPF Transition Offset** (1 January 2022–31 December 2022), a one-year wage offset of 0.25%–0.5% for companies for every local worker they employ aged 55 to 70.

WorkPro: Job Redesign and Flexible Work Arrangements

WorkPro was launched in April 2013 to support companies in making their workplaces more productive and progressive so as to attract and retain older or economically inactive Singaporeans. It replaced three prior schemes with similar objectives, viz. the Work-Life Works! Fund, Flexi-Works!, and ADVANTAGE!

WorkPro was enhanced in July 2016 with the following components:

— Age Management Grant (up to $20,000 per older worker) for the implementation of age management practices at the workplace

— Job Redesign Grant (up to $300,000) to support job redesign projects targeted at older workers
— Work-Life Grant (up to $160,000) to support adoption of flexible work arrangements for all workers

Companies that tapped on other grants viz. the Inclusive Growth Programme or Capability Development Grant for their job redesign projects could apply for the Job Redesign (Rider), upon project completion if the project had a positive impact on older workers.

With employers today having a better appreciation of the need for age-friendly workplaces and job redesign to create more inclusive workplaces, WorkPro has been discontinued. Other schemes such as the Enterprise Development Grant and Productivity Solutions Grant continue to support job redesign efforts.

Looking Ahead: Further Ways to Boost Employment of Older Workers

Although the rise in older worker employment over the past decade has been significant, there may still be scope to eke out further gains. Former MOM Deputy Secretary Kok Ping Soon (2019) noted that nearly half of seniors remained outside the labour force despite being in "relatively good and fair health".[44]

While Singapore's labour force participation and employment rates among older workers are already among the world's highest, there is still room for part-time employment rates and female employment rates among older workers to increase (Table 8.7).

For seniors without a financial need to continue working, more part-time job opportunities may persuade them to stay in the workforce. One possibility is for the government to curate suitable job opportunities, including part-time ones, for seniors, or appoint a partner organisation to do so. For instance, seniors with professional or corporate experience could be engaged as business advisors, career coaches, or life coaches, providing them an opportunity to share their experience with business owners or younger executives. However, care must be taken not to typecast seniors as only being suitable for certain kinds of jobs.

Table 8.7 Employment Rates Among Older Residents by Gender and Full-Time/Part-Time (2020)

Age Group	Male Employment Rate (%)	Female Employment Rate (%)	Full-Time Employment Rate (%)*	Part-Time Employment Rate (%)*
55–59	83.2	61.7	63.4	9.9
60–64	73.9	50.7	49.6	11.4
65–69	56.5	35.8	33.1	11.8
70 and above	26.0	12.6	11.6	7.2

**Note*: Data pertain to residents in full-time/part-time employment as a percentage of the resident population in the respective age groups.
Source: Manpower Research and Statistics Department, MOM.

Another possibility is to provide career matching services tailored to seniors, notwithstanding that seniors are already served by the publicly funded Career Centres under Workforce Singapore (WSG) or the National Trades Union Congress Employment and Employability Institute (NTUC's e2i) (see next section).

According to Kok (2019), under half of seniors aged 55 and above who had enrolled in WSG or NTUC-e2i courses in 2016 completed their training. He therefore proposed developing training course packages customised for different profiles of seniors and infused with senior-centric pedagogy.

While the DRC already provides significant impetus for companies to hold on to older workers, Kok suggested that the government consider providing a bonus DRC to companies in selected sectors that commit to restructuring in order to be more age-friendly. However, this would have to be weighed against the objective of reducing reliance on foreign workers.

At the end of the day, mindsets towards ageing, both on the part of employers and workers, are vital in the drive to increase productive longevity. As Kok summarised, "The focus will be to turn the push ('you have to work longer') into a pull ('there's important work you want to do') and transform the desire to be 'free from work' to one of being 'free to work'."[45]

Facilitating Employment and Career Transition

For a socio-economic model centred on self-reliance and work as social security, active labour market policies are a prerequisite. The government has to pull out all stops to facilitate job matching and reskilling for new jobs, particularly as the economy restructures and the risk of structural unemployment grows. Facilitating the quick re-entry of displaced workers into employment is also important in preventing unemployment "hysteresis" or scarring, whereby extended periods without employment may lead to loss of job skills and erosion of employability.

The **Adapt and Grow initiative** is as an umbrella scheme for employment facilitation, under WSG, addressing what former Minister for Manpower Lim Swee Say dubbed job "**mismatches**", due to gaps in skills, wage, or other expectations, and "**missed matches**", due to workers and employers failing to find each other despite being fairly good fits.

The initiative comprises: (a) **career matching services** offered by state-funded Career Centres, along with a national jobs portal called MyCareersFuture.gov.sg, to address missed matches and (b) **employment support programmes** to plug gaps and address mismatches.

With the launch of Adapt and Grow initiative in 2016, special effort has been made to reach out to PMETs, as Career Centres had previously been associated, in the public mind, with support for rank-and-file workers. The PMET share of employed residents has risen steadily from 52.5% in 2010 to 59.9% in 2020. As PMETs have more specialised skills, should they be displaced or retrenched, they may face greater difficulty finding new jobs that can offer equivalent pay or make use of their skills (Figure 3.10). While company-specific skills may be less transferable to a new employer, a greater concern is technology and restructuring eliminating the need for certain jobs and skills. The latter requires PMETs to be reskilled for new job roles or occupations, and is a major focus of Adapt and Grow programmes.

Career Matching Services

Unlike countries such as Australia, where state-funded employment facilitation has been outsourced to the private/non-profit sectors, the public sector continues to provide job matching services in Singapore. Three of the five national Career Centres are run by WSG, a government statutory board, and the remaining two by NTUC's e2i.

Professional career coaches at these centres provide career counselling and equip jobseekers with job search skills, such as interview and résumé-writing skills. They refer jobseekers to suitable job opportunities, or to Adapt and Grow programmes as needed. In FY2019, about 65% of jobseekers registered with WSG and e2i career centres were placed in jobs within six months.[46]

Since the outbreak of the COVID-19 pandemic, 24 satellite centres, called SGUnited Jobs and Skills Centres, have been set up nationwide to complement the five Career Centres. These centres offer career advisory and guidance, boosting ground outreach while referring jobseekers who require more in-depth career coaching to the Career Centres.

Partial Outsourcing to Career Matching Providers

In 2017, the government engaged two foreign private sector job agencies, Ingeus (headquartered in Australia) and MAXIMUS (headquartered in the US), to complement the PMET job matching efforts of the five Career Centres on a two-year pilot initiative. This came after prior pilots involving four local employment agencies had yielded poor placement outcomes.

Ingeus and MAXIMUS (known as Career Matching Providers) were selected based on their professional focus, capabilities, and track record in working with governments abroad. It was hoped that they would enrich the diversity of career matching services supported by the government by bringing in know-how and exchanging best practices on service delivery with the existing Career Centres. They operate on an outcome-based payment model, with payment for every eligible PMET jobseeker placed into employment.

In 2019, WSG reported that the Career Matching Providers had performed satisfactorily, with placement success rates "very comparable" with those of WSG and e2i Career Centres.[47] Hence, the pilot has been extended.

Looking Ahead: Further Outsourcing?

In Singapore, the bulk of job matching still takes place without state intervention or support through the large number of private employment agencies and private job portals.

Anyone, employed or otherwise, can approach the WSG or e2i Career Centres for assistance regardless of income level or employment status. However, many Singaporeans prefer to leverage their own networks or go through private sector intermediaries before turning to the Career Centres for help.

The annual placements of around 31,000 in 2018 and 2019 through the Adapt and Grow initiative (comprising placements through career services as well as employment support programmes) are a small fraction of the total number of job switches that take place annually.[48] Even among the long-term unemployed, where there is a stronger case for state intervention, many find jobs without government help.

With the success of the Career Matching Providers, there may be scope to expand outsourcing of state-funded employment assistance. Funding private employment agencies for placements of all unemployed jobseekers would increase government expenditure considerably without necessarily improving outcomes. It may, however, be possible to engage private employment agencies to do more for vulnerable jobseekers such as those who are older or long-term unemployed.

As private employment agencies are paid by firms to find suitable candidates for them, they adopt a firm-centric approach rather than the jobseeker-centric approach of the Career Centres and Career Matching Providers. Funding employment agencies for placement of vulnerable jobseekers is possible if it can be reconciled with the employment agencies' client-centric business model and can be done in a way that does not incur excessive deadweight funding on the part of the government. Being able to measure the "delta" effort or outcomes from such funding would be critical.

In response to COVID-19, MOM is appointing selected employment agencies as SGUnited Jobs and Skills Placement Partners to help local jobseekers secure jobs and traineeships (details in Chapter 11). Under this initiative, funding support will be given to placement partners to place mature jobseekers, long-term unemployed jobseekers, or persons with disabilities into jobs and traineeships. This will create additional pathways for vulnerable local jobseekers to access professional career matching services to land employment or training opportunities.

National Jobs Portal: MyCareersFuture.gov.sg

The National Jobs Bank was created for employers to advertise positions to facilitate job matching with locals before applying for an Employment Pass under the Fair Consideration Framework. In 2018, it was revamped and rebranded as MyCareersFuture.gov.sg, a jobs portal that aims to provide local jobseekers with a fast and smart search service, matching them to jobs that best fit their skill sets and highlighting jobs that are eligible for government support under the Adapt and Grow programmes. The portal is also able to recommend jobseekers to employers and allow employers to sort applicants based on skills fit and experience.

MyCareersFuture.gov.sg is not intended to supplant private sector job portals, but to serve as a complementary offering tailored to the needs of local jobseekers. It is also a source of data on jobseeker trends, job vacancies, and matching efforts.

Adapt and Grow Programmes

Various employment support programmes under the Adapt and Grow initiative provide wage and training support to address gaps in skills, wage, and job expectations.

Among these, the most significant are the **Professional Conversion Programmes (PCPs)** which were first launched in 2007. These support PMET career conversions by providing salary support and course fee subsidies. Under PCPs, individuals are hired by a participating employer and typically take up a full-time course to acquire the necessary skills required for the job.

Employers who hire Singaporeans under PCPs are eligible for salary support of 70% of monthly salary during the period of full-time training, subject to a grant cap, and higher salary support of 90% of monthly salary, at a higher grant cap, for hiring Singaporeans either aged 40 and above or long-term unemployed (25 weeks or more).

Most PCPs are "**place and train**" programmes whereby the employer must first hire a worker and place the worker on training in order to be eligible for support. This avoids the risk of the training not eventually leading to a job. In some instances, the government recognises that training ahead of demand may be necessary, given a lack of immediate hiring opportunities despite good long-term industry prospects. In such cases, an "**attach and train**" (or "train and place") PCP may be launched, although these form the minority of PCPs.

Since 2016, WSG has gone upstream to offer **Redeployment PCPs** to help workers at risk of restructuring to be redeployed to new job roles within the same firm or industry. This has helped the Institute of Banking and Finance to partner various banks to retrain frontline bank tellers for new roles in digital banking and advisory services.

To support restructuring and keep structural unemployment at bay, WSG has ramped up PCPs aggressively in recent years, from placements of around 1,300 in 2016 to nearly 5,000 in 2018 and about 4,500 in 2019. Non-PMET workers are similarly supported under equivalent rank-and-file conversion programmes.

Other Adapt and Grow programmes include:

— **Career Support Programme**, which until September 2020 (when it was superseded by a new Jobs Growth Incentive) provided wage support to companies that hired retrenched mature or long-term unemployed PMET workers

— **Career Trial**, which allows employers and jobseekers to assess job fit through a short-term trial, during which the government provides jobseekers with an allowance. If the jobseeker is offered formal employment after the trial, there is also salary support for employers, and a retention incentive for those who stay in the job.

— **P-Max**, which provides a grant to help SMEs better recruit, train, and retain PMETs

Further Support for Mature Workers

Although unemployment and long-term unemployment rates have been fairly low and stable (Figures 2.4, 2.5), there remain concerns for mature and older workers.

Table 8.8 Incidence of Retrenchment (Number of Retrenchments per Thousand Local Employees) by Age

Age Group	2017	2018	2019	2020
Below 30	2.3	2.1	1.6	7.3
30–39	6.9	5.0	4.5	9.8
40–49	9.9	7.7	7.5	12.7
50 and above	8.1	6.0	6.2	12.9

Source: Labour Market Report 2019, Manpower Research and Statistics Department, MOM.

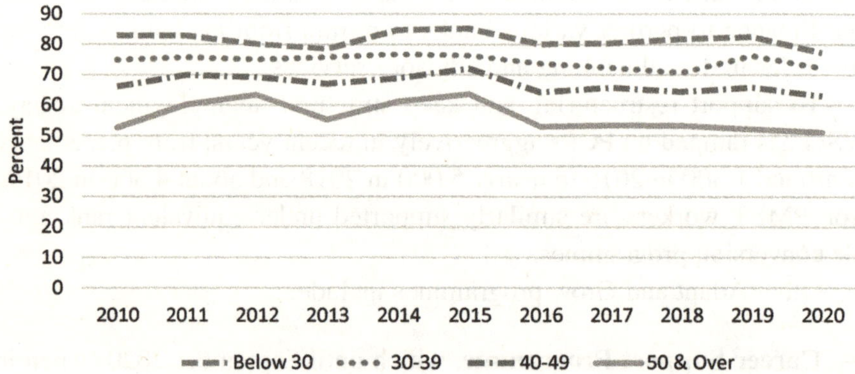

Figure 8.8 Re-entry Rate of Retrenched Residents into Employment, 6 Months Post-Retrenchment

Source: Labour Market Survey and administrative records, Manpower Research and Statistics Department, MOM.

First, mature and older workers are more likely to be retrenched than younger ones (Table 8.8).

Second, the re-entry of retrenched resident workers into employment has been on a slight downward trend even before COVID-19, with older workers finding it more difficult to re-enter employment (Figures 3.10, 8.8).

This is consistent with data suggesting that older workers take longer to find jobs. The median duration of unemployment of citizens aged 50 and above was 12 weeks in June 2019, against eight weeks for all unemployed citizens.[49]

While Adapt and Grow Programmes such as PCPs and the Career Support Programme already provided higher training and wage support for mature jobseekers aged 40 and above, the Unity Budget in 2020 introduced a further hiring incentive for employers of mature jobseekers who have undergone an eligible reskilling programme. This was subsequently replaced, from September 2020, by the Jobs Growth Incentive, which supports firms to accelerate hiring of their local workforce with a special focus on mature workers (see Chapter 11 for details). An additional SkillsFuture Credit of $500 was also given to every Singaporean aged 40 to 60 years in 2020, over and above the broad-based top-up of $500, for use in selected reskilling programmes at continuing education and training (CET) centres.

Looking Ahead

With the economic fallout from COVID-19 stretching into 2021 and economic restructuring proceeding at a relentless pace, helping workers who are displaced to get back into employment quickly will be even more important than before.

Constantly changing skills requirements will also necessitate a "switching infrastructure" or system that allows rapid reskilling for new job roles. Workers will have to be nimble and adaptable, leveraging the strong foundational skills acquired in early life, as well as the collective support of the CET/SkillsFuture and employment facilitation ecosystem, to refresh their skills and stay relevant.

At the same time, they will need a robust safety net to tide them over periods of unemployment, as discussed in Chapter 5, providing the time, space, peace of mind, and motivation to pivot to new opportunities.

Employers must also play their part. With workforce growth decelerating and job roles transforming, it will be harder to find workers with the perfect match of skills and experience for the job. If the inflow of foreign workers is to remain sustainable, employers will need to be open to workers who may not already have all the requisite skills and experience but who are prepared to top up their skills and learn on the job. This is undoubtedly challenging given the short time-to-market that many firms face, but a commitment to forward workforce planning and building up their local workforce will be increasingly vital for firms operating in Singapore.

Endnotes

1. Since 1978, Singapore has only experienced two strikes: by shipyard workers in 1978 and bus drivers in 2012.
2. Organisation for Economic Co-operation and Development (OECD), "Foreign Born Population," OECD Migration Database, accessed 2 May 2021, https://data.oecd.org/migration/foreign-born-population.htm.
3. Source: 2011 Census, UK Office for National Statistics (ONS).
4. Gulf Labour Markets, Migration, and Population (GLMM) Programme, "Percentage of Nationals and Non-Nationals in GCC Countries' Employed Populations (2015)," accessed 2 May 2021, https://gulfmigration.org/media/graphs/GLMM%20-%20Website%20-%20GCC%20Graph%206%20-%2008%20Nov%202013.pdf.
5. Lim Swee Say, speech at Tripartite Alliance for Fair and Progressive Employment Practices' 10th Anniversary Event, 16 November 2016.
6. Ravi Menon, "Economic Dynamism Amidst Demographic Change," speech at the Institute of Policy Studies Singapore Perspectives 2018 seminar, 22 January 2018. The 2013 Population White Paper had projected that resident workforce growth would contribute about 0.1 percentage points to average workforce growth per annum from 2020 to 2030.
7. Comments attributed to then-Minister of State (Education and Communications & Information) Sim Ann at a dialogue organised by the National University of Singapore Society on 19 August 2015 were cited in Tan Tam Mei, "Population Still Hot Button Issue," *New Paper*, 20 August 2015.
8. Ministry of Finance, "Employers to Receive First Tranche of Wage Credit Scheme Payouts by End March 2014," press release, 18 March 2014.
9. By comparison, local professional, manager, executive, and technician (PMET) numbers increased by about 35,000 a year between 2014 and 2019.

Figures cited by Josephine Teo, speech at the debate on the President's Address, 1 September 2020.

10. Chia Yan Min, "Scope for 'Selective' Flexibility in Foreign Manpower Policy: Lim Swee Say," *Straits Times*, 9 March 2018.
11. Hariz Baharudin, "Pilot Scheme to Facilitate Hiring of Foreign Talent in Tech Firms," *Straits Times*, 31 July 2019.
12. Josephine Teo, speech at the debate on the President's Address, 1 September 2020.
13. In April 2021, NTUC Secretary-General Ng Chee Meng indicated that NTUC was considering the possibility of "ring-fencing" certain jobs for Singaporeans, such as in the human resources sector.
14. David Card and Alan Krueger, "Minimum Wages and Employment: A Case Study of the Fast-Food Industry in New Jersey and Pennsylvania," *American Economic Review* 84(4) (1994): 772–93.
15. David Neumark and William Wascher, "Employment Effects of Minimum Wages and Subminimum Wages: Panel Data on State Minimum Wage Laws," *Industrial and Labour Relations Review* 46(1) (1992): 55–81.
16. In a 1978 survey, 90% of economists polled agreed that the minimum wage decreased employment among low-skilled workers (J. R. Kearl, Clayne Pope, Gordon Whiting, and Larry Wimmer, "A Confusion of Economists?" *American Economic Review* 69(2) (1979): 28–37). A similar survey of American Economic Association members in 2000 found that only 46% agreed with the statement in full, and another 28% agreed with provisos (Dan Fuller and Doris Geide-Stevenson, "Consensus Among Economists: Revisited," *Journal of Economics Education* 34(4) (2003): 369–387).
17. See, for instance, Hristos Doucouliagos and T. D. Stanley, "Publication Selection Bias in Minimum-Wage Research? A Meta-Regression Analysis," *British Journal of Industrial Relations* 47(2) (2009): 406–428; Marco Hafner, Jirka Taylor, Paulina Pankowska, Martin Stepanek, Shanthi Nataraj, and Christian Van Stolk, "The Impact of the National Minimum Wage on Employment: A Meta Analysis," *RAND Europe* (2017).
18. David Neumark, "The Employment Effects of Minimum Wages: Some Questions We Need to Answer," NBER Working Paper No. 23584, revised October 2017.
19. Jeffrey Clemens, "Making Sense of the Minimum Wage: A Roadmap for Navigating Recent Research," *Policy Analysis* 867 (May 2019).
20. OECD, *Employment Outlook 2015* (Paris: OECD Publishing, 2015), 34–52.

21. Doruk Cengiz, Arindrajit Dube, Attila Lindner, and Ben Zipperer, "The Effect of Minimum Wages on Low-Wage Jobs," *Quarterly Journal of Economics* 134(3) (2019): 1405–1454.
22. José Azar, Emiliano Huet-Vaughn, Ioana Marinescu, Bledi Taska, and Till von Wachter, "Minimum Wage Employment Effects and Labor Market Concentration," NBER Working Paper No. 26101, July 2019.
23. Christian Dustmann, Attila Lindner, Uta Schönberg, Matthias Umkehrer, and Philipp vom Berge, "Reallocation Effects of the Minimum Wage: Evidence from Germany," working paper, 2019, http://sarkoups.free.fr/dustmann719.pdf; Peter Harasztosi and Attila Lindner, "Who Pays for the Minimum Wage," *American Economic Review* 109(8) (2019): 2693–2727.
24. Dara Lee Luca and Michael Luca, "Survival of the Fittest: The Impact of the Minimum Wage on Firm Exit," NBER Working Paper No. 25806, May 2019.
25. John Addison, McKinley Blackburn, and Chad Cotti, "Minimum Wage Increases in a Recessionary Environment," *Labour Economics* (2013): 30–39; Jeffrey Clemens and Michael Wither, "The Minimum Wage and the Great Recession: Evidence of Effects on the Employment and Income Trajectories of Low-Skilled Workers," *Journal of Public Economics* 170 (2019): 53–67.
26. Congressional Budget Office, "The Budgetary Effects of the Raise the Wage Act of 2021," https://www.cbo.gov/system/files/2021-02/56975-Minimum-Wage.pdf.
27. Senior Minister Tharman noted, in a forum on jobs and skills at the Singapore Perspectives conference organised by the Institute of Policy Studies on 12 January 2021, that half of the bottom 10% of workers were above the age of 55, and of these, two-thirds did not complete secondary school.
28. Singapore participated in Round 2 of the survey in 2014–2015. See OECD, *The Survey of Adult Skills: Reader's Companion, Third Edition* (Paris: OECD Publishing, 2019) and OECD country note on Singapore (https://www.oecd.org/countries/singapore/Skills-Matter-Singapore.pdf). The performance of older people in Singapore contrasts with that of 15–24-year-olds who performed better than the OECD average in literacy and had the highest average score among participating countries in numeracy.
29. Leong Chi Hoong, Ong Pinchuan, Tan Di Song, and Kuhan Harichandra, "The Impact of the Workfare Income Supplement Scheme on Individuals' Labour Outcomes," *Economic Survey of Singapore Second Quarter 2014* (Singapore: Ministry of Trade and Industry 2014, 27–36). Elastic labour demand would increase the negative impact of a minimum wage on employment.
30. Josephine Teo, speech at the Debate on the President's Address, 1 September 2020.

31. Linda Lim, "The Economic Case for a Minimum Wage: A Conversation with Linda Lim," interview by Kwan Jin Yao, 25 July 2020, https://www.academia.sg/academic-views/minimum-wage-conversation/.
32. Economist William Baumol suggested that wages will still grow in jobs with little or no productivity increase, in response to rising wages elsewhere. This is known as "Baumol's Cost Disease".
33. Zaqy Mohamad, speech at Ministry of Manpower Committee of Supply Debate, 3 March 2021.
34. National Wages Council Guidelines 2017/18.
35. National Wages Council Guidelines 2018/19.
36. Figures cited by National Trades Union Congress' then-Deputy Secretary-General Koh Poh Koon in October 2020. The figures cited are not based on take-home pay, for which it is necessary to subtract employee Central Provident Fund (CPF) contributions rather than add in employer CPF contributions.
37. Figures cited by Senior Minister of State (Manpower) Zaqy Mohamad on 3 November 2020 in response to Parliamentary Questions by MPs Jamus Lim and Liang Eng Hwa.
38. Josephine Teo, speech at the Economic Society of Singapore Annual Dinner, 22 August 2019 (Number of citizens aged 65 and over in 2020 updated with data from the Department of Statistics).
39. Ibid.
40. Lim Swee Say, Retirement and Re-employment (Amendment) Bill Round-Up speech, 9 January 2017.
41. Wong Pei Ting, "The Big Read in Short: Re-employment a Mixed Bag for Older Workers," *TODAY*, 31 August 2019.
42. Lee Zen Wea, Huang Jirong, and Guo Jiajing, "Impact of the Retirement and Re-employment Act on Older Workers' Employment Outcomes," *Economic Survey of Singapore First Quarter 2017* (Singapore: Ministry of Trade and Industry, 2020): 45–50.
43. Tripartite Workgroup on Older Workers, *Strengthening Support for Older Workers*, report of the Tripartite Workgroup on Older Workers, 2019.
44. Kok Ping Soon, "Reimagining Productive Longevity," *Ethos* 20 (Singapore: Civil Service College, 2019): 5–21.
45. Ibid., 18.
46. Ministry of Finance (MOF), *The Revenue and Expenditure Estimates for the Financial Year 2020/2021* (Singapore, MOF, 2020). See Head S — Ministry of Manpower key performance indicators.
47. Kenneth Cheng, "Foreign Job-Matching Agencies Get 1-Year Extension from Govt after 'Satisfactory' Placement Record," *TODAY*, 18 December 2019.

48. The number of locals entering employment averaged about 137,000 in each six-month period from 2017 to 2019 (source: Ministry of Manpower administrative records and Labour Market Survey), with an even larger number switching jobs.
49. Ministry of Manpower, "Singapore Citizens in the Labour Force," occasional paper, 23 January 2020.

Chapter 9

Capturing Value from Economic Growth

The ability to sustain good socio-economic outcomes for citizens depends critically on Singapore's ability to make a living amid competition from both advanced and emerging economies. In the Socio-Economic Flowchart (Figure 1.3), this is necessary for upstream employment and incomes. Economic activity also generates profits and tax receipts, adding to the wealth of business- or equity-owning citizens and providing the state with resources for social spending and redistribution.

Value Capture

Economic activity is only useful to a country insofar as value can be captured from it. This applies to economy activity performed in Singapore by firms based here, as well as economic activity abroad by Singapore-owned or Singapore-based firms.

Pathways to Value Capture

Value can be captured through various channels, including:

1. **Profits**: income through shareholding (whether widely distributed shareholding in listed companies, concentrated in the hands of a Singaporean owner as in some privately held firms, or via Temasek portfolio companies)

2. **Employment**: good jobs and incomes for Singaporeans
3. **Tax receipts**: used for public spending or to build up national reserves
4. **Strategic linkages**: clustering/hub effects, forward and backward linkages and adjacencies. Interdependencies create stickiness and can be a sustainable competitive advantage for Singapore.
5. **Capabilities**: these form the basis of competitiveness and future value capture

These channels are highlighted in the lightly shaded boxes in the Value Creation and Capture Flowchart for domestic economic activity (Figure 9.1).

The total economic impact of an investment or new economic activity is not limited to the **direct impact** from jobs and incomes generated. There is also the **indirect impact** arising from demand for goods and services supplied by other industries and firms and the **induced impact** arising from household spending of the income earned. This secondary impact can be quantified by multipliers in input-output tables.

Apart from the obvious considerations of market size, opportunities, and business costs, the attractiveness of Singapore to both local and foreign companies is affected by a suite of factors highlighted in the darkly shaded boxes, which the government can influence through investment in physical or digital infrastructure, manpower development, regulations, as well as support in the form of grants, tax incentives, financing support, and procurement. These also shape business conditions that support the

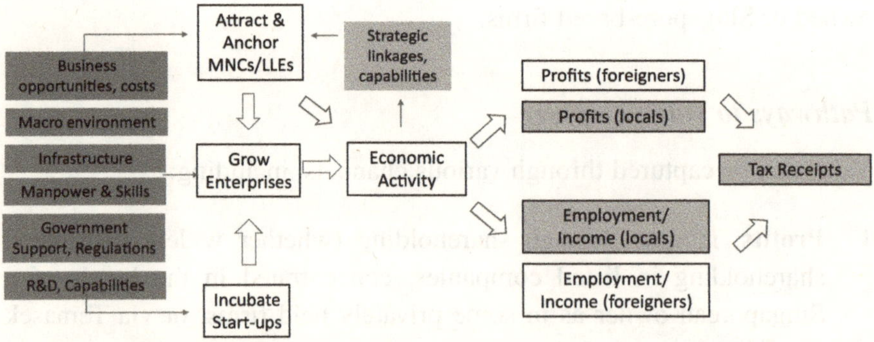

Figure 9.1 Value Creation and Capture Flowchart

growth of firms, whether through domestic scaling-up or internationalisation. Government support may be targeted at automation, productivity enhancement, training, building of corporate capabilities, innovation, and internationalisation.

However, it is not my intent to embark on a comprehensive discussion of these economic levers, which would take another book to satisfactorily explore. Instead, the focus here will be on Singapore's economic structure — the mix of enterprise types and sectors that make up the Singapore economy, which affects the country's growth potential, economic resilience, and job opportunities. Economic structure depends on the government's overarching economic strategy and must be informed by value capture. We will then consider how Singapore can optimise productivity and incomes amid population constraints. The chapter concludes by highlighting the realities and trade-offs confronting Singapore in its choice of economic future.

Singapore's Economic Structure

Looking Back: Tigers of Different Stripes

Singapore, like the other East Asian "tiger" economies, enjoyed rapid economic growth through export-led industrialisation. Between 1960 and 1985, real income per capita increased by more than four times in each of the tiger economies. Some scholars have pointed to the role of state-directed industrial policy in explaining the East Asian "Miracle".[1] Other commentators prefer to emphasise sound macroeconomic policy, investment in education and technology, as well as the accumulation and efficient allocation of capital and labour.[2]

The Asian tigers, though, were never cut from exactly the same cloth. Singapore's export strategy was founded on attracting foreign multinational corporations (MNCs), whereas South Korea and Taiwan protected domestic production and incentivised exports, for example, through export credit subsidies. Like Singapore, Hong Kong kept taxes low and promoted free trade, but was more laissez-faire in its approach to economic development and less reliant on foreign MNCs.

After a brief experiment with import substitution in the early 1960s, Singapore pursued an export-led strategy in earnest from 1965, adopting a highly open stance towards foreign investment. This was necessary to overcome the limitations of Singapore's small domestic market, low savings, and lack of industrial capabilities. At a time when many developing countries viewed MNCs as exploitative, Singapore actively wooed MNCs to set up manufacturing operations in Singapore. This effort was spearheaded by the Economic Development Board (EDB), which had been set up in 1961 by Goh Keng Swee, Singapore's then-Minister for Finance and economic architect. Besides offering attractive tax incentives, no restrictions were imposed on equity ownership, foreign exchange controls, or the repatriation of capital; MNCs could freely borrow from the domestic capital market and were not obliged to transfer technology to local firms.[3] As Prime Minister Lee Hsien Loong put it, "We decided if by exploiting us they created jobs for us, and they generated markets for us, and they brought technology and organisation... so be it."[4]

Over time, differences among the tiger economies became more pronounced as national priorities and strategies diverged. Whereas Hong Kong saw its manufacturing mostly hollowed out through offshoring to mainland China, especially after 1997, Singapore retained substantial manufacturing activity on its shores with a succession of national economic strategy reviews affirming the centrality of manufacturing in anchoring value chains. Beginning with general manufacturing and electronics, Singapore deepened and diversified its manufacturing base to include petrochemicals in the 1980s and pharmaceuticals in the 1990s, even while it grew its services sectors as a "second engine" of the economy.

While manufacturing has remained important to South Korea, Taiwan, and Singapore, the domestic private sector has played a bigger role in South Korea and Taiwan, whereas Singapore's manufacturing sector has been dominated by MNCs and government-linked companies.

In parallel with its MNC strategy, Singapore developed its own national champions in the form of government-linked firms such as Singapore Telecommunications, Keppel Corporation, DBS, ST Engineering, Singapore Airlines, and Neptune Orient Lines. Many of these were former state-owned monopolies and had acquired considerable financial clout, experience, and track record before they were corporatised.

The 1980s and 1990s saw Singapore's economy open up further compared with South Korea and Taiwan. There was a wave of privatisation, the aim being to inject competition and gradually divest government ownership of entities operating in the commercial space. In sectors deemed strategic, such as banking, telecommunications, and airlines, the government retained control via the state-owned sovereign wealth fund Temasek Holdings, although Temasek's business decisions are guided by commercial considerations rather than directed by the state. The government-linked companies, or GLCs, were rechristened Temasek-linked companies, or TLCs. In sectors deemed non-strategic, the government divested its stake entirely, an example being the Public Works Department, which became CPG Corporation.

The United States-Singapore Free Trade Agreement (USSFTA), signed in 2003, was a significant milestone in the opening up of Singapore's economy. The USSFTA obligated Singapore to ensure that TLCs acted in accordance with commercial considerations and were not influenced by the government. While Singapore had acceded to the World Trade Organization Agreement on Government Procurement in 1994, the USSFTA brought many more statutory boards under rules to prevent government procurement from discriminating in favour of local enterprises. A new statutory board, the Competition Commission of Singapore (now Competition and Consumer Commission of Singapore), was also set up to administer the 2004 Competition Act.

While Singapore's TLCs remained strong, alongside the many MNCs present here, few truly multinational companies have arisen from the private sector. Unlike the Korean *chaebols*, which have attained global leadership positions in consumer electronics and cars, Singapore does not boast significant international players apart from the TLCs and a few real estate firms and banks, which are at best regional players.

This has led to calls for a shift away from an economic model dominated by MNCs and TLCs to build up a strong private enterprise sector. Even in this, opinions differ as to the best strategy to develop private enterprise. Some continue to place faith in state-guided industrial policy, looking to the government to identify winners and channel resources to build up competitiveness in key sectors. Others believe that the government should simply step aside to allow private enterprise to take centre stage.

Singapore's Enterprise Mix

MNCs have been the driving force behind Singapore's economic development since the 1960s, providing jobs, technology, organisation, and market access that have enabled Singapore to achieve accelerated economic development. However, over the past decades, lower-end manufacturing operations, such as hard disk production,[5] have shifted out of Singapore. Although these activities have been replaced by higher-end manufacturing, design, and research and development (R&D) (for example, in the biomedical industry), the latter employ fewer workers and cannot fully make up for the loss of lower-end manufacturing employment. Singapore has also succeeded in attracting MNCs to locate their global or regional corporate headquarters and R&D facilities in Singapore.

TLCs are Singapore's national champions. Corporations such as Singtel, Sembcorp, DBS, and CapitaLand are major regional or international players. These companies started from a position of dominance within the Singapore market; leveraging their track record and acquiring expertise with government backing, they spread their wings and made inroads into markets abroad. While Temasek retains majority shareholding or a controlling stake in TLCs deemed strategic, these companies typically have a broad-based shareholding structure and run on a commercial basis. Other former government-linked corporations have been divested or privatised in full or in part.

SMEs employ about 70% of the workforce and contribute over 40% of nominal value added (Table 9.1). They have a critical role to play in the enterprise ecosystem, whether as suppliers or service providers to large enterprises, contributors to the diversity of lifestyle and retail offerings, or potential large local enterprises themselves.

Table 9.1 Enterprise Mix by Size (2020)

	Number of Enterprises	Employment	Value Added
SMEs	99%	70%	43%
Non-SMEs	1%	30%	57%

Source: Ministry of Trade and Industry.

Table 9.2 Enterprise Mix by Ownership (2020)

	Number of Enterprises	Employment	Value Added
Local Enterprises	81%	68%	36%
Foreign Enterprises	19%	32%	64%

Source: Ministry of Trade and Industry.

While MNCs continue to play a major role in Singapore's enterprise ecosystem, the desire to grow more large local enterprises (**LLEs**) has gained impetus over the years. A perennial concern is that footloose MNCs may relocate their headquarters and research centres nearer to major markets and production centres such as China. Former Permanent Secretary (Finance) Ngiam Tong Dow (2006), in emphasising the need for Singapore to "grow (its) own timber", observed, "The MNCs have contributed a lot to Singapore but they are totally unsentimental people. The moment you're uncompetitive, they just relocate."[6]

Another motivation is to develop indigenous corporate and innovation capabilities as a national competitive advantage. Michael Porter (1990) noted that "a development strategy based solely on foreign multinationals may doom a nation to remaining a factor-driven economy.... At some stage in the development process, the focus should shift to indigenous companies. In Singapore and Ireland, my view is that the shift has been too little and too late."[7]

Tan Kim Song and Manu Bhaskaran (2015) argued that stronger local enterprises and "inherent capacity" would strengthen Singapore's structural resilience to economic shocks and make it more likely for Singapore workers to prosper in the long term.[8] They contrasted the supporting role played by SMEs within Singapore's industrial ecosystem with the core of globally competitive SMEs in Germany, Japan, South Korea, and other export-oriented economies which have produced a stream of globally-competitive national giants.

However, growing LLEs from the ranks of SMEs has proved challenging, despite the efforts of industry promotion agencies including SPRING Singapore and International Enterprise Singapore, which have since 2018 merged to form Enterprise Singapore.

In its heydays during the 1990s and early 2000s, home-grown technology firm Creative Technology went toe-to-toe with Apple for a share of the global portable media player market. However, the company's fortunes waned in the late 2000s. Water treatment and environment solutions firm Hyflux won infrastructure projects in Southeast Asia, China, and the Middle East, but ran into financial difficulties and filed for creditor protection in 2018. The likes of Banyan Tree, Osim, and BreadTalk have also expanded beyond Singapore's shores, but cannot match the TLCs in terms of size and global reach. With the rise of the digital economy in the 2010s and influx of private equity funding, however, Singapore-based corporations such as Grab and Sea Limited (formerly known as Garena) have expanded rapidly, holding out promise to become major international players.

Growing and Capturing Value from Home-Grown Enterprises

A major challenge faced by SMEs is lack of scale, given Singapore's small market size. Observers have also pointed to the difficulty SMEs face in gaining a foothold in sectors dominated by MNCs and TLCs, with little protection from foreign competition. A common complaint is that public agencies do not give smaller or newer firms a chance to secure government contracts. Another is the perceived monopoly of talent by the public sector and MNCs, with SMEs generally unable to match the salaries offered by the government and large firms. In calling for a rebalancing of support between MNCs and SMEs, Tan and Bhaskaran (2015) suggested that "the actual and effective assistance provided to SMEs paled in comparison to that offered to MNCs and GLCs because of the latter's perceived ability to expand GDP on a larger scale."[9]

While the government has stood firmly behind the MNC/TLC strategy that has brought Singapore much success thus far, it has redoubled efforts to grow local enterprises in parallel through support for capability building, innovation and internationalisation, as well as help with loan and equity financing.

The 2010 Economic Strategies Committee chaired by then-Minister for Finance Tharman Shanmugaratnam set a target of doubling the number of "globally competitive companies", defined as local firms with revenue exceeding $100 million, from around 500 in 2009 to 1,000 by 2020.[10] The Committee on the Future Economy (CFE), co-chaired by Ministers Heng Swee Keat and S. Iswaran, articulated the government's intent to help high-growth enterprises scale up and internationalise through targeted support, including access to networks, mentors, technology, and financing. According to the CFE report released in February 2017, there were around 800 companies with revenue exceeding $100 million, up from 560 in 2009.[11]

Notwithstanding, growing Singaporean multinationals is not an end in itself. It is worth noting that South Korea, despite its many global conglomerates, has a lower median income than Singapore (Table 2.2). Finland's economic tribulations following the decline of Nokia are also instructive.[12] It takes more than highly productive national champions to achieve high incomes and inclusive economic growth for citizens.

Even if local SMEs were to succeed and grow into global champions, there is no guarantee that the bulk of value they create will accrue to Singapore. Some of these firms will be acquired by multinationals or foreign investors. Even those that remain in local hands may decide to locate production and operations in lower-cost countries or countries with larger markets. Their R&D may be done abroad in countries such as China or India, where there is an abundant supply of skilled engineers and scientists. In short, growing national champions from the private sector may not yield benefits for Singapore and Singaporeans even if these companies succeed in scaling globally.

There are, of course, examples of global companies that are world-beaters but yet retain strong ties and identification with their country of origin. Many derive branding value from their association with their home country. An example is IKEA, which is closely identified with Scandinavian design. To maximise the contribution from potential home-grown multinationals, these firms need to be firmly rooted in Singapore, creating good jobs for Singaporeans and contributing to a strong enterprise ecosystem here through their supply chain networks, supplier development, their ability to bring Singapore SMEs overseas, or their contribution to R&D.

Between GDP and gross national product (GNP), the former is likely a better barometer of economic success. Location has a stronger nexus to broad measures of national economic well-being — economic activity creating jobs and generating spillover benefits through supply networks and agglomeration. That said, ownership is not without value even if economic activity takes place abroad. Wealth accruing to Singaporean owners is more likely to be spent in Singapore, and corporate headquarters and the nexus of supporting services are more likely to be located in Singapore if the company's owners are living here.

How TLCs Can Add and Capture Value for Singapore

Notwithstanding concerns, over the years, about TLCs crowding out other private enterprises, the Temasek model has two important advantages: Singapore ownership and control (with returns accruing to the state, in particular), and the ability of TLCs to leverage Temasek's resources, reputation, and network to spread their wings abroad. Given the limitations of scale and resources faced by private sector players and the advantage of ownership, a case could be made to nurture a second wave of globally competitive companies through Temasek.

This could be done by bringing promising medium-sized Singapore companies in strategic sectors under the Temasek fold or by setting up companies to commercialise the output of applied research institutes. With Temasek's backing, resources, and corporate expertise, the likelihood of growing strong international companies would be greater. Furthermore, their links back to Singapore would be guaranteed. At the very least, earnings would accrue to the state's reserves and can be used for the benefit of Singaporeans. There is potential to gain more than just income from equity. These firms could play a role in strengthening indigenous capabilities, human capital, and the national innovation system, which could significantly augment Singapore's competitive advantage.

To support its aim of doubling the number of firms with revenue over $100 million by 2020, the 2010 Economic Strategies Committee recommended catalysing the supply of patient (or long-term) growth capital for Singapore-based SMEs of up to S$1.5 billion by 2020, with half (up to $750 million) supplied by the government.

Consequently, the **Co-Investment Programme (CIP)** was launched in 2010. Under this programme, the government co-invests, with Temasek Holdings and the private sector, in promising Singapore-based firms. The

CIP comprises a direct investment fund managed by Heliconia, a wholly-owned subsidiary of Temasek set up for this purpose, as well as a fund-of-funds with private equity firms as limited partners. Heliconia and its feeder funds have invested in several firms with considerable potential, including Razer, a gaming hardware firm, and Hope Technik, a home-grown robotics manufacturing firm.

CIP-supported firms have found Temasek's involvement useful not just for capital, but also to leverage the Temasek brand and network. Mentoring by experienced business leaders is another key value-add provided by the limited partners. From the "Singapore Inc." viewpoint, Heliconia is able to identify synergies and opportunities for collaboration among its portfolio companies, for instance helping a fire protection solutions company and bathroom fittings company tap opportunities in overseas building projects.

The CIP has made progress in grooming promising Singapore enterprises for international expansion while keeping them firmly rooted in Singapore. A second tranche of funding for CIP was set aside in Budget 2014, along with an SME Mezzanine Growth Fund which was further expanded in Budget 2016. By 2019, when the third tranche of funding for CIP was announced, the government had already set aside $400 million in capital, catalysing about $1.3 billion of funding for SMEs.

Notwithstanding the utility of Temasek involvement, other pathways to business growth and success should not be discounted. In recent years, the abundance of global venture capital and private equity has enabled some Singapore-based companies to invest heavily in technology and people so as to leapfrog the competition, penetrate overseas markets, and scale rapidly.

Capturing Value from Start-Ups and Scale-Ups

The start-up scene in Singapore has generated considerable buzz and international attention of late. US-based organisation Startup Genome ranked Singapore 14th among the world's top start-up ecosystems in 2019, behind only Tel Aviv and Moscow in Asia. In the blockchain and fintech subsectors, Singapore ranked fourth and fifth, respectively. Local linkages were cited as a particular strength of Singapore.

The government has been heavily involved in catalysing and nurturing this ecosystem, with **Enterprise Singapore** the public agency in charge of start-ups. In 2016, the government formed **SG Innovate** to help scientists build deep tech start-ups through investment, commercialisation support, and connections. In 2018, **Startup SG** was created to represent the interests of the start-up community and showcase itself both locally and overseas. Its programmes include **Startup SG Equity** (which co-invests with venture capital funds), **Startup SG Accelerator** (supports incubators and accelerators), **Startup SG Talent** (attracts and facilitates entry of tech talent), and **Startup SG Network** (connects the ecosystem through an online portal). The **Startup SG Founder Programme**, which provides mentorship and a capital grant for first-time entrepreneurs, was re-introduced in 2017 and enhanced in 2020.

As at 2020, Singapore is home to 3,800 technology start-ups.[13] About 150 venture capital funds such as Jungle Ventures, Golden Gate Ventures, and Temasek's Vertex Venture Holdings are active here, along with several international start-up accelerators and incubators, such as Startupbootcamp Fintech and Rockstart. Singapore start-ups attracted $14.3 billion in funding in 2018 and $8.5 billion in 2019, but this figure fell to $5.5 billion in 2020 due to the COVID-19 pandemic.[14]

While the direct economic contributions of start-ups in terms of value added and jobs created has been modest so far, a 2015 PricewaterhouseCoopers (PwC) report forecast that Singapore's tech-enabled start-ups could potentially contribute up to 2% of GDP directly and provide 168,000 jobs by 2035.[15] Start-ups may also indirectly contribute to the economy, such as by helping to increase the productivity of other firms and creating demand for suppliers and service partners.

A frequently cited measure of success of an entrepreneurial ecosystem is the volume and value of exits. Prominent exits include video-streaming website Viki, acquired by Japanese company Rakuten for US$200 million in 2013, and live chat provider Zopim, which was acquired by US-based Zendesk for US$30 million in 2014. However, this raises questions as to whether Singapore captures value if a home-grown firm is acquired by a foreign multinational.

A foreign acquisition is not necessarily a poor outcome for Singapore if the firm retains substantial economic activity here. Furthermore, founders who have successfully exited often remain plugged into the start-up scene in Singapore, contributing their resources and experience as angel investors or mentors.

Another concern is that successful enterprises such as Razer have turned to overseas stock exchanges for listing due to the prospect of higher valuations abroad. While Singapore misses out on the financial and legal services that accompany a public offering, other business activities that the firm has in Singapore are not necessarily imperilled by a foreign listing. What may matter more is whether Singapore continues to offer a competitive value proposition to the firm for activities such as manufacturing, R&D, marketing, or distribution. Razer, for instance, has announced plans to open a new Southeast Asia headquarters in Singapore, creating a thousand jobs.

It has been suggested that for GDP contribution and job creation, it is more efficient to focus on companies in the scale-up rather than start-up phase. A report commissioned by the UK's Information Economy Council identified a focus on scale-ups (defined as "enterprises with average annualised growth in employees (or in turnover) greater than 20% a year over a three-year period, with 10 or more employees at the beginning of the observation period") as the key to securing national competitive advantage.[16] EDB has made efforts to attract promising global SMEs to Singapore. In this, EDB Investments (EDBI) plays a role, using strategic investments in high-potential firms to bring them here and anchor them within the Singapore ecosystem. In 2019, a Scale-up SG programme was launched to help Singapore companies with a proven track record to scale up effectively, and become market leaders and eventually future global champions.

All said, a vibrant enterprise ecosystem needs both the start-up feedstock as well as a healthy pool of scale-ups. Start-ups also provide a means through which research and development done in universities and research institutes can be commercialised, creating pathways to value for Singapore's considerable investment in R&D.

Capturing Value from MNCs and Foreign Direct Investment

Notwithstanding efforts at developing local start-ups and enterprises, attracting MNCs and foreign direct investment (FDI) remains integral to Singapore's economic strategy.

In the early years following Singapore's independence, MNCs played a critical role in creating jobs to absorb the supply of labour. They also brought expertise to Singapore, allowing the economy to rapidly climb the value chain. In terms of jobs and capabilities, the value proposition of FDI was clear.

Over time, however, manufacturing investments in Singapore have become more capital-intensive, yielding less in terms of job creation. Singapore has become a high-cost economy, less suited for manpower-intensive production but with strengths in high-end manufacturing and technology. While EDB has set a medium- to long-term target of attracting fixed asset investment of S$8 to $10 billion a year, with another $5 to $7 billion in total business expenditure, it only expects corresponding job creation of between 16,000 and 18,000 jobs. In 2020, EDB attracted fixed asset investment commitments totalling $17.2 billion (its highest since 2008), which are expected to create over 19,000 jobs.

It can no longer be expected that most investments which the EDB secures will create a large number of good jobs. These investments may still be worthwhile if they bring in new technology or know-how, catalyse adjacent industries, or generate high value added (VA) that can be captured in Singapore.

Value capture from foreign investments will increasingly take the form of strategic linkages and the anchoring of capabilities (Figure 9.1). Multinationals have traditionally anchored industry clusters — building up an ecosystem of suppliers, service providers, and clients. As EDB becomes more selective in the investments it brings in, it must ensure that these investments contribute to building up key industry clusters to give Singapore a sustainable competitive advantage. This refers to strong economic clustering that keeps firms rooted in the ecosystem, much in the way the City of London exerts a gravitational pull on financial and professional services firms.

Capability transfer is something Singapore has done well in and must continue to emphasise. In the 1970s and 1980s, EDB set up the Japan-Singapore Institute, French-Singapore Institute, and German-Singapore

Institute in collaboration with the respective foreign governments to raise the technical skills of the local workforce to meet the manpower needs of MNCs. In the early days of industrialisation, Singapore had to rely more on skilled foreigners in a variety of roles. Over time, more of these jobs were taken over by Singaporeans who had acquired skills through formal training as well as experience on the job. The role that MNCs have played in building up indigenous human capital over the years should not be underestimated.

This must continue if Singapore is to capture value from MNC investment in a new era of emerging technologies. Firms should be given latitude to import talent in areas where there is a lack of skilled local manpower, but the aim must be to achieve greater localisation over time. In 2017, EDB launched the **SkillsFuture Leadership Development Initiative** with the goal of training 800 potential business leaders over three years. While complete localisation is not a tenable objective for any global city, there ought to be more Singaporeans acquiring skills and taking up corporate leadership positions in the coming years.

Agglomeration and Hub Strategy

As a major sea and air transport node, Singapore has built a cluster of economic activity around its seaport and airport, including trade, logistics, financial, business, and other professional services. This has enabled Singapore to leverage its connectivity to entrench economic advantage. Besides physical connectivity, Singapore seeks to plug itself into the world through pursuit of free trade. An ardent supporter of regionalisation through ASEAN and multilateralism through the World Trade Organization, Singapore has also signed a considerable number of bilateral free trade agreements (FTAs) with its trading partners, beginning in the early 2000s during George Yeo's tenure as Minister for Trade and Industry.

The hub strategy has been integral to Singapore's economic development over the years, sustaining Singapore's manufacturing base and anchoring value chains here.

In 2000, Jurong Island was officially opened. It had been formed from the amalgamation of seven offshore islands through land reclamation to provide a home for Singapore's petrochemical industry. As at 2020, Jurong Island has attracted investments of over $50 billion, with over 100 global petrochemical and speciality chemical companies forming part of its integrated ecosystem, along with utilities and logistics services providers. The common location enables upstream refineries to sell feedstock to downstream manufacturers while facilitating outsourcing and sharing of common services for economies of scale.

A major foray into the biomedical sciences was made with the construction of Biopolis in 2003. Led by then-Chairman Philip Yeo, Singapore's Agency for Science, Technology and Research (A*STAR) wooed top international scientists, research labs, as well as major pharmaceutical companies to set up shop in Biopolis. Biopolis anchors the entire R&D value chain for the life sciences, from basic drug discovery to clinical development and medical technology research. It houses an array of public and private biomedical research institutes, alongside corporate tenants.

Other location-based clusters include Fusionopolis for ICT, media, physical sciences, and engineering, and Launchpad@Ayer Rajah for start-ups.

Hub networks extend beyond firms, suppliers, and distributors, encompassing financial, accounting, legal, marketing, and other business services as well. The availability and quality of these services contribute to successful industrial clusters. Access to high-quality research and investment capital also matters. Singapore must itself be an attractive location for corporate executives, business owners, and investors to call home as the presence of these decision-makers is a key part of this strategy.

The clustering of economic activity has the potential to reap economies of agglomeration through interdependencies, network, and scale effects. Major industry players help to build up supply networks and in turn enjoy the convenience, choice, and niche services from an extensive array of suppliers and service providers. Value is captured throughout the ecosystem, whose sustainability depends on the density of linkages that constitutes "stickiness". To this end, industry and research clusters should be leveraged to develop indigenous capabilities and intellectual property, adding further to "stickiness" and facilitating value capture.

Where it is not feasible or desirable to locate an entire industry value chain in Singapore, the aim has to be for Singapore companies to establish themselves in strategic niches in the value chain from which they may not be easily dislodged.

Sectoral Diversification and Its Limits

Another key question regarding Singapore's future economic structure pertains to the mix of industries and extent of diversification that is optimal for Singapore.

Given Singapore's roots as an entrepot port, shipping and commerce have been a key part of Singapore's economy from colonial times to the present, although the share of these activities in GDP has fallen as other industries have developed.

From the 1960s to 1980s, manufacturing anchored Singapore's export-oriented industrialisation policy. Beginning with general manufacturing, Singapore added to its industry mix electronics in the 1970s, petrochemicals in the 1980s, and pharmaceuticals in the 1990s. This was primarily driven by the desire to find new engines to power growth.

Within each industry, too, Singapore moved up the value chain from labour-intensive activities to more capital-intensive and higher-skill activities. The electronics sector, for instance, upgraded from personal computer assembly and hard disk drive manufacturing to higher-end semiconductor production, design and assembly, as well as hard disk media and integrated device manufacture. Moving up the value chain was a conscious strategy as well as a natural consequence of economic development given the rise in manpower and business costs as Singapore developed.

The 2001 collapse of the dot-com bubble, followed by a global electronics downturn from 2001–2002, resulted in significant retrenchments in the electronics sector and underscored the need for further economic diversification. The 2000s saw Singapore's economic strategy shift from an efficiency-driven phase to an innovation-driven phase, as Singapore was now closer to the technological frontier and needed to develop its own research and innovation capacity. Efforts were also made to position Singapore as a global city by strengthening international linkages and welcoming global talent to its shores.

The 2003 Economic Review Committee (ERC) report recommended building a diversified economy powered by manufacturing and services as twin engines of growth. Over time, the services sector grew in importance as the second engine of growth. Logistics, financial, and professional services developed to support shipping and manufacturing, particularly as MNCs set up regional and global headquarters in Singapore. Rising incomes also spurred the development of retail, food services, and property services.

The ERC report also identified exportable services such as finance and professional services, as well as education and healthcare, as key growth areas. This led to the Global Schoolhouse initiative, with the aim of bringing in 100,000 foreign educators and students, and the Singapore Medicine initiative, which aimed to make Singapore a hub for medical tourism. The mid-2000s saw a retreat from these two initiatives. First, the swelling population made it difficult to absorb more foreign students and their families. Second, healthcare resources, especially manpower, were stretched by growing domestic needs and the burgeoning private healthcare sector, which needed little additional encouragement from the government to attract foreign patients.[17]

In 2005, a controversial decision was taken to develop two "integrated resorts" with casino licenses in Singapore, with the stated aim of boosting the tourism industry in the face of strong regional competition. It was also in line with economic diversification: the two resorts were expected to create 35,000 jobs directly and indirectly, as well as achieve Singapore's goal of becoming a vibrant international city. The integrated resorts were completed and began operations in 2010.

The share of services in Singapore's GDP climbed from 61.4% in 2000 to 70.1% in 2020, with significant growth in business services and finance. After remaining in the ballpark of a quarter of GDP since 1990, the share of manufacturing in GDP has fallen to around a fifth of GDP since 2008 (Figure 9.2).

The manufacturing sector itself is fairly well diversified. Electronics remained the largest cluster in 2019, accounting for over a third of VA and output, but other clusters including biomedical were also significant contributors (Table 9.3).

Unsurprisingly, the manufacturing sector's share of resident employment has declined steeply from 25.8% in 1990 to 9.6% in 2020, as higher-VA, more capital-intensive activities such as pharmaceutical

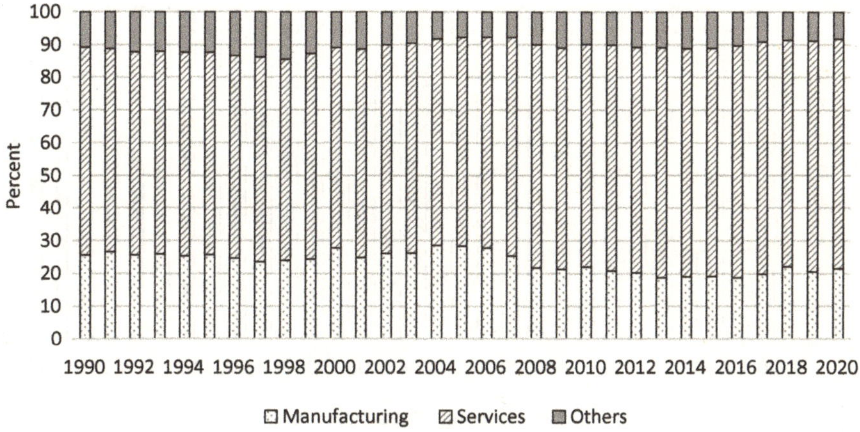

Figure 9.2 Share of GDP

Source: Singapore Department of Statistics.

Table 9.3 Singapore's Manufacturing Clusters (2019)

Cluster	Number of Establishments	Value Added ($ billion)
Electronics	229	39.4
Chemicals	418	11.9
Biomedical	147	12.4
Precision Engineering	2,717	12.4
Transport Engineering	1,202	8.3
General Manufacturing	4,304	8.3

Source: Census of Manufacturing Activities, Economic Development Board.

production have replaced labour-intensive manufacturing activities over time (Figure 9.3). Going forward, employment in manufacturing can be expected to contract further as production becomes increasingly automated and capital-intensive.

Notwithstanding, the government intends to sustain Singapore's manufacturing base as a vital part of the economy. The 2017 Committee on the Future Economy report recommended keeping a globally

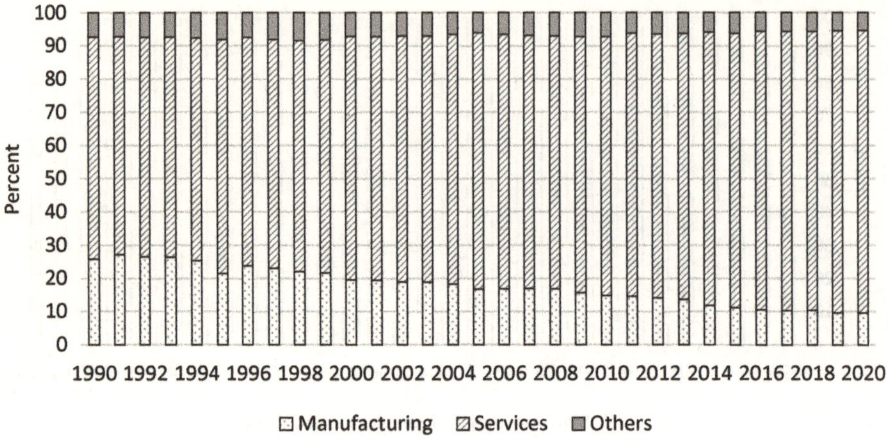

Figure 9.3 Share of Resident Employment

Source: Ministry of Manpower, Singapore Department of Statistics.

competitive manufacturing sector that contributes around 20% of GDP in the medium term. This was in view that manufacturing is a source of good jobs and productivity growth, generating strong spillovers to the rest of the economy. The report also highlighted the importance of manufacturing in diversifying Singapore's production base and exports. In 2021, the government reaffirmed its commitment to keeping manufacturing at about a fifth of GDP over the medium term, with plans to grow the sector by 50% over the next 10 years.

A key benefit of economic diversification is increased resilience to supply or demand shocks in any one sector. For instance, during the COVID-19 pandemic, the biomedical industry buoyed Singapore's exports as countries around the world stockpiled medicine and pharmaceutical ingredients.[18]

However, given Singapore's land and population constraints, there are limits to the range of economic activities that Singapore can take on. Some have even asked whether Singapore ought to forgo certain economic clusters such as petrochemicals, given its carbon footprint, land take, and heavy reliance on foreign manpower. Others have suggested that Singapore focus its efforts on key sectors where Singapore has greater potential to excel.

On Picking Winners and Losers

If there is to be greater focus, the question is whether this should be market-led or state-directed. In times past, the government has actively identified the "next big thing" — petrochemicals and life sciences, for instance. This has entailed courting of foreign investment, attracting talent, ramping up training in relevant areas, and building major infrastructure such as Jurong Island and Biopolis.

In Budget 2015, the government articulated five key growth clusters, namely advanced manufacturing, applied health sciences, smart and sustainable urban solutions, logistics and aerospace, as well as Asian and global financial services.[19] The 2017 Committee on the Future Economy report similarly cited increased demand for finance, hub services, logistics, healthcare, digital economy, and advanced manufacturing.[20] However, these are broad areas which Singapore was already engaged in.

Perhaps it is not realistic in the current context to identify a major new area of investment such as petrochemicals or life sciences. First, Singapore's population and workforce constraints are such that it cannot ramp up manpower significantly in a new growth area without correspondingly reducing manpower in other areas or becoming less diversified. Second, there are no obvious major new areas to enter, given that Singapore's economy is already fairly diversified.

Rather, any changes are likely to be intra-sectoral, altering the mix of activities within each manufacturing cluster or services sector. For instance, within finance, it could be the balance between trading and compliance, or among front-office, mid-office, and back-office work. Within ICT, there could be greater emphasis on data analytics and cybersecurity, themes pertinent to Singapore's Smart Nation initiative and global growth areas. Within manufacturing, it could be industry 4.0, robotics, and 3D printing, among others.

Indeed, to speak of sectors as such may not be appropriate, given the blurring of lines between traditional sectors. Increasingly, we hear of the "servitisation" of manufacturing. As Toh Mun Heng (2016) pointed out, manufacturing companies such as Rolls Royce have increased the services content in their product offerings as a way of differentiating their products.[21] This could include R&D, maintenance repair and overhaul, as well as parts management. Likewise, boundaries between telecommunications companies, broadcasters, and media content providers have broken down with the emergence of technologies such as television streaming and Voice over Internet Protocol.

For some, the call to focus is not just about identifying new opportunities but also about de-emphasising or downsizing certain industries given Singapore's overall factor constraints. This could be driven by market forces such as rising rents and wages forcing low margin activities offshore. In fact, it may be wise for the government not to write off any industry. Few would have predicted the success of Singapore's ornamental fish and furniture industries given the high labour and land costs in Singapore. And yet the furniture industry has experienced a resurgence through a focus on design and smart marketing.[22] In his maiden Budget speech in 2016, then-Minister for Finance Heng declared that "there is no such thing as a sunset industry, only sunset thinking." He referred to a "spirit of enterprise" as the key factor behind the success of any business, regardless of industry.[23]

Notwithstanding, the government wields various resource levers to direct economic activity — through the allocation of land earmarked for specific industries, grants and incentives given to attract and develop economic activities, and the sizing of intake into various courses in the universities and polytechnics.

What concerns policymakers is the rapid growth of low-productivity domestic services sectors, which has seen their share of GDP rise, dragging down Singapore's overall productivity growth. For instance, there could be too many subscale retail and food and beverage establishments, while the healthcare sector could balloon as the population ages. There is also a conscious urging of young people to take up science and engineering instead of flocking towards the more lucrative finance and real estate sectors which are associated with wealth management rather than wealth creation.

In Singapore, dirigisme and free market ideology co-exist in an ever-shifting equilibrium as the state seeks to shape economic strategy while leaving room for market forces to direct the allocation of resources efficiently.

The challenge is one of intervening judiciously, whether by setting the rules of the game, providing information to economic agents or applying resource allocation levers — so as to allow for the smooth functioning of markets within the state's broad strategic arc while minimising the likelihood of market failure.

Raising Productivity and Incomes Under Population Constraints

With workforce growth slowing in Singapore, sustained economic growth depends on productivity growth. Wage increases can only be sustained without a loss of competitiveness if there is concomitant growth in labour productivity.

However, the measurement and interpretation of productivity figures is far from straightforward. First, there are various alternative measures of labour productivity: VA per worker, VA per hour worked, or even physical measures of productivity such as the rate of task completion per worker. Second, labour productivity growth is heavily influenced by economic cycles which could mask the underlying trends and issues. Labour productivity tends to fall during a downswing as employers are slow to shed workers, and to rise during an upswing as previously hoarded labour is used more productively. Year-to-year growth in productivity may hence be less meaningful than tracking productivity growth over a longer horizon.

Third, a measure such as VA per worker or VA per hour worked is subject to the limitations of VA or GDP as a measure of economic activity. For instance, the booking of corporate profits could lift headline GDP and productivity even if the bulk of the returns accrues to shareholders abroad.

Finally, there could be compositional effects in the denominator of an indicator like VA per worker. For instance, aggregate productivity could be depressed even if every worker becomes more productive, if less productive or marginal workers enter the workforce. On the other hand, the exit of less productive workers from the workforce, for instance due to severe unemployment, could conversely boost productivity without an increase in general welfare.

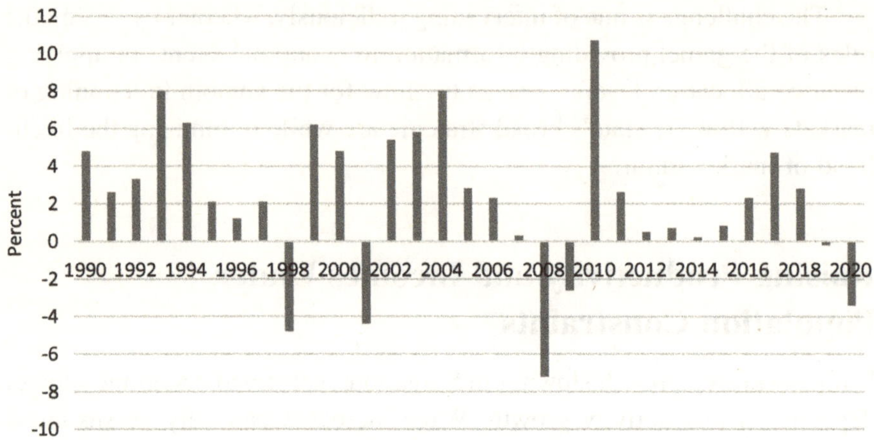

Figure 9.4 Real Growth in VA per Worker

Source: Singapore Department of Statistics, Ministry of Manpower.

Hence, any interpretation of Singapore's productivity figures must be done with care.

From 1989–1999, real VA per worker grew by a compound average of 3.1% per annum (Figure 9.4). However, from 1999–2009, labour productivity growth slowed to 1.4% per annum. In 2010, there was a rebound in real VA per worker growth on the back of exceptionally strong GDP growth as Singapore's economy rebounded from the 2008–2009 financial crisis.

Singapore's real labour productivity growth averaged 2.5% per annum between 2009 and 2019, within the 2%–3% target set by the Economic Strategies Committee in 2010. However, excluding the 2010 rebound, real VA per worker growth averaged 1.6% per annum between 2010 and 2019.

If we look instead at real VA per actual hour worked (AHW), which is more comparable internationally, the picture is somewhat better.[24] In terms of real VA per AHW, productivity grew at 2.9% per annum from 2009 to 2019 and 2.3% per annum from 2010 to 2019 (Figure 9.5).

A few points are worth noting.

First, there has been a secular slowdown in productivity growth in many other advanced economies. According to a McKinsey Global Institute study, average labour productivity growth (VA per hour worked) in the United States and six advanced European economies slowed to

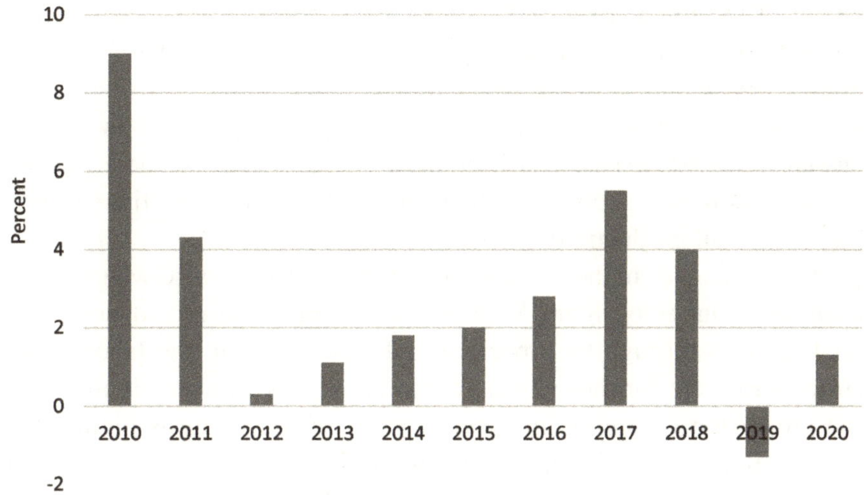

Figure 9.5 Real Growth in VA per Actual Hour Worked

Source: Ministry of Trade and Industry.

0.5% per annum from 2010–2014, down from 2.4% per annum a decade earlier (2000–2004).[25] The study attributed this to three factors: the waning of a productivity boom that began in the 1990s, persistent weak demand and uncertainty following the Global Financial Crisis, and digitisation, which had cannibalised incumbent products and services while not yet yielding measurable productivity gains.

There is debate on whether it takes time for innovation to show up in productivity growth, and whether measured productivity is reflective of actual gains. "Techno-pessimists", such as American economist Robert Gordon, have suggested that recent technological progress has not been as impactful as previous innovations and improvements in industrial organisation.[26] This is not the place to enter into such a debate, but Singapore is nonetheless in good company when it comes to slowing productivity growth.

Second, a key driving force in Singapore's aggregate productivity performance over the past decade has been the faster growth in employment and hours worked in less productive, domestically oriented sectors compared with more productive, externally oriented sectors. Studies by Ministry of Trade and Industry (MTI) economists (Fan & Teo, 2017; Teo

& Ong, 2018; Toh & Ting, 2020) found that a negative "shift share" effect dragged down overall productivity growth from 2009 to 2016, although productivity within most sectors improved.[27] While the shift share effect turned positive from 2016 to 2019 with strong employment growth in the outward-oriented finance and insurance, and ICT sectors, the continued growth in domestic services as the population ages may continue to be a drag on overall productivity growth.

Third, changes in the composition of the workforce also weigh on the headline productivity figure. With generous support for employers to hire older workers through the Special Employment Credit, the labour force participation rate for those aged 65 and above has climbed significantly. The proportion of seniors in the workforce in Singapore is higher than most developed countries apart from South Korea and Iceland (Table 8.5). The tight labour market and more stringent Dependency Ratio Ceilings may have also prompted hiring of more marginal Singaporean workers, depressing labour productivity.

Then-Minister for Finance Tharman pointed out, in rounding up the 2014 Budget Debate, that Singapore has taken an inclusive approach in restructuring where productivity is not achieved through the shedding of less productive workers.[28] This has made it more challenging to see a rise in measured productivity.

Total Factor Productivity

A critique of Singapore's development that dates back to the early 1990s is that Singapore's economic growth has been largely driven by growth in factor inputs (i.e. labour and capital) rather than productivity. In a well-known paper, Alwyn Young (1992) characterised Singapore's economic growth from 1966 to 1990 as almost entirely attributed to capital accumulation and workforce growth, with growth in total factor productivity (TFP) playing a minimal role.[29]

While the large-scale mobilisation of capital and labour has accounted for the bulk of Singapore's growth over the years (Figure 8.2), growth in TFP has picked up, accounting for a larger share of GDP growth in recent decades (Table 9.4) This reflects the significant investment in education and training, as well as research, innovation and enterprise, particularly in

Table 9.4 Contribution of TFP Growth to GDP Growth by Decade

	1973–1979	1979–1989	1989–1999	1999–2009	2009–2019
Annualised Real GDP Growth (%, CAGR)	6.7	7.4	6.9	5.1	4.8
Annualised TFP Growth (%, CAGR)	−1.4	1.6	0.8	1.0	1.0

Source: Singapore Department of Statistics.

recent years. Given constraints on labour force growth, TFP growth will become an increasingly important driver of Singapore's economic growth, underscoring the importance of continued investment in skills and innovation.

Characterising the Population Constraint

The central economic challenge facing Singapore is one of optimising economic outcomes under population constraints. For most of Singapore's history, there was no supply-side constraint in the form of limits to immigration and population growth. The way to maximise citizens' incomes was to grow high-VA sectors and train Singaporeans to take up high-paying jobs in these sectors while topping up manpower in lower-VA sectors with foreigners.

Given the need to keep population growth sustainable, however, two other considerations come into play. First, the number of foreigners in essential but lower-VA sectors such as domestic services must be contained. Second, the high-VA sectors typically require many foreigners to plug gaps in expertise, and their numbers too will have to be managed.

As outlined in Chapter 8, the influx of foreign workers must be calibrated in view of land, infrastructure, and societal constraints. Population growth that runs ahead of infrastructure and land supply will result in congestion on trains, roads, and public spaces, and steep increases in the cost of property and land. Societal constraints are perhaps even more binding given Singaporeans' sentiments regarding job competition, which is the greatest pain point in regard to the foreign workforce.

There are other social frictions too. Singaporeans' feeling of being outnumbered by foreigners in workplaces and residential areas would be exacerbated if foreigners fail to integrate well. Some have pointed out that the preponderance of foreigners in frontline service poses challenges arising from language barriers and cultural differences. There could also be disamenities associated with foreign worker congregation points near residences, although this can be ameliorated by careful planning of foreign worker accommodation and transport capacity.

Finally, an over-reliance on foreign manpower would be inimical to economic and social resilience, as discussed in Chapter 8.

Hence, it is necessary to constrain the growth of the foreign workforce, which would in turn constrain the growth of the overall workforce. This implies that in times of strong external demand, Singapore may not be able to take up all the economic opportunities that present themselves. Potential investments may have to be forgone, resulting in the creation of fewer PMET jobs here. The workforce may not be able to support such a diverse range of economic activities, thus reducing economic resilience and job opportunities in specialised areas. More Singaporeans will have to take on jobs in lower-VA domestic sectors to meet essential needs as foreign worker inflow is tightened. On the plus side for local workers, the labour market is likely to remain tight, with upward pressure on wages likely as the economy recovers from the effects of the COVID-19 pandemic.

The supply-side constraint poses new challenges as Singapore's economy enters a mature phase of growth. Manpower shortages in essential services could drive up costs for businesses and consumers as well as erode cost competitiveness if productivity growth does not keep pace with wage growth. There could be increased underemployment if the economy is unable to create enough PMET jobs to meet the aspirations of Singaporeans. Average wages would certainly be lower than in the unconstrained growth scenario. With Singapore's GDP growth rate confined to a more modest range compared with the past, the economy may be at risk of slipping into a recession more frequently.

While GDP or income per capita is more pertinent to economic well-being, absolute GDP size as well as the real growth rate of GDP affect Singapore's geopolitical clout as well as attractiveness to businesses seeking to expand. It is important to sustain optimism about Singapore's growth prospects to avoid adverse feedback loops from outflow of talent and investments, which would further shrink the workforce.

Evidently, there is a trade-off between the social pain points and economic costs. Two questions follow.

First, what population growth rate is feasible and socially acceptable, taking into account what can be done to ease the population constraint by growing the Singaporean workforce organically, and by lowering the social cost of taking in foreigners? Second, what steps can be taken to optimise economic outcomes (i.e. maximise economic growth and incomes) given the population constraint?

Easing the Population Constraint

While land is finite and population cannot expand forever, increasing the local-born population and labour force would ease the population constraint in a more socially acceptable way than ramping up immigration. This could entail improving fertility, increasing labour force participation rates, and encouraging the return of overseas Singaporeans. Despite generous pro-family support, however, Singapore faces an uphill battle to raise birth rates. While labour force participation, especially among older workers, has increased significantly over the past few years, there is a limit to how much further this can be raised as Singapore already has among the highest proportion of elderly in employment among developed nations (Table 8.5). On a one-off basis, the shortening of National Service duration and steps taken to minimise the wait between National Service and university/polytechnic enrolment have given a modest boost to the workforce.

A second strategy is to alleviate the land/infrastructure and social pain points arising from immigration so as to make it more acceptable to Singaporeans (Table 9.5).

The social pain points arising from immigration are hardly uniform. There are different issues associated with different groups of foreigners and they matter differently to Singaporeans of different age and education levels, for example:

- — The young polytechnic graduate competing for a job
- — The mid-career PMET who is unhappy at being bypassed for promotion

Table 9.5 Strategies to Address Population Pain Points

Constraints and Pain Points	Strategies: Existing and Potential
Land/space and infrastructure constraints	— Expand infrastructure capacity especially transport, housing, hospitals
Social constraints	
(i) Perception that foreigners are taking away jobs and/or suppressing incomes, made worse by perception that foreign employers in Singapore are discriminating against Singaporeans and favouring their compatriots	— Strengthen human resource practices and safeguard fair employment through the Fair Consideration Framework — Develop locals proactively, e.g. through the SkillsFuture Leadership Development Initiative
(ii) Singaporeans feeling outnumbered by foreigners especially in residential areas or workplaces with high concentration of foreigners, especially where foreigners fail to integrate well or where Singaporeans are unaccustomed to foreigners' cultural traits and habits	— Integrate foreigners/new citizens and increase Singaporeans' acceptance of diversity — Address sensitive issues of sub-ethnicities — Consider breaking up foreigner concentrations in residences and workplaces
(iii) Communication difficulties arising from large number of foreigners in frontline service due to language barriers and/or cultural differences	— Enhance frontline experience by ensuring adequate representation of Singaporeans in service roles e.g. hospital front desk roles — Equip foreign service staff with language skills and knowledge of local cultural sensitivities
(iv) Discomfort with congregation of foreign workers near residences (linked to infrastructure)	— Expand number of purpose-built foreign worker dormitories and activity centres — Better manage transportation of foreign workers from dormitories to workplaces

— The mature worker who has been retrenched
— The Singaporean unhappy that a service staff can only speak Mandarin, etc.

Hence, it may not be appropriate to present the population constraint as a single binding target for the whole economy, such as a cap in the number of foreigners or proportion of the workforce that foreigners comprise. A more nuanced approach would be to take into consideration the composition of foreign workforce in terms of skill-level and nationality and whether the pain points of various citizens have been adequately addressed.

For instance, it cannot be assumed that with improvements in construction productivity, every Work Permit holder shed from the construction sector will permit the hiring of one more Employment Pass holder as Singaporeans may perceive a greater job threat from the EP holder than the foreign construction worker.

While it is possible to naturalise more foreigners to bring the ratio of Singapore Citizens to foreigners to any desired level, this would not reduce the likelihood of encountering people who look and sound different from Singapore-born Singaporeans. Naturalisation does matter in that the next generation of naturalised Singaporeans will be Singapore-born and will grow up here. However, the immediate solution has to be better integration of foreigners and new citizens into society, along with gradual acceptance that Singapore-born Singaporeans will eventually be the minority.

Optimising Economic Outcomes from Constrained Population Growth

Having assessed what would be an appropriate envelope for the inflow of foreign manpower, the next question is how productivity, economic growth, and incomes can be maximised subject to Singapore's population and workforce constraints.

One way to approach this is to group Singapore's economic sectors into three broad categories:

(a) **High-VA Exportable Sectors**: these are manufacturing and services sectors with high VA/growth which offer a high proportion of skilled jobs commanding good wages. They tend to be exportable sectors such as ICT, financial and professional services, advanced manufacturing, and biomedical sciences.
(b) **Essential Domestic Sectors**: these are sectors which have traditionally been low VA but are needed to support growing domestic needs due to population growth in recent years as well as Singapore's rapidly ageing population, e.g. healthcare and early childhood education.

(c) **Other Sectors**: these include food services, retail, general manufacturing, and other sectors that tend not to have high VA or exportable content, and need not expand rapidly to keep up with societal needs.

This is in fact an oversimplification. In each sector, there would be progressive, high-growth firms as well as low-productivity/low-VA firms. For instance, retail and food establishments, such as BreadTalk and Charles and Keith, have expanded rapidly through internationalisation. Conversely, not all firms in high-VA sectors are progressive. Nevertheless, this simple construct will facilitate the identification of optimisation strategies for the economy.

Given constraints on population growth (subject to the earlier caveat that it would be too simplistic to set a single, binding numerical target), Singapore's manpower flows over time can be summarised in Figure 9.6. Broadly speaking, this assumes that local manpower freed up from certain sectors can be redeployed in other sectors.

The following strategies could help to optimise jobs and incomes for Singaporeans subject to overall workforce constraints:

(1) **Grow and localise quality jobs in high-VA sectors**
Investment attraction and enterprise development can spur job growth in high-VA sectors. The share of quality jobs held by Singaporeans may be increased by calibrating the inflow of foreigners into such jobs or by enhancing the skills and capabilities of Singaporeans to make them more competitive.

(2) **Restructure away from low-VA sectors**
The government could facilitate restructuring away from low-VA sectors in order to free up manpower and resources for new growth areas.

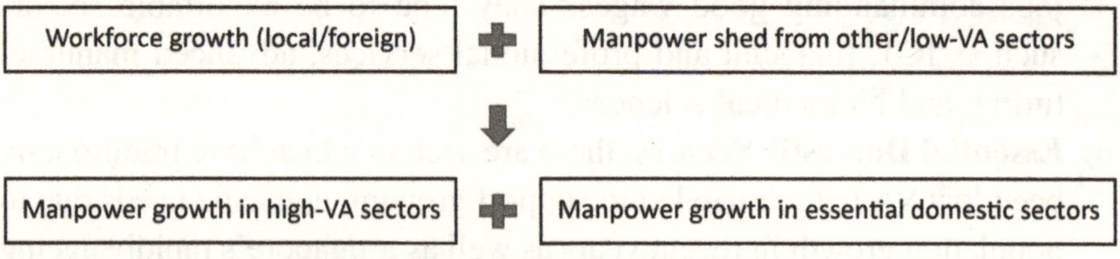

Figure 9.6: Manpower Flow Identity

Within each sector, there can also be a shift from lower-VA to higher-VA parts of the value chain.

(3) **Increase productivity, especially in the essential domestic sectors**
Increasing productivity, especially in the essential domestic sectors, can free up manpower and reduce dependency on foreign workers. Higher productivity will also enable wages to be raised (strategy 4) without significantly eroding competitiveness.

(4) **Raise wages and redesign jobs, especially in the essential domestic sectors**
In order to meet national needs (e.g. healthcare for the ageing population) without bringing in even more foreigners, Singaporeans will have to take up many of the jobs in the essential domestic sectors. Higher wages, along with job redesign, can make these jobs more attractive to citizens, whether to younger Singaporeans entering the workforce or displaced PMETs.[30] This will mitigate the aspirations gap as well as potential structural unemployment, and is vital for the alignment of aspirations, skill sets, and job profiles in the economy.

Some of these strategies may move the needle more than others; an in-depth look at each sector is required to determine what is feasible in terms of restructuring, localisation, productivity, and job redesign. In particular, it would be useful to take reference from the localisation rates and productivity levels that other advanced economies and cities have managed to achieve.

Recent efforts corresponding to these strategies are outlined and discussed below.

Strategy 1a: Growing High-VA Sectors

To grow the economy, the MTI family of agencies has pursued a strategy of attracting investments, transforming industries, creating new enterprises, and helping enterprises to internationalise. Attracting MNCs, particularly those in high-VA sectors Singapore hopes to anchor, remains core to Singapore's economic strategy. This has been complemented, particularly in recent years, by vigorous efforts to spur the creation of new enterprises, particularly in deep-tech areas, and helping them to internationalise.

To optimise resources, more aggressive support in terms of grants, tax incentives, manpower, and land allocation has been directed towards growth areas such as advanced manufacturing and ICT, as well as more productive firms which are typically account-managed by sectoral champion agencies. For instance, firms that require flexibility to bring in foreign manpower to fulfil critical roles may seek the assistance of their sectoral agencies.

Strategy 1b: Localising Quality Jobs

At the broadest level, the calibration of foreign worker inflow, such as through qualifying salary thresholds for employment pass holders, provides an impetus for firms to hire local workers. To stamp out discriminatory hiring practices, particularly against locals, the Fair Consideration Framework has been strengthened over the years, as described in Chapter 8. On the other hand, progressive employers committed to nurturing the Singaporean core, promoting complementarity between local and foreign employees, and strengthening knowledge transfer, may qualify for the Human Capital Partnership programme, which provides fast-lane access to enterprise- and workforce-development schemes.

A key limb of the localisation effort is to encourage and incentivise firms to develop their Singaporean core. The Ministry of Manpower's (MOM's) **Capability Transfer Programme** (launched in 2017 and extended to 2024) provides funding and manpower support to firms that engage foreign experts to transfer global skills to the local workforce. There is a suite of education and training initiatives, including those under the SkillsFuture umbrella, to build up the skills and capabilities of Singaporean workers. Of note, the **SkillsFuture Leadership Development Initiative** encourages firms to build up a pipeline of Singaporeans with the potential to take on senior leadership positions in firms. On their part, employees must be willing to take on overseas postings to gain the experience needed to assume regional or international leadership positions in due course.

To take these efforts further, one possibility is to set targets for localisation or skills transfer as part of eligibility or evaluation criteria for incentives offered to companies, or consider adopting a points-based system for skilled immigration that takes into account availability of trained locals, as outlined in Chapter 8.

Strategy 2: Restructuring Away from Low-VA Sectors

Restructuring away from low-VA sectors could be left to market forces. Given the tight labour market and limited supply of land, the prices of factors of production would be bid up by more productive sectors and firms, squeezing out less productive sectors, assuming that the government does not intervene to prop up the laggards.

Proactive efforts to rechannel resources from the less productive to the more productive sectors and firms could accelerate the process but may be controversial. For instance, the government could differentiate manpower control measures by sector or industry or calibrate the release of land for specific industrial or commercial uses. Regulatory levers could also be employed, such as by imposing licensing requirements or tightening regulatory standards to constrain the growth of certain sectors.

A shift from broad-based to targeted assistance for firms could also accelerate the exit of less productive firms or the consolidation of less productive sectors while tilting support to the more progressive sectors and firms. This would have the further advantage of lowering fiscal cost.

A related concern has to do with jobs deemed unproductive even if they are high-paying. For instance, some are concerned that too many young people are becoming real estate agents and financial insurance advisors. The worry is that Singapore could become a society of wealth managers rather than wealth creators if scarce manpower is directed towards such jobs at the expense of science, engineering, or entrepreneurship. On the other hand, jobs in finance and real estate pay well and appeal to Singaporeans. They are also a channel through which the spillovers from wealth in Singapore can benefit a broader group of Singaporeans.

It may, however, be heavy-handed to deploy strong regulatory levers to shrink such sectors unless the regulations are required to protect the public in the first place. Instead, the government could support efforts at disintermediation, i.e. removing the need for agents to go between buyers and sellers to the extent that this is possible through technology or standardised products. Given that the availability and attractiveness of estate agent and financial advisory jobs are closely correlated with asset cycles, preventing the emergence of property and asset bubbles is key. To avoid becoming a rentier economy, it is important to ensure that jobs in science and engineering, as well as jobs in essential service sectors, are rewarding and attractive enough to Singaporeans so that they can hold their own against the allure of wealth management and estate agency.

Strategy 3: Increasing Productivity

Given that wage growth must be underpinned by higher productivity in order to be sustainable, raising productivity is a key strategy for all sectors in the economy, as highlighted by the Economic Strategies Committee.

The National Productivity and Continuing Education Council (NPCEC), a tripartite committee chaired by then-DPM Tharman, was set up in April 2010 to boost skills and enterprise productivity. Subsequently, NPCEC was split into a National Productivity Council and a SkillsFuture Council to give dedicated focus to the SkillsFuture initiative. In 2016, the two councils were remerged to form the Council for Skills, Innovation and Productivity, which has subsequently become the Future Economy Council chaired by former Finance Minister (now DPM) Heng Swee Keat.

"Industry Transformation Maps" (ITMs) have been developed for 23 industries to spur growth and strengthen competitiveness through productivity, jobs, skills, innovation, trade, and internationalisation. Building on work started by the NPCEC, the ITMs bring together firms, industry associations, unions, and government agencies to find ways to boost productivity in each sector, whether by encouraging skills development, reviewing regulations, or setting up industry-level platforms and shared services.

Ways to increase productivity include:

- Capital deepening
- Upgrading the skills of local and foreign workers
- Investing in technology or organising production/businesses more efficiently
- Sharing services or achieving scale economies
- Leveraging cross-sector support or horizontal enablers

While Singapore is close to the productivity frontier in certain highly productive exportable sectors, it lags behind the global leaders in other sectors, suggesting significant scope for productivity catch-up.

There are, however, challenges and trade-offs in the productivity drive. A key factor underpinning productivity is the design of infrastructure, systems, and processes. For instance, a central kitchen or centralised dishwashing facility could raise productivity among restaurants in a mall but may not have been planned for in the design of older malls. Likewise, the potential for efficient in-building logistics and distribution could be constrained by building design and it may be prohibitively expensive to retrofit old malls or hotels. Sometimes, efforts at improving efficiency at a particular location could push the problem elsewhere. For instance, outsourced food production may require more frequent transportation and lead to road congestion.

Even with rising productivity in every sector, there could still be a decline in aggregate productivity if less productive sectors are expanding faster than more productive sectors. Should higher productivity manufacturing clusters grow less quickly than services, it will mean that maintaining or raising Singapore's overall productivity growth will become yet more challenging.

Strategy 4: Raising Wages and Redesigning Jobs

The government may directly raise wages in professions such as nursing and education where it is the largest employer,[31] or indirectly in any sector of the economy by calibrating foreign worker inflow. In addition, the government has made targeted interventions to help low-wage workers through the Progressive Wage Model, which sets wage floors and ladders in selected low-wage sectors (see Chapter 8).

Redesigning jobs is integral to restructuring and necessary to forestall structural unemployment or underemployment on a significant scale. Traditional manufacturing and middle-skill professional jobs are being displaced by restructuring and globalisation, and potentially by technology in many sectors. An important receptacle for displaced workers, especially PMETs, would be the essential domestic sectors such as healthcare where needs are still growing and technology is not able to replace human workers in the immediate horizon. Otherwise, Singapore will be faced with both unemployed PMETs as well as heavy reliance on foreign workers in the essential domestic sectors.

While MOM's Adapt and Grow initiative, described in Chapter 8, provides considerable support for career conversion, there remain significant barriers to the successful transition of PMETs to the essential service sectors. Pay is an issue, as is prestige, given that many of the jobs in these sectors are occupied by lower-skilled, lower-wage foreigners. To overcome these barriers requires a simultaneous raising of wages accompanied by job redesign to make these sectors more productive and attractive to Singaporeans. These efforts could be undertaken as part of the manpower plan under each sector's ITM.

Summarising the Approach

The strategies described in this section are summarised in Figure 9.7.

These strategies are subject to inherent trade-offs and constraints:

— **Growth and localisation**: Insistence on localisation beyond a point could erode competitiveness and make Singapore less attractive to MNCs. Singapore's attractiveness to new industries and firms could also be constrained by competition from other economies.

— **Restructuring**: Too quick a pace may result in structural unemployment if displaced workers cannot be reskilled quickly enough. The

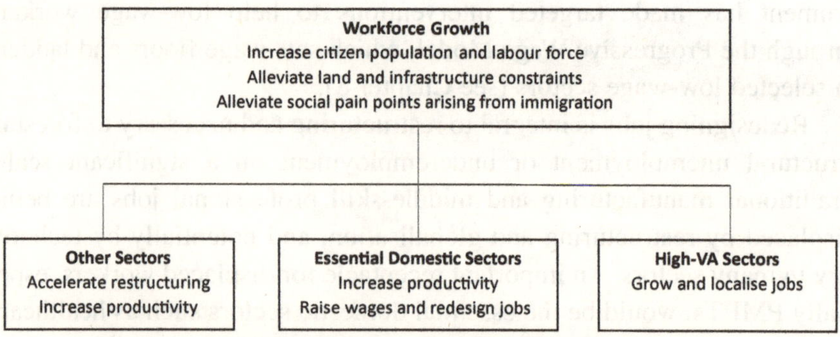

Figure 9.7: Strategies for Workforce and Economic Optimisation

pace of restructuring from low-VA to high-VA sectors, besides being constrained by population, will be constrained by the skills mix and how quickly workers can be reskilled for new roles.

— **Productivity**: While raising productivity is a no-regret move, there could be bottlenecks from training capacity, technological limitations, or firms' resistance to change.

— **Better wages/job redesign**: Raising wages without a concurrent increase in productivity could lead to cost inflation and a decline in competitiveness.

Singapore must continue to attract investments and nurture enterprises, especially in growth areas such as advanced manufacturing, green technologies, and professional services, which can create good jobs and instil confidence in Singapore's future.

However, a significant number of Singaporeans will not be able to find employment in these new growth clusters. First, many of these sectors will be capital, technology, or knowledge-intensive with high VA but low employment. Localisation of quality jobs in these sectors is only possible up to a point as multinationals may not find it attractive to remain in Singapore without access to global talent. Furthermore, in the near term, older workers who have had little formal education may lack the foundations to acquire the skills needed for knowledge-intensive jobs in the new industries.

At the same time, Singapore faces urgent and growing needs in essential domestic sectors, needs which cannot be met entirely by foreign workers due to population constraints. Singaporeans will have to fill many of the jobs in the essential domestic sectors, especially healthcare. Other domestic service sectors such as food services may also require more Singaporeans as aggregate population constraints bite.

The needs in these sectors can be moderated by restructuring and productivity improvements, but only partially. In the near to medium term, there will continue to be strong demand for rank-and-file jobs, especially in domestic service sectors where automation cannot readily substitute for manpower.[32]

With many more Singaporeans pursuing university degrees, whether at government-funded or private institutions, the gap between aspirations and the jobs actually available could widen. If left unaddressed, there could be a significant number of disgruntled underemployed graduates.

The singularly pressing issue, then, is to be able to attract Singaporeans, both new workforce entrants as well as mature workers displaced by restructuring or technology, into blue-collar or service work that has traditionally been shunned by locals. Manpower scarcity will drive up wages, narrowing the wage differentials between blue-collar and white-collar work. Still, there is a role for the government in facilitating the wage adjustment that needs to take place and supporting the redesign of jobs to blur the traditional distinction between PMET and non-PMET work. Mindsets regarding blue-collar work will have to change in tandem with higher wages and better working conditions. People in such jobs must become knowledge workers who are comfortable working with technology and automation, which play a part both in increasing productivity and improving working conditions.

In order not to drive up costs too quickly, the rise in wages should be accompanied by an increase in productivity. Hence the importance of raising skills, pursuing innovation, leveraging technology, redesigning business processes for greater efficiency, and adopting manpower-lean formats wherever possible.

It can be argued that Singapore has overachieved, in terms of GDP and incomes, relative to the country's collective skills thanks to excellent infrastructure, Singapore's hub status, and a conducive business environment. Compared with the OECD average, Singapore has a larger proportion of adults with low literacy and numeracy skills (according to the OECD Survey of Adult Skills), dragged down by those in the older age group (55 to 65 years).[33] Singapore's economic future will depend on whether the skills and productivity of its people catch up with the world's best, as well as whether Singapore can continue to command a location premium which translates into an income premium for citizens.

Transforming Perspectives

Several shifts in perspectives are required for Singapore's economic transition, given Singapore's population and workforce constraints.

The first is that **a vibrant society, in Singapore's context, can no longer be defined by youthfulness**. Singapore will become an increasingly aged society surrounded by countries with more youthful demographics. It must adapt to become an aged, vibrant society. Mindsets regarding ageing must evolve. The only way to keep the population profile relatively young would be to take in significantly larger numbers of young immigrants, which would be outside the bounds of social and political acceptability.

The second is that **fewer people in Singapore will look or sound local**. There will be an ever-shrinking share of locally born and bred people in Singapore. Efforts to attract overseas Singaporeans back to Singapore can mitigate this, but only to an extent. Even if the rate of immigration is not increased, and foreign worker inflows are carefully calibrated, the share of naturalised citizens, permanent residents, and work pass holders will continue to go up. Singaporeans must get used to living and working with people who do not appear or sound local, even if they hold pink identity cards. The alternative is a declining population size, similar to the situation in Japan, and far outside the currently envisaged population trajectory.

The third is that **the perception of what is a good or desirable job will have to change**. Not all Singaporeans can compete globally in high-tech, knowledge-intensive areas, regardless of how good our education system is. Even if foreigners are shut out from Singapore, there is no escaping global competition as much knowledge work can be done remotely. A significant proportion of Singaporeans will need to make a living from high-touch, domestic services jobs such as in healthcare, eldercare, community services, and hospitality, which cannot be easily automated or offshored. These will have to be transformed into jobs with good pay and status to simultaneously address Singapore's foreign worker dependency while meeting the career and wage aspirations of locals.

Finally, there must be recognition of the trade-off between Singapore's openness to foreign professionals and wealth and the location premium that Singapore can command in terms of job opportunities and incomes. Singapore's openness to skilled foreigners affects the range and depth of economic activities that can take place in Singapore and consequently the pull of Singapore as a global city through economies of agglomeration. This affects opportunities for Singaporeans in high-growth knowledge sectors, as well as in service sectors where many Singaporeans will find employment. The more Singapore is welcoming of foreign capital and wealthy immigrants, the more well-paying jobs there will be in wealth management, fine dining, and other services catering to the wealthy which should continue to do well even as e-banking, takeaway food, and self-service gain traction. On the other hand, if Singapore dials back on global wealth and talent attraction in favour of an economy and society with greater local orientation, Singaporeans would have to accept a reduction in the range of such jobs and the location-specific premium they would command.

Endnotes

1. Dani Rodrik, "The 'Paradoxes' of the Successful State," *European Economic Review* 41(3–5) (1997): 411–442.
2. World Bank, *The East Asian Miracle: Economic Growth and Public Policy Main Report* (New York: Oxford University Press, 1993).
3. Toh Mun Heng, "Singapore's Trade in Value Added: Importance and Implication of Information from the OCED-WTO TiVA Database," paper for the 24th International Input-Output Association Conference, 2016.
4. Lee Hsien Loong, speech at the Economic Club of Washington, 23 October 2017; Zakir Hussain, "Singapore Succeeded by Staying Open to MNCs: PM," *Straits Times*, 24 October 2017.
5. Chia Yan Min, "How Hard Disk Drive Sector Lost Its Mojo," *Sunday Times*, 17 August 2014.
6. Ngiam Tong Dow and Simon Tay, *A Mandarin and the Making of Public Policy* (Singapore: NUS Press, 2006), 23.
7. Michael Porter, *The Competitive Advantage of Nations* (New York: Free Press, 1990), 679.
8. Tan Kim Song and Manu Bhaskaran, "The Role of the State in Singapore: Pragmatism in Pursuit of Growth," *Singapore Economic Review* 60(3) (2015): 1–30.
9. Ibid.
10. Economic Strategies Committee, *Report of the Economic Strategies Committee: High Skilled People, Innovative Economy, Distinctive Global City*, February 2010, https://www.yumpu.com/en/document/view/8312324/full-esc-report-ministry-of-finance.
11. Committee on the Future Economy (CFE), *Report of the Committee on the Future Economy: Pioneers of the Next Generation*, February 2017, https://

www.mti.gov.sg/-/media/MTI/Resources/Publications/Report-of-the-Committee-on-the-Future-Economy/CFE_Full-Report.pdf.

12. According to the Research Institute of the Finnish Economy (ETLA), Nokia accounted for 4% of Finnish gross domestic product (GDP), and almost half of GDP growth, in 2000. See Jyrki Ali-Yrkkö, ed., *Nokia and Finland in a Sea of Change*, ETLA (Helsinki: Taloustieto Oy, 2010). See also Edwin Lane, "Nokia: Life After the Fall of a Mobile Phone Giant," *BBC News*, 18 March 2016.
13. Heng Swee Keat, Unity Budget Statement, 2020.
14. Tan See Leng, speech at the Action Community for Entrepreneurship Community Day, 30 March 2021.
15. PwC, "Singapore's Tech-Enabled Start-Up Ecosystem," (Singapore: PwC Consulting, 2015) https://www.pwc.com/sg/en/microsite/media/assets/startup-google.pdf.
16. Sherry Coutu, *The Scale-Up Report on UK Economic Growth*, a special report to the UK government, November 2014.
17. Jonathan Tan, "Re-inventing Singapore's Medical Tourism Industry," *Perspectives@SMU*, 26 February 2016, https://ink.library.smu.edu.sg/cgi/viewcontent.cgi?article=1180&context=pers.
18. Ovais Subhani, "Pandemic Powering Demand for Singapore's Pharma Exports," *Straits Times*, 29 August 2020.
19. Tharman Shanmugaratnam, Budget Statement, 2015.
20. CFE, *Report of the Committee on the Future Economy*.
21. Toh, "Singapore's Trade in Value-Added."
22. Singapore Furniture Industries Council, "A Look at Singapore's Flourishing Furniture Industry," Singapore Information Services, accessed 2 May 2021, http://www.insis.com/articles/se/a-look-at-singapore-s-flourishing-furniture-industry.
23. Heng Swee Keat, Budget Statement, 2016.
24. Since 2015, the Ministry of Trade and Industry (MTI) has released figures on value-added (VA) per actual hour worked (AHW), which has become more relevant given the increase in the proportion of part-time workers and cyclical changes in hours worked by full-time employees. AHW refers to the actual time spent by employed persons on work activities, regardless of whether the hours are regular in nature or whether they are paid for.
25. Jaana Remes, James Manyika, Jacques Bughin, Jonathan Woetzel, Jan Mischke, and Mekala Krishnan, *Solving the Productivity Puzzle: The Role of Demand and the Promise of Digitization* (McKinsey Global Institute, February 2018).

26. Robert J. Gordon, "Why Has Economic Growth Slowed When Innovation Appears to Be Accelerating?" NBER Working Paper No. 24554, April 2018.
27. Fan Shir Li and Marsha Teo, "Drivers of Labour Productivity Growth Trends in Singapore: An Update Using Value-Added per Actual Hour Worked," *Economic Survey of Singapore 2016* (Singapore: Ministry of Trade and Industry, 2017): 88–98; Marsha Teo and Ong Swee Joo, "A Shift Share Decomposition Analysis of Labour Productivity Growth in Singapore," *Economic Survey of Singapore 2017* (Singapore: Ministry of Trade and Industry, 2018): 18–25; Benjamin Toh and Jessica Ting, "Drivers of Labour Productivity Growth in Singapore 2009–2019," *Economic Survey of Singapore Third Quarter 2020* (Singapore: Ministry of Trade and Industry, 2020): 42–54.
28. Tharman Shanmugaratnam, Budget Debate Round-Up Speech, 2014.
29. Alwyn Young, "A Tale of Two Cities: Factor Accumulation and Technical Change in Hong Kong and Singapore," *NBER Macroeconomics Annual 1992* (1992). However, Kee Hiau Looi (2004) pointed out that conventional measures of total factor productivity (TFP) assume perfect competition and constant returns to scale. Taking into account observed market power and non-constant returns to scale technology, she estimated a significantly larger productivity contribution in Singapore's economic growth. See Kee Hiau Looi, "Estimating Productivity When Primal and Dual TFP Accounting Fail: An Illustration Using Singapore's Industries," *Topics in Economic Analysis & Policy, Berkeley Electronics Journal* 4(1) (2004): 1193.
30. The Lien Foundation Long-Term Care Manpower Study (2018) found that long-term care workers, including nursing aides and healthcare assistants, were paid less than their counterparts in Hong Kong, South Korea, Japan, and Australia.
31. In 2021, for instance, the Ministry of Health announced a 5%–14% rise in monthly base salaries for nurses, following previous pay hikes in 2014 and 2015.
32. A 2015 survey by Singapore Chinese Chamber of Commerce and Industry found that 89% of firms wanted to hire rank-and-file workers compared with 69% that wanted to hire Institute of Technical Education/polytechnic graduates and 63% that wanted to hire university graduates.
33. OECD country note on Singapore: https://www.oecd.org/countries/singapore/Skills-Matter-Singapore.pdf.

Chapter 10

Financing State Spending

Finance is central to the work of the government. The sustainability of public spending is vital to ensure that public programmes can continue to run, and investments in infrastructure and people can be made into the future. This chapter describes how Singapore has expanded and diversified its revenue sources over time and discusses options to provide for continually growing expenditure needs.

Singapore's fiscal principles and practices have contributed to a healthy budgetary position over the years. These include keeping the public sector lean, focusing on public outcomes instead of spending, intervening upstream to minimise the need for downstream expenditure, and having government spending reinforce individual and community efforts.

From the late 1960s to the 1990s, the Singapore government turned in persistent, sizeable budget surpluses. Revenue expanded as Singapore's economy grew while public spending remained conservative. The government was the proverbial prudent saver, living well below its means and accumulating reserves for the future.

Since the early 2000s, however, the picture has changed. Public expenditure has increased sharply, with the overall budget surplus averaging just 0.1% of GDP from FY2001 to FY2010 and 0.9% of GDP from FY2011 to FY2019.[1] The government's cash surplus, which includes land sales as well as actual investment and interest income (items which are not reflected in the government's conservatively defined overall budget balance[2]), fell from around 10%–20% of GDP in the 1990s to around 0%–10% of GDP in the 2000s and 2010s.[3]

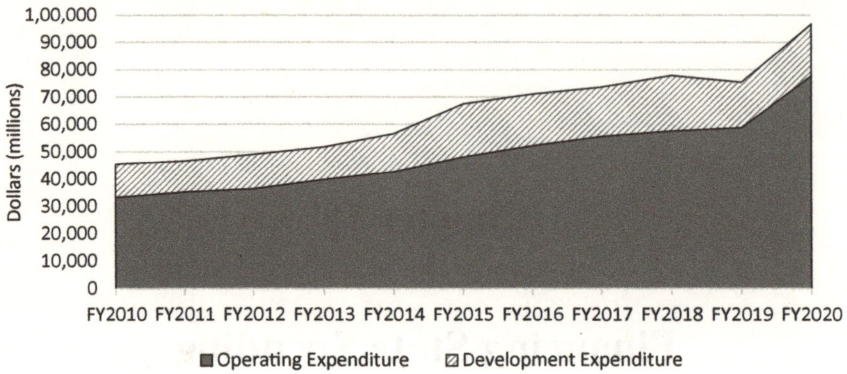

Figure 10.1 Total Government Expenditure (Excluding Special Transfers)

Source: Ministry of Finance.

From FY2020 to FY2019, total government expenditure (excluding special transfers[4] and spending from endowment and trust Funds) rose from $45.3 billion to $75.3 billion (Figure 10.1). As a percentage of GDP, government expenditure has drifted up from an average of 13.6% from FY2010–FY2014 to an average of 15.4% from FY2015–FY2019. Spending on healthcare has tripled, from $3.7 billion in FY2010 to $11.3 billion in FY2019.[5] It jumped to over $16 billion in FY2020 amid the COVID-19 pandemic, overtaking spending on education and even defence for the first time.

It is to be expected that social spending will rise as Singapore matures as a nation. First, healthcare needs, and hence spending, will rise as the population ages. Just as in the life cycle of individual, a period of accumulation over the working years is followed by a period of "dissaving" or drawing down in old age, there is a life cycle pattern to a nation's expenditure. The analogy, of course, cannot be taken too far, for the nation never retires and must continue to sustain itself.

Second, greater redistribution and additional social transfers such as the Workfare Income Supplement have become necessary to keep inequality at bay and help Singaporeans cope with the rising cost of living.

Hence, a shift in fiscal position, from persistent surpluses to a more balanced budget, is only natural as Singapore and its society mature.

Reserves Protection Framework

The reserves protection framework serves as a key safeguard of Singapore's fiscal sustainability.

Singapore's first Prime Minister, Lee Kuan Yew, had always been concerned about the inherent tendency towards fiscal profligacy in democratic political systems. This led the government to initiate changes to the Constitution in 1991 to create the office of an Elected President whose role is to safeguard the nation's reserves comprising physical (land and buildings) and financial assets. Accompanying this was a set of rules regarding the protection of reserves, which was codified in a 1999 White Paper.

In essence, public expenditure in each term of government is capped at the revenues the state raises within the term (called current reserves). Any drawdown of reserves accumulated in previous terms of government (called past reserves) requires the approval of the Elected President. At the end of each term of government, any surplus is locked up as past reserves. Land and financial assets can only be disposed of at fair market value; the net proceeds accrue to past reserves and cannot be used for current expenditure. If an asset is sold below fair market value, the government is required to top up the shortfall from current reserves to avoid a draw on past reserves. Furthermore, the government may not borrow without the approval of the President and Parliament, except for the issuance of government securities that are strictly intended to develop the Singapore bond market and provide a return to Central Provident Fund (CPF) savings. Under this two-key system, the President can check the excesses of a profligate government to prevent it from frittering away the hard-earned reserves built up over the years.

Given the strictures placed on the government in regard to spending, it is prudent for the government to budget for surpluses in the first couple of years into each new term of government so as to create buffer for unanticipated spending or revenue shortfalls. This is to ensure that the books are balanced across the full term of government. Consequently, there would be a tendency to draw down the remaining current reserves before the term of government expires, quite apart from any political impetus to share surpluses with citizens in the run-up to a general election.

One way that the government may set aside funds from current reserves for future use is through endowment and trust funds, which are set up by law for specific purposes. These include the Lifelong Learning and ComCare Endowment Funds, as well as the Pioneer Generation and National Productivity Funds. These serve to alleviate the fiscal burden on future governments by providing for various economic and social needs through current budget surpluses. Spending from government endowment and trust funds amounted to $4.4 billion in FY2019.

The past reserves shield Singapore's currency from speculation while insulating Singapore from financial and economic crises without the need to turn to debt markets or multilateral lending agencies. The understanding has been that the President's approval to draw on past reserves would be sought sparingly, only in moments of utmost need. Only on two occasions since 1991 have past reserves been drawn upon: to finance contingency measures during the 2008–2009 Global Financial Crisis and during the 2020–2021 COVID-19 pandemic.

Although there was no legal or constitutional obligation for the government to do so, the $4 billion drawn in 2009 was returned in full to the past reserves in February 2011, a decision which drew applause from both sides of the House during the 2011 Budget Debate.

Arguably, there had been no need for the government to dip into past reserves for the crisis contingency measures in 2009. This turned out to be a shrewd move nonetheless. It was a tangible demonstration to Singaporeans of the utility of the past reserves as a fallback for rainy days. Given the depth of the financial crisis, described at the time as the worst the world had seen since the Great Depression, it was undoubtedly an apt cause for activating past reserves. It was a case of "If not now, then when?" The use of past reserves demonstrated that the reserves were not merely a theoretical insurance, but could actually be withdrawn in times of need.

The COVID-19 pandemic saw the government seek approval to draw on past reserves thrice within FY2020: $17 billion for the Resilience Budget (second Budget of 2020), $4 billion for the Solidarity Budget (third Budget), and $31 billion for the Fortitude Budget (fourth Budget), amounting to $52 billion in total. While most countries borrowed to finance COVID-19 support measures, Singapore was able to tap on its reserves, underscoring the utility of the accumulated savings.

Financing Current Expenditure from Investment Returns

In fact, the reserves are more than a safeguard to be called upon in times of crisis. A considerable portion of the government's current spending derives from the returns on investing the reserves.

While a number of other advanced countries spend a significant part of the state budget servicing debt, Singapore is in the privileged position of deriving extra revenue from the savings built up by generations past.

Before 2001, dividends and interest income from investing the reserves were taken into the government's annual budget for spending. In 2001, the **Net Investment Income (NII) framework** was introduced. Under this framework, the government could spend only up to 50% of actual dividends and interest income after deducting debt servicing and investment-related costs. This was to support the continued growth of reserves.

Since then, there have been two major changes in legislation to provide more revenue from the reserves for the government budget. The first was the introduction of the **Net Investment Returns (NIR) framework** in 2008. The NIR framework expanded the definition of investment returns to total returns, including capital gains (both realised and unrealised) of assets under GIC (formerly known as Government of Singapore Investment Corporation) and the Monetary Authority of Singapore, while assets under Temasek Holdings remained under the NII framework. To smooth out expenditure and make budget forecasting easier, the amount available to the government of the day is based on expected long-term real returns rather than actual year-to-year investment returns. Otherwise, there could be a spike in government spending whenever the market is in bull territory, and conversely a shrinkage in expenditure when market sentiment is weak. The remaining half of the real returns which cannot be spent are reinvested to grow the reserves so as to keep pace with the growth of Singapore's economy.

The second change was the **inclusion of Temasek's assets in the NIR framework** from FY2016.[6] This expanded the income stream from the reserves significantly, from just over 2% of GDP to an expected 3% of GDP. The Net Investment Return Contribution (NIRC) jumped from

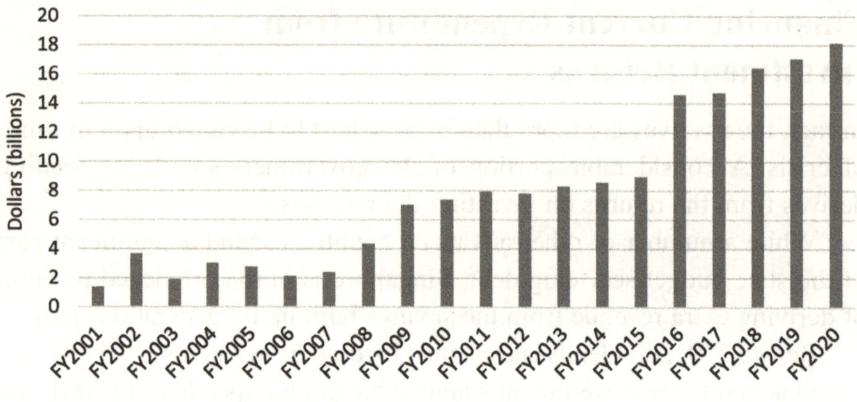

Figure 10.2 Net Investment Returns Contribution to Government Budget

Sources: Ministry of Finance; "50 Years of the Singapore Budget," *Straits Times*, https://graphics.straitstimes.com/STI/STIMEDIA/Interactives/2015/02/budget_singapore_2015/index.html.

about $8.9 billion in FY2015 to over $14.6 billion in FY2016, becoming the single largest revenue source in the government budget ahead of corporate income tax and Goods and Services Tax (GST) (Figure 10.2). It has since risen to $17.0 billion in FY2019 and $18.1 billion in FY2020, making up around a fifth of government revenue (operating revenue + NIRC).

Extra-budgetary cash flows in the form of **capital receipts** (comprising mostly revenue from land sales) and **investment and interest income** are not available for spending under the reserves protection framework. These amount to tens of billions of dollars each fiscal year. For instance, capital receipts came in at $11.5 billion in FY2019, offset by land-related expenditure of about $2 billion in FY2019, fairly close to the sums in FY2018. Interest and investment income was about $30 billion.

Diversifying Revenue

Singapore's public revenue base has been broadened and expanded over the years. Long-term fiscal planning has given the government a strong position from which to launch economic and social development programmes as well as ensure their sustainability amid rising expenditure needs.

For several decades after Singapore's independence, the government's revenue derived mainly from personal and corporate income tax. The Goods and Services Tax (GST) was introduced in 1994 to diversify the revenue base and enable, for competitive reasons, a reduction in corporate and personal income taxes. Notwithstanding the Economic Development Board's tax incentives to attract multinationals to Singapore, the government felt that it was important to lower corporate and personal income taxes to keep Singapore competitive vis-à-vis other economies, in particular Hong Kong (see Chapter 4). Consequently, the corporate income tax and top marginal personal income tax rate, which had been as high as 40% before 1986, were brought down to 17% and 20%, respectively, by 2010 (Figure 4.1).

From a fiscal perspective, a key advantage of a consumption tax such as GST is that it is less strongly correlated with economic cycles compared with other forms of taxes. Personal and corporate income taxes tend to be more strongly procyclical, i.e. rising and falling in tandem with economic growth, which makes the health of the government's coffers dependent on the state of the economy. During economic downturns, lower firm profits and wages pull down income tax revenue at a time when public expenditure demands tend to be elevated. Consumption and hence GST are also likely to fall, but not by as much. GST therefore adds ballast to the state purse, enabling the government to better ride out fluctuations in economic performance. Moreover, GST would offset the shrinkage of the tax base as the population ages and retirees leave the workforce.

GST is also considered to be an efficient tax in that it does not distort economic decision-making as much as other forms of taxation. It is for these reasons that most countries today (including all OECD countries except for the US, which uses a sales tax instead) employ some form of GST, which is sometimes called value-added tax (VAT).

Since the 2000s, fiscal policy changes have been aimed at growing revenue as well as redistributing income. Anticipating a structural increase in expenditure, the government added new streams of revenue and enhanced existing streams well ahead of expenditure needs (Figure 10.3).

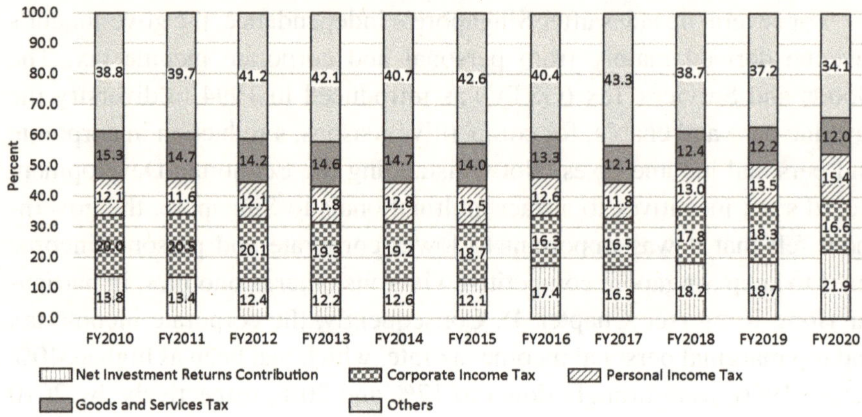

Figure 10.3 Breakdown of Government Revenue Sources

Source: Ministry of Finance.

GST, which had remained at 3% since 1994, was raised to 4% in 2003 and 5% in 2004 following the recommendations of the Economic Review Committee. It was further increased to 7% in 2007. Consequently, GST overtook personal income tax in annual collections up to FY2018 when it fell behind personal income tax once again.

In Budget 2018, then-Minister for Finance Heng Swee Keat announced that GST would be raised from 7% to 9% sometime in the period 2021–2025, with the commitment that the government would "carefully assess the prevailing economic conditions as well as our needs at that point" before moving to raise GST.[7] This was principally motivated by the need to support higher recurrent spending, especially on healthcare, with the proportion of Singaporeans aged 65 and above set to increase from about 15% in 2019 to 25% in 2030. In view of the COVID-19 pandemic and economic impact, it was announced in the Budget 2020 speech that the GST hike would not take place in 2021, but would still be necessary by 2025.

The largest expansion in revenue has come from the introduction of the NIR framework in 2008 and its expansion to include Temasek in 2016. These moves have allowed the government to tap significantly more on the investment returns on the reserves, which have become the largest source of revenue for government spending at around $18 billion in FY2020.

Asset taxes have also been progressively increased in Budget 2010 and Budget 2013. As outlined in Chapter 4, these include higher tax rates on more expensive residential properties and cars. Although less significant in revenue terms, these serve to address wealth inequality, particularly as Singapore does not impose taxes on capital gains unlike a number of other advanced economy jurisdictions.

The sharp rise in property prices post-2009, along with a high volume of transactions, has given government coffers a significant boost. So too have vehicle taxes and Certificate of Entitlement (vehicle ownership license) premiums, although the government has stressed that these sources are highly cyclical and cannot be depended on in the medium- to longer-term to remain at elevated levels.

In 2014, the government raised sin taxes on liquor and tobacco, ostensibly for health and social reasons and to keep pace with inflation. To help meet Singapore's carbon emissions pledge, a carbon tax has been imposed on large emitters (those producing 25,000 tonnes or more of greenhouse gas emissions a year, which account for about 80% of Singapore's emissions) from 2019 onwards. Set at an initial $5 per tonne of greenhouse gas emissions, the tax is projected to rise to $10–$15 per tonne by 2030. The government expects revenue of close to $1 billion over the first five years of implementation but is prepared to spend more than this on emissions abatement within the same period.[8]

Financing Social Spending

With recurrent public expenditure on healthcare rising as the population ages, as well as the need to strengthen social security given economic uncertainty and income volatility, the question is how this should be financed.

While the NIRC underscores the tremendous fiscal advantage Singapore enjoys, one may question how much more Singapore ought to rely on NIRC, given that it has become by far the largest revenue source, accounting for about a fifth of the budget. For reasons of sustainability and prudence, the government prefers that consumption and social support be funded from current revenue as a matter of principle. Will current and future generations of Singaporeans become like the proverbial trust-fund kid, dependent on the previous generation's largesse? Or do Singapore's present infrastructure and social investment needs make it entirely reasonable for the government to use more of the resources at its disposal for these ends?

Singapore's approach to safeguarding its reserves for future generations stands in stark contrast to that of the US and other advanced economies, which have increasingly relied on borrowing to fund deficits, particularly amid the COVID-19 pandemic. The "secular stagnation" hypothesis advanced by former US Treasury Secretary Lawrence Summers posits that a global savings glut has led to structurally depressed real interest rates across the world.[9] With real interest rates negative and the cost of debt servicing declining as a share of GDP, Jason Furman and Lawrence Summers (2020) have suggested that rising public debt per se may not be a concern or constraint in the medium term for the United States and other countries in a similar situation.[10]

Donald Low (2014) argued that the Singapore government ought to draw a larger share of the investment returns from the reserves to fund social spending, both from the perspective of intergenerational equity as well as efficiency. He pointed out that a significant part of Singapore's reserves was generated from fiscal surpluses during the 1980s and 1990s when the baby boomer generation was economically active. Now that they are entering retirement, it would be fair to flow back more of the investment returns on reserves rather than store up more for future generations who would be better educated and richer than the current generation. Rather than raise tax rates, he argued, "the government should first ask itself whether investing the nation's savings abroad yields superior returns than spending them on its own people."[11] This call to weigh up social returns to financial returns can be compared with a company considering whether to reinvest cash in the business or to seek returns on financial assets.

The Workers' Party has proposed that instead of raising GST, the government could explore other sources of revenue such as tapping on land sales revenue or raising the NIR limit from 50% to 60% of the expected long-term investment returns on reserves. Given that industrial land sales are typically for leases of 30 years or less in order to facilitate land use recycling, it may be argued that land sales are a renewable source of income.

The drawdown for COVID-19 has put a dent in Singapore's reserves. Depending on the trajectory of economic recovery, there may well be a need for further budget deficits in the near future. The investment climate is also far from certain, although equity and asset prices remain buoyant in 2021. As of 31 March 2021, GIC's 20-year annualised real rate of return stood at 4.3%, an increase from the 2.7% in 2019.[12] Over a longer time horizon, however, the rate has been trending down since the early 2000s. Temasek's total shareholder return has also come down over the decades, although the one-year return shot up to 24.53% in the year ending 31 March 2021.[13] The question then is how much more the Singapore government should increase its structural dependence on NIRC vis-à-vis shoring up other sources of revenue such as GST, which now makes up a smaller proportion of revenue compared with a decade ago.

This is, I suggest, a matter of individual judgment and risk appetite. There is no one answer that all fair-minded Singaporeans would converge on. It is a political judgment to be made by the elected government of the day. Informed public debate is possible only to the extent that investment returns can be reliably projected and would depend on what the government deems appropriate to disclose.

Financing Infrastructure Development

Notwithstanding the fiscal space bought by the inclusion of Temasek Holdings in the NIR framework and the planned increase in GST to 9% by 2025, the potential need for further revenue to meet growing public expenditure demands remains a key fiscal concern.

Besides healthcare and social spending, expenditure on infrastructure consumes a large share of total government spending. In recent years, these have included the building of new roads and mass rapid transit (MRT) lines (the rail network will double from 178 km in 2016 to about 360 km in 2030[14]) as well as the construction of Changi Airport Terminal 5, a mega project which could cost tens of billions. Climate change adaptation, to protect Singapore against rising sea levels, is also expected to require public spending in the order of $100 billion over the next hundred years.[15]

One possibility is to consider **allowing a broader set of land and infrastructural investments to be funded from past reserves**. Currently only a limited set of land-related expenditure can be funded from past reserves, for example, land reclamation as well as land acquisition for the Selective En Bloc Redevelopment Scheme and MRT stations, as these are deemed to be merely converting past reserves from one form (cash and financial assets) to another (land).

This is prudent from a fiscal standpoint, but it also means that infrastructural improvements are financed by the government of the day, whereas the resulting increase in land value accrues to past reserves. A case could be made to finance some types of infrastructural or strategic investments from past reserves. After all, in managing one's personal finances, it would not be imprudent to set aside a portion of one's savings for investments to increase future earning capacity. In the corporate world, companies may likewise invest their cash reserves to seize growth opportunities and generate future revenue.

Another option available to the government is **borrowing, whether through loans or the issuance of public debt or infrastructure bonds**. The low interest rate environment has made this an attractive proposition for many countries with sizeable infrastructure needs.

Since the 1990s, development spending in Singapore has been mostly funded by operating surpluses. The government indicated that it issued bonds only to develop the financial markets and not because it needed to borrow.

Budget 2019, however, saw the government embrace debt as part of the financing mix for long-term infrastructure. Then-Minister for Finance Heng Swee Keat noted that "for these large and lumpy expenditures where the benefits span many generations of Singaporeans, paying for them through some borrowing is fairer and more efficient."[16] With the President's concurrence, the government would be able to provide a guarantee for the loans so as to lower financing costs.

Under the Significant Infrastructure Loan (Singa) Act passed in 2021, the government plans to issue new Singa bonds (subject to a limit of $90 billion, with annual interest payments capped at $5 billion) to finance long-term infrastructure with high upfront costs. These include new MRT lines, as well as pumping stations and tidal walls for protection against rising sea levels. Green bonds will also be issued under the Act for selected public projects related to sustainable development, such as Singapore's first integrated solid and waste water treatment facility.

Whether borrowing is preferable to drawing on past reserves depends on whether the government can borrow at lower cost than the returns it expects to make on its investments. Taking commercial loans could also instil financial discipline in these major development projects.

Notwithstanding, Minister Heng made clear that the government would not borrow to fund recurrent expenditure in areas such as healthcare, education, and security. For fiscal prudence, these would continue to be funded from recurrent revenue such as the GST.

A third option for infrastructure financing to turn to **public-private partnerships (PPPs)**, which refer to arrangements such as "build-finance-operate" or "build-own-operate" whereby the government engages a private sector entity or consortium to finance, develop, and operate infrastructure in return for a commitment to purchase the public services generated from the infrastructure. In these arrangements, the private sector typically raises funding for the project so that the government incurs no upfront cost.

PPPs have been used in countries such as the UK, Canada, and Australia for a wide range of infrastructure projects including schools, hospitals, roads, and prisons. They are also popular in developing countries, given the draw of mobilising private finance to supplement public funds in meeting infrastructure needs.

During the early to mid-2000s, the Singapore government entered into a number of PPPs to develop an incineration plant, a water recycling plant, a technical education college (the Institute of Technical Education College West), and, most ambitious of all, the Singapore Sports Hub. Singapore was attracted to PPPs not for fiscal reasons, but for the perceived advantages of private sector involvement in such projects including risk sharing, financial and project management discipline, integration of operational considerations into project design, as well as private sector access to technology and networks.

While the government can avoid upfront costs through a PPP arrangement, a contingent liability is created with the government committed to a stream of payments over a period of time, typically 20 years or longer. A 2018 United Nations report noted that private finance is more expensive than public finance, and that PPPs may "incur high design, management and transactional costs due to their complexity and the need for external advice".[17] A study by the UK National Audit Office found that the UK's Private Finance Initiative model was more expensive and less efficient than public financing for infrastructure projects.[18]

A major challenge that arises from PPPs is the long-term nature of the relationship entered into between the government and private sector entities. Needs change over time, as does technology, which may require the terms of the agreement to be updated or adjusted. This may entail constant renegotiation and may constrain operational flexibility unless the product or service delivered is a standard one with little need for variation over time. Having multiple stakeholders and priorities, as was the case with the Singapore Sports Hub, may add to the challenge. It is telling that in the 2010s, PPP projects in Singapore have been mostly confined to NEWater (high-grade reclaimed water) and desalination plants where there are clearly defined deliverables and measurable quality standards.

In 2016, the Ministry of Transport indicated that it would not consider PPP for the development of Changi Airport Terminal 5. This would allow the government to retain tighter control over this strategic asset without the complication of dealing with a private sector partner whose priorities may clash with strategic considerations.

In view of the COVID-19 impact on air travel, construction of Changi Airport Terminal 5 has been put on hold for at least two years while the government studies how the pandemic will change the aviation sector. However, other infrastructure projects will still require substantial fiscal outlays, necessitating government borrowing or new approaches to public financing in the coming years.

Growing the Economy, Containing Expenditure

Seeking new revenue and means of financing is not all the government must do to keep its finances on an even keel. Two other efforts must proceed in parallel: keeping the economy competitive and growing in order to generate public revenue, and keeping expenditure in check.

The first of these is not entirely within the government's control, but there is much the state can do to promote growth such as keeping regulations business-friendly and investing in skills and key economic infrastructure. The tax system should be kept competitive, as should Singapore's manpower policies, to nourish the goose that lays the golden egg.

Prudent spending is as important as growing revenue in the overall fiscal scheme. While social expenditures will rise as the population ages and the government steps up social support, there is still considerable potential for saving across the range of public programmes. What is needed is a hard-nosed appraisal of all government spending on social, community, and economic programmes and to sunset those which are less effective. Over time, there could be an accumulation of well-meaning programmes that incur significant deadweight losses by incentivising people and firms to do what they would have done by themselves anyway. It is therefore important to take a root-and-branch approach to the culling of programmes that have not proven effective.

This requires robust programme evaluation and governance frameworks. Public agencies should conduct systematic pre- and post-implementation reviews and strengthen the loop between evaluation and resourcing. By objectively appraising programmes for value for money, agencies can cut losses on programmes whose efficacy has fallen short or whose relevance has diminished. This is not to say the government should adopt a short-termist approach that fails to recognise that some gains are less tangible or are realised only over a long horizon. Too often, however, the path of least resistance is to let programmes continue to run regardless of their efficacy or relevance.

In Singapore, the Ministry of Finance (MOF) is working with ministries to implement programme evaluation frameworks and build up the necessary capabilities. These efforts complement the oversight role of the Public Accounts Committee and the Auditor-General's Office.

Much can be learnt from good practices abroad. For instance, evidence-based policymaking is well-developed in the UK. The UK Alliance for Useful Evidence comprises independent research bodies and consultancies, a network of thematic What Works Centres, and government bodies, all of which supply evidence that can inform policy.

Just as important as sunsetting existing programmes is to prevent the proliferation of programmes that are poorly designed, duplicative, or likely to incur considerable deadweight cost from the outset. This can be achieved through rigorous programme evaluation at the design stage, taking in lessons learnt from previous programmes with similar objectives in Singapore and other parts of the world. A judicious balance should be struck between rigorous evaluation to prevent wastage and allowing room for policy experimentation to try out new, untested initiatives.

There is also something to be said for across-the-board cuts. Budget 2017 introduced a permanent 2% cut to the budget caps of all government ministries to force prioritisation of programmes and spur greater efficiency. At such a margin, modest compared with the UK government's post-2010 austerity drive, it is unlikely that public services would be adversely affected.

What is critical is whether the budget cuts will succeed in encouraging government agencies to seek not just incremental improvements in productivity but also new and better ways of achieving public outcomes. In the UK, for instance, austerity was accompanied by innovations that enlisted behavioural economics and psychology to improve government policy and services while reducing costs. Several Singapore agencies such as the Ministry of Manpower, Land Transport Authority, and Inland Revenue Authority of Singapore have already used behavioural insights and design thinking to improve public services and policy outcomes, but a greater push from the budget management angle could potentially spur greater action.

Another important dimension is design and project management, particularly for big-ticket infrastructure projects where there is considerable scope for cost savings, or conversely cost overruns if poorly conceptualised, designed, or managed. In 2011, MOF set up the **Centre for Public Project Management** to review the scope, design, and cost reasonableness of project proposals above $100 million and optimise projects to achieve value for money. Projects estimated to cost above $500 million are put through a Gateway Process (inspired by the UK) where they undergo several phases of review by the **Development Projects Advisory Panel** (DPAP). The DPAP comprises experienced public officers, academics, and industry experts who review the project scope and requirements and advise public agencies on how to optimise design and procurement before the projects are put up to a ministerial committee for approval. In particular, projects are optimised for lifecycle costs and not just upfront development costs. Information communications technology projects are likewise reviewed by the **Public Sector Infocomm Review Committee** to ensure financial discipline and increase the likelihood of successful project outcomes.

Singapore public finances are in an enviable position of strength. However, a maturing economy and society will subject the system to greater strain in the years ahead, necessitating prudent forward planning and disciplined expenditure to secure the city-state's future.

Endnotes

1. Inclusive of the exceptional spending in FY2020, the overall budget surplus averaged –0.6% from FY2011 to FY2020.
2. Overall budget balance refers to total government revenues less total government expenditures inclusive of special transfers, top-ups to endowment and trust funds, and the Net Investment Return Contribution. This conservative definition of budgetary position means a lower surplus or larger deficit is recorded than under the International Monetary Fund's Government Finance Statistics.
3. Sources: Singapore Department of Statistics; Lee Kok Fatt, *Singapore's Fiscal Strategies for Growth: A Journey of Self-Reliance* (Singapore: World Scientific Publishing, 2017), 59.
4. In FY2019, special transfers (such as the Wage Credit Scheme and Bicentennial Bonus) excluding top-ups to endowment and trust funds amounted to a further $1.7 billion or 0.3% of GDP. Spending from government endowment funds (such as ComCare) and trust funds (such as the Pioneer Generation Fund) came to another $4.4 billion.
5. Excludes expenditure from government endowment and trust funds such as MediFund, ElderCare Fund, and the Pioneer Generation Fund. Healthcare expenditure would be even higher if such spending were included.

6. Temasek had a net portfolio value of $381 billion as of 31 March 2021.
7. Heng Swee Keat, Budget Debate Round-Up Speech, 2018.
8. Ibid.
9. Lawrence Summers, "U.S. Economic Prospects: Secular Stagnation, Hysteresis, and the Zero Lower Bound," *Business Economics* 49(2) (2014): 65–73.
10. Jason Furman and Lawrence Summers, "A Reconsideration of Fiscal Policy in the Era of Low Interest Rates," discussion draft, 20 November 2020, https://www.piie.com/system/files/documents/furman-summers2020-12-01paper.pdf.
11. Donald Low, "New Options in Social Security," in Donald Low and Sudhir Thomas Vadaketh, eds., *Hard Choices: Challenging the Singapore Consensus* (Singapore: NUS Press, 2014), 129.
12. GIC, *Report on the Management of the Government's Portfolio 2020/21*, https://www.gic.com.sg/wp-content/uploads/2021/07/GIC_AR_PDF_210723.pdf.
13. Temasek Holdings, *Temasek Review 2021*.
14. Heng Swee Keat, Budget Debate Round-Up Speech, 2016.
15. Lee Hsien Loong, National Day Rally, 2019.
16. Heng Swee Keat, Budget Statement, 2019.
17. Philip Alston, "Extreme Poverty and Human Rights," report of the Special Rapporteur on Extreme Poverty and Human Rights, (26 September 2018), 11, https:// undocs.org/A/73/396.
18. National Audit Office (NAO), *PFI and PF2*, report by the Comptroller and Auditor General (London: NAO, 2018).

Chapter 11

Pandemic, Politics, and Pathways to the Future

There is little doubt that Singapore's future will be shaped by the COVID-19 pandemic that continues to ravage the economy, as well as the political milieu in which public policy will be developed. This chapter surveys some of the implications of COVID-19 and the 2020 general election, before making concluding observations on how Singapore's socio-economic system and society may evolve in the years to come.

COVID-19: Impact and Implications

The COVID-19 pandemic that engulfed the world in 2020 and plunged Singapore into its deepest recession on record has profound implications for Singapore's socio-economic system and outcomes, not just in the near term but also into the medium term and beyond.

As a highly open, trade-dependent economy, Singapore has been particularly hard hit by COVID-19. Travel restrictions were first imposed on countries and regions affected by the early outbreak of COVID-19, and progressively widened to cover all short-term visitor arrivals by the end of March 2020. This brought the aviation and tourism sectors, significant contributors to Singapore's economy, to a standstill, while disrupting the supply of manpower to firms across all sectors. The "Circuit Breaker", a partial lockdown imposed from 7 April to 1 June 2020 to curb local transmission of the virus, took a heavy toll on small businesses. During this period, shops were shuttered, while food and beverage outlets were open only for takeaway. Even after the Circuit Breaker ended, restrictions on many activities remained, with limits imposed on the size of public gatherings. Following an outbreak of the virus in foreign worker dormitories in April 2020, many foreign workers were only allowed to resume work months later.

Singapore suffered its worst-ever quarterly GDP contraction (–13.3% year-on-year) in the second quarter of 2020, followed by a 5.8% contraction in the third quarter. GDP for the full year contracted by 5.4%, the largest decline on record.

COVID-19 Support Measures

Like many other countries, Singapore committed tremendous fiscal resources to stem the economic fallout of COVID-19. This was done through an unprecedented five Budgets in FY2020, drawing on Singapore's past reserves for only the second time ever. In total, $92.9 billion was set aside for COVID-related support measures for businesses and households, amounting to 19.2% of GDP (Table 11.1). The overall budget deficit for FY2020 at $64.9 billion, or 13.9% of GDP,[1] was the largest in Singapore's history. The President gave assent to draw up to $52 billion from past reserves, significantly more than the $4.9 billion approved for the 2009 Global Financial Crisis.

Financial help for households and individuals was a blend of universal support and progressive support which was automatically disbursed depending on income and household type.

Universal benefits included:

- **Solidarity Payment**: $600 for every adult Singaporean, $300 for every adult permanent resident/long-term visit pass plus (LTVP+) holder
- $100 for every Singapore household with at least one citizen
- $300 for citizen parents with at least one Singaporean child aged 20 and below
- $100 for citizens aged 50 and above
- **Solidarity Utilities Credit**: $100 for every Singaporean household

Table 11.1 Singapore's COVID-19 Support Measures and Cost

	Major Support Measures: Individuals/Households	Major Support Measures: Employers	Cost of COVID Support Measures
Unity Budget (18 February 2020)	Care and Support Package (cash payouts, Workfare Special Payment, grocery vouchers, additional GST Voucher, service and conservancy charges rebate)	Stabilisation and Support Package (Jobs Support Scheme (JSS) support at 8% of wages, enhanced Wage Credit Scheme, corporate tax rebate)	$6.4 billion
Resilience Budget (26 March 2020)	— Enhanced Care and Support Package (tripled cash payouts, increased Workfare Special Payment) — Temporary Relief Fund, COVID Support Grant — SGUnited Jobs and Traineeships — Self-Employed Person Income Relief Scheme (SIRS)	— Higher JSS support of 25%–75% depending on sector — Sectoral support packages for aviation, tourism, land transport, arts and culture — Enhanced property tax rebate, rental waivers, financing (cash flow) support	$48.4 billion (+$17 billion draw on reserves)
Solidarity Budget (6 April 2020)	— Expanded eligibility criteria for SIRS — Topped up cash payout to form $600 Solidarity Payment for all citizens	— 75% JSS support for all sectors in April and May 2020 — Foreign worker levy waiver and rebate — Enhanced financing support	$5.1 billion (+$4 billion draw on reserves)
Fortitude Budget (26 May 2020)	— Solidarity Utilities Credit — SGUnited Jobs and Skills Package including mid-career traineeships, skills programmes, Jobs Growth incentive	— Extended JSS — Extended foreign worker levy waiver and rebate for firms unable to resume work — Deferred increase in older worker Central Provident Fund contribution	$33 billion (+$31 billion draw on reserves)

(Continued)

Table 11.1 (*Continued*)

	Major Support Measures: Individuals/Households	**Major Support Measures: Employers**	**Cost of COVID Support Measures**
		— Expanded rental relief for small and medium-sized enterprises, government tenants — Digital Resilience Bonus	
Ministerial Statement (17 August 2020)	— Extended COVID Support Grant — Widened eligibility for Workfare Special Payment	— Extended and stepped down JSS depending on sector — Further support for aviation and tourism	No additional outlay ($8 billion from Budget savings elsewhere)
Total Sum			**$92.9 billion ($52 billion draw on reserves*)**

*$42.7 billion of the $52 billion was utilised in FY2020, with the balance to be deployed in FY20201, along with a further expected $1.7 billion draw on reserves.

Benefits with progressive features under the **Care and Support Package** included:

- Additional cash support of $300 for middle-income Singaporeans and $600 for lower-income Singaporeans (excluding those who own two or more properties)
- Grocery vouchers for citizens living in one- or two-room HDB flats, additional utilities rebates for HDB households
- Service and conservancy charge rebates of between 1.5 and 3.5 months for all HDB households, depending on flat type
- **Workfare Special Payment** of $3,000 to Workfare recipients, both employees and self-employed

There was also support for those who had lost jobs or suffered pay cuts of 30% or more (to broaden support beyond existing ComCare schemes) and who met means-tested criteria:

- The **Temporary Relief Fund** was a one-off support of $500 provided on application in April 2020 for local workers with prior gross monthly household income of $10,000 (or per capita income of $3,100) or below
- The **COVID-19 Support Grant** provided a cash grant of up to $800 per month for three months on application for local employees who met income and property value qualifying criteria and who agreed to actively participate in job search or attend a training programme

For households, the **Courage Fund** provided a one-time sum of up to $1,000 to households with family members affected by COVID-19 (i.e. contracted COVID-19 or were on quarantine/leave of absence/stay-home notice) and with a loss of household income of at least 10%, also with qualifying household income criteria.

Affected union members could receive another sum (up to $300) through the National Trades Union Congress Care Fund. Grants for the ethnicity-based Self-Help Groups and community development councils were also increased to facilitate localised efforts to help those in need.

To keep local unemployment at bay, the **Jobs Support Scheme (JSS)** was introduced in the Unity Budget. The scheme was similar in design to the Jobs Credit Scheme employed during the Global Financial Crisis, but with significantly higher support. JSS provided employers with wage support of 25%, 50%, or 75% of the first $4,600 of gross monthly wages, depending on sector, to encourage the retention of local workers. Support of 75% was provided to firms in all sectors during the Circuit Breaker in April and May 2020. JSS was extended to cover wages paid up to September 2021, with support for better-performing sectors phased out from December 2020 and progressively lowered for other sectors.[2] By February 2021, over $25 billion had been committed to JSS, supporting over 150,000 employers.

For self-employed persons (SEPs) who would not benefit from JSS, the following programmes were introduced:

- The **SEP Training Support Scheme** provided an enhanced training allowance ($10 an hour) for eligible courses
- The **SEP Income Relief Scheme (SIRS)** provided a total of $9,000 in three instalments to self-employed citizens with prior annual net trade income of not more than $100,000. Additional eligibility criteria based on spousal income, property value, and ownership applied. SIRS was extended to SEPs who also had employment income of not more than $2,300. Support was provided automatically to about 100,000 SEPs who had previously declared income to the Inland Revenue Authority of Singapore or the Central Provident Fund Board, or on application for those who had not. SIRS did not require a commitment to training or job search, unlike the ComCare schemes or the COVID-19 Support Grant.

SIRS was unusual in that it did not require a commitment to training or job search unlike the ComCare schemes or even the COVID-19 Support Grant.

In total, about $10 billion was set aside for social and household support. This included the Temporary Relief Fund, COVID-19 Support Grant, and SIRS, which together helped more than half a million people.

To help defray costs for employers of foreign workers (Work Permit and S Pass holders), particularly as many could not be repatriated due to travel restrictions, the government provided the following:

- **Waiver of foreign worker levy** due in April and May 2020
  - Extension at 100% in June and 50% in July for firms not allowed to restart business

    o Extension at 100% from June to September, 75% in October, 50% in November, and 25% in December for construction, marine, and process firms
- **Foreign worker levy rebates** of $750 per worker in April and May
    o Further rebates of $750 in June and $375 in July for firms not allowed to restart business
    o Further rebates of $750 in June, $375 from July to September, and $90 from October 2020 to December 2021 for construction, marine, and process firms

Impact on the Labour Market

Retrenchments and unemployment climbed as the recession worsened. The resident unemployment rate reached 4.8% in September 2020, slightly below the previous recessionary high, before falling to 4.4% by December (Figure 11.1). Retrenchments rose to 9,120 in the third quarter of 2020, totalling 26,110 for the full year (Figure 11.2). However, the incidence of retrenchment remained below previous downturn peaks (Table 11.2). 81,700 employees were placed on shorter work weeks or temporary layoffs in the second quarter of 2020, compared with 26,500 in the first quarter of 2009 during the Global Financial Crisis.[3] Between March and July 2020, over 220,000 workers at 6,300 firms had their pay

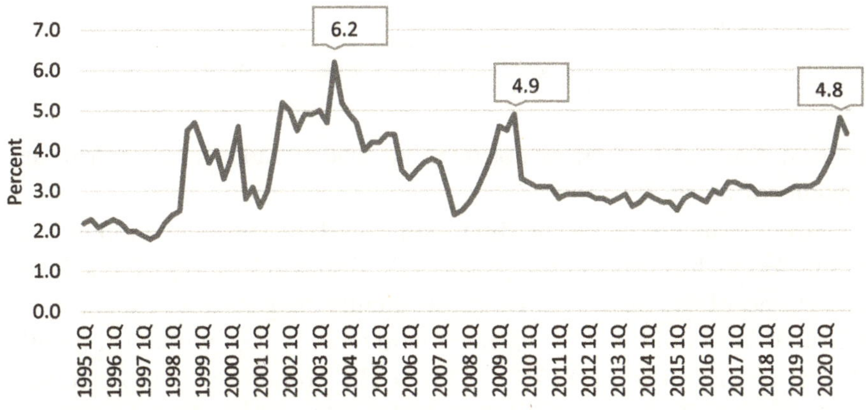

Figure 11.1 Quarterly Resident Unemployment Rate (Seasonally Adjused)

Source: Manpower Research and Statistics Department, MOM.

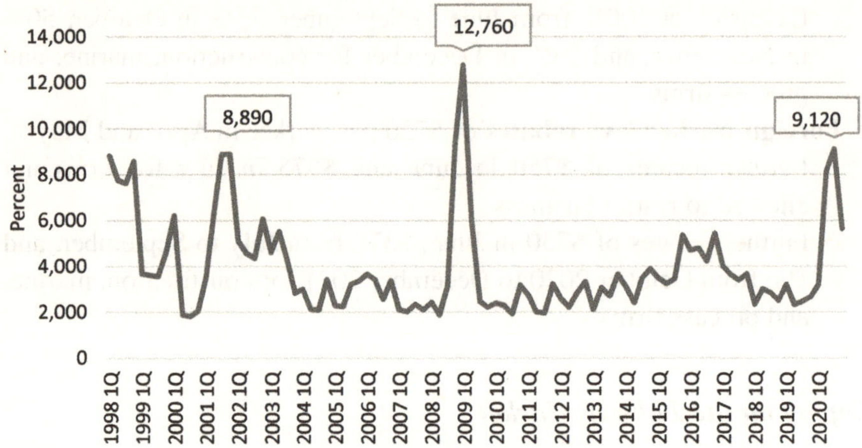

Figure 11.2 Quarterly Retrenchments

Source: Manpower Research and Statistics Department, MOM.

Table 11.2 Incidence of Retrenchment

Year	Incidence of Retrenchment (per thousand employees)
1998: Asian Financial Crisis	32.7
2001: Dot-com Bust	26.3
2003: SARS	16.7
2009: Global Financial Crisis	14.2
2020: COVID-19	12.8

Source: Manpower Research and Statistics Department, MOM.

reduced based on mandatory notifications that excluded smaller firms and pay cuts of under 25%.

After contracting in the first half of 2020, resident employment rebounded in the third and fourth quarters, surpassing pre-pandemic levels by the end of the year. However, job quality may have declined: while 93.6% of local university graduates found employment within six months of graduation (up from 90.7% in 2019), the proportion of those in full-time, permanent employment fell to 69.8% (down from 81.7% in 2019).[4] Likewise, the full-time permanent employment rate of polytechnic fresh graduates declined from 61.1% in 2019 to 52.0% in 2020.[5]

Budget support measures have helped to mitigate the job market fall-out. According to government estimates, these measures could save or create about 155,000 jobs in 2020 and 2021, stemming the rise in resident unemployment rate by about 1.7 percentage points and preventing the economy from contracting by a further 5.6% in 2020 and 4.8% in 2021.[6]

The **Tripartite Advisory on Managing Excess Manpower and Responsible Retrenchment** was updated in March 2020. Along with the recommendations of the **National Wages Council**, which were released in March and October 2020, this provided guidance to firms on cutting wages in a responsible way in order to preserve jobs.

A **National Jobs Council** chaired by Senior Minister Tharman Shanmugaratnam was set up to identify and develop job opportunities and skills training amid the COVID-19 situation. A key concern was to prevent unemployment "scarring" — the long-term adverse impact on employability and earnings arising from unemployment, particularly early in one's career.[7] The Council set the goal of creating close to 100,000 job, traineeship, and skills training opportunities for local workers within 12 months under the **SGUnited Jobs and Skills Package**. This involved mobilising public sector agencies, employers, unions, and training partners to offer opportunities in different sectors, catering to every skill level.

Jobs created included part-time and temporary positions to manage COVID-related operations and meet manpower shortfalls due to travel restrictions, as well as long-term positions in both the public and private sectors. As in previous major downturns, public sector hiring was brought forward to absorb manpower, with the public sector committed to providing 15,000 of the target of 40,000 jobs to be created for the year.

Traineeships for fresh graduates and mid-career workers, offered by companies under the SGUnited Traineeships/Mid-Career Pathways Programme, attracted 80% government support for training allowances up to a cap. In addition, there were subsidised full-time training courses delivered by continuing education training centres such as universities with an allowance for trainees provided by the government.

By the end of 2020, nearly 76,000 locals had been placed in jobs or training opportunities through the SGUnited Jobs and Skills package.[8] Of these, about three in four secured jobs.

Others turned to entrepreneurship for a living. Data from the Accounting and Corporate Regulatory Authority showed that around

5,500 to 6,400 new businesses were formed monthly between June and October 2020, up from around 5,300 a month in the corresponding period the year before.

Economic Outlook and Implications

Entering 2021, COVID-19 continues to afflict the world. The periodic resurgence of the disease, stoked by more contagious and deadlier strains of the virus, has kept economies in stop-start mode. While progress has been made with mass vaccination underway in many countries, it will take time for herd immunity to be achieved.

In the meantime, international travel remains crippled, with the aviation, hospitality, and tourism-related sectors still in distress.

To secure the future of Singapore Airlines, Temasek Holdings led a multi-billion dollar recapitalisation of the company in 2020 to shore up its finances for the turbulent ride ahead. The government also gave Singaporeans domestic tourism credits (called SingapoRediscovers Vouchers) totalling $320 million. While domestic tourism cannot make up for the loss in foreign visitor spending, it can at least provide some support for the battered tourism sector to help it retain capabilities for the eventual recovery.

While the global economy is poised for a robust rebound in 2021, economic volatility is expected to persist into the medium term as countries continue to struggle with the health and economic fallout. Geopolitical tensions between the US and China are adding to uncertainty, inducing the reconfiguration of cross-border production and supply chains. As a small, highly trade-dependent economy, Singapore is particularly vulnerable to the vicissitudes of external demand.

With tens of billions already spent, government support measures such as JSS are set to taper off as the economy recovers. This support was vital in the early stages of the pandemic fallout to keep jobs and capabilities in place and prevent a sudden surge in layoffs. However, a process of adjustment is inevitable as some jobs in tourism and hospitality will not return anytime soon. A measure of "creative destruction" is, in fact, necessary for the economy to emerge stronger post-COVID. Some firms will shutter while others will have to pivot to new opportunities, releasing workers from employment. The SGUnited Jobs and Skills Package is intended to cushion the impact on workers, providing them with retraining while being paid an allowance. Notwithstanding, the government has to be alert to a possible spike in business insolvency and layoffs as COVID-19 support and temporary relief from contractual obligations are withdrawn.

Government support has pivoted from holding workers in place via the JSS to encouraging companies to hire local workers via a **Jobs Growth Incentive (JGI)**. Under this scheme, companies that expand their local workforce between September 2020 and September 2021 inclusive receive wage subsidies for new locals hires, with mature workers receiving higher support (50% co-funding for 18 months, compared with 25% for 12 months for those under 40 years). By February 2021, JGI had supported the hiring of over 270,000 locals. Up to 35,000 traineeships and training opportunities will also be made available through the extension and enhancement of the SGUnited Jobs and Skills Package announced in Budget 2021.

Income Security and Unemployment Support

In such a period of heightened volatility, income security becomes pertinent to a large segment of the workforce beyond the group of low-income residents eligible for ComCare assistance. While the COVID-19 Support Grant and SIRS have expired in December 2020, there remains a structural need for support going into 2021 as the economic impact of the pandemic continues to be felt.

This has taken the form of the **COVID-19 Recovery Grant** with stepped-down support and more stringent eligibility criteria compared with the COVID-19 Support Grant and SIRS to target those in greater need. Support is also contingent on effort to seek employment or undertake training (for the unemployed) or to reach out to clients and businesses (for the self-employed).

In the medium term, alternatives to straight-out government support could take the form of unemployment insurance or CPF unemployment savings, but these would take time to develop and implement. A social dividend could also perform the role of helping individuals or families tide over episodes of unemployment.

Inequality

In the aftermath of the Global Financial Crisis of 2008–2009, income inequality moderated or plateaued in a number of countries. *The Financial Times* reported that two in three economies saw a fall in inequality from 2008 to 2013 as measured by income or consumption growth of the bottom 40% compared with the total population.[9] In the US and China, the income share of the top 1% levelled off after a long period of increase while the income share of the bottom 50% flattened after a lengthy decline. Globally, the financial sector, which was at the heart of the crisis, contracted. In the UK and Switzerland, economies with a significant financial sector, the income Gini coefficient (pre-taxes-and-transfers) fell significantly after 2008 after having risen for some years in the run-up to the Global Financial Crisis.

Wealth inequality, in all likelihood, also moderated substantially as equity and asset prices plunged. From their respective 2007 peaks to 2009 troughs, the Dow Jones Industrial Average, S&P 500, and NASDAQ each declined by more than 50%. It would take over five years for the Dow Jones Industrial Average and S&P 500 to claw back their losses. The Nikkei 225, the FTSE 100, and the Straits Times Index fell by 61%, 48%, and 62%, respectively, from 2007 peak to 2009 trough.

By contrast, the COVID-19 pandemic has seen inequality head in the opposite direction. Some analysts have referred to a "K- shaped" recovery due to the uneven impact of the outbreak on different industries and income groups across the world. Data compiled by the International Labour Organization showed that in the first half of 2020, average wages actually rose in a number of countries such as the US, Canada, and France as lower-income workers suffered disproportionately high job losses.[10]

In Singapore, real median gross monthly income from work for full-time employed residents declined by 0.4% between June 2019 and June 2020 whereas real income at the 20th percentile fell by 4.6%.[11] Households in the bottom 10% experienced a 6.1% real decline in average monthly household income from work (per household member, inclusive of employer CPF) in 2020, significantly more than households in other deciles, which experienced declines of between 1.4% and 3.2%.[12] The PMET unemployment rate for residents rose by 0.6 percentage points to 3.5% in June 2020 compared with a 1.7 percentage point increase in the non-PMET unemployment rate to 6.4% over the same period.[13]

This reflects the higher incidence of job and income losses in sectors and occupations with larger concentrations of low-income, non-PMET workers whose work often requires them to be on-site. By contrast, PMETs in higher-paying jobs, where work can be done remotely, have been relatively insulated. The Ministry of Manpower reported that about half of the workers affected by cost cutting measures from March to July 2020 were from accommodation and food services, construction, as well as wholesale and retail — sectors which had below median wages to begin with.

A study by DBS economists on the bank's database of 1.2 million customers found that lower-income earners (those earning $2,999 and below) accounted for nearly half of customers who suffered income declines of more than 10% (Table 11.3) in May 2020.[14] Of this group, about half saw their income decline by more than 50% and about two-thirds had emergency funds of three months or less. Higher-income earners, the data showed, were relatively less affected.

Besides employees and freelancers, small business owners have also suffered income losses. Those providing in-person services have been affected by the Circuit Breaker and social distancing measures while SMEs, in

Table 11.3 Breakdown of DBS Customers Who Suffered Income Declines of Over 10% by Salary Range and Emergency Funds (May 2020)

	Emergency Funds				
Salary Range	**< 1 Month**	**1–3 Months**	**4–6 Months**	**> 6 Months**	**Total**
≤ $2,999	**22%**	**11%**	5%	11%	**49%**
$3,000–$4,999	11%	6%	3%	6%	26%
$5,000–$6,999	5%	3%	1%	3%	12%
$7,000–$9,999	2%	1%	1%	2%	6%
≥ $10,000	2%	2%	1%	3%	8%
Total	42%	22%	12%	24%	100%

Source: DBS Asian Insights.

general, are less well-equipped with the digital capabilities to tap on e-commerce compared with larger enterprises.[15]

While the Gini coefficient of household income from work remained unchanged at 0.452 in 2020, large fiscal transfers lowered the post-tax-and-transfer Gini coefficient from 0.398 in 2019 to 0.375 in 2020 (Figure 2.9). However, wealth inequality is likely to have expanded, given rising asset prices in Singapore and other markets.

After an initial drop of between 30% and 40% from their February 2020 peaks to March 2020 troughs, the S&P 500 and Dow Jones Industrial Average reached all-time highs by August and November 2020, respectively. The technology-oriented NASDAQ fared even better, powering to a series of record highs from June 2020 onwards. US stock market exuberance was propelled by a flood of liquidity provided by the US Federal Reserve, along with massive fiscal stimulus, even as the real economy foundered. Consequently, US household wealth climbed to a record high in the second quarter of 2020.[16]

The Shanghai Composite Index, too, reached one-year highs in July 2020. The Morgan Stanley Capital International All Country World Index had entered positive territory, year-to-date, by August 2020 although the London FTSE, Hong Kong Hang Seng, and Singapore's Straits Times Index remained some distance below their pre-COVID highs despite their respective rebounds.

In Singapore, where much of household wealth is held in property, residential property prices held steady through the COVID-19 outbreak. The Private Residential Property Price Index fell a mere 1.0% in the first quarter of 2020, before rebounding strongly to finish the year at an all-time high (Figure 3.3). Again, the contrast with the Global Financial Crisis is stark. Then, the property price index fell by 8.3% between the second and fourth quarter of 2008; by the second quarter of 2009, it had declined 24.9% from its 2008 peak. The HDB Resale Price Index gained 5% in 2020, ending the year within 8% of its 2013 peak (Figure 3.4). Eighty-two resale flats were transacted at over a million dollars in 2020, a record that looks set to be surpassed in 2021 with 53 such transactions in the first quarter of the year.

There will likely remain strong structural support for asset prices in the medium term, given the US Federal Reserve's commitment to maintain low interest rates until economic recovery is well under way and there is a sustained increase in general price inflation, beyond asset price inflation.[17]

At the household level, the shift towards more home-based learning may put students from lower-income households at a disadvantage to their better-off peers. They tend to have less space and privacy at home and may lack good information technology equipment or stable Internet connections. While schools had moved quickly to provide routers, laptops, and tablets to students who needed them during the Circuit Breaker, the COVID-19 pandemic underscored the importance of the home environment and household resources in supporting students' learning and educational outcomes.[18]

As equity and asset prices continue to rally in response to global stimulus measures and anticipated economic recovery, both wealth and income inequality need to be closely monitored. Otherwise, there is a risk that the progress made in recent years could unravel, putting the social compact under greater strain.

Community Giving and Volunteerism

On a positive note, the COVID-19 pandemic spurred community support in the form of giving and volunteerism. Donations to the Community Chest, Community Foundation of Singapore's Sayang Sayang Fund, as well as through the SG Cares application and Giving.sg platform, totalled $90 million from January to May 2020, comparable to the amount received for the whole of 2019 by the Community Chest and Giving.sg.[19] Individuals and businesses stepped forward to offer help in various ways such as distributing masks, delivering food to seniors and vulnerable families, and showing appreciation for frontline workers. Over 13,000 Singaporeans signed up as volunteers through the SGUnited portal set up for those who wanted to contribute.

Foreign Worker Dependence, Business Costs, and Productivity

The travel curbs necessitated by COVID-19 have drawn attention to the risks of foreign worker dependence.

On 18 March 2020, Malaysia implemented the Movement Control Order (MCO) which barred Malaysians from travelling out of Malaysia and non-Malaysians from entering the country. This left thousands of Malaysian daily commuters unable to return to Singapore to work. Employers in Singapore had to find ways to plug the resulting labour shortfall, while others scrambled to find accommodation for their Malaysian workers who remained in Singapore or who chose to enter Singapore prior to the MCO taking effect.

This episode highlighted that a strategy of using Johor or Riau as a base to accommodate daily commuting workers, so as to lower housing costs, is not without risks. Firms employing such workers in essential services will have to rethink their workforce strategy.

The rapid spread of COVID-19 in foreign worker dormitories also shone a spotlight on housing arrangements for the nearly 300,000 foreign workers residing in dormitories.[20] The government announced that new purpose-built dormitories would be developed over the next one to two years with more living space and amenities per resident for safe distancing and greater resilience to public health risks.[21] Sing Tien Foo, director of the Institute of Real Estate and Urban Studies at the National University of Singapore, suggested intensifying land use to allow for high-rise dormitories albeit at significantly higher construction and running costs.[22] In any case, the cost increase from improved standards for foreign worker accommodation is likely to be shared by government, employers, and dormitory operators and factored into firms' workforce planning decisions.

In regard to foreign worker dependency and housing, cost savings and efficiency may have to be traded off for greater resilience and workers' welfare. With travel restrictions still in force in 2021, COVID-19 may provide the impetus for workforce localisation and investment in automation to raise labour productivity, putting the economy on a stronger footing for the future.

Digitalisation and Remote Working

The pandemic has accelerated digitalisation in commerce by bringing more businesses and consumers on board e-commerce and digital payments. More employers are also embracing work-from-home arrangements, which will have implications for commercial real estate demand, traffic volume, as well as demand for digital technologies such as videoconferencing. The Emerging Stronger Taskforce, set up under the auspices of the Future Economy Council, identified digital transformation, changing consumer demands, and a greater focus on sustainability as among the key shifts that could provide new economic opportunities for Singapore in the post-pandemic world.[23]

Global City and Air Hub Status

Singapore's total population dipped by 0.3% between June 2019 and June 2020, the first decline since 2003.[24] This was due to a 2.1% (35,800) fall in the non-resident population as many foreign workers who were out of employment left Singapore while new workers could not enter.

Globally, MNCs are rethinking their production and supply chains in light of the pandemic, as well as mounting US-China tensions. Reshoring or locating production nearer to end markets are among the options considered.

It remains to be seen how attractive Singapore continues to be to foreign expatriates in a post-pandemic world. Many foreigners living in Singapore have been cut off from their loved ones back home as a result of international travel restrictions. For some, part of the draw of working in Singapore has been the opportunity for frequent travel to Southeast Asian destinations as well as a packed calendar of international sporting and entertainment events held here. Employers, too, may prefer to employ workers in situ in other countries rather than bring them to Singapore.

COVID-19 has made virtual meetings a norm for many businesses and other organisations, which could reduce the demand for air travel in the medium term and beyond. The International Air Transport Association has projected that air travel will not return to pre-COVID levels until 2024. Even if Singapore retains its air hub status through the COVID-19 crisis, the volume of visitors and transit travellers could be lower for some time to come. A lasting reduction in demand for meetings, incentives, conventions, and exhibitions (MICE) would also affect Singapore as a preferred MICE destination.

If COVID-19 results in a dial-back in globalisation, the willingness to work abroad, or international travel, Singapore's global city allure could lose its shine.

Fertility

The impact of COVID-19 on Singapore's marriage and fertility rates has compounded what is already an existential challenge for the nation. With couples putting off decisions to tie the knot or start families — whether due to financial insecurity or safety concerns over visiting hospitals and clinics during this period — there were about 10% fewer marriages in 2020 compared with 2019, while the total fertility rate fell from 1.14 in 2019 to a historic low of 1.1 in 2020.[25] This will likely have a long-term impact on Singapore's population and workforce size.

To encourage parenthood, a Baby Support Grant of $3,000 will be given to parents of Singaporean children born from 1 October 2020 to 30 September 2022 on top of existing incentives under the Marriage and Parenthood Package, which includes a Baby Bonus cash gift of up to $10,000. The government has also increased financial support through matching grants in the Child Development Account for parents who have a second child from 2021.

Developing a Conducive Political Milieu

Socio-economic policy is never devised in a vacuum. It is shaped by the political environment, which determines policy priorities and sets limits on the types of policies and programmes that can be feasibly implemented.

Park Chan-ung and Jung Dongchul (2007) identified "democratization" as an important factor in explaining the divergent paths taken by East Asian economies in their welfare spending and development since the 1980s.[26] Christian Aspalter (2006) also contended that competition in democratic elections had led to an increase in welfare commitments in Taiwan and South Korea. Regarding Singapore, he attributed the stable and "linear" development trajectory of the welfare state to "the stability of the Singaporean polity, the strong grip on power of the People's Action Party (PAP) and the immense economic success of the small island state over the past few decades".[27]

A dominant PAP government in the 1960s and 1970s was able to push ahead with a socio-economic system centred on individual responsibility.

Even with Singapore's extraordinary economic progress, founding Prime Minister Lee Kuan Yew noted that "it was difficult to counter the seductiveness of welfare promises by the opposition during elections."[28]

Increases in mandatory savings through the CPF system were only possible with strong economic growth and low inflation, which returned the PAP government large majorities in successive elections from 1968 to 1980. With a strong political mandate, Lee was able to push through amendments to the Land Acquisition Act in 1973 which allowed the government to acquire land for housing development at below market rates.

It may be argued that the PAP's entrenched position insulated the government from the populist pressure to increase social transfers common in other democratic systems. This enabled the government to pursue strategies aimed at sustaining long-term growth instead.

The PAP's political dominance was at its zenith from 1968 to 1981 when it held all seats in Parliament until Workers' Party Secretary-General J. B. Jeyaretnam wrested away a single seat in a 1981 by-election.

While there is little doubt that the PAP government in those days enjoyed genuine popularity due to rising living standards, some have argued that the PAP's dominant position also owed, in no small part, to a "climate of fear" (Ortmann, 2011) where Singaporeans were afraid of being involved in Opposition politics or even voting against the PAP.[29] In an open letter to the Prime Minister in 2007, Singaporean author Catherine Lim wrote, "There is much anecdotal evidence to suggest that it could become pure paranoia, as seen in the many coffeeshop stories about Singaporeans... not voting for the opposition in the general election for fear of being found out and losing their homes, jobs, promotions etc."[30]

This climate of fear appears to have receded significantly since the 2011 general election. As K. Kesavapany, then-director of the Institute of South East Asian Studies, observed, "This election was important also because the climate of fear that was said to pervade Singapore politics was shed, for all to see. Voters made their views and feelings known in both the traditional and the new social media with an intensity that could not have existed in a climate of fear."[31] External observers such as Stephan Ortmann (2011) also acknowledged that Singapore had transformed into a "competitive authoritarian regime" with "meaningful contestation for ruling power for the first time".[32]

The past decade has seen more professionals and executives with successful careers step forward to join the political fray as Opposition candidates. The more prominent parties are now able to attract volunteers and funding in contrast to the days when their leaders had to raise funds by hawking books in street corners.

The result has been a more hotly contested political space. The PAP's vote share swung from 66.6% in 2006 to 60.1% in 2011, when it lost a group representative constituency (a multi-member constituency) for the first time. Notably, there had been public unhappiness then due to train congestion and long waiting times for HDB flats as infrastructure had not kept up with population growth, along with the high-profile escape of a terrorism suspect from custody.

In 2015, for the first time, the PAP faced contests in every constituency during a general election. Its vote share rebounded to 69.9% in 2015, which some commentators attributed to the outpouring of emotion at the recent passing of Singapore's first Prime Minister Lee Kuan Yew, as well as a feel-good factor surrounding the nation's 50th anniversary celebrations.

In 2020, amid the COVID-19 pandemic, the PAP's popular vote share fell again to 61.2%, confounding expectations that a "flight to safety" during the crisis would boost the ruling party's vote share.[33] This time, however, there were few obvious failings in policy delivery, leading some pundits to speculate that the dip in vote share reflected the electorate's wish for alternative voices in Parliament, as well as a desire among young voters for greater fairness and transparency in the political arena.

It would, however, be unwise to read too much into the electoral swings in 2011, 2015, and 2020. In each general election, whichever the constituency and contesting Opposition party, at least 20%–30% of votes are claimed by the Opposition. Conversely, the PAP has always managed to garner around 40% or more of the votes. The balance comprises swing votes, which may be influenced by issues of the day, as well as the perceived quality of the Opposition party and its candidates.

It is likely that a significant proportion of swing voters prefer the PAP government to remain in power but desire to have an Opposition presence in Parliament (as fully elected Members of Parliament) to keep the ruling party on its toes. Such voters could have been influenced by bookie odds of questionable authenticity which circulated via mobile messaging ahead of the 2015 general election — these appeared credible as the PAP had lost by-elections in Hougang and Punggol East following the 2011 general election; or by predictions of an Opposition wipe-out in the 2020 general election — again credible, given previous instances of perceived flight to safety. Just one in 10 voters swayed by such considerations would be sufficient to account for the 10 percentage-point swings in the PAP's vote share in both 2015 and 2020. This makes it difficult to discern secular trends, including voting patterns among younger Singaporeans and new citizens, as well as changing political proclivities as citizens grow older, all of which bear watching.

Absent a pervasive climate of fear, and with the democratisation of the media landscape via the rise of social media, a popular vote share that has fluctuated between 60% and 70% in the past three elections is a fair indication of the level of support the ruling party enjoys. Among the disaffected, there is clearly a segment of the electorate that is concerned about jobs, income, and costs, the so-called bread-and-butter issues, and whose interests a democratically elected government must respond to.

Singapore's Leftward Tilt

Then-DPM Tharman Shanmugaratnam observed in April 2013 that the Cabinet's thinking had shifted "left-of-centre":

> If I compare our thinking in Cabinet, or the weight of thinking in Cabinet, when I first entered politics about 11 years ago, I would say the weight of thinking was centrist but there were two flanks on either side of it. There were some who were a little right-of-centre, and there were some a little left-of-centre. Now I would say the weight of thinking is left-of-centre. You still get diversity of views in Cabinet, but the centre of gravity is left-of-centre.[34]

The slew of social support measures introduced after 2011, while welcomed by many citizens and commentators, also generated disquiet among conservatives. At a ministry staff forum some years ago, a senior colleague asked whether the shift towards a more welfare-oriented approach had been overdone, expressing concern that it was undermining the principle of self-reliance. In the 2015 Parliament debate on the Budget Statement, then-Nominated MP Chia Yong Yong warned, "If we lean too much to the left, there will be not much left."[35]

Yet, to attribute the leftward shift in government thinking entirely to the results of the 2011 general election would not be fair. Workfare, arguably the most significant enhancement to Singapore's social security system, had been implemented well before 2011 while the tightening of foreign worker inflow was set in motion in 2010. The government had been aware of the driving forces (described in Chapter 3) that necessitated greater social support and had begun taking steps to address them.

Some observers saw the Pioneer Generation Package, introduced in 2014, as a move to win over the politically important constituency of senior voters ahead of the 2015 general election. As outlined in Chapter 5, there are sound welfare and equity justifications for this programme. If political pressure does in fact lead to good policy, so much the better.

In this regard, one must hope that greater Opposition presence in Parliament following the 2020 general election will generate robust and constructive policy debate that will yield effective policy ideas and solutions, particularly to tackle the myriad socio-economic challenges Singapore faces.

While alternative voices in Parliament and society at large can play a salutary role in identifying policy blind spots, and keeping the government responsive to the electorate, there is also the risk that intensifying political pressure may spur populism and reduce the space for long-term policy planning. Still more dangerous is ideological polarisation, which can break down trust within society if stoked by divisive politics and left to fester.

With mature democracies such as the US afflicted by the excesses of partisan politics, from governmental gridlock to societal polarisation, there are few obvious role models for Singapore to follow.

However, the results of the 2020 general election and the government's response offer hope for Singapore. The electorate seemed to differentiate among the political contestants, with the ostensibly more credible parties performing significantly better. Following the election, Prime Minister Lee Hsien Loong announced that Workers' Party

Secretary-General Pritam Singh would be formally designated Leader of the Opposition and given additional manpower support and resources to perform his role. This was with the expectation that the Opposition would contribute more to Parliamentary debate and put forward credible policy alternatives for the government to consider.

For Singapore to succeed, it is incumbent on all political parties and the electorate to uphold a culture of responsible, fact-based public discourse, prioritising the national good over partisan interests. If Singapore, continuing a tradition of exceptionalism, can evolve its own brand of competitive, constructive democracy, this would be a significant advantage for the country as it navigates the challenges that lie ahead.

A Forward Agenda for Socio-Economic Policy

At the opening of the 14th Parliament, President Halimah Yacob outlined the new government's priorities. Among them was "to consider carefully how to strengthen our safety nets, to give Singaporeans more assurance coping with life's uncertainties" and "to do so in a way that is financially sustainable for future generations".[36] The COVID-19 pandemic provides an opportunity to revisit assumptions and recalibrate policies for the future.

What could a forward agenda for socio-economic policy look like? With Workfare and Silver Support, the main pieces of Singapore's social security system are already in place. The government can continue to increase coverage and support through these schemes as needed.

An area deserving of attention is how to support temporarily or structurally displaced workers amid economic volatility and restructuring. Options include unemployment insurance or unemployment savings through CPF, supplemented by government top-ups for the less well-off. It is also important to get more self-employed persons into the CPF system so that they can accumulate savings for their medical needs and retirement. Stronger incentives may be needed to encourage CPF contributions, including tying government transfers to contributions.

Going beyond the confines of the current model, one possibility is to provide a social dividend, tiered according to wealth, with the aim of boosting solidarity, enhancing financial security, and mitigating inequality by giving Singaporeans an additional stake in the nation's economic progress. Depending on how the dividend is sized, it could streamline social assistance by replacing the panoply of existing support schemes, but would incur significant additional fiscal cost.

Education and employment facilitation will remain key priorities in the future socio-economic model. Schools must equip students with a positive attitude towards learning, which will carry them through life, and foundational skills they can build on. A well-oiled lifelong learning and employment facilitation system is needed to continually retrain and re-skill workers to keep up with job demands.

Further reducing reliance on low-skilled foreign workers is a must to drive productivity and raise local wages across the economy, while recognising that Singapore cannot divest the bulk of the foreign workforce without shrinking the breadth of its economic activity. As for skilled foreigners, the balance must be found between assuring Singaporeans of fair opportunities for jobs and career development, and keeping Singapore open to reap the considerable advantages that come with being a global city.

Depending on the trajectory of income and wealth, driven by global forces, more progressive taxes on wealth and incomes may be required to preserve fairness and social cohesion, with taxes on wealth preferred to taxes on income from work. This would require better ways of assessing household and personal wealth.

Finally, public agencies must be zealous in managing expenditure — not tight-fisted when money ought to be spent, but constantly checking the bureaucratic tendency towards excess. Low-cost options should be preserved in public services and amenities so that they can be enjoyed by all Singaporeans. There must be strong effort to develop and sustain common spaces, which are so important in forging a shared national identity.

The future will throw up all manner of challenges that will test the creativity, resilience, and solidarity of Singaporeans. The role of the government will not recede even as other societal stakeholders step up as equal partners. Working hand-in-glove with society must be a trusted government, with instincts honed through constructive political competition. Policymaking should be flexible and adaptive, with policies distilled through the contestation of ideas, monitored for effectiveness, and refined, enhanced, or discarded as appropriate.[37]

The Future Envisioned

The yardstick of Singapore's success, now and into the future, will be its progress in human development — unlocking potential and enabling self-actualisation for as many Singaporeans as possible, to the greatest extent possible. This will require economy and society to be dynamic, inclusive, and sustainable, enabled by a nimbler, fairer, and stronger socio-economic system.

If plans for the future economy materialise, Singapore can remain a **dynamic** economy excelling in high-tech, sustainable, and creative industries with significant value creation and capture through research, design, and innovation. Economic dynamism will bring opportunities for Singaporeans to earn a living and contribute in ways they find meaningful. Singapore will become an increasingly aged society, but one with active and well-educated seniors, not unlike Japan and parts of Western Europe today.

As a city plugged into global flows of goods, services, capital, talent, and ideas, Singapore's economic growth can transcend the constraints of land or even population size. Technology will enable Singapore-generated business ideas and solutions to reach the world, opening access to burgeoning markets overseas. This requires speed and flexibility to adapt to changing market conditions and seize opportunities wherever they may be found.

Successful entrepreneurs, business leaders, and highly skilled professionals will play a key role in wealth generation. Some will be local-born Singaporeans, but many others will be from abroad. Singapore cannot afford to close its doors to foreigners if it is to retain its place as one among a number of leading cities in the world. It will need a critical mass of talent and wealth, some rooted here and others transient but contributing nonetheless to Singapore's economy and society.

Such an economy, high cost with the presence of wealthy foreigners, will only be socially and politically acceptable if the majority of Singaporeans can share in the nation's prosperity.

With high asset prices and economic rewards increasingly concentrated among those possessing skills and talents in global demand, the upward pressure on inequality will be relentless. Even with sufficient resources to be distributed to all citizens, there is still the question of how to redistribute fairly without undermining the work ethic, while keeping the majority of Singaporeans productively engaged. Just as critical is how to give Singaporeans financial security and assurance amid the vicissitudes of economic cycles and life. It is impossible to be fast without being fair — without an **inclusive** society, trust will break down and the social compact will unravel. A robust, well-designed social security system must therefore complement opportunities for economic contribution. At stake is both social cohesion and the culture of responsibility towards self, family, and society.

Some Singaporeans will thrive in capital- and knowledge-intensive sectors. Others will do well as gig workers in creative industries. Still others will find good employment in services such as retail, dining, wealth management, and professional services. In these areas, the concentration of wealth in Singapore will add a premium to location-specific services, enabling Singaporeans to earn more than those with comparable skills elsewhere.

However, there will also be many middle-income Singaporeans whose jobs are displaced by technology or migration of industries to lower-cost countries. Successive cohorts of Singaporeans will be more highly educated and it will become increasingly challenging to meet their aspirations for good jobs commensurate with their skills and education.

At the same time, opportunities lie in sectors with heavy foreign manpower reliance, where technology cannot fully replace people in the medium term. In the healthcare sector, needs are expected to grow as the population ages and becomes more affluent. Jobs in healthcare, community, and personal services will have to be made more attractive to Singaporeans both young and old. More locals must find employment in areas where technology cannot easily replace humans, such as in domestic-oriented services, where they would earn good pay as knowledge workers leveraging technology and working alongside machines to augment their productivity.

For the system to be **sustainable**, there needs to be a match between labour demand and supply, without excessive growth in foreign manpower. The crux of the matter is whether the transformation of jobs can keep pace with the transformation of the economy. Blurring the traditional lines between white-collar and blue-collar work is a necessary part of the transition towards a stronger, more sustainable socio-economic system.

From the starting point of heavy reliance on low-skilled foreign manpower, a better equilibrium can be envisioned, but the way forward will not be painless. Costs would rise with higher incomes, but this can be mitigated by higher productivity from better skills and adoption of technology. The nature of service that a consumer can expect may change — it would be more technology-enabled and less manpower-dependent — but quality need not be compromised.

In short, the ticket to dynamic, inclusive, and sustainable development would be to seize the opportunities offered by technology and the global economy, while redesigning essential services jobs to make them more attractive and rewarding for Singaporeans. There must be respect for every job, with decent pay and working conditions, so that all workers can take pride in their jobs and give of their best. Also necessary are common spaces and affordable living options, so that no group feels priced out of participation in mainstream society. Finally, there must be adequate financial security for citizens up and down the income distribution, and across life stages, with ample opportunities to pursue self-actualisation.

The Singapore System would require, as Senior Minister Tharman has suggested, the core values of both the Left and the Right — the "social empathy and solidarity" advanced by the Left, together with the "ethic of personal responsibility and effort" espoused by the Right[38] — *personal effort with collective support,* in short.

Consider this vision for Singapore: a nation abounding with opportunities where citizens find fulfilment in their chosen vocation, assured of collective support for their needs, even as they strive to build better lives for themselves, their families, and the community. We may never fully get there, but it will take a refreshed socio-economic system — faster, fairer, and stronger — to get us closer.

Endnotes

1. Revised figures as at 16 February 2021.
2. JSS support was temporarily increased for firms in sectors affected by more stringent safe management measures from May 2021.
3. Monetary Authority of Singapore (MAS), *Macroeconomic Review October 2020* (Singapore: MAS, 2020).

4. Source: Joint Autonomous University Graduate Employment Survey 2020.
5. Source: Polytechnic Graduate Employment Survey 2020.
6. Heng Swee Keat, ministerial statement, 5 October 2020. See also Christopher Saw, Koh Wen Jie, Foo Xian Yun, and Clement Lee, "Impact of the Circuit Breaker and Budget Measures in Response to COVID-19," *Economic Survey of Singapore Second Quarter 2020* (Singapore: Ministry of Trade and Industry, 2020): 42–48. According to the MAS *Macroeconomic Review October 2020*, monetary policy would help reduce economic contraction by another 1.1% in 2020 and 0.8% in 2021.
7. See, for instance, Wiji Arulampalam, Paul Gregg, and Mary Gregory, "Unemployment Scarring," *Economic Journal* 111(475) (2001): FF577–584. Graduating in a recession may depress earnings for 10 years or more, according to some studies: Lisa Kahn, "The Long-Term Labor Market Consequences of Graduating from College in a Bad Economy," *Labour Economics* 17(2) (2010): 303–316; Philip Oreopoulos, Till von Wachter, and Andrew Heisz, "The Short- and Long-Term Career Effects of Graduating in a Recession," *American Economic Journal: Applied Economics* 4(1) (2012): 1–29.
8. Heng Swee Keat, Budget Statement, 2021.
9. Cardiff Garcia, "How Global Income Inequality Has Shifted Since the Crisis," *Financial Times*, 12 August 2017.
10. International Labour Organization (ILO), *Global Wage Report 2020-21: Wages and Minimum Wages in the Time of COVID-19* (Geneva: ILO, 2020).
11. Manpower Research and Statistics Department, Ministry of Manpower (MOM), *Labour Force in Singapore 2020* (Singapore: MOM, 2021).
12. Singapore Department of Statistics, "Real Change in Average Monthly Household Income from Work per Household Member (Including Employer CPF Contributions) Among Resident Employed Households by Deciles, 2020."
13. Ibid.
14. Irvin Seah, Yeo Kee Yan, Lim Rui Wen, Lorna Tan, Yong Woon Bing, and Chung Wei Le, "Same Storm, Different Boat: Impact of COVID-19 on Financial Wellness in Singapore," *DBS Asian Insights Sector Briefing* 89, 2020.
15. Ling Hai, Co-President of Mastercard Asia-Pacific, quoted on the enterprise digital divide in Global-is-Asian, "How Are Singaporeans Spending During the Pandemic?" *Global-is-Asian*, 19 November 2020, https://lkyspp.nus.edu.sg/gia/article/how-are-singaporeans-spending-during-the-pandemic.
16. US Federal Reserve, *Z.1 Financial Accounts of the United States Second Quarter 2020*, Federal Reserve Statistical Release, 21 September 2020.

17. US Federal Reserve, Federal Open Market Committee statement, 17 March 2021.
18. Sandra Davie, "COVID-19 Shows Children's Well-Being and Success Depends Not Just on More than Just What Happens in School," *Straits Times*, 28 May 2020.
19. Ministry of Finance (MOF), *Singapore Public Sector Outcomes Review 2020* (Singapore: MOF, 2020).
20. Josephine Teo, remarks at the Multi-Ministry Task Force press conference, 14 April 2020, https://www.moh.gov.sg/docs/librariesprovider5/2019-ncov/delivered-remarks-by-manpower-minister-josephine-teo-at-mtf-press-conf-14-apr-2020.pdf.
21. "Improved Standards of New Dormitories for Migrant Workers," Singapore government, 8 June 2020, https://www.gov.sg/article/improved-standards-of-new-dormitories-for-migrant-workers.
22. Lim Yan Liang, "Rethinking Dorms: Next Steps for Foreign Worker Housing in Singapore," *Straits Times*, 4 June 2020.
23. Emerging Stronger Taskforce, *Emerging Stronger Taskforce Report*, May 2021, https://emergingstronger.sg/assets/pdf/EST%20Report_Single%20Page.pdf.
24. National Population and Talent Department (NPTD), Strategy Group, Prime Minister's Office et al., *Population in Brief 2020* (Singapore: NPTD, 2020), https://www.strategygroup.gov.sg/files/media-centre/publications/population-in-brief-2020.pdf.
25. Chew Hui Min, "Singapore's Fertility Rate Falls to Historic Low in 2020," CNA, 26 February 2021, https://www.channelnewsasia.com/news/singapore/singapore-total-fertility-rate-tfr-falls-historic-low-2020-baby-14288556.
26. Chan-ung Park and Dongchul Jung, "The Asian Welfare Regimes Revisited: The Preliminary Typologies Based on Welfare Legislation and Expenditure," paper prepared for the 4th International Conference on Restructuring Care Responsibility. Dynamics of Welfare Mix in East Asia, 20–21 October 2007, University of Tokyo, Japan.
27. Christian Aspalter, "The East Asian Welfare Model," *International Journal of Social Welfare* 15(4) (2006): 290–301.
28. Lee Kuan Yew, *From Third World to First: The Singapore Story: 1965–2000* (Singapore: Times Editions, Singapore Press Holdings, 2000).
29. Stephan Ortmann, "Singapore: Authoritarian but Newly Competitive," *Journal of Democracy* 22(4) (2011): 153–164.
30. Catherine Lim, open letter to the Prime Minister, 4 November 2007, https://pseudonymity.wordpress.com/2007/11/05/.

31. K. Kesavapany, "Reflections on the Singapore General Elections," East Asia Forum, 12 May 2011, https://www.eastasiaforum.org/2011/05/12/reflections-on-the-singapore-general-election/.
32. Ortmann, "Singapore: Authoritarian but Newly Competitive."
33. In an interview shortly before the 2020 general election, National University of Singapore Associate Professor Bilveer Singh, a long-time observer of Singapore politics, was quoted as saying, "It is without a doubt that GE2020 will be a landslide victory for the PAP. In fact, the opposition may be entirely annihilated this election. Singaporean voters will run back to papa." In Nelle Ng, "This NUS Professor Predicts that GE2020 Will Be a Landslide Victory for the PAP," Kopi, June 29, 2020, https://thekopi.co/2020/06/29/bilveer-singh-predicts-will-be-a-landslide-victory-for-the-pap/.
34. Tharman Shanmugaratnam, as quoted in Aaron Low, "Cabinet: More Left-of-Centre Now, Helping the Lower-Income," *Straits Times,* 19 April 2013.
35. Chia Yong Yong, as quoted in Chong Zi Liang, "Singapore Budget 2015: NMP Chia Yong Yong Questions Calls for More Flexibility in CPF Withdrawals," *Straits Times*, 3 March 2015.
36. Halimah Yacob, Address for the first session of the Fourteenth Parliament, 24 August 2020. https://www.istana.gov.sg/Newsroom/Speeches/2020/08/24/Address-by-President-Halimah-Yacob-for-First-Session-of-the-Fourteenth-Parliament.
37. As policy ideas need time to foment and may gain traction as circumstances change, it would be prudent for the government not to put out statements ruling out any particular policy, from which it would be hard to walk back later.
38. Tharman Shanmugaratnam, "Making Ours an Uplifting Society," *Straits Times*, 16 January 2021.

Index

Lightning Source UK Ltd.
Milton Keynes UK
UKHW041221120821
388716UK00001B/3

9 789811 236532